Scotland's
CASTLE CULTURE

Scotland's
CASTLE CULTURE

Edited by Audrey Dakin, Miles Glendinning and Aonghus MacKechnie

First published in Great Britain in 2011 by
John Donald, an imprint of Birlinn Ltd

West Newington House
10 Newington Road
Edinburgh
EH9 1QS

www.birlinn.co.uk

ISBN: 978 1 906566 33 3

The publishers gratefully acknowledge the support
of Historic Scotland, The Russell Trust, the Strathmartine
Trust, the Architectural Heritage Society of Scotland,
and The Royal Commission on the Ancient and Historic
Monuments of Scotland towards the publication of
this book

British Library Cataloguing-in-Publication Data
A catalogue record for this book is available
on request from the British Library

Typeset and designed by Mark Blackadder

Printed and bound in Britain by
Bell & Bain Ltd., Glasgow

Contents

Acknowledgements

We are extremely grateful for the help we received from others, our benefactors, friends and colleagues, in both sponsoring and compiling this book and we acknowledge their generosity here.

The Architectural Heritage Society of Scotland and Edinburgh College of Art were the co-sponsors of the 2009 Castle Culture conference from which this book derives. Special thanks to Geoffrey Stell who worked closely with us to shape the conference.

Without the support of Historic Scotland, The Russell Trust, The Strathmartine Trust and The Royal Commission on the Ancient and Historical Monuments of Scotland this book could not have come into being.

At Historic Scotland, the following were helpful: Michelle Andersson, Malcolm Bangor-Jones, Sean Conlon, Barbara Cummins, Noel Fojut, Simon Montgomery, Dara Parsons, Michael Pearce, John Raven and Ian Thomson. Other individuals to whom we are indebted for their help are Anne Martin, Derek Smart, Lachie Stewart, Shannon Fraser, Murdo MacDonald, Michael Lynch and Mary Turner.

Lastly, we would like to thank our families for their forbearance while the book was taking shape.

Stirling Castle, Forework Gate: conjectural restoration by David M Walker 1994. Built c. 1500–10 for James IV, the gatehouse had six lofty round towers. Its still–extant entrance resembled a triumphal arch, recalling the Imperial imagery used by the Stewart kings from the 1460s. This imagery is seen elsewhere today with Imperial crown spires such as that of Edinburgh's St Giles' Cathedral / High Kirk, and the main meaning was that Scotland's own monarchy was in charge of the kingdom. (© David M Walker / Aonghus MacKechnie)

List of Contributors

IAIN ANDERSON runs the Threatened Building Survey within the Royal Commission on the Ancient and Historical Monuments of Scotland. He studied architecture and architectural history at the Glasgow School of Art and has previously worked within the Historic Scotland Inspectorate.

IAN BEGG is an architect with historical interests who lives in Plockton. Apprenticed with Sir Robert Lorimer's one-time chief assistant, he worked with Neil and Hurd architects in 1951, becoming sole partner in 1963 until the firm merged with L A Rolland and partners in 1965. In 1984, he set up the firm of Ian Begg Architect. He has taught at several schools of architecture, notably the Strathclyde school.

AUDREY DAKIN is an architect. She is currently working for the Scottish Historic Buildings Trust as a Project Officer. She previously worked at the National Trust for Scotland as a Project Officer for the Little Houses Improvement Scheme, at the Architectural Heritage Society of Scotland as Chief Officer and at Historic Scotland as Conservation Architect and Conservation Bureau Manager. While at Historic Scotland, she managed research projects and edited technical publications including the Rural Buildings of the Lothians Guide for Practitioners.

JOHN GIFFORD has been in charge of the Buildings of Scotland Research Unit since 1980. He is author of *William Adam* (1989), author or co-author of six of the published volumes in *The Buildings of Scotland* series, and contributor to a seventh. He is currently writing *Dundee and Angus* (forthcoming, 2012).

MILES GLENDINNING is Director of the Scottish Centre for Conservation Studies and Professor of Architectural Conservation at Edinburgh College of Art (University of Edinburgh). He has published extensively on Modernist and contemporary architecture, and on modern housing.

IAN GOW is Chief Curator at the National Trust for Scotland and formerly Curator of Architectural Collections at the National Monuments Record of Scotland. He is Honorary Curator and an Honorary Fellow of the Royal Incorporation of Architects in Scotland. He has published extensively on the decorative arts and architecture of Scotland.

SIMON GREEN is an architectural historian working in the Survey and Recording Section of the Royal Commission on the Ancient and Historical Monuments of Scotland. He is the Honorary Secretary of the Society of Architectural Historians of Great Britain and the Chairman of The Architecture Advisory Panel of The National Trust For Scotland.

AONGHUS MACKECHNIE is Historic Scotland's north region Head of Heritage Management. His published work has been mainly on the architecture of the Renaissance–Early Modern periods, and the culture of Gaeldom.

ANN MACSWEEN is head of a casework team in Historic Scotland dealing with historic buildings and monuments. She is an archaeologist and a planner with a special interest in Scotland's prehistory. Her publications include a book on the history of Skye and joint editorship of five volumes of modern Scottish history for the University of Dundee and the Open University.

JOHN MALCOLM holds a BA and an MLitt in Archaeology from the National University of Ireland, Galway. He was the National University of Ireland Travelling Student in Archaeology from 2005 to 2008, based at the University of Glasgow. He has been an Inspector of Ancient Monuments and Senior Heritage Management Officer for Historic Scotland since 2008.

CHARLES MCKEAN FRSE is Chairman of Edinburgh World Heritage, Professor of Scottish Architectural History, University of Dundee, and a member of the Heritage Lottery Fund Scottish Committee. He was previously Secretary and Treasurer and Chief Executive of the Royal Incorporation of Architects in Scotland, and Chairman of the National Trust for Scotland's Buildings Committee. His publications include *The Scottish Château* (2001) and several volumes of the Royal Incorporation of Architects in Scotland regional guides.

ROBERT J. MORRIS is Emeritus Professor of Economic and Social History at Edinburgh University. He has spent all of his tax-paying life in Scotland and written extensively about towns and civil society – key aspects of Scotland's history. He has walked his camera around urban and rural Scotland and is currently planting an apple orchard in Berwickshire.

MICHAEL MOSS is Research Professor in Archival Studies at the University of Glasgow, board member of the National Trust for Scotland and the National Archives of Scotland, and a member of the Lord Chancellor's Advisory Council on National Records and Archives. His publications include *The 'Magnificent Castle' of Culzean and the Kennedy Family* (2002), and (as co-author) *Nelson's Surgeon: William Beatty, Naval Medicine and the Battle of Trafalgar* (2005).

ALLAN RUTHERFORD is employed in Historic Scotland's Heritage Management Directorate. His PhD research focused on the Scottish medieval castle and he has published (as co-author) on the history of castle restoration in Scotland.

GEOFFREY STELL, an architectural historian with specialist interests including castles, towers and fortifications, was Head of Architecture at the Royal Commission on the Ancient and Historical Monuments of Scotland until his retirement in 2004. He is now an honorary lecturer in the Department of History, University of Stirling, and a visiting lecturer in the Department of Architecture, Edinburgh College of Art. He also serves on the Scientific Council of Europa Nostra.

DAVID WALKER, formerly Chief Inspector of Historic Buildings with Historic Scotland, is Emeritus Professor of Art History at the University of St Andrews and Director of the *Dictionary of Scottish Architects 1840–1940*. His publications include *The Architecture of Glasgow* (1968, revised 1987) (co-author) and contributions to numerous volumes in the *Buildings of Scotland* series and the Royal Incorporation of Architects in Scotland regional guides.

DIANE WATTERS is an architectural historian who works at the Royal Commission on the Ancient and Historical Monuments of Scotland (RCAHMS) and teaches at the Scottish Centre for Conservation Studies, Edinburgh University. A specialist in twentieth-century architecture and conservation in Scotland, she has undertaken a succession of research-based publications for RCAHMS, and is currently compiling a volume on Scotland's historic school architecture pre-1880.

Midmar Castle, Aberdeenshire: drawing by David M Walker as it was in 1961, long-empty but intact and unaltered. The walled garden was then leased to the Forestry Commission as a nursery for Midmar Forest. (© David M Walker / Forestry Commission)

Introduction

Miles Glendinning and Aonghus MacKechnie

This castle hath a pleasant seat:
the air nimbly and sweetly recommends itself
unto our gentle senses.[1]

This book's aim is to set out the story of Scotland's castles. They have been with us for nearly a millennium, and their history over that period is charted here not only through their evolving built forms but also through the frequently changing attitudes towards them during the centuries since castles were first considered necessities. At various times, they were esteemed, abandoned, demolished, mimicked in new designs, documented or drawn and studied as primary historical documents, reoccupied and protected as state monuments. In these pages, all these stages in the history of the castle, as an idea and as a built reality, are touched on, sometimes repeatedly.

What, though, is a castle? We have sidestepped that question in this book, and have simply taken 'castle' to represent anything stone-built and castellated, or castle-like, thus embracing castles of enclosure, residential towers or tower houses, castle-revival houses, and castellated non-domestic structures. That diversity of built form is matched by the diversity of approaches taken by the many scholars who have contributed to this volume, reflecting their own perspectives and specialisms. For instance, Michael Moss' paper on Culzean is informed by his background as an archivist, and is strongly document-based; while as a practising architect, Ian Begg's approach highlights the challenges of repair, business and construction. However, the authors all seek to challenge accepted norms and introduce fresh ideas and new ways of addressing their subject. Some of the new perspectives focus on dispassionate analysis, as in the statistical comparisons contained in Geoffrey Stell's paper; at the other extreme lie some more consciously contentious approaches to the subject, such as the attempt to analyse the Inveraray castle project through the prism of contemporary politics.

A strong theme running through the book is that of conservation, which is mostly viewed as a positive rather than negative factor. Two papers in particular – Robert Morris' paper on Edinburgh and Ann MacSween's on Craigievar – highlight the interventions of antiquarians and preservationists. Most contributors come from the mainstream of architectural history, whether 'castellologists' specialising in the earlier period (such as Geoffrey Stell, Allan Rutherford and John Malcolm), or country house specialists of the eighteenth and nineteenth centuries, such as David Walker, Ian Gow and Simon Green. The paper by Diane Watters covers the more recent period of transition from centuries dominated by new construction of castles, to the twentieth-century age of state-driven castle conservation.

The remainder of this Introduction sets out to do two things: first, to give a more detailed overview of the contents of the book and the contributions of the specialist writers involved; and second, to provide a wider historical context for those analyses, by sketching out the evolution of the historiography of the Scottish castle since the late seventeenth century.

Overview of Contents

The book is arranged in the form of two complementary sequences of papers. Part I comprises a strictly chronological succession of chapters stretching from the Middle Ages to the present day, each providing an overview of general architectural and cultural trends over a substantial chronological period. Part II contains a series of individual case studies of key monuments, in most cases spanning several phases of use, reuse and restoration, and thus less tidily separated in chronological terms.

The first part of the book begins by considering the emergence of the castle as a coherent Scottish building type. From around the eleventh century, Celtic cultural systems were superseded by a new centralised royal power, whose authority was implemented through a social hierarchy of feudal knights holding land as part of a military 'contract' in service of the crown. This new elite comprised Norman families invited to Scotland, who introduced the motte-and-bailey formula, built from the time of David I (r.1124–53) until the thirteenth century. A typical motte, such as that at Inverurie, comprised an earthen mound with timber structures above. From the twelfth and thirteenth centuries, in turn, this class of defensive place of authority was gradually superseded by the stone castle. The 'Norman' settlement formula of 'motte/castle – church – town' was, however, to remain standard, until a changing society from the later seventeenth century required the church and town to be set apart

from the elite residence, as exemplified at eighteenth-century Inveraray.

The introduction, development, character and meaning of medieval and Renaissance Scottish castles is discussed by Geoffrey Stell in his overview chapter. It reviews questions such as the societal relationships between people and castles, and the terminology associated with them. He poses the question 'Is Scotland truly a land of castles?', buttressing his conclusions with appendices setting Scottish examples alongside their peers in England and Wales. Our earliest castles (such as Castle Sween) were built from the twelfth century for regional magnates, but the thirteenth century is identified by Stell as the key transition point, with a sequence of massive lordly castles of enclosure such as the Douglas castle of Bothwell, planned around a donjon tower nucleus.

Bothwell is the subject of the first of the case-study chapters of Part II, by John Malcolm and Allan Rutherford, who resoundingly endorse Douglas Simpson's earlier judgement that it constitutes one of the 'foremost secular structures of the Middle Ages in Scotland'. Their reappraisal – which reassesses the importance of the de Moray contribution to its building – charts its complex incarnations, from its beginning as Scotland's biggest medieval castle to its modern role as a monument. Malcolm and Rutherford underline the fact that such castles were part of a wider, so-called 'Anglo-Norman' trend, rather than modelled on specific prototypes: Bothwell was long regarded as modelled upon Coucy-le-Château, built for Alexander II's father-in-law. But their key point, based on an assessment embracing wider contexts than previously considered, is that its history must be more complex than has previously been thought – including the fourteenth-century reconstruction of its donjon, the Moray Tower.

After 1296 and the opening of the Wars of

Independence, the new castles became English military bases and thus military architecture. But from around 1306, Robert I, 'the Bruce', showed that these buildings were vulnerable to attack, and most were wrecked by the Scots themselves to deny bases to the English. A more monolithic type of residential stone tower (developed from the donjon tower) became prevalent from the time of David II (r.1328–71) who built David's Tower at Edinburgh Castle c.1368–72, a massive tower house dominating the town. This model of a tower as royal or lordly residence was fashionable elsewhere, notably at Vincennes (c.1360–70), which similarly part-projects beyond the defences which clasp it. This pattern was still seen as appropriate for a royal residence when James V's Holyrood tower was built in the 1520s, and essentially the same formula developed into the sixteenth- to seventeenth-century tower house.

The issue of whether castles were chiefly 'power statements' built by the rich and sophisticated, or whether they actually served a military purpose, is a debate that has rumbled on for nearly a century and that still forms a key theme in both Stell's and McKean's chapters. The overall consensus in this book combines both interpretations, reflecting the fact that most castles were built in peacetime but had on occasion to play a military role, during times of warfare or feuds. Castles defending the realm, such as Stirling, Edinburgh or Dumbarton, were intended to be the most powerful. At Edinburgh, for instance, Oliver Cromwell wrote with some surprise of the castle's extensive fortifications following his negotiated capture of it in 1650:

> I think, I need to say little of the strength of the place; which, if it had not come in as it did, would have cost very much blood to have attained, if at all to be attained . . . I must needs say, not any skill or wisdom of ours, but the good-will of

God, hath given you [the English parliament] this place.[2]

In Chapter 2, Aonghus MacKechnie reviews the period when asymmetrical castles were becoming rejected as residences, in response to the growing architectural dominance of classicism, the style based on scholarly study of Roman and Greek antiquity. Instead of vertically proportioned towers with complex skylines inspired by informal local precedent, the newly fashionable classicism depended on a more apprehensible set of governing principles, such as uniformly proportioned facades and profiles, and use of the 'Orders'. Although Scottish attempts at evoking classical forms began as early as the fifteenth century, only in the seventeenth century would classicism's architectural ideals establish a decisive dominance.

The Renaissance period set out a tripartite period division: the antique, or classical, which was revered; the 'Dark Ages' that followed the collapse of the Roman Empire; and the (then) present day, important because it was inspired by antiquity. In Scotland, this Renaissance reverence for Roman constructions was seen in sixteenth-century Kinneil and Callendar Park, where in each case the house's positioning responded to the adjacent ancient Roman wall.

In MacKechnie's chapter, we trace the way in which the gradual emergence of a symmetrical, castellated style in the late sixteenth century, as exemplified by Newark's north quarter of 1597, was overtaken by events after 1603, when James VI emigrated to become James I of England and Ireland. From that point, a new emphasis on English models became dominant, and remained a powerful influence into the next century and beyond. Indeed, the ogee-domed turret roofs of Tudor–Jacobean England became an integral part of 'Scottish tradition', to the extent that the 'Scots Jacobean' style was embraced as a key element in the repertoire of revivalist architects such as Sir Robert Lorimer (1864–1929).

By the closing decades of the seventeenth century, an era of proto-Enlightenment and proto-Romanticism, classical houses were replacing castles, allowing the latter to find a new use as a focus for tradition-minded sentiment. From this developed both castle revival and castle conservation. But the shift from practical modern use to sentimental relics was not a simple or unitary one: throughout the late seventeenth and early eighteenth centuries, there were repeated attempts to revive 'Castle Culture', and castellated style, as an expression of the pride and power of old landed families. The climax of that movement was the castellated enhancement of the royal palace of Holyrood in the 1670s; there, the imagery expressed the lineal antiquity and legitimacy of an absentee monarch. The same legitimising process was then, in turn, embraced by key dynastic families in the late seventeenth century, while the early and mid eighteenth century witnessed a more complex pattern of rejection and almost simultaneous revival of the 'castle' as landed residence.

The general overview of this period in MacKechnie's Part I chapter is complemented by three chapters in Part II, which trace the complex story of the seventeenth- and eighteenth-century castle as exemplified by three key cases: Glamis, Blair and Inveraray.

Charles McKean sees Glamis Castle (rebuilt 1668–84 by Patrick, earl of Strathmore) as the 'earliest, noblest and *most Scottish* expression of Scottish Baroque'. He contests the frequent interpretation of Glamis as 'throwback architecture' in comparison to contemporary fashion in England, arguing that 'its rightful place in Scottish cultural history has been concealed by the way Scottish architectural history has been constructed over the last two centuries'. McKean also focuses on the landscape, surroundings and setting of Glamis,

emphasising the importance of considering such buildings in these wider structural contexts.

John Gifford's study of Blair encapsulates this book's theme. As an ancient Comyn family castle that had been enlarged incrementally, competing eighteenth-century proposals concluded with its de-castellation in 1747 to create a classical house; while the transformation of 'Blair Castle' to 'Atholl House' went full circle when, from 1869, it was recast as a Baronial castle. Gifford sees rejection of the state apartment (a suite for a possible royal visit) as a key aspect of the planning of Blair. The intention had once been to create one, but the abolition of heritable jurisdictions after the 1745–6 rising seemed to transform the duke's role from a local 'sub-king' within a feudal hierarchy to part of a post-absolutist Whig oligarchy. Gifford suggests the ultimate decision to omit a state apartment sits within that context, and might exemplify a change in the way the social and political order was viewed by Scots in those years.

Aonghus MacKechnie argues that Inveraray, begun in 1745 for the 3rd duke of Argyll, likewise reflected changing political context, although in a different way. Almost contemporary with Blair, Inveraray was an early Gothic Revival castle. What was the reason for that stylistic choice? On the one hand, we could argue that we are dealing with a continuation of the castle revival of the late seventeenth century, as exemplified in the castellated rebuilding of residences such as Drumlanrig. But on the other hand, Inveraray was built in the age of a still-new, still-fragile union with England for a politician who had helped create that union, and who hated Jacobitism and its associated risk to the union. Did being pro-union mean internalising English values? If so, the use of Gothic at Inveraray may represent a conscious echo of the Whig nationalist associations of Gothic in England, as exemplified by, say, Stowe. Inveraray also exemplified the other contemporary structural changes to society and landscape, notably in its creation of a new planned town, industry and ornamented estate policies.

During the same years in the eighteenth century, the march of Enlightenment and stress upon the rational was also becoming complemented by 'Romanticism', a reactive movement grounded in emotion and feeling. The enduring power of this movement in Scotland was exemplified by two authors writing a century apart: Allan Ramsay (1686–1758) and Sir Walter Scott (1771–1832). At the opening of the eighteenth century, Ramsay wrote in Scots, seeing it as a potential casualty of union: he wanted to invigorate it to ensure its survival. Scott, on the other hand, wrote his narratives in English and used Scots as a Romantic badge of the past, as Enlightenment Scotland bade it farewell. Likewise, Tobias Smollett (1721–1771), from Dunbartonshire, studded his novels with Scots people and settings, which he hailed as 'agreeably romantic beyond conception'. Robert Adam, a child of the Enlightenment, was also influenced strongly by Romanticism, and clearly delighted in old buildings and castles, which could serve him as models for the new. Robert and his brothers James and John reintroduced such elements as crow-steps, castellated round turrets and bartizans, as well as concealed roofs behind crenellated parapets – an arrangement possibly derived from that at Edinburgh Castle. The brothers' first castellated venture was a version of Inveraray, at Douglas Castle (1757), but from the 1770s they launched in earnest into their new breed of castles, for example at Wedderburn (1771–5) for Patrick Home.

Romanticism was an even clearer influence in the creation of Balmoral, which is the subject of the sixth case-study chapter in Part II, by Simon Green. His account confirms Balmoral's uniquely prestigious status within Victorian Scotland, as the first new royal 'seat' in the country since the seventeenth century. The driving force of the project was Albert, the prince consort, who

had ideas of his native, Romantic-period Germany in mind – ideas which aligned closely with the contemporary cult of the Romantic Highlands. The castle was built wholly anew on a site adjoining its predecessor, but set so as to obtain better views of the Cairngorm Mountains. The new Balmoral was designed so as to appear an organic multi-phase building – an approach that represented a step away from the post-Adam Picturesque Romanticism of David Hamilton, James Gillespie Graham and William Burn, whose work is described in David Walker's overview account, forming the sixth chapter in Part I of this book. The nearest precedent for Balmoral, in fact, was Scott's Abbotsford – not least as the Linlithgow Palace-style porch included at Abbotsford also appeared at Balmoral – although Balmoral's profile was exaggerated by contrasting a mammoth tower (like Hoddom Castle – or, more immediately, Ayton of 1851) between miniaturised wings, each element suggesting a separate building phase.

Green contrasts Balmoral with Albert's other creation, Osborne House in England, whose design was Italianate classical, and he explores the differing ideas which produced such contrasting designs. Most surprising, perhaps, was the fact that the building of Balmoral was made possible by a private bequest to Queen Victoria in 1852.

Balmoral was part-inspired too by the impact of the 'Sobieski Stuarts' (brothers called Hay who claimed to be royal Stuarts) and the precedent of their 'Highland home'. Such was the brothers' personal impact that in 1839 the 14th Lord Lovat (whose forebear, the 11th Lord Lovat, had been hanged in 1747 during anti-Jacobite reprisals) built for them a crow-stepped 'royal' mansion on the isle of Eilean Aigas on the Beauly River, complete with twin-throned and antlered hall, Jacobite trophies and Stuart memorabilia.[3] In 1842, the brothers published, from a supposedly ancient manuscript, what they claimed to be the authentic codification of clan tartans: *Vestiarium Scoticum*. The association of tartan with ancient clan elites was already established, as it was – since George IV's visit to Edinburgh in 1822 – with the monarchy; but now there were both Highland and Lowland tartans, all supposedly 'ancient', for consumption by a widening community of Romantic-period castle builders – including the 'Highland Queen', for Balmoral.

In Chapter 3, Ian Gow and Aonghus MacKechnie discuss the period that followed Inveraray's contruction, and the more widespread reintroduction of newly built castles. Theirs is the only chapter to be dominated by a single individual. This was Robert Adam, the critical figure in Romanticised castle revivalism in Scotland. Adam's castles constitute a legacy of the first order of importance, and he was profoundly influential, both during his lifetime and afterwards, through people like John Paterson and Richard Crichton, Alexander Laing and others. The authors then highlight the shift from Adam's symmetry towards a still-Romantic Picturesque asymmetry, characterised by, say, David Hamilton's Castle Toward (1820–1). The key building, though, that heralded the 'Scotch Baronial', the subject of David Walker's Chapter 4, was Sir Walter Scott's Abbotsford, begun around 1817.

The enjoyment of castle ruins continued throughout this period, and at Castle Toward there were two, each treated differently. Old Castle Toward – a tower plus unvaulted domestic wing and courtyard, main residence of the Lamonts – had been despoiled by the Campbells in 1646 and never reoccupied. The main drive to the 1820s castle was carried along the base of the slope beneath the old castle and, probably around the same time, the ruins were stabilised to ensure their survival. Closer to the new castle stood the remains of the Campbell house of Auchavoulin. Less exists of that castle, but one high wall was retained and a part was converted as a rustic

feature incorporating reset stone fragments, possibly from an old chapel which once stood nearby.

Another important innovation noted in Chapter 3 is the reoccupation of previously abandoned castles and a revaluing of old buildings. A catalyst in all this was James MacPherson's *The Works of Ossian*, published from 1760, whose Romantic drama was influential in many cultures elsewhere.

One possible external influence exerted by Scotland's Castle Culture during this period was the emergence in late eighteenth century Germany of 'Romantic Rhineland'. *Ossian* had been quickly popular in Germany, and was translated into German in 1764. Scotland's mountains, lochs and Picturesque castles found their counterpart in the hill-slope castles of the Middle Rhine. These had been mostly wrecked by Louis XIV's invasion of 1689, but French control was ended from 1814 when Marshall Blücher's Prussian army joined the forces ranked against Napoleon, and from around the 1820s these old castles were being reconstructed for reoccupation. Members of the Prussian royal family were at the forefront of this move to reoccupy the castles, possibly the best known being Stolzenfels (1835) by Karl Freidrich Schinkel, who had of course visited Scotland and the Highlands. The similarity in approach that developed in both Romantic Highlands and Romantic Rhineland can be illustrated by two navigational towers: Port Ellen Lighthouse, a design by David Hamilton in 1832 (Figure 1) and the Mäuseturm ('Mouse Tower') near Bingen, reconstructed in 1856–8; for each is a near blank-walled asymmetrical tower with a castellated asymmetrical superstructure.

In Chapter 4, David Walker traces the diverse strands of 'Scotch Baronial' architecture from 1830 to 1914, whose debates and changing ideas attracted numerous talented architects and inspired a vast number of buildings. The key figure overall was William Burn, but the period was opened by the diverse contributions of W H Playfair in Edinburgh and David Hamilton in Glasgow. Walker's chapter highlights the contrasting regional character of Baronial in Edinburgh, where David Bryce led the way, and in Glasgow, supplementing this traditional polarisation with characterisations of the north and north-east. By the early twentieth century, according to Walker, discussion of modern castellated architecture had become highly polarised. Some attacked Baronial houses as 'sham castles', while others, headed by Sir R R Anderson, 'saw the Scots Renaissance as a rich architectural language, its revival no different in principle from that of the Italian Renaissance, and a lot closer to home'. Walker's chapter, by contrast, unambiguously celebrates the richness of nineteenth-century Baronial from a historical and conservation perspective, lamenting how many buildings were lost during the twentieth century that today's generation might have valued.

But by then, as Diane Watters points out in the fifth overview chapter of Part I, the state had already stepped onto the scene with the first Ancient Monuments Act in 1882. The period covered by her chapter is dominated by the state's increasing role during the twentieth century, notably with the introduction of 'listing' through another Act in 1947, implemented from 1948. Scheduling castles as monuments, and listing them as historic buildings, combined the nineteenth-century 'French' system of direct state upkeep with the new twentieth-century mechanism of planning control. But the early twentieth-century age of imperialist pride also saw the beginning of a new wave of privately financed castle restoration projects (contemporary with major ecclesiastical restoration projects at Iona and Paisley Abbeys). More recently, a new wave of privately financed castle reoccupation began, facilitated by the 'wealth creation' policies of the Tory government of 1979–97 – the restorers in

FIGURE I
Port Ellen Lighthouse (1832) designed by David Hamilton (Arra Fletcher)

such cases often being enthusiastic middle-class professionals with no family or 'clan' links to the castles concerned.

Iain Anderson illustrates this theme of early twentieth-century reoccupation through a double case-study chapter in Part II, which traces the restorations of two long-ruined medieval clan castles in the West Highlands: Duart and Eilean Donan. Duart, the principal MacLean castle, was purchased in 1911 by a MacLean (Sir Fitzroy MacLean), by whom it was restored in a scheme by the leading architect J J Burnet. The scheme was completed in 1916, but MacLean had already formally 'reoccupied' the castle in a grand 1912 ceremony 'to witness the re-crowning of a Chief and the rebirth of a Clan . . . That Castle of Duart', it was reported triumphantly, 'is once more occupied by its chief'.[4] Castle reoccupation and 're-crowning' ceremonies such as this formed part of the wider 'neo-Celtic' movement of the turn of century, and provided rich owners with a means of advertising ancient lineal status. But, as Anderson shows, Eilean Donan Castle is better known still. The MacRae clan had been Constables of the Castle from 1511, and four centuries later, around 1911, its tattered fragments were acquired by a descendant, Lieutenant-Colonel John MacRae-Gilstrap, and re-created above base level for reoccupation between 1913 and 1932. The architect was an experienced restorationist, George MacKie Watson. This twentieth-century intervention, strongly recalling the creative castle restorations by nineteenth-century French architect Viollet-le-Duc, rather than the 'Anti-Scrape' conservation ideologies or dogmas of William Morris and the Society for Protection of Ancient Buildings, was one of the most important episodes in the history of Scottish Castle Culture.

Ian Begg's paper, which concludes the sequence of case-study papers in Part II of the book, is authored by a practising architect who has both restored and built Scottish castles. Begg tells us something of his own career before proceeding to relate the story of the building of his own castle-like home, Raven's Craig, near Plockton, intended as 'a modern house with the feel of an old tower [that] would feel good and strongly protective'. Begg sets that project in the context of his other flamboyantly castellated projects of the 1980s and 1990s, including the St Mungo museum in Glasgow and the Scandic Crown Hotel in Edinburgh's High Street, both of which are highly characteristic of the Postmodern era in attempting to echo a historical context through 'in keeping' style rather than modern contrast. Begg defends this work articulately against the habitual Modernist (and post-Venice Charter conservationist) criticism of 'pastiche' design. The second part of Begg's paper relates an even more startling attempt to translate this approach to the rampantly modernising environments of contemporary China, in a project for new 'Scottish castles' amidst new Chinese vineyards.

Telling the Story of Scotland's Castle Culture: A Short Historiographical Overview

The historiography of Scotland's castles reflects the wider evolution of cultural attitudes through the years and centuries. This is bound up with changing concepts of modernity, antiquarianism or preservationism, and also with changing political world outlooks. Was Scotland's culture to be valued? And if so, which elements of that culture? Or should it be regarded as problematic, maybe an embarrassment, because it did not comply with norms set elsewhere? And how did these values change over time?

It becomes increasingly easy to answer such questions when dealing with recent times, especially the twentieth century with its profusion of published sources, but the historiography of Scotland's Castle Culture can be traced back, albeit via fragmentary snippets, to the late seventeenth and early eighteenth centuries – a time when many castles were losing their status or practicality as residences, and being reconstructed or replaced, while others were acquiring new roles as ornamental historical artefacts to be viewed and visited. These contemporary values were vividly illustrated in Captain John Slezer's *Theatrum Scotiae* (1693), a series of architectural views, and in other views (such as George Heriot's Hospital and Gordon Castle) that he intended for future publication. Slezer, a military man originally from a German-speaking part of Europe, and from 1671 chief engineer in Scotland, holds a key place in Scotland's architectural and castles studies because he documented both newly reconstructed castles (Glamis, Thirlestane) and old castles, whether in use (Stirling, Edinburgh) or abandoned and in ruins (Bothwell, St Andrews). Slezer was uncompromising in his praise of his subject matter:

> It's a Matter worthy of one's enquiry, how a Nation, as SCOTLAND, so much addicted to *Military Arts*, and so constantly engaged in both Foreign and Domestick Wars, should have been in a Capacity to erect such superb Edifices as that Kingdom abounds with.[5]

St Andrews Cathedral, in its heyday, had been 'one of the best of the Gothic kind in the world', and even comparable to St Peter's in Rome. This kind of fulsome, uncritical praise was only typical of the time: contemporary descriptions tended to speak positively about gentlemen's residences, whether castles or not. To John Hodge in 1722, for instance, Newark (Selkirkshire) was 'a pretty castle'.[6]

Slezer omitted to mention his collaboration with another key antiquarian, Sir Robert Sibbald (1641–1722), who in 1707 wrote:

> Amongst the Sciences and Arts much improved in our time, the Archeologie, that is the Explication and Discovery of Ancient Monuments, is one of the greatest use.[7]

Early antiquarianism focused almost exclusively upon Roman or prehistoric remains, but medieval survivals were also increasingly valued. For example, Sir John Clerk of Penicuik (1676–1755), the noted politician, classical scholar and antiquary, persuaded Lord Sinclair in 1739 to finance repairs to Rosslyn Chapel (which had been built by a Sinclair ancestor), and oversaw the work personally. In his appreciation of castles, Clerk drew a distinction between intact towers, which he liked, and a hybrid case such as Thirlestane Castle, partly classicised in the 1670s, which Clerk criticised as 'a great building of a vile Gothick taste'.[8] These first harbingers of the love of castles were combined at times incongruously with the 'improving' Whig contempt for the obsolete, pre-eighteenth-century past. William Adam's projected *Vitruvius Scoticus* (unpublished until 1812), a proud parade of Scottish modernity and of his own architecture, contained almost exclusively classical designs – the exception being Taymouth, a crow-stepped castle already made symmetrical, for which he had designed symmetrical wings. Artists connected to the government army in 1745–6 paid some attention to old buildings, and old Inveraray Castle is at the centre of Paul Sandby's view of the town.

Notwithstanding Inveraray's Gothic Revival design, replacement of castellation with classicism continued apace until the 1770s and the building of new 'ancient' castles by Adam and his brothers. By now, the values expressed in the published accounts of travellers had begun to shift from aggressive modernity to a general Romanticism – a world-view, however, that covered wide variations. For Dorothy Wordsworth in 1803 and

1822, ruined castles were chiefly of interest as an integral part of broader landscapes of the Picturesque or Sublime: on her 1822 tour to Inveraray, the only castle to rouse her interest was Newark.[9] To Walter Scott, whom Dorothy befriended, castles were by contrast invigorating, primary historic documents: tangible documents of history. And to John E Bowman, on his Scottish tour of 1825, the old seaboard castles of northern Argyll echoed the sublimity of the scenery and, in their collapsing state, symbolised the transience of all phases of history. He anticipated that eventually a castle such as Duart, 'though now in a state of dilapidation, may no longer remain, to mark to future ages the barbarous manners of the ancient Highland chieftains, before the all subduing hand of time levels them with the base of the eternal hills on which they stand'.[10]

By now, however, the idea was growing that the decay of castles was not inevitable, but could be arrested. For contemporaries of Bowman's, such as Sir Walter Scott and Lord Cockburn, not only was it desirable to retain old castles, but it was now a duty. Lauriston Castle's owner, Thomas Allan, first planned to demolish the tower but was pressurised by his friend Lord Cockburn to retain it. Cockburn's prolifically expressed views well expressed a Castle Culture in transition towards conservation. When Allan declared his plans, Cockburn thundered:

> I require nothing to convince me that the plan is bad – and I am perfectly determined not to be convinced that it is good. I never yet have seen any one old monument destroyed . . . without being followed, when it is too late, by sorrow and reproach. The last you won't escape – God save you from the first. The worthy old tower! . . . Depend upon it, the demolition is totally unnecessary, and even necessity, or what is called so – that

is, the temporary convenience of a new domicil – is no justification. If you can clap two centuries of time on top of a new house the day it is built, it may not be profane to extinguish two centuries by pounding an old one.[11]

Walter Scott's comments on Lauriston also mixed modernity and preservationism, as he recorded in his visit of 1827:

> Went with Tom Allan to see his building at Lauriston, where he has displayed good taste – supporting rather than tearing down or destroying the old chateau . . . The additions are very good and will make a most comfortable house. Mr Burn, architect, would fain have had the old house pulled down, which I wonder at in him, though it would have been the practice of most of his brethren.[12]

Cockburn also sternly criticised the more impersonal neglect of ruined Highland structures, such as Kilchurn Castle, where there was

> still enough of turret, and window, and ivy remaining to render it perhaps in as perfect a stage for preservation, as a ruin, as it ever has been or can be. But what murder it is undergoing! . . . Not one sixpence . . . or one moment of care has ever been bestowed on either of the two duties of protecting or of cleaning. [The cause was the owner] being reconciled to what ought to be felt shameful; till at last he who would give £500 for a hearthrug or £5000 for a Gothic dairy, stares at the idea of expending a shilling on arresting the decay of the only thing he may happen to possess which painting or poetry think worthy of their notice.[13]

In comments such as these, we have almost arrived at the modern concept of the national duty to care for historic buildings in the abstract, although, in contrast with contemporary France, there was not yet any concept that the state should take charge of this work.

To Scotland's greatest castle historians and surveyors, David MacGibbon and Thomas Ross, castles were tangible documents of national history – a history still firmly based on a narrative of progress and Improvement from a primitive, even if also romantic, 'Baronial' past: 'Nothing can be more interesting and instructive than to follow the records of our national history contained in these old castles.'[14] They argued that regnal union with England in 1603 had brought about 'an enlightening and civilising effect on Scotland generally, by bringing it into contact with a richer and more polished people, and in this way many improvements were gradually imported from the south into the domestic arrangements and architecture of the country'.[15] The wars of the seventeenth and eighteenth centuries, however disruptive, represented a kind of progress, by tending 'to obliterate old feuds and knit the nation together with a common purpose'.[16]

MacGibbon and Ross, living in an age of high empire as well as continuing Improvement, naturally felt it a historian's patriotic duty to broadcast the virtues of British unionism, propagate the concept of a pre-union Scotland fettered by war, and condemn Jacobitism and Highlanders as primitive and disruptive. In this they were in tune with contemporary orthodoxies. Mar Castle, for them, was in 1746 'one of the principal garrisons for keeping the Highlanders in order'.[17] It had before then been 'burnt by the natives'.[18]

By the early twentieth century, this worldview had lost its confident swagger, and a more balanced, scholarly approach was beginning to take its place. W Mackay Mackenzie's *The Medieval Castle in Scotland* (1927), for instance,

grappled with the subject in an earnest, scholarly way. There was still, however, a pervasive assumption that pre-union castle architecture, however technically ingenious, was unsophisticated and 'late'. More generally, the relative economic and political decline of Scotland during the interwar depressions led to a subtle downplaying of the entire Scottish architectural heritage, or its conflation with English architecture. For example, although Robert Adam featured prominently in Nikolaus Pevsner's *An Outline of European Architecture* (1943), he was presented as an 'English' architect. And John Summerson's *Architecture in Britain*, first published 1953 and still in print today as a standard student text, covered pre-1707 Scotland in a somewhat patronisingly worded appendix.

By the late 1960s, however, the gradual emergence of a separatist rather than unionist Scottish nationalism was beginning to undermine the credibility of this approach. In 1967, for example, T W West's *A History of Architecture in Scotland* argued that, despite the monumental labours of authorities like MacGibbon and Ross, 'most British writers on architecture generally have paid scant attention' to Scotland. West praised the researches of antiquarians such as W Douglas Simpson or chief government archaeologist Stuart Cruden.[19] However, this generation still retained some of the old attitudes: in 1986, Cruden argued of Scottish medieval church architecture that: 'It must be acknowledged that it is an inferior architecture, the fag-end of the international European tradition.'[20] For Cruden, Scotland's castles, however richly picturesque, still also told a gloomy tale of backwardness, incessant troublemaking, and a much-extended medieval period, with no story of a 'Renaissance'.

By 1986, such attitudes had been left far behind by the onward march of Scottish architectural and cultural politics. Already, in the 1960s and 70s, John Dunbar had twice looked afresh at castles in his *The Architecture of Scotland* (1966, revised 1978) and found a more positive narrative in his overviews, which he presented in dispassionate, scholarly terms. Others, such as George Hay, also took a refreshing approach. For Hay, Scotland's Renaissance was perhaps 'late'; but the same was true of other countries. As for individual castle studies, there was an extensive series of government guidebooks, allied to numerous essays in the *Proceedings of the Society of Antiquaries of Scotland*, notably by W D Simpson and Harry Gordon Slade. Archaeological analyses replete with supplemental documentary references characterised the Royal Commission (RCAHMS) series of county-based *Inventories*, which began in 1908. The swansong of the series, the seven-volume *Argyll* (1971–92) forcibly re-emphasised the significance of the seaboard medieval castles of that region. The late eighteenth and early nineteenth-century 'castle revival', too, was covered in mainstream architectural history studies and publications by numerous authors.

The political failure of the 1979 devolution referendum was followed by a compensatory upsurge in nationalistic cultural enterprises of all sorts, including architectural history – in effect, a dramatically telescoped mirror-image of the post-1707 Whig elite's denigration of 'primitive' Scottish culture. Scottish documentary history was substantially enhanced by the widely available John Donald series of in-depth studies published by John Tuckwell, and university Scottish History departments were burgeoning. There was, for instance, Allan Macinnes' Highlands-oriented course at Glasgow; at St Andrews, Norman MacDougall inaugurated a series of new royal biographies with his *James III* and *James IV*, continued at Edinburgh by Michael Lynch and Julian Goodare. Most fields of Scottish cultural history saw ambitious overview publications, including a four-volume *History of Scottish Literature* (1987, edited by Cairns Craig), Duncan

MacMillan's *Scottish Art: 1460–1990* (1990), John Purser's *Scotland's Music* (1992, revised 2007) and a *History of Scottish Architecture* (1996, by Miles Glendinning, Ranald MacInnes and Aonghus MacKechnie). All of these books volubly protested against any suggestion that Scottish patterns could any longer be shoehorned into interpretations based on English or British culture. Other significant architectural publications included the multi-authored booklet *The Architecture of the Scottish Renaissance*, which accompanied the 1990 RIAS exhibition, and Deborah Howard's *Scottish Architecture from the Reformation to the Restoration, 1560–1660* (1995).

In the specific field of Castle Culture, the consequence was an escalating wave of reinterpretation, arguing for the 'internationalism' and sophistication of Scottish designers and patrons, and condemning the old 'warlike' and 'primitive' interpretation of Scottish castles in ever more extreme terms. James IV's Stirling forework gate, for example, was now seen not as a coarsely battlemented fortress entrance but as the British-truncated remnant of a 'Roman'-style triumphal arch, part of a complex array of imperial symbolism within the Scottish monarchy from James III's time onwards. In a series of publications in the 1990s, Ian Campbell proselytised on the linked concepts of a 'Scottish Romanesque revival' in the fifteenth century and an early Scottish participation in the wider processes of the 'Renaissance' in Europe. This audacious interpretation proposed the dramatic catapulting of castellated buildings such as Linlithgow Palace from 'Baronial' backwardness to the front rank of international architectural development. Cruden's model of a Scotland stumbling behind England was now replaced by one of a proudly 'European' Scotland, marching in the forefront of not only the wider European Renaissance, but also many other later, international architectural trends.

The vehement attacks on the old Summerson approach to Scottish architectural history continued to rumble on for a time, until it could be certain that the monster had been finally and irreversibly slain. The very title of Charles McKean's *The Scottish Chateau* (2001) suggested a special emphasis on the dignity and 'European' sophistication of the Scottish castle. A decade further on, McKean's chapter on Glamis Castle in Part II of this book further elaborates on that argument, protesting that to assess Scottish castles or architecture from an (English) '"Palladian perspective" is a nonsense approach to understanding Scottish architectural culture of the century between 1650 and 1750'. By this stage, any negative comments about any aspect of Scottish architecture by English writers were seen as unacceptable. Even the sedate writings of (Sir) Howard Colvin, the leading establishment figure among English/British architectural historians, were criticised for suggesting that, by the late seventeenth century, 'the tower house was an anachronism'. Faced with this bristling militancy, the response of some English historians was defensive: in 1995, for example, Giles Worsley, chronicler of country houses, complained that 'to write about Scottish architectural history is to enter a minefield of nationalist passions, both contemporary and modern'.[21]

But, like its early eighteenth-century unionist mirror-image, the 1980s and 1990s world outlook of 'resurgent' cultural nationalism was neither homogeneous nor uncritical, and the castle might still find itself in the firing line – in the same way as castles were often praised by otherwise uncompromisingly zealous eighteenth-century Improvers such as Sir John Clerk. The twentieth-century Gaelic poet Sorley MacLean, for example, turned on its head the Walter Scott tradition of romanticising the castle-owning landed classes in his 1938 poem 'Ban-Ghàidheil' ('A Highland Woman'), launching an assault upon a Gaelic society dominated by (perhaps absentee) landlordism and a complicit Church:

*An t-earrach so agus so chaidh
's gach fichead earrach bho'n an tùs
tharruing ise 'n fheamainn fhuar
chum biadh a cloinne 's duais an tùir.*
· · ·
*mheal ise an dubh-chosnadh cruaidh;
is glas a cadal suain an nochd.*

This Spring and last Spring
and every twenty Springs from the beginning,
she has carried the cold seaweed
for her children's food and the castle's reward
· · ·
the hard Black Labour was her inheritance
grey is her sleep to-night.[22]

For MacLean, the 'castle' was a symbol not simply of inherited division and inequality, but of active oppression and cruelty.

At the end, perhaps the strongest feature not only of the historiography of Scotland's Castle Culture but of the wider attitudes towards the castle over the centuries, is this ever-changing diversity. Ever since the Middle Ages, people have passionately valued, and also at times passionately criticised, Scotland's castles for a wide range of reasons – cultural, visual, practical and emotional – sometimes all at the same time, and with the balance never remaining static for long. That stimulating but sometimes jarring diversity has continued into recent decades, as MacLean's attack demonstrates. Even as 'restoring owners' up and down the country were lovingly bringing ruins back into life, the opposite trend also still fitfully flared: in 1980, the remains of Cathcart Castle, which had outlasted its successor house, were reduced to a three-foot high stump by the City of Glasgow District Council; and as recently as 2002, the owner of the sixteenth- to nineteenth-century Lanrick Castle demolished it altogether, defying the formidable apparatus of modern conservation legislation and government controls. There was, and is, no monolithic view of castles, and in that respect our generation is no different from those of previous centuries.

PART I

Eight Centuries of Castle Culture:
A Chronological Survey

CHAPTER ONE

Foundations of a Castle Culture: Pre-1603

Geoffrey Stell

First created and brought to maturity when military values prevailed among warrior aristocracies, medieval castles, whether built of earth and timber or stone and lime mortar, have long been perceived as products of social and political turbulence and as veritable machines of war. Such allegedly 'real' castles, where function is considered to have exactly matched form, have traditionally been seen as mighty and impregnable -looking centres of lordship and authority that endured for as long as they remained fit for military or defensive purpose.

The experience of many major castles in Scotland, as elsewhere, has conformed to this image, and whether by design or default they found themselves caught up in the thick of war, besieged and often scarred by slighting or mining. The Stewart (later royal) castle of Rothesay on Bute was almost certainly the object of the first recorded siege on Scottish soil in 1230 when it was attacked by forces shipped in by a Norwegian fleet. English garrisons in mighty Bothwell Castle (see Chapter 7) were attacked and the castle damaged by Scots in 1314 and 1337, and there is good reason to believe that the missing rear half of the donjon is evidence of deliberate slighting on the part of Andrew Murray, not an easy undertaking either physically or psychologically, for the rightful owner of the castle. The castle at St

Andrews, subject of a fourteen-month artillery siege of the Protestant assassins of Cardinal Beaton in 1546–7, has bequeathed remarkable evidence of the besiegers' mine, thwarted by the defenders' counter-mine. St Andrews was badly damaged but, over centuries of intermittent Anglo-Scottish warfare, few suffered more than Lochmaben Castle, a strategic gateway to south-west Scotland which has come down to us as a tough-looking relic of national conflict and local family feuding.

The single most destructive phase in the history of Edinburgh Castle occurred in April and May 1573 when it was being held on behalf of Queen Mary against an English-backed force of 'King's Men' led by Regent Morton, an event that is depicted in a near-contemporary woodcut, first published in 1577 (Figure 2). Several siege batteries were trained on the castle, and the most spectacular effect of the bombardment was to bring down one of the most prominent residential buildings, the then 200-year-old David's Tower. This lofty tower, an icon of late medieval Scottish kingship, fell in two stages, burying the great well of the castle on its second collapse. In the rebuilding operations, which Morton himself authorised immediately following the siege, its much-reduced ruins, surviving to just above first floor level, were encased within the Half-Moon Battery where they were eventually rediscovered

FIGURE 2
Edinburgh Castle: woodcut of siege of 1573 (from
Raphael Holinshed, *The Chronicles of England,
Scotland and Ireland* (1577 and later editions))

FIGURE 3
Siege tower: engraving by Emmanuel Viollet-le-Duc
(from *Dictionnaire raisonné de l'architecture française*
(1858–68) and *An Essay on the Military Architecture of
the Middle Ages* (1860))

in 1912, over three centuries later.

Such episodes have reinforced the view that
castles were essentially products of societies and
regions that were to a greater or lesser degree
militarised and where defence or, at the very least,
security and protection were paramount. No
small wonder perhaps that the overall form and
features of castles came to be regarded as strictly
functional and evolutionary, undergoing modifi-
cations in response to attacking strengths and
defensive needs. Castle studies were long dominated by issues of design typology and military
capability, while military strategy was likewise
seen as the key to determining and understanding
a castle's location.

For more than a century from the middle
decades of the nineteenth century these views
prevailed among successive generations of castle

scholars, who were interpreting fortifications
whilst the world was preparing for, or actually
engaged in, warfare, and when there was much
contemporary discussion about – and practical
application of – concepts of attack and defence.
One of the earliest, most influential and prolific
proponents of such views was French architect
and theorist Eugène Emmanuel Viollet-le-Duc
(1814–1879). He acquired – and indeed still
enjoys – considerable status, and was able to put
into physical effect, most notably at Carcassonne
and Pierrefonds, his unambiguously military
theories about castles, specialising in the imaginative reinstatement of lost upper works, especially timber hoardings and roofs. His dramatic,
sketched interpretation of a belfry siege tower is
worthy of a Hollywood stage set at its most
extravagant (Figure 3).

FIGURE 4
Castle Fraser, Aberdeenshire: Dr W Douglas Simpson
illustrating a talk, 1956 (© RCAHMS, SC 802341)

FIGURE 5
Doune Castle, Perthshire: south façade of hall and
gatehouse, 1985 (© RCAHMS, SC 798573)

In Britain as a whole, not only Scotland, the
military standpoint reached its peak in the person
of Dr William Douglas Simpson (1896–1968),
who stands out as an uncompromising protagonist
of such views (Figure 4). Simpson's mother was
German, and through her he had close family
links with East Prussia, an area from where in the
1930s he and his generation were confronted with
the contemporary reality of mobile, ruthlessly
efficient, professional armies. Such influences
became patently manifest in his theories about the
effects of 'livery and maintenance' and so-called
'bastard feudalism' – that is, the employment of
paid retainers – on late medieval castle design.

Late fourteenth- and fifteenth-century castles
such as Doune (Figure 5) and Tantallon were the
initial settings for Simpson's application of these
'keep-gatehouse' theories, prompted by his obser-
vation that the inner gates of their gatehouses
might be secured from within the gatehouse
passage. He concluded that, in the event of unpaid
retainers running amok within the courtyard
through lack of pay and/or excess of drink, the
owner or custodian had the means to shut himself
off from them. The owners were thus taking as
much defensive precaution against unruly staff
within as against potential attackers without.
These theories, which took no account of
postern gateways, of which even a drunken
retainer would be aware, were patently absurd –
but they were very persuasive at the time, and
were written into most of Simpson's prodigious
and influential output, larded with emotive references to the 'rampant ruffianism among the old
Scottish baronage' and the treachery and fickle-
ness of the 'jackmen' or bullies' in their employ.

Until comparatively recently it was also held as axiomatic, following the Bayeux Tapestry model, that castles were necessarily products of periods of social and political turbulence and violence. Certainly, there were campaigns of conquest involving the building of castles, especially of earth and timber. But, demonstrably, castle and tower building generally was more related to periods of social and economic stability and to the expression of wealth. Serious practical investments in time, money and materials applied to the creation of all castles and towers, and those erected in stone were particularly demanding of resources and organisation. Where they were part of a campaign, such costly structures were mainly intended to put the seal on military conquest. In the last quarter of the thirteenth century, King Edward I of England (1272–1307) expended a fortune on such a castle-building programme in North Wales, spending about £80,000, then a considerable sum, on eight major castles. The greatest of these was Caernarvon, begun in 1283 but never quite finished.

More obviously than most, Caernarvon shows what a great part symbolism played in medieval castle design and construction. By planting its huge bulk in the ancient centre of Gwynedd, Edward was not just making a crude statement of English royal power; rather, he was symbolising reconquest, and even ancient imperial associations. The castle embraced an earlier Norman motte built by the earl of Chester, while in 1283 what were believed to be the mortal remains of the body of Magnus Maximus, father of the Roman emperor Constantine and subject of an ancient Welsh romance, were reburied in the church. The architecture of Caernarvon Castle is loaded with Roman imperial symbolism. Its unusual but distinctive polygonal towers and banded masonry were quite clearly intended to imitate the tile-laced Theodosian wall of Constantinople, a message confirmed by the

triplet of eagle turrets above the principal or Eagle Tower. Belief was almost greater than reality as a motivating force in the Middle Ages and, in the hands of a ruthless and wealthy monarch such as Edward I, symbolism became a powerful political tool. Thankfully, as described below, money, time and mortality ensured that he never had the opportunity to create such a castle of the emperors in Scotland.

No coded messages, merely an obvious delight in aesthetic and decorative powers and charms, conveyed especially by their skylines of ornate crenellations and turrets, are what emerge from some contemporary illustrations of castles, most famously those of a series of French chateaux in the *Très Riches Heures*, a Book of Hours painted for the Duc de Berry by the Limbourg brothers between 1413 and 1416. What is less well known is that by the first half of the fifteenth century Scotland may well already have been regarding such features in much the same way, as appears to be demonstrated by the instructive case of mighty Borthwick Castle. There, in 1430, William Borthwick, its original builder and loyal supporter of King James I, was granted special licence to construct a castle in a place commonly called the Mote of Lochorwart. Like other Scottish licences to crenellate, the Borthwick licence appears to reflect a bond of political trust, and traditions of royal service were maintained by later generations of the family, including William's son, who probably completed the castle in the middle of the fifteenth century. Significantly, like at least one other surviving example, the licence included provision for the construction of 'defensive ornaments at the wall-head' ('in summitate ornamentis defensivis'). Even in the fifteenth century, it seems, battlements and turrets were already viewed as symbols of lordship and authority, as much, if not more, than practical means of defence.

Even from before the age of the castle, the

FIGURE 6

Arbroath Abbey, Angus: engraving of gatehouse range (from Francis Grose, *The Antiquities of Scotland* (1789–91), © RCAHMS, SC 498324)

emphasis that society has placed on status, ceremony, display and symbolism in architecture can never be underestimated. The corollary is that, while accepting that defensive considerations may have been critical determinants of castle design in certain times and locations, we can no longer share the confidence of earlier generations of military castellologists to assert that function necessarily followed form. Indeed, we have to be prepared to accept that castellated appearances might be deceptive, probably more often than not. For the past few decades the academic spotlight has thus been placed on the ways in which social, economic and institutional life has impinged upon the building, use and development of castles. Indeed, as expressions of lordship and institutional authority, castle-like forms have even extended into the realms of what is conventionally classified as church architecture. Arbroath Abbey (Figure 6), for example, was one of a select group of monastic houses that acquired rights of regality jurisdiction, the highest form of judicial authority under the crown, and it is thus no coincidence that the castle-like architecture of the rebuilt gatehouse and adjacent range at Arbroath, culminating in the corner Regality Tower, corresponds closely in date with the assumption of these rights in the late thirteenth century, a symbolic statement directed at the townsfolk of the adjacent abbot's burgh as much as anyone. Symbolism, albeit of a different source and inspiration, also certainly underpins the martial, castle-like appearance of the fifteenth-century west front of St Machar's Cathedral, Aberdeen.

In line with current environmental interests, much of the academic emphasis is now on the castle's place in the physical landscape, and upon its associations, *qua* the country house and estate centre, with yards, ancillary demesne buildings, gardens, ponds and parks – all the accoutrements, in other words, of a later country mansion or laird's house. Indeed, in terms of their domestic planning and landscape context, the ways in which many Scottish castles and towers became country houses in the later medieval and early modern eras was not as radical a transformation as was once thought. However, as McKean has recently pointed out, the transition from castle to country house has been confused partly by the fact that contemporary Scottish nobles and lairds themselves persisted with the idea of evoking a warlike heritage through architectural trappings and martial fashion accessories such as gun loops, and partly through a deliberate renaming of houses as castles, a point referred to more fully below. One result has been that, judging by their outward castle-like forms and their display of symbols of ancestry, authority and defence, it has become almost impossible to draw any meaningful line between survival and revival among many of the numerous and often grandiose 'fortified' houses of the latter half of the sixteenth century. Many of these, especially the grander piles such as Fyvie Castle and Castle Fraser, may indeed be better understood as conscious products of a precocious, first-phase castle revival which was already well under way by 1603. Ironically, thanks to their inclusion in the highly influential books of illustrations by Robert Billings, *The Baronial and Ecclesiastical Antiquities of Scotland* (1848–52),

many of these very same buildings became the models for another generation of castle builders three centuries later (see Figure 7).

Setting aside these specific Scottish issues, it is clear that questions of form, function and symbolism have general international application in relation to castle and tower architecture. Deciding between what might have been for real use and what for show is not a peculiarly Scottish matter of castle interpretation. However, given that this country came to stand, as it undoubtedly did, at the European forefront of castle revival in the eighteenth and nineteenth centuries, what was so special about Scotland and about the attitude to the castle in medieval and Renaissance Scotland? What pointers are there towards a Castle Culture taking firm and enduring root here? Several tests might be used in an attempt to address these questions exhaustively, but they have been reduced here under four main sub-headings for the purposes of an initial analysis: the importance of numbers; designations; 'Scottishness'; and the meaning of castles to contemporary Scots.

1. Under *numbers*, the questions are both absolute – is Scotland truly a land of castles? – and relative – do we have more or fewer castles than our neighbours? In order to gain some crude initial idea of a general census, four published sources were consulted. Though using different criteria, and of variable status as works of reference, these works share a common aim of attempted comprehensiveness. The results, which are described and tabulated in Table 1, show an enormous range, extending from 754 to as high as 2,763, the latter figure reflecting a completely unrestricted view of date and type, modern as well as medieval. Two sources, however, present relatively closely matched four-figure assessments: Salter with 1,026; and the Collins map, initially with 1,186 later increased to 1,250.

FIGURE 7

Castle Fraser, Aberdeenshire: engraving by Robert W Billings (from *The Baronial and Ecclesiastical Architecture of Scotland* (1848–52))

A second table (Table 2) breaks down the castle 'genus' in Scotland into two of its constituent 'species': timber castles and stone-built tower or fortified houses, again based on published sources that have aimed at a degree of comprehensiveness. The gap between two of the sources in relation to tower houses reflects a variation in definition and approach, but the aggregate of the higher figure (674) and that eventually arrived at for the timber castles (317) is closely approaching the 1,000-plus figures in Table 1, a shortfall that would almost certainly be made up by other castle types not listed here. At this stage little can thus be definitively asserted about over-

all numbers of castles and towers in Scotland, timber as well as stone, but a figure of about 1,200 would appear to constitute a reasonable working hypothesis or starting point for further research.

A third table (Table 3) presents a geographical view of published numbers in parts of two regions that are known to have been relatively heavily castellated: the area of the western seaboard that lay within Argyll, and the West March of the Anglo-Scottish border. The subject of the most comprehensive published survey in modern times, the former county of Argyll is known to have contained 89 castles within its boundaries. An equally thorough review of all

TABLE 1
General Censuses of Medieval Castles and Fortifications in Scotland

MacGibbon and Ross
Date-range | 'From the twelfth to the eighteenth century'
Types | Masonry castles, towers and houses
Numbers | 754 (omitting buildings in towns, churches and sundials), 426 of which were classified as tower houses by J G Dunbar (see below)

Macgregor
Date-range | '1150 AD and the end of the seventeenth century'
Types | Masonry castles, towers and fortified houses
Numbers | 1,186 increased to 1,250 in 1985 edition

Salter
Date-range | 'Between 1100 and the 1630s'
Types | Timber and masonry castles, towers and fortified houses
Numbers | 1,026

Coventry
Date-range | Unrestricted
Types | Timber and masonry castles, towers, fortified houses and mansion castles
Numbers | 2,763 (2001 edition)

Sources: David MacGibbon and Thomas Ross, *The Castellated and Domestic Architecture of Scotland* (5 vols, 1887–92); D Ronald Macgregor, [Map of] *The Castles of Scotland* (1974 and later); Mike Salter, *Discovering Scottish Castles* (1985); and Martin Coventry, *The Castles of Scotland* (1995 and later).

TABLE 2
Censuses of Selected Castle Types in Scotland

Tranter
Date-range | c.1400–c.1650
Types | Masonry towers and houses
Numbers | 554, plus 120 noted as 'much-altered structures'

Dunbar
Date-range | Fourteenth to early seventeenth centuries
Types | Masonry tower houses
Numbers | 426

Stell
Date-range | Twelfth to fourteenth centuries
Types | Timber castles
Numbers | 239 (188 + 48 possible + 3 doubtful), increased to 317 (259 + 53 possible + 5 doubtful) on republication in Stringer, *Essays on the Nobility* (1985) when list included ringworks

Sources: Nigel Tranter, *The Fortified House in Scotland* (5 vols, 1962–70); John G Dunbar, 'Tower-Houses', in Peter McNeill and Ranald Nicholson (eds), *An Historical Atlas of Scotland c.1400–c.1600* (1975), derived from MacGibbon and Ross (above); and Geoffrey Stell, 'Provisional List of Mottes in Scotland', in *Château Gaillard*, vol. 5 (1972).

TABLE 3
Censuses of Castles in Selected Regions of Scotland

RCAHMS, Argyll

Date-range	Twelfth to seventeenth centuries
Area	Former county of Argyll
Types	Timber and masonry castles, towers and fortifications
Number	89 (cf. 58 in 1985 edition of Collins map above)

RCAHMS, Eastern Dumfriesshire

Area	Eastern Dumfriesshire
Date-range	Twelfth to seventeenth centuries
Types	Timber castles and masonry castles and towers
Number	14 timber castles (5 of which later converted to stone); 7 moated or ditched enclosures; 2 early stone castles; 123 towers or sites of towers and cognate structures

Maxwell-Irving

Date-range	Fourteenth to seventeenth centuries
Area	Dumfriesshire and eastern Galloway
Types	Masonry towers and fortified houses
Number	90 (increased to 92 on reprinting in 2006)

Sources: RCAHMS, *Inventory of Argyll* (7 vols, 1971–92) and RCAHMS, *Argyll Castles in the Care of Historic Scotland* (1997); RCAHMS, *Eastern Dumfriesshire* (1997); Alastair M T Maxwell-Irving, *The Border Towers of Scotland: The West March* (2000 and 2006).

castle types, including known sites, that was conducted in one area of the western Borders produced an overall tally of 146, while a specific study of the towers of the West March listed 92. Though actual numbers are not cited, the sheer density of all categories of sixteenth- and seventeenth-century defensible houses – towers, bastles and peles (known sites as well as standing remains) – in the Anglo-Scottish border region as a whole is well reflected in the distribution map published by Philip Dixon to accompany his important 1979 article, 'Towerhouses, Pelehouses and Border Society', in the *Archaeological Journal* (Figure 8).

No attempt has been made here to provide comparative figures for Ireland, where the overall picture is still emerging through active research. For England and Wales, however, there have been scholarly attempts to list and describe all the castles, made first by the late David James Cathcart King, and then by Philip Davis, his continu-

ator on 'The Gatehouse' website, the core of which is formed by King's original list and supporting documentation. An updated overall figure for castle and fortifications of all kinds in England (Table 4) is 4,637, comprising 2,390 certain and 2,247 possible examples, with an additional 537 doubtful attributions. For Wales (Table 5), the corresponding figures are, respectively, 905, 527, 378 and 215. According to this census, Northumberland was the most densely castellated of all former English counties, and by a very long way. King listed 131 surviving castles and towers, plus 102 that are known to have disappeared, making an overall total of 233. Second and third were Yorkshire and Shropshire with corresponding overall figures of 124 and 112 respectively, together roughly the same as Northumberland.

Admittedly lacking some of the categories included in these lists, on this showing Scotland

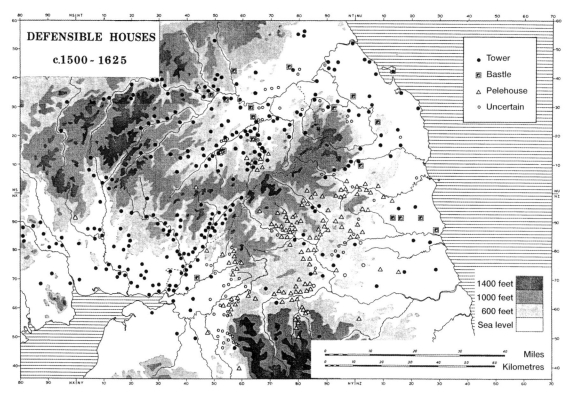

DEFENSIBLE HOUSES

c.1500 - 1625

• Tower
▣ Bastle
△ Pelehouse
○ Uncertain

1400 feet
1000 feet
600 feet
Sea level

Miles
Kilometres

FIGURE 8

Anglo-Scottish Borders: map of defensible houses c.1500–1625 (from *The Archaeological Journal*, vol. 136 (1979), © Philip Dixon and The Royal Archaeological Institute)

emerges with 150–350 per cent less than the English totals, and some 20–25 per cent more than those of Wales, figures that appear to be roughly proportionate to the countries' landscapes and populations. In a British Isles context, though, Scotland does not appear to stand out as an especially castellated country, except in the more militarised, one-time frontier zones, such as the western seaboard and the Anglo-Scottish Borders. It is thus difficult to sustain the notion that a Castle Culture simply grew out of a land where castles and towers were particularly numerous.

2. These comparative figures serve also to highlight part of the problem of *designation*, the second of our sub-headings: what kinds of structure have

been defined and counted as castles, towers and fortifications? Have like been compared with like, or have numbers been distorted by differences in terminology and understanding? Castle studies have traditionally been dominated by taxonomic approaches, almost all of the sub-classifications such as 'tower house', 'hall house' and 'enclosure castle' being of modern invention and application, part of a lingua franca used by castellologists in their international studies of castles of western Europe and the Crusader kingdoms. Scotland, however, has been subjected to more than its proportionate share of semantic variants, especially among its later (that is, sixteenth-century) towers and halls, so the task of defining and counting these has become unusually difficult. As

TABLE 4
Census of Medieval Castles and Fortifications in England

Category	Certain	Possible	Total	Doubtful
Timber castle	735	505	1240	292
Masonry castle	468	88	556	20
Tower house	117	60	177	8
Pele tower	224	197	421	32
Bastle	185	289	474	18
Chain tower	11	1	12	0
Fortified manor house	181	504	685	69
Fortified church	41	67	108	8
Fortified town/village	143	127	270	23
Palace	154	310	464	18
Artillery fort	100	44	144	6
Linear defence	5	14	19	2
Siege work	26	22	48	16
Uncertain type	0	19	19	26
Totals	2,390	2,247	4,637	537

TABLE 5
Census of Medieval Castles and Fortifications in Wales

Category	Certain	Possible	Total	Doubtful
Timber castle	278	191	469	125
Masonry castle	173	33	206	8
Tower house	1	9	10	2
Pele tower	5	12	17	2
Bastle	0	6	6	1
Fortified manor house	19	17	36	14
Fortified church	3	15	18	1
Fortified town/village	32	29	61	5
Palace	11	16	27	2
Siege work	2	6	8	4
Artillery fort	2	0	2	0
Uncertain type	1	44	45	51
Totals	527	378	905	215

Sources for Tables 4 and 5: David James Cathcart King, *Castellarium Anglicanum*, an index and bibliography of the castles in England, Wales and the islands (2 vols, 1983) and Philip Davis on 'The Gatehouse' website: http://homepage.mac.com/philipdavis/lists.html

will be shown below, most, if not all, of these works appear to belong to a self-conscious, first phase of castle revival, so there is really no difficulty in accepting them under a generic banner of castles and towers, much in the same way as wide varieties of hound were to Macbeth 'clept / All by the name of dogs'.

Unambiguous terms such as 'castrum', 'turris' and 'aula' certainly abound in the medieval record, but contemporary terminology does not provide the hoped-for clarity in the sixteenth and seventeenth centuries, given that the documents often contain a heterogeneous and repetitive mix of terms like 'fortalice' or 'manor place', general expressions that appear to denote legal and institutional status rather than actual physical forms and appearances. Also, to add further confusion to the issue of designation, as Charles McKean has pointed out, the 'castle' appellation did make a significant return during this period when, as signifiers of patrons' noble rank or pretension, houses with simple territorial names came to be retitled as castles. Thus, for example, Strathbogie, Gloom, Drumminor, Bog o'Gight (or The Bog), Muchall, Freuchie and Pettie became, respectively, Huntly Castle, Castle Campbell, Castle Forbes, Gordon Castle, Castle Fraser, Castle Grant and Castle Stewart. However, setting this trend against a background where defence and security remained fine matters of degree, not kind, where dangerous circumstances might still call such features into play, and when symbolism retained the power it had always had, there seems little reason to deny the wishes of contemporary patrons in placing rebranded and early revival or pastiche forms of 'castle' among the ranks of those which had exhibited similar ambiguities for centuries.

3. By 1603, then, Scottish castles, like those in other countries, had long exhibited a mixture of functionalism and symbolism in their architec-ture, a fusion that will always confound those seeking to distinguish 'real' from 'pretended' castle-like forms. This country is not unusual in lacking precise descriptive terms to define its towers and 'strong houses', but natives and visitors alike appeared to be predisposed towards viewing many of them as 'castle-wise'. Certainly, there is little evidence to suggest that a 'castle' conveyed any sense of opprobrium or out-of-date or out-of-fashion values, probably quite the opposite. So, how far did 'Scottishness', or any degree of distinc-tive architectural and social identity, lie behind this long-standing acceptance of, or even a renewed predilection for, castles and towers? Was medieval and early modern Scotland especially distinguished by its contribution to castellated architecture, and hence eager to retain and proudly flaunt the form?

At even a superficial titular level, the first answers to these broad questions reveal a funda-mental split between three approaches, each of which conveys subtle but significant differences in meaning: 'castles *of* Scotland', 'castles *in* Scot-land' and 'Scottish castles'. 'Castles of Scotland' is how David MacGibbon and Thomas Ross described their subject, prefacing their five-volume 1887–92 work with the following: 'The history of our Scottish castellated and domestic architecture is, in its main features, somewhat similar to that of France and England, although to a considerable extent modified by the more unsettled and less prosperous condition of the country. This, however, had the effect of introduc-ing and developing some varieties of style, which give a distinctly native and picturesque character to the later periods of our domestic architecture.' Of their fourth period (1542–1700), they further wrote: 'In the earlier part . . . the Scottish style was in universal use. Some indications of the Renais-sance feeling gradually began to appear . . . and towards its close the native style had been completely driven from the field by the foreign

FIGURE 9
Bothwell Castle, Lanarkshire: aerial view from south-west, 1968 (© RCAHMS SC 498076)

invader.' Arguing for 'castles in Scotland', William Mackay Mackenzie began his 1927 work with this revealing explanation: 'The specific subject of the book is the castles of Scotland, but it must not be forgotten that these constituted merely a province in the castle building area of western Europe. *Scotland invented nothing in this field* [my italics], though of course it moulded what it borrowed to its own desires. Thus . . . references to such structures elsewhere become necessary in the course of explanation.' An unequivocal spokesman for the 'Scottish castle' was Stewart Cruden, who in 1960 wrote of 'a stubborn adherence to a native partiality for vertical building'

from the end of the fourteenth century. He further elaborated: 'The tower-house, typical castle of the Scottish Later Middle Ages, is in fact derived from the great gatehouses which distinguish their last phase. Thus the first part of the long story with its medieval European background merges in the late fourteenth century into the second part in which native propensities prevail and foreign influences are accepted with reservations.'

Unilaterally, none of these bold and confident standpoints retains uncritical acceptance today. To later generations of castellologists the evidence has appeared much more complex, multi-faceted and ambiguous. Where questions of ethnic or national distinctiveness have been addressed, they have tended to be answered in ways which point to one or other of these approaches, or a fusion of all three. No one approach commands the entire field, but that is not to say, *pace* Mackenzie, that important and identifiably Scottish architectural contributions and blends did not emerge in the later medieval and early modern periods.

In terms of their design and features, if not building materials, classic courtyard castles such as Dirleton and Bothwell (see Chapter 7) (Figure 9) would not have been out of place in other medieval kingdoms. The earliest known stone enclosure castle, Castle Sween in Knapdale, would certainly not have stood out in contemporary Ireland; nor, as has long been recognised, would the later thirteenth-century Comyn stronghold of Inverlochy have been conspicuously different from the Edwardian castles of North Wales. Kildrummy, too, starting out as a plain polygonal enclosure with oddly projecting chapel, was later enlarged and elaborated with angle-towers and double-towered gatehouse of characteristic Edwardian style – not surprisingly, given that this second phase may well have been of English design and workmanship, possibly even closely modelled on Harlech itself.

Variant forms of enclosure castle were worked out in a nascent *Gàidhealtachd* along the western seaboard, where castles of the MacDougall and MacDonald heirs of Somerled became established in areas of retreating Norwegian influence, often occupying sites which bore names or other evidence that hinted at ancient occupation and that modified the polygonal geometry of the castles. Within their curtain-walled circuits were all the internationally recognisable components such as towers, turrets, donjons, halls and gatehouses, but they formed a more irregular and less formulaic assemblage. Dates of construction and development also

appear to have stretched over a much longer period than elsewhere, extending from thirteenth-century Dunstaffnage (Figure 10) to fifteenth-century Duntrune (Figure 11), through Mingary, probably of c.1300 or later, and mid fourteenth-century Castle Tioram (Figure 12), whose parent structure appears to be more of a hall than a tower.

The distinctive identity and sense of place that these castles were beginning to show became even more marked among curtain-less island castles, which came on record in the fourteenth century. The type is best represented by Finlaggan on Islay, centre of the powerful MacDonald Lordship of the Isles from the second quarter of the fourteenth century through to their forfeiture in 1493. Comprising hall, chapel, numerous service and other buildings, together with an offshore Council Isle, Finlaggan, like many others in the Hebrides, stands on an island in a freshwater loch, looking much more like a nucleated urban or rural settlement than a castle (Figure 13). Others of this collective domestic character occupy offshore islands and, like Dùn Chonaill, were even regarded as 'strong' castles, though it must have been a strength that was more nature-derived than man-made. Island dwelling was a common feature of late medieval Irish life, but few there appear to have achieved the status and physical development of many of those found among the islands of Scotland's western seaboard.

In Scotland, hall-centred castles, conventionally termed 'hall houses', also enjoyed a longevity, if not continuing status, that appears to have contrasted with most of their Irish counterparts. Aros on Mull is one of a group that probably belong to the fourteenth-century MacDonalds rather than their Macdougall predecessors. Dundonald in Ayrshire, one of the ancestral seats of the Stewart family, belongs mainly to the fourteenth century in its existing form, and its elongated plan, converted out of an earlier gatehouse,

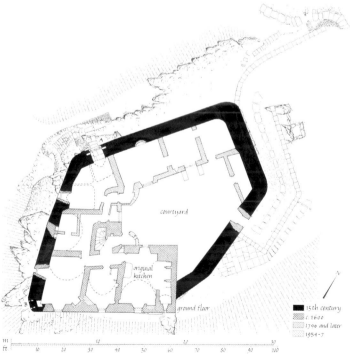

FIGURE 10
Above. Dunstaffnage Castle,
Argyll, from north-east, 1972
(© RCAHMS, SC 359685)

FIGURE 11
Left. Duntrune Castle, Argyll:
ground floor plan, 1990
(© RCAHMS, DP 069242)

FIGURE 12
Above. Castle Tioram, Inverness-shire, from north-east, 1926 (© RCAHMS, SC 1201437)

FIGURE 13
Right. Finlaggan Castle, Islay, Argyll: site plan, c.1981 (© RCAHMS, SC 427389)

FIGURE 14
Dundonald Castle, Ayrshire, from west, 1897 (© RCAHMS, SC 1171770)

boasts two great halls, one above the other, a work undertaken by Robert II (r.1371–90), first of the family's royal dynasty (Figure 14). Like Kindrochit in Mar, also by Robert II, many such hall-centred establishments in Scotland appear to have had associations with hunting and hunting forests.

Other distinctively Scottish variations were also worked upon the theme of the great hall as the public and ceremonial adjunct to the private residential tower. From the fourteenth century Scots nobles re-engaged with what was already a well-worked formula elsewhere and built such halls, integrated or detached, at periods when public duties and display came to be of paramount importance to them. For the fifteenth century alone, such halls can be found associated with castles such as Balgonie, Balvenie, Bothwell

(see Chapter 7), Crichton, Dean, Dirleton and Innis Chonnell, all of whose owners were of considerable political standing and usually of close royal association. At Dean Castle, Kilmarnock, for example, the scale and likely date of a heavily restored great hall range, detached from a large early fifteenth-century tower, appear to mark the zenith of the quasi-royal fortunes of the Boyds of Kilmarnock in the middle decades of the fifteenth century. Having secured control of the young, fatherless James III in 1466, Robert, Lord Boyd used his royal authority virtually to run the government of the kingdom from Kilmarnock for the next three years, his ambitions coming to an abrupt end in 1469 when James began his personal rule (Figure 15).

Whereas in England such halls came to be

FIGURE 15
Dean Castle, Kilmarnock, Ayrshire, from south, 2009 (© RCAHMS, DP 059993)

associated with grand manor houses and palaces, in Scotland they remained firmly within a castle context, reaching their apogee in the royal castles of Edinburgh and Stirling, one forming part of a palace block, the other standing relatively detached within the castle precincts. Also in contrast to the evidence from elsewhere, here the relationship between hall and tower percolated well down the landholding scale and persisted through the sixteenth and much of the seventeenth centuries. In Scotland, horizontal planning belonged just as much to the architecture of the Middle Ages as it did to that of the Renaissance and, as indicated below, hall building ultimately came within the reach of even the lowliest of lairds.

Like Ireland, late medieval Scotland warmly espoused what came to be labelled the 'tower house', and it is easy to agree with Cruden about the predominance of Scottish tower-building practices and use between the fourteenth and seventeenth centuries. Whilst considerably more towers appear to have been erected in Ireland, Scottish builders carried the type to greater physical and social heights, developed it in many more ways and made use of such structures over a much longer period. With Ireland, England and elsewhere, there is also a contrast in the early background and origins. Apart from a temporary mid twelfth-century Scots contribution to Carlisle Castle, tower building in Scotland itself was established within a political framework in

FIGURE 16
Edinburgh Castle: siege of 1544 showing Forework and David's Tower (from Cotton MSS, Augustus I, vol. 2,
© The British Library, C 08281-06)

which towers associated with the Norman, Angevin and Plantagenet empires, relatively plentiful and conspicuous elsewhere, were completely absent. This lack of precedent gives special interest and distinctiveness, intrinsically and comparatively, to the sources, development and distribution of the designs of Scottish towers as they emerged from about the middle of the fourteenth century onwards.

The tower created in Edinburgh Castle from 1367 by David II (1329–1371) appears to be one of the key progenitors of the entire Scottish genre (Figures 16 and 17). Entombed beneath the Half-Moon Battery, there is not enough left of its layout, particularly of the upper floors, to be certain of the original access arrangements at

what came to be known as David's Tower, but the possible use of forebuildings appears to hark back to Norman and Angevin models. Its original L-shaped layout, subsequently brought to a square or oblong, might have had some influence on immediately succeeding generations of Scottish towers, such as that at nearby Craigmillar on the southern outskirts of Edinburgh, and its physical links to a nearby palace and hall block points towards the later integrated tower and hall designs discussed above. As an iconic expression of Scottish kingship, the height and dominance of David's Tower must clearly have had a general symbolical significance that was not lost on all ranks of landholding society. When completed under David's successors in the latter half of the

FIGURE 17
Edinburgh Castle and esplanade from east, c.1955 (© RCAHMS, SC 1172625)

fourteenth century, the tower was the largest, loftiest and most conspicuous feature of the new eastern forework of the castle, commanding a view which embraced the mile-distant royal abbey of Holyrood, soon to become the preferred royal residence in Edinburgh.

As at Threave Castle in Galloway, other first- and second-generation towers erected by the greater Scottish magnates from about the middle of the fourteenth century also show faint echoes of Anglo-Norman and Angevin tower design in their access and formal reception arrangements. Whatever the sources, however, other priorities soon made themselves manifest. The kitchen, and by inference catering and banqueting, was an early facet of domestically inspired Scots design, a marked contrast with Irish towers in which identifiable kitchens are conspicuously absent. Though of an uncommon, acute-angled parallel-

ogram plan with rounded corners, late four-teenth-century Neidpath Castle typifies many of its generation in possessing a kitchen in the wing of its 'L-plan' layout, adjacent to the lower or screens end of the hall on the first floor of the main block (Figure 18). Equally tellingly, it is clear that the main purpose of a wing added after only a few decades to the late fourteenth-century oblong tower at Clackmannan was to create a kitchen on the first floor immediately adjoining the hall (Figure 19). In a group of towers in south-western Scotland, the kitchen was even more closely juxtaposed, being located within the body of the hall itself, within the screens or serv-ice area at the opposite end from the main fireplace. But for integrated domestic design Borthwick Castle, which dates from the second quarter of the fifteenth century, best exemplifies how classic medieval plans were interpreted and

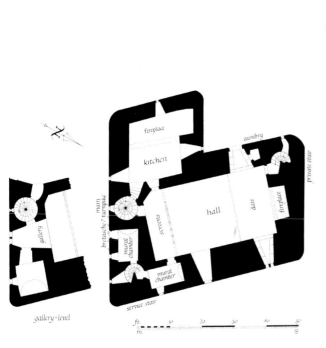

gallery-level

shaped into towered forms that were distinctively Scottish (see Figures 20 and 21). Borthwick consists of an elongated and vaulted hall block fronted by a pair of towers: one, which contained the kitchen and a stack of 'centrally heated' chambers above, was connected directly to the lower or service end of the hall; the other effectively served as a solar tower with a vertical suite of superior chambers correspondingly linked to the upper or dais end of the hall. As was almost universal throughout Scotland until the later decades of the sixteenth century, the principal public room or laird's hall was on the first floor, while the upper two or three floors were generally sub-divided into the main retiring and sleeping chambers. In Irish towers by contrast, the principal room, a hall-cum-gallery, was almost invariably on the top floor.

A distinctive form of extended tower that

FIGURE 18
Above left. Neidpath Castle, Peeblesshire: reconstructed first floor plan, c.1966 (© RCAHMS, DP 043862)

FIGURE 19
Above right. Clackmannan Tower, Clackmannanshire, from south-west, c.1928 (© RCAHMS SC 723772)

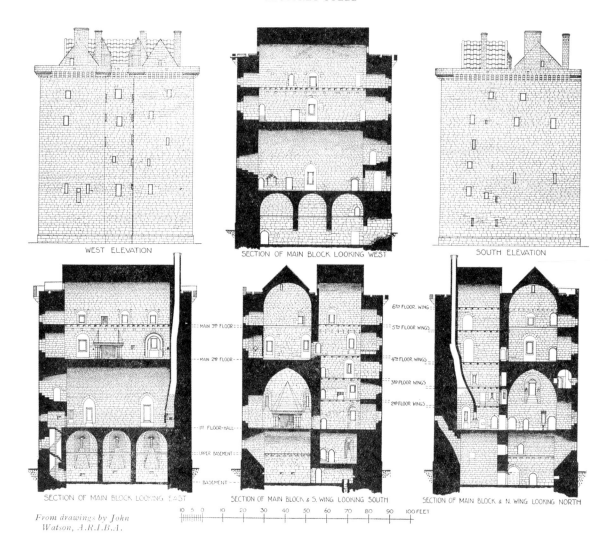

WEST ELEVATION

SECTION OF MAIN BLOCK LOOKING WEST

SOUTH ELEVATION

SECTION OF MAIN BLOCK LOOKING EAST

SECTION OF MAIN BLOCK & S. WING LOOKING SOUTH

SECTION OF MAIN BLOCK & N. WING LOOKING NORTH

MAIN 3ʳᵈ FLOOR

MAIN 2ᴺᴰ FLOOR

1ˢᵀ FLOOR-HALL

UPPER BASEMENT

BASEMENT

6ᵀᴴ FLOOR. WING

5ᵀᴴ FLOOR WINGS

4ᵀᴴ FLOOR WINGS

3ᴿᴰ FLOOR WINGS

2ᴺᴰ FLOOR WINGS

From drawings by John Watson, A.R.I.B.A.

10 5 0   10   20   30   40   50   60   70   80   90   100 FEET

appeared in many parts of Scotland from around the middle of the sixteenth century was the one later dubbed the 'Z-plan', a layout which incorporated angle-turrets flanking the main block at diagonally opposite corners. This staggered and generally elongated design permitted a doubling or tripling of internal accommodation, with well-organised, corridor-linked services in the basements and suites of halls and chambers in the main block and wings above. Scotland was certainly not alone in applying or adapting such designs, but even where they may have been of demonstrable foreign origin it is not easy to view such structures as mere pastiches. Drochil in the Borders is a case in point. Built in the 1570s by the Regent Morton, and evidently incomplete at the date of his execution in 1581, Drochil was designed with lodgings disposed on either side of a central corridor that may have formed a gallery on the top floor (Figure 22). Unique and exotic in Scotland at that date, this double-pile plan was almost certainly derived from the highly influen-

FIGURE 20
Opposite. Borthwick Castle, Midlothian: elevations and sections (from RCAHMS, *Inventory of Midlothian* (1929), © RCAHMS, SC 1233681)

FIGURE 21
Above. Borthwick Castle, Midlothian: engraving by Robert W Billings (from *The Baronial and Ecclesiastical Architecture of Scotland* (1848–52))

tial anthologies of Renaissance architecture then being produced by Jacques Androuet du Cerceau. The result, however, was not an undisguised French chateau but a tower-like hunting lodge which is manifestly a Scottish blend, certainly in external appearance and construction.

The adaptation of foreign and native became a conspicuous feature of a phase which amounted to a celebration of tower architecture from about the third quarter of the sixteenth century onwards. The blending and revivalism took many forms, but symbols of lineage and nobility were much in evidence and attention was lavished upon gatehouses. Rowallan, for example, a relatively modestly sized laird's residence, was remodelled in the 1560s when it assumed the character of a miniature royal castle or lodge. That was when the stepped approach, flanked by twin drum towers, was created and a royal armorial placed over the front door (Figure 23). Clearly replicating on a domestic scale the palace layout and double-towered frontispieces of royal works

FIGURE 22
Drochil Castle: Peeblesshire: engraving by Robert W
Billings (from *The Baronial and Ecclesiastical Architecture of Scotland* (1848–52))

such as Stirling Castle, the remodelled Rowallan
was obviously intended to symbolise a distant
connection with the royal family through Elizabeth Mure, daughter of Adam Mure of Rowallan
and first wife of Robert II. The frontage of
Tolquhon was another – perhaps even more
striking – specimen of symbolism and royal association. A Forbes residence with a tower since the
early fifteenth century, Tolquhon was much
enlarged and re-fronted with a pseudo-military

gatehouse between 1584 and 1589 by William Forbes, royal tenant-in-chief (Figure 24). He proudly inscribed his achievement and displayed the arms of his king, who was obliging enough to come and visit Forbes' 'new wark' in 1589.

The vogue for towers and revival of castle-like forms persisted well into the seventeenth century and expressed itself in widely varying forms. At one extreme was Craigievar Castle (1610–26) (see Chapter 15), very much a rich Aberdeen merchant's self-indulgent fantasy, with ornate, parapet-less upper works and a few token gun ports. Behind the external display, however, is a stepped L-plan layout set out on traditional lines, the same, age-old vertical stacking of rooms above a late sixteenth-century scheme aborted by a previous owner at first floor level (Figure 25). Roughly contemporary with Craigievar is Coxton Tower, a small, plain tower just over 7 metres square on plan. Started in the late sixteenth century but not finally finished until about 1621 (and then incorporating a later marriage stone of 1644), Coxton was built in a style that would have done credit to a medieval laird (Figure 26). Why it should have assumed such an old-fashioned form remains imperfectly understood but, like Scotstarvit in Fife, it serves to demonstrate that archaism remained a significant force in Scottish tower design well into the seventeenth century.

One basic underlying characteristic of Scots tower building in all its forms was its broad social basis; not the exclusive preserve of any single caste, it embraced all echelons of landholding society from the monarch downwards. In parts of the Borders, a number of the lesser towers may even have been the products of 'kindly tenants', dating from around the period in the sixteenth century that they were beginning to convert their leases into more permanent and secure forms of feu tenure. Towers were most certainly associated with the lowliest sixteenth- and seventeenth-century landholders known as 'bonnet' lairds, an anachronistic term devised by Sir Walter Scott, but one which conveniently defined a small farming landholder who, alongside his servants, worked his lands himself, and who tended to wear a bonnet or cap, not the hat of the gentry. As exemplified by surviving structures at Isle (1587) and Barns (c.1576) (Figure 27), theirs were diminutive three-storeyed tower residences, measuring as little as 7 by 6 metres on oblong plan. Some retain vestiges of the steadings that served as their everyday working environments, while some, such as Easter Fordel, also aped grander fashion by their association with correspondingly small, usually single-storeyed, hall ranges.

It would of course be a mistake to assume that the defences of Scots towers were everywhere withering away in the name of fashion and art in the latter half of the sixteenth century. The West March was one area where, as late as the 1560s, tower houses were being built and equipped unequivocally for defence as well as residence. Height, bulk and firepower, together with a beacon platform and outlook tower, were deemed essential, not decorative accoutrements, for the Maxwell stronghold of Hoddom, described in a report of 1565 as a 'fort'. It has walls of almost 3 metres in thickness, and was equipped with a formidable array of gun ports at both parapet and basement levels, one of which still retains the wooden stock of a hand-held gun. Outside Scotland, there can be few such unambiguously defensive private residences of this date and bulk. Indeed, reflecting local patterns of feuding and thieving, interspersed by periods of national emergency and outright military conflict between Scotland and England, a continuing need for vigilance and security meant that fire beacon platforms, bells and watch-turrets, though not unknown elsewhere, became especially characteristic of towers along much of the Anglo-Scottish frontier. Likewise, prevalent in, but not exclusive to, this region were the walled enclo-

FIGURE 23
Right. Rowallan Castle, Ayrshire: south-east
frontage, 1993 (© RCAHMS, SC 358173)

Figure 24
Below. Tolquhon Castle, Aberdeenshire: north-west
frontage, 2003 (© RCAHMS, SC 961133)

Figure 25
Opposite. Craigievar Castle, Aberdeenshire, from
south, 1973 (© RCAHMS, SC 357706)

FIGURE 26
Opposite. Coxton Tower, Moray, from south-west, 1997 (© RCAHMS, SC 710990)

FIGURE 27
Above. Barns Tower, Peeblesshire: drawing by Alexander Archer, 1838 (© RCAHMS, DP 065688)

sures or refuges known as barmkins, which were sometimes equipped with a tower, and bastles, a term applied to strongly constructed farmhouses with dwellings set above byres, larger and smaller versions of which were also known as strong houses and pele-houses respectively. Though not the region with the densest distribution of known towers – that claim belongs to the east-central Lowlands – the Border zone boasts some especially dense local clusters of towers, especially along the Kirtle Water and in the valley of the Allan Water north of Galashiels, where the close

grouping conveys a strong sense of 'neighbourhood watch'. In parts of the Anglo-Scottish Border, towers even appear to have been the products of a local economy based upon cattle thieving, modern research having demonstrated the direct links between the profits of cattle raiding and investment in tower building, principally by the Armstrongs, Elliots and Grahams, builders of many of the erstwhile and relatively densely packed towers in the West March.

Within what can be perceived as broad 'national' norms, Scots towers thus display many contrasts in scale, detailing and emphasis, in itself a distinctive characteristic. Marked variations in their geographical distribution across Scotland appear to reflect a complex web of social, economic and tenurial conditions, and there are discernible contextual and regional differences in the forms and functions of their associated enclosures and ancillary buildings. With all their local and regional variations, however, towers had emerged and developed from the fourteenth century onwards in ways that, taken together with all the other categories described above, constitute a castellar heritage that is distinctively Scottish. Throughout, there were parallels – and contrasts – with other countries, most notably with Ireland, but from about the middle of the sixteenth century there appears to have been a significant parting of the architectural ways from those of all neighbours when the Scots began to embellish old or new imported designs in the conscious re-creation of castle-like forms.

4. So, finally, *what had castles come to mean to Scots* by about the time of the Union of the Crowns in 1603? However variously defined and configured, such buildings were clearly enjoying a renewed popularity, and contemporary attitudes must thus speak for themselves. Castle-like structures continued to offer a tried and tested set of designs that were practically convenient in balancing domesticity with a measure of defence, but architectural symbolism clearly remained a potent force. The later cult of the castle may have grown out of a fertile sense of what these buildings had come to represent in general historical terms by the turn of the seventeenth century, namely, freedom from oppression, the exact opposite of what castles are normally thought to have stood for. It would be far-fetched to suggest that, generically, such buildings were somehow viewed as architectural counterparts to the Declaration of Arbroath of 1320, but positive attitudes towards them do seem to

have grown up during the long period of intermittent conflict between the medieval kingdoms of Scotland and England that has been dubbed the Three Hundred Years' War (1296–1603). Indeed, those experiences may have served to reinforce even older attitudes and traditions.

There is one general factor that may have had a long-term bearing on Scottish attitudes: of the medieval and later castles which stand at the hearts of what became the four capital cities of the British Isles, Edinburgh's is the exception. In London, as is well known, Duke William of Normandy built a fortress immediately following his victory at Hastings in 1066. Then, in 1078, he authorised the construction of the mighty White Tower, core of what became the principal castle of medieval England and what, to this day, remains an abiding symbol of the Norman Conquest. In Wales, Cardiff followed in the wake of conquest, a Norman castle being established in the ruins of a Roman fort in 1081. It consisted of two large wards with a motte placed between them, later topped by a shell-keep. The conquest of Ireland began a century later, in 1169, and was led initially by a few powerful knights, Hugh de Lacy establishing control of most of south-eastern Ireland through power bases in Drogheda, Trim and Dublin. King John won Dublin for the English crown, and in 1204 he authorised the building of a royal castle there, the south-eastern or Record Tower being one of its few surviving visible remains.

The origins and development of Edinburgh Castle are significantly different. Occupation of the castle rock goes back into prehistory, and literary evidence of about AD 600 points to 'Eidyn' as the setting for a hall-like residence of a British king of the Gododdin. Eventually forming part of Anglian Northumbria, the buildings on this prominent rock site probably witnessed phases of conquest and change in the kingdom-forming processes of the ninth-eleventh centuries, but by the twelfth century and the reign of King David I (r.1124–53) Edinburgh had emerged as one of the most prominent castles of the Scottish realm. Its earliest surviving architecture, the chapel of St Margaret, is in the Romanesque style and spirit associated elsewhere with Anglo-Norman conquest, but this and other buildings of the early castle were built not by conquerors but by kings of the native Canmore dynasty, their building works being products of their own inclination and invitation, not undertaken at the point of an alien sword.

Conquest eluded later English attempts, although King Edward I came closest to effecting permanent occupation. For a period in and after 1304 it seemed that the kingdom of Scotland, like the principality of Wales previously, was at his mercy. He had retaken Stirling Castle, and the Forth Valley – which he rightly perceived as the country's strategic throat – found itself ringed by a series of military strongpoints established or planned at Linlithgow, Polmaise, Menstrie and Inverkeithing, together with a huge prefabricated pontoon that had been shipped to the middle reaches of the River Forth. Lacking the accustomed resources, the English campaign faltered, and resurgent Scottish resistance eventually provoked Edward, later commemorated as 'Scottorum Malleus' ('Hammer of the Scots'), into making one further attempt in 1307. His death during the campaign and in sight of Scotland eventually proved to be a crucial turning point in Anglo-Scottish relations, but not until the so-called 'Rough Wooings' of the 1540s was Scotland again so uncomfortably close to being conquered militarily, a process in which many key castles and fortresses would undoubtedly have become instruments and symbols of alien conquest.

Only one Scottish castle and associated burgh permanently suffered the fate of military conquest: Berwick upon Tweed. By far the most important burgh of thirteenth-century Scotland,

Berwick was initially taken by Edward I in 1296 and then passed backwards and forwards between the Scots and the English until, in 1482, the town, castle and a surrounding pale were annexed by English forces on what proved to be a permanent basis. Later, in 1557, a Franco-Scottish refortification of the fortress at Eyemouth, a short distance to the north of Berwick, alarmed the English so much that they wrapped their conquered enclave in one of the most advanced and expensive artillery fortifications in Europe. Berwick apart, however, by 1603, when the previously warring kingdoms found themselves joined in dynastic union, Scotland proudly regarded itself as unconquered. Indeed, the period of the Union of the Crowns was marked by the appearance of an inscribed Latin motto: 'Nobis haec invicta miserunt CVI [centum sex] proavi', roughly translated as 'a line of 106 kings have left us this unconquered'.

For the most part, Scottish castles and towers had not been closely associated with the manifold processes of military colonisation and were thus not perceived as products or symbols of foreign domination. Against such a background there was little to inhibit, and perhaps much to encourage, future generations from private castle-mansion or tower building, reconstruction or restoration. Certainly, by the late seventeenth and early eighteenth centuries, when Scotland was moving again in the direction of castle revival, it was entirely in keeping with the zeitgeist that Sir John Clerk of Penicuik (1676–1755) should be able to refer to such old towers as 'the honour and pride of a country'.

There is, however, an important sequel. A second, much more military, strand in Scotland's Castle Culture was rooted not in the Middle Ages but in the first half-century after 1603. In 1651, Oliver Cromwell (1599–1658), who became Lord Protector of England, Scotland and Ireland in 1653, completed the remarkable objective that

Edward I and others had signally failed to achieve, namely, complete military control of Scotland. Though it proved to be a relatively short-lived episode, the Cromwellian era witnessed the beginnings of the militarisation of key castles such as Edinburgh. Within a few decades, Scotland also then found itself heavily implicated in a long struggle for and against the reinstatement of the ousted Stewart dynasty, and North Britain, as it was known, became *the* front line of a long war fought from 1688 to 1746, with the bulk of the new artillery forts, barracks and militarised castles established across the Lowlands and Highlands.

The castles appear not to have been perceived as alien agencies, except by disaffected Jacobites, and the Scots once again took to adapting the castles-cum-forts in their own fashion, particularly the two major castles of Stirling and Edinburgh, which became regimental headquarters. Through imperial campaigns and two world wars, Scotland came to espouse the military cause of Great Britain in a manner, style and effectiveness that was completely disproportionate to its size. One enduring legacy of this proud tradition has been to create a special culture of Edinburgh Castle, which has become the setting for a national monument to the war dead and background to world-famous military ceremonies and parades. In this age of mass tourism, few are unaware of Edinburgh's daily one o'clock gun, the annual 21-gun salutes to celebrate the monarch's birthday, and the festival-time military tattoos on the castle esplanade.

CHAPTER TWO

1603–1746: Castles No More, or *'the Honour and pride of a Country'*?

Aonghus MacKechnie

Introduction

By the early seventeenth century, castles were no longer the ideal for new house building by elites throughout much of Western Europe, and the new fashion was for classical houses. In Scotland, castles continued being built, but by then in parallel with new fashions introduced from England from 1603 through the court. By the late seventeenth century classicism was fashionable, and Scotland was thus in the mainstream. But Scotland, in contrast to elsewhere, found it difficult even then to part with her Castle Culture. Reasons for this perhaps included reaction to the replacement in 1689 of her 'ancient' monarchy, followed by incorporating union with England in 1707. From that point, nationalism, martial virtue and so on were transferred to a new British nationalism. But whilst one Scottish reaction was to celebrate the union as a demonstration of Scotland's modernising achievement, another view grew stronger which held that Scotland's culture and commerce had suffered, its culture was being lost, and that something should be done about that. This chapter concludes with a focus on these polarities as they interfaced, the influence upon architecture and castles arising from the conflict between rational progress (what the winners had done) and Romanticism (what the losers were left with), and the compromises between the two.

Background

We have seen that David II's Tower (1360s–70s) at Edinburgh Castle, following the fashion exemplified by, say, Vincennes (near Paris), presented the detached residential tower as the ideal elite residence, and that in Scotland this 'tower house' model was long-lived. This changed during the seventeenth century, when the domestic ideal instead became the classical house or urban tenement. This chapter examines that change, but considers too the early stages of castle revival, a process which was to divide into several phases and which forms the basis of the subsequent chapters of this book.

Castellation was also popular for civic and religious architecture because it denoted authority. Musselburgh's tolbooth (?c.1590), for instance, looked like an enormous tower house. Edinburgh's rebuilt mercat cross (1617) was castle-like, but castellation was rejected firmly by civic Edinburgh with, above all, the new Canongate Church (1688), a counter-Reformation design and thus classical. When Dairsie was built (1621) as a model Episcopal church with a castle-like corbelled

belfry, ecclesiastical fashion had already changed to classical, often with Gothic windows, though crow-steps (Fenwick, 1641) remained popular (Figure 28). Dairsie's castellation, in alliance with 'primitive' Gothic tracery, intended to help convey the antiquity of Episcopacy, was, though, a one-off, and rejected by Presbyterians.

Scottish culture and education had long embraced classicism's paradigms but, concerning architecture, a more directly martial imagery had been favoured. Two things drove change: fashion, in an increasingly dynamic society; and attitudes towards security. Castles were symbolic statements of power, wealth, authority and sophistication, as well as a practical form of security. They were not designed for warfare but for the normality that was peacetime (albeit in times of war they were useful and quick to feature), and to obviate threat from the primary contemporary risks of feuding rivals or opportunist gangs. Following James VI's inheritance of the crowns of England and Ireland in 1603, feuding in Scotland was being stamped out (albeit a process slower in some parts, notably the Highlands). The need for personal security and security of possessions (such as vital land charters) consequently diminished, leading the castle in that respect towards obsolescence. Signifiers of castle architecture – bartizans, corbelling, etc – were incrementally abandoned, albeit crow-steps clung on in the regions. The classical house was to fulfil Modernist needs. The castle, long the badge of continuity and lineal legitimacy, was relegated to an inferior role, but it proved too valuable to reject totally, especially amongst the long-established elite families.

This account therefore covers not the rejection of the castle alone, but also the rise of the classical house. It is suggested that the process was a largely top-down 'diffusionist' one, because the paradigms were mostly for courtiers who had access to the foremost designers, craftsmen and cash, as well as first-hand knowledge of other countries.

Contemporary terminology is unhelpful in defining the term 'castle' for our period. The Privy Council in 1605, for instance, referred to Newbie as 'the plaice and fortalice', the 'hous' and the 'castell', all for the same property and in the same year. And Caerlaverock was that same year denoted both a 'castell' and 'plaice'.[1] Other terms included 'strong house', and 'fortalice'. This chapter takes 'castle' as embracing castellated, normally residential and towered structures. The term 'chateaux' is unsatisfactory, because it suggests that Scotland's castles were an offshoot of French architecture – which they were not. They remained unambiguously Scottish in character, with distinctive silhouettes and upper-level ornamentation contrasting with plainer mass walling below, as exemplified by Amisfield (1600) or Craigievar (1626) (see Chapter 15). The flow was away from skylines as the focus of exterior statement towards façade ornamentation, as classicism's principles displaced those of castle builders. Even interior plans were laid out symmetrically with mirrored apartments, as at, say, Kinross.

The concept of a castle as a strong centre was shown in 1600 when James ordered that certain south-west houses be occupied for peace enforcement. Consequently Spedlins' superstructure was remodelled in 1605, with bartizans. This new work was externally symmetrical, while a

FIGURE 28
Opposite. Dairsie Church, Fife: the pitched roof was an eighteenth-century addition (© RCAHMS, SC 507840)

FIGURE 29
Above. Linlithgow Palace, West Lothian: showing grid-windowed north quarter by James Murray, and parkland setting (© Historic Scotland)

spinal corridor introduced symmetrical interior planning to the otherwise orthodox tower.

As artillery developed, castles became not more but less military. For example, Caerlaverock's mighty thirteenth-century castle was modernised in the 1620s–1630s as a residence for the earl of Nithsdale. Its eastern arm was rebuilt, with the new courtyard front resembling Linlithgow Palace's north quarter (1619), while to light important new interiors, big windows were punched through the outside curtain wall (Figure 29). This conflicted with its original builders' intentions, but to Scotland's seventeenth-century castle builders the threats and psychological imagery had changed, and lairdly living demanded big windows.

These castles normally had rich interiors. Balloch (remodelled c.1600; since renamed Taymouth), for instance, had portraits of kings in the hall, family portraits in the chamber of dais beyond; furnishings including a bed valance now in the Burrell Collection. And as patrons demanded higher design standards, use increased of architectural publications to inform new design, particularly for features such as doorways – necessarily classical, like their published models.

By the 1580s, the developing interest in classicism informed the reconstructions of Crichton (from 1581), Newark (1597), Hamilton (1595) and Fyvie (from 1596). These castles exemplified a wish to 'reform' from within the Castle Culture itself. The paradigm of the new classicism was Stirling's Chapel Royal (1594), designed presumably by William Schaw (d.1602), King's Master of Works and best known as the founder of modern freemasonry (Figure 30). Yet around 1600 – surely again involving Schaw – Queen Anne built a Queen's House at Dunfermline: it was high, turreted and castle-like astride a gateway which – as an accompanying inscription carefully pointed out – pre-existed. Here was royal sanction awarded both to innovative scholarly classicism and to the castellated traditionalism which highlighted royal continuity and legitimacy.

Prestigious buildings then, normally, were stone-built and had barrel-vaulted ground floors, with the main floor, or *piano nobile*, on the floor above. At, say, Kellie, and Newark, a stone stair within the main entrance – positioned, as was typical, on the junction of two wings at right-angles – led to the main floor (Figure 31). Frequently, the inner (or 're-entrant') angle contained a turnpike to the upper levels, corbelled and conical-roofed as at Fenton (late sixteenth century) and Ferniehirst (1598), emphasising that these were castles. Castle Menzies (1571–7) and Elcho (completed c.1600) each had a massive main structure, with the entrance in a notably smaller jamb (wing) on one side (Figure 34).

This formula of an 'L-plan' front – a main block plus subordinate entrance wing in, crudely, an L-shape – was modified and, by the 1620s, the main block and jamb tended to be more equal in size. The entrance was no longer in a wing but set in the angle stair turret, which now rose not from corbels but from the ground, as at the seventeenth-century royal palace stair turrets. We will return to this L-plan type, which continued into the modern age.

The post-castle trend is clearer from three 1600s houses built by loyal government officials close to James, and very possibly involving Schaw or his successor as Master of Works, Sir David Cunningham of Robertland. Robertland (d.1607) was briefly royal surveyor in England, but his architectural contribution remains unclear.

FIGURE 30
Opposite top. Chapel Royal, Stirling Castle: main front (© Historic Scotland)

FIGURE 31
Opposite bottom. Newark, Renfrewshire (© Historic Scotland)

1600s Innovations

Scone Palace, begun c.1602 for Sir David Murray of Gospertie on forfeited Gowrie lands gifted to him by James, was an early 'post-castle'. Horizontally proportioned, its front symmetrical with set forward centre and ends, only crow-step gables survived from the castle-builder's repertoire. Accommodation included a King's Room, while a 160-foot long gallery wing presented a new scale and need for horizontal planning.

Culross Abbey House (1608; heightened 1680s) was built for Edward Bruce, Lord Kinloss (1548/9–1611), Master of the Rolls in England. It introduced a combination of features which were soon standard: square corner pavilions as seen in England or France, probably ogee-domed, a gridded flat façade with window pediments and string courses, a parapet set on continuous rather than individual corbels, and evidently a flat leaded roof. Like the Chapel Royal it was innovatively classical: aedicule-windowed in the manner of the Italian renaissance and, unusual in Scotland, it was unvaulted, spine-walled and two rooms deep (contrasting with 'the castle', which was typically one room deep). Culross in its terrace-garden setting seems reminiscent, in miniature, of the Villa d'Este; but, more so than Scone, it was a classical house and not a castle.

The regnal union (1603) enabled another of James VI's Scots given high office in England, George Home, earl of Dunbar, to build a new house within the post-frontier Berwick Castle. Berwick was considered obsolete in the context of union, the new house symbolising an anticipated end to conflict between Scotland and England. But three months from a formal opening planned for St George's Day 1611, Dunbar died.

FIGURE 32
Opposite. Linlithgow Palace, West Lothian: courtyard view of north quarter (© RCAHMS, SC 800009)

Only some sculptured elements survive, incorporated in Berwick's 1650s church. Dunbar's house was colossal, described at the time as 'a sumptuous and glorious palace', and seemingly in the form of an English mansion, with mullioned and transomed windows and parapeted flat roofs for taking in the views. Its 'surveyor and builder' in 1611 was James Murray, Robertland's successor as Master of Works. Murray, laird of Kilbaberton (today called Baberton) since 1612 and knighted by Charles I in 1633, was another diligent servant loyal to the crown, and – as Schaw had once been – he became the dominant figure in Scottish architecture until his death in 1634.

In 1613, Alexander Seton (1555–1622), Chancellor and builder of Fyvie, built a suburban villa at Musselburgh: Pinkie House. A long wing with a gallery comparable with Scone's was added to the pre-existing tower, with a two-storeyed bay window in the south gable from where the site of the Battle of Pinkie – fought in 1547 between English and Scots – might be viewed from the context of new amity with England. A (Latin) garden inscription announced:

> There is nothing here to do with warfare; not even a ditch or rampart to repel enemies, but in order to welcome guests with kindness and treat them with benevolence, a fountain of pure water . . . He [Seton] has brought everything together that might afford decent pleasures of heart and mind. But he declares that whoever shall destroy this by theft, sword, or fire, or behaves in a hostile manner, is a man devoid of generosity and urbanity, indeed of all culture, and is an enemy to the human race.

Seton highlighted two threats to his place of peace: warfare – for which preparation was unnecessary, presumed irrelevant following regnal union – and risk from hostile people intent on theft and destruction. Pinkie spoke of James VI's agenda of Solomonic peace and of union. Pinkie's message (albeit the sixteenth-century tower was retained) was that fortified castles were of the feuding and warring past; villas were now a desirable option, and numerous examples near Edinburgh, such as Baberton, were to follow. Pinkie's battle site was assigned a new role, as a physical monument to a less enlightened, forever-gone age and to union, while the castle's martial 'language' was subordinated by newly fashionable ideals of neo-Stoicism which, as Michael Bath has shown, dominated the interior design.

Pinkie's tower was altered to fit the new grid-windowed garden front and string courses, but on the courtyard (west) front, the old jamb and consequently Pinkie's hybrid character was emphasised, with a flat roof, ogee-domed corbelled turrets and square bartizans on the tower's north gable.

James' Visit

James visited Scotland in 1617. Extravagant preparations kept Murray busy at the palaces from 1615. Falkland's galleries were given flat roofs, but more was done at Holyrood and Edinburgh Castle's palace. The experimental classicism of the 1580s–1600s was giving way to a more English-looking architecture, reflecting the new closeness with England. James' demand for conformity between his kingdoms in all things as part of his plan to create a *Magna Britannia* or Great Britain had architectural consequences. This was shown most clearly by re-creating Holyrood's chapel on an English Episcopal model, with Murray in charge but fittings, and craftsmen including Nicholas Stone and Matthew Goodrich, sent from London. And, of course, James VI's 1611 Bible had made English the language of worship.

The dominance of Edinburgh's palace in High Street views was amplified by reconstructing and defining the most visible element. Like Culross, it has string courses, pedimented windows and a parapeted flat roof, here terminated by ogee-domed square bartizans. This was not a de-castellation but a modernisation partly in line with English norms, as evident from the façade's resemblance to Bolsover Little Castle, built only two to three years earlier. Edinburgh's ogee-turrets and mullioned and transomed window further indicate ideas imported from English architecture (precisely as French architecture had been the model for James V's 1530s Falkland Palace). Inside the palace, English-type deep-relief plaster ceilings were installed, and symbolism of union was emphasised.

Decorative plaster ceilings were novel in Scotland when introduced to the royal works in 1617. Until then, decorative ceilings were normally painted, with numerous themes, allegorical, dynastic, intellectual and religious, reflecting something of the owner. At Pinkie, for instance, the gallery scheme seemingly included an image of the patron. Scone had images of hunting, of courtiers, featuring James in every scene. The new-style ceiling ornament, by contrast, conveyed some classical imagery ('worthies' such as Alexander, at The Binns (1620s)) but its consistent main theme was Britishness, Stuart monarchy and union. In a spirit of 'unionist nationalism' a Latin inscription was introduced – '106 forefathers have left these to us, unconquered'. This stressed Stuart royal legitimacy and the proud fact that Scotland had given England her king. Such ceilings became popular, sometimes (as at Craigievar, The Binns and Winton) in conjunction with overmantel armorials. But non-domestic ceilings might still be painted: notably Skelmorlie Aisle, Largs (1638) and Grandtully (1630s – where, again, the message was of Stuart unionism).

FIGURE 33
Baberton House, Edinburgh: restored view depicted in drawing from David MacGibbon and Thomas Ross, *Castellated and Domestic Architecture of Scotland*, vol. 4 (1892)

Three Houses, James Murray and a Court Architecture

Murray built himself not a castle, but a villa. Baberton, dated 1622 and 1623, duplicated the 'L-plan' formula, creating a symmetrical U-shaped plan (the space between infilled 1765) (Figure 33). Corbelled stairs occupied the inner angles, but castellation was otherwise rejected: pitched roofs minus parapets, skews instead of crow-steps, finials over the angles instead of bartizans. Ceiling plasterwork bore unionist symbolism.

Elements and ornament from Baberton were reproduced at Pitreavie (Figure 35) and Winton, the three houses forming a group.

Pitreavie (1620s/30s), an enlarged version of Baberton, was built for Sir Henry Wardlaw, friend of Kilbaberton and fellow official in the royal works. Wardlaw was also father-in-law to Sir Anthony Alexander, who in 1629, having travelled abroad to study architecture, was conjoined in post with Murray. Pitreavie, like Baberton, had corbelled stairs tucked within each inner angle, but its image, like Babarton, was of post-castellation.

Winton (1620–7), by contrast, possibly befit-

FIGURE 34
Elcho Castle, Perthshire:
general view showing
entrance
(© Historic Scotland)

FIGURE 35
Above. Pitreavie, Fife: prior to nineteenth-century additions (© RCAHMS, SC 1106518)

FIGURE 36
Opposite. George Heriot's Hospital, Edinburgh (© RCAHMS, SC 710871)

ting the old landed status of the patron, George, 8th Lord Seton and 3rd earl of Winton, was rich and modern, but profiled to look like an old Scots castle: asymmetrical – when symmetry was the established prestigious model – wings of unequal size, one flat-roofed with a parapet whose detail replicated English examples such as Haddon Hall, and other English-looking features including tall chimney flues. Inside, the main spaces had elaborate plaster ceilings, while the hall fireplace is a richer version of Baberton's.

Castellated or uncastellated, these houses

were near Edinburgh, where there was stronger competition concerning modernising fashion and where security was less a concern than in more 'remote' regions, their builders anticipating a law-abiding future. They had no ostentatious defences such as the prominent gunholes at, say, Dalcross (1619–21).

Here was a court, or courtier, architecture, using the same architects, designers or craftsmen. The group included non-domestic buildings – George Heriot's Hospital (begun 1628, involving William Wallace, King's Master Mason) has a collegiate character with corner 'tower houses', parapeted and turreted; but these towers had also symmetrical elevations, pedimented windows and string courses (Figure 36). Crow-steps were made into enrichments, with chimneys given tall individual flues as at Winton.

Edinburgh's Parliament House, designed by Murray (1632), resembled domestic architecture, being L-planned with an angle stair, hall in the main block and smaller spaces in the jamb (Figure 37). It was laden with Stuart unionist iconography, underlined by palace-like square bartizans, ogee domes and flat roofs, the courtyard-facing parapets pierced and English-looking. The flat roof denoted prestigious modernity, but also authority, the same symbolism as Michelangelo's Capitoline buildings in Rome. Above all, its hybrid classical–castellar form, like Heriot's towers, emphasised the value of Scottish culture to progressive elites.

From the 1600s many Plantation settlers in Ireland took with them Scottish concepts and, evidently, designers – as seen at, say, Tully (for Sir John Hume after 1610), Castle Monea (for Malcolm Hamilton, 1618–19), or Castle Balfour (for Sir James Balfour, 1618). Sir Hugh Mont-

FIGURE 37
Above. Parliament House, Edinburgh: drawing by
John Elphinstone in Hugo Arnot's *The History of
Edinburgh* (1788) (© RCAHMS, SC 426674)

FIGURE 38
Opposite. Scotstarvit Tower, Fife
(© RCAHMS, SC 1204556)

gomery (who in 1623 married Anthony Alexander's sister Jean) was another builder, whose projects included the family's north aisle and tower added to Newtonairds Priory.

Other Options

Besides new 'courtier' architecture were other ideals. People often retained castles in occupation, perhaps extended, and traditionalist builders built new castles. Seton Castle, for instance, with vast rooms including a 'Samson's Hall', held its prestige as one of Scotland's grandest buildings and was an important base for both James (1617) and Charles (1633) on their Scottish visits. There Murray was knighted, and salvaged sculpture suggests he possibly designed work there too. Much smaller than Seton, but similarly retaining its status, was Scotstarvit Tower (Figure 38). Built c.1500, it was altered in 1627 and a castellated new superstructure added. The client for this reconstructed and traditional-looking castle was Sir John Scott (1585–1670), a distinguished, forward-looking intellectual who worked on the Blaeu Atlas project (the Atlas was published 1654) and

48

whose works included a Latin verse anthology (*Delitiae Poetarum Scotorum*) published in 1637.

But old castles were increasingly problematised; disguised, often, especially if lacking ancestral value. For instance, Argyll's Lodging in Stirling was rebuilt 1632–3 by its new owner, Sir William Alexander – Anthony's father – in anticipation of Charles' visit (Figure 39). The old castle became one corner of a new classical U-plan house whose front had a grid of richly sculptured openings. The building was no longer a castle, something further amplified in 1674 when it was completed like a French *Hôtel*, U-planned with high gated wall enclosing the fourth side, the gateway design from an Italian pattern book by Allesandro Francini.[2]

Some castles were (like Spedlins) modernised

by reconstructing the upper levels. Comlongan's superstructure was rebuilt in 1624 with a symmetrical south front with duplicate profiles to a new gallery and square cap-house opposite – a possible reference to Edinburgh's Palace, but with Scottish crow-steps, the result being a traditional castle. Preston Tower on the other hand was heightened (1626) with a two-storeyed, grid-windowed and symmetrical block, the roof parapeted and probably flat: again, reflecting the architecture of Edinburgh's palace, but here more closely.

The more obvious means of increasing a castle's accommodation was to add a wing, and many were constructed in the seventeenth century; but it was important to builders that the tower remained dominant, as at Midhope, Hills

and Kirkconnel, where at each a gateway also survives, set at right angles to the main front.

But castle building was still 'normal'. For example, two neighbouring Highland castles, Dalcross and Castle Stuart/Petty (c.1619), were within the castle tradition, albeit the latter responded to ideas of symmetry in its plan and Gordon Castle-like angle oriels. In the north-east a wave of castle building or upgrading took place, including Craigievar, Castle Fraser (Ian Bel, Thomas and James Leiper master masons), and Coxton (pre-1644). Castle culture was still vigorous, while open platform-roofed turrets represented the influence of the new architecture.

Hill House in Dunfermline (1621–3) was hybrid: a castellar L-planned hall block and jamb, but with classicising façades. In the new fashion

FIGURE 39
Opposite. Argyll's Lodging, Stirling: general view
(© Historic Scotland)

FIGURE 40
Above. Braemar Castle, Aberdeenshire: showing 1620s tower with anti-Jacobite fortifications
(© Historic Scotland)

of Culross and the palaces it had string courses and pedimented window heads while, further responding to the new interest in English models, its flat-roofed stair turret has silhouetted lettering.[3] Innes (1640–53, by William Aytoun, master mason at Heriot's) was similar, its parapet modelled on Parliament House, with Baberton-inspired finials over the angles.

Another inventive way of classicising the L-plan formula was by setting the entrance diagonally (like the polygonal turrets in the Heriot's courtyard), creating a symmetrical splay plan. Possibly introduced at Braemar (1628) (Figure 40) and used at Parliament House, today's exemplar is Glamis (see chapter 8), whose avenue currently shares the doorway's same diagonal axis. Crichton House (?c.1650, Crichton Castle's successor), and Auchenbowie (1666) had polygonal turrets, and again the windows are regular and gridded with stripped façades, the gables crow-stepped. Staney-hill Tower (?1620s), however, buckle-quoined, court-style and with entrance turret, jamb and wing similarly sized in the new manner, had its door on the same alignment as the main house, a grand gateway at the end of an avenue. This splay-plan model lived on, as shown below.

An architectural debate of 1632 between Sir Robert Kerr and his grandson Sir William, Lord Kerr of Newbattle and earl of Lothian, concerned Ancrum. Both agreed that work was needed, but they disagreed over what this should be, and a 'pro-castle' versus 'anti-castle' issue arose.

The wings might be modernised without debate. But Kerr wanted the tower retained as both a physical security and status symbol. 'By any meanes,' he wrote, 'do not take away the battelment, as some [advised] . . . me . . . to do, as Dalhoussy your nyghtbour did, for that is the grace of the house, and makes it looke lyk a castle, and henc so nobleste, as the other would make it looke lyk a peele.' The family could be proud of its castle, because it represented authority, lineal

antiquity and entitlement, which they wished others to see. And it looked good. A stripped, plain 'peel' tower would convey the wrong messages.

This concept of the tower being little valued as main residence whilst prized as a security and symbol was an important marker in Castle Culture. At Amisfield, say, the tower (1600) is beautiful, strong and a castle; but in 1631, a new classical house was built only a few metres distant. And at Drum, a low domestic wing with Culross-like pavilions was added to the tower (1618).

Civil Wars

Challenges to royal authority from the late 1630s brought war, while the years of English military occupation (1650/1–1660) halted major projects, save for churches, colleges and star-shaped English fortifications such as Inverness and Ayr. Many castles were temporarily given duties as military architecture.

Glasgow's new court-style college, begun in 1630, was wholly uncastellated and tenemental. At Aberdeen, though, the new college's Cromwell Tower (1657–8) resembled a tower house, as if conceived to resemble Heriot's.

Restoration

The restoration of royal authority in 1660 and of parliament, as well as the return of exiled elites and of the old norms, brought a return to new building. Leslie Castle (1661–3), a traditional L-plan enclosed by a moat plus drawbridge, suggests that its builder envisaged a return to the old architecture, while at the likewise L-planned Clounie Crichton Castle (1666), an almost completely symmetrical interior plan anticipated what lay ahead.

Most new houses were classical and symmetrical, with crow-steps almost the only element of castellation's repertoire to remain in occasional use. England, France and Holland all provided models, but the greatest authority of all was Louis XIV's Versailles.

Amongst the first to build anew was Sir John Gilmour at his newly acquired Craigmillar Castle, from 1661. Gilmour reconstructed the north quarter as a two-storey uncastellated wing, unvaulted, the main apartment at ground level. The adjoining tower was, or was soon, no longer for elite living. Instead, it became a picturesque, historical appendage for viewing, for in 1689 Prestonfield's south front was aligned upon it.

The new fashion was at first led by the Mylne family of master masons, and possibly the brothers Sir Robert (Master of Works 1660–1668) and Sir William Moray, and also Sir William Bruce, appointed Surveyor in 1671. Leslie House (1667–72) and Panmure (1672) were amongst the first of this new generation, as was Bruce's own Balcaskie House (c.1670–4). Such houses often had balustraded end-gabled or U-plan fronts, with a third, centre gable (following Scone) on longer-façaded examples, such as Panmure, built wholly anew on a new site and thus an 'ideal' unconstrained by pre-existing walling. Balcaskie was a 1630s L-plan tower made (almost) symmetrical by adding a duplicate wing and pavilions, thus creating a U-plan front following Baberton or, say, Careston. Crow-steps indicated that an earlier castle was incorporated, though differing floor levels rendered the front gables – almost imperceptively – different. Both Bannockburn House (1674) and Philpstoun (1676) were given similar end-gabled façades.

From here on came a string of post-castellated classical houses, or 'anti-castles', with Bruce the dominant person in Scottish architecture, working often with the king's master mason, Robert Mylne (d.1710). Money was again avail-able for building, with officials in lucrative government posts becoming prominent builders, above all John Maitland, duke of Lauderdale (1616–82). Bruce reconstructed a series of houses for Lauderdale, featuring two castles. Brunstane House (c.1672–5) was his suburban Edinburgh villa. Thirlestane Castle (c.1670–7) was Lauderdale's main Scottish seat (Figure 41) (his other main house was Ham House, near London), and notwithstanding Bruce's classical veneer, it remained clearly a castle. At Lennoxlove (then called Lethington) the old tower, though altered in 1626 and 1673–4, was retained as the dominant element.

The crown stirred briefly into the old role of seeking to lead fashion by reconstructing Holyrood Palace. Lauderdale had Bruce appointed Surveyor, and he reconstructed Holyrood, working there until 1678 (Figure 42). A failed parliamentary union attempt, a need to maintain what James VI had called 'some show of a court', and the palace's condition (it was then partly a burnt-out ruin, partly Cromwellian barracks and thus offensive to Charles) all combined to make reconstruction seem necessary. Following 1660s precedent it was balustraded between the ends, but Holyrood combined ideas from elsewhere (notably the tiered pilasters modelled on Amsterdam's town hall), while the decision to retain and duplicate James V's 1520s castellated tower – for concealment was an option – depicted a visual link between the absentee Charles II and Scotland's ancient royal line. Perhaps already that tower was associated with Queen Mary, but regardless, the old Scottish Castle Style here found a new, propagandist value, underlining Stuart entitlement to reign. The tower's duplication, paradoxically (albeit an old idea), was necessitated by the modernist, classicist demand for symmetry – a need which extended so far as to design a huge nave-and-aisles stables block correspondent with the old Abbey Church. But Holyrood, in contrast

FIGURE 41
Above. Thirlestane Castle, Berwickshire: engraving from *Theatrum Scotiae* by Captain John Slezer (© RCAHMS, SC 695492)

FIGURE 42
Opposite. Holyrood, Edinburgh, main front, James V tower on left: engraving from *History of Edinburgh* by William Maitland, 1753 (© RCAHMS, SC 891890)

FIGURE 43
Overleaf. Kinneil House, West Lothian, main front: photograph taken pre-1930 (© RCAHMS, SC 1216078)

to broadly coeval counterparts in England, the Low Countries or France, was, externally, prominently castle-like, while inside it resembled contemporary English elite work, with craftsmen, as in 1617, sent from the English royal works.

Accompanying the new classical architecture was the introduction of the state apartment. These were rich apartments with big linear plans built in the hope that a king would visit. They provided another reason for dispensing with castles, which were typically too small to accommodate a state apartment. Thirlestane Castle, though, was already big, sufficient to contain one, which was simply superimposed upon the main living apartment, the stately interiors decorated by craftsmen from the royal works, whom Bruce also engaged at Balcaskie.

This 're-forming' approach was popular. At

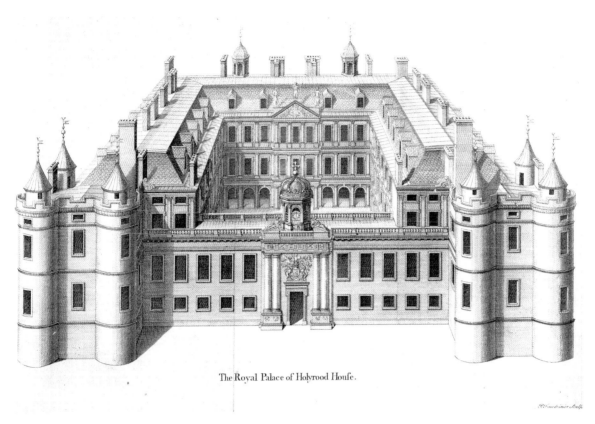

The Royal Palace of Holyrood House.

Kinneil and Hatton, for instance (both probably 1670s), pre-existing towers were given balustraded flat roofs and Bruce-like or English-looking lanterns. Kinneil, for the duke of Hamilton, was given a classical but still towered, gridded façade and end pavilions; while the crow-stepped north wing was retained (Figure 43). Hatton House was rebuilt for Lauderdale's brother, Lord Hatton, who succeeded Bruce as royal surveyor. There, the tower was enwrapped in corner-turreted lower wings, the design anticipating Inveraray (see Chapter 9).

Meanwhile, Bruce produced more innovative designs, including Dunkeld (c.1676–84), for the 1st marquess of Atholl, and Moncrieffe (1679 – attributed), and, for himself, Kinross. Moncrieffe and Dunkeld, tripartite-planned (ie, with twinned flue-bearing cross-walls), were each plain, reliant on proportion for effect, having simple 'squarish' footprints, gridded façades and piended/hipped roofs, quoined corners and ornament confined to the doorway. The model seems to have been English (as the profiles, Moncrieffe's quoins and Dunkeld's roof lantern all suggest) or possibly Dutch. It's unknown how far client or architect proposed introducing this house-style; but Dunkeld – should we believe the sometimes fallible evidence of a Slezer print – also had a parapet and corner bartizans, indicating either the value of tradition or a perceived higher risk of attack. Gordonstoun (insecurely dated) was another classical house built during the broad period with bartizans, though these are terminations to flanking wings. Granton House (near Edinburgh) had a symmetrical splay-plan tower whose south front was remodelled, perhaps before 1700, with a

centre-doored symmetrical façade, and the barti-zans retained.

The earl of Annandale consulted Bruce in 1694 concerning Craigiehall. An area was defined to contain new house, courts and parterres; but Bruce required the old house's demolition, unless the whole ensemble was moved so that it would not disrupt the symmetry of the formal design. Bruce advocated classical symmetry: 'Where I make any designe I have no regard to irregular planting, office houses, or any other old matter wch are oblique & not agreeable to a modish & regular designe.'[4]

Bruce was succeeded in the royal works by Mr James Smith (c.1645–1731) (the 'Mr' signify-ing that he was university educated), who seems, like James Gibbs after him, to have left for Rome to become a priest but returned as an architect. Smith was a contractor to Bruce at Holyrood, by around 1681 *de facto* a royal architect (the survey-orship being *de jure* with Hatton), appointed formally in 1683. At his own Whitehill (1686) – renamed Newhailes – Smith introduced a sepa-rate type of classical house: one room deep (like a castle in that respect) with centre-pedimented façades, the main apartment compacted in to a spiralled rather than linear progression, recalling the L-shape disposition of earlier years.

Smith's father, also James and a contracting mason, built Kilravock's south quarter (1665–7, with Robert Nicolson) like an old castle with corbelled corner and off-centre stair turret. However, it was for the younger Smith's knowl-edge of continental – especially French and Ital-ian – architecture that patrons engaged him. For both Bruce's and Smith's clients wanted an archi-tecture resembling not past Scottish ideals, but English or European paradigms. New castles were increasingly unwanted. Three prominent excep-tions were Thirlestane, Drumlanrig and Glamis, where Castle Culture was vigorously reasserted by patrons wishing to stress old landed status.

Castles Reasserted and Rejected

Glamis (see Chapter 8) was rebuilt for the earl of Strathmore, who was determined not to occupy a 'prison'-like castle but a modern house, whilst retaining elements he had always liked.

Drumlanrig was remodelled 1679–89 for the duke of Queensberry as a simultaneously modern but 'ancient'-looking dynastic castle (Figure 44). Paradoxically, it combined the then two, but opposite, formulae – castellation and a forest of skyline turrets, plus a classical giant Order in a symmetrical composition.[5] Like Heriot's, Drum-lanrig was corner-towered with ogee domes and flat 'tower house' roofs; but its frontispiece was modelled more explicitly on Holyrood, whose centrepiece has a giant royal crown – here, substi-tuted by a vast ducal coronet.

Whose design Drumlanrig was is unknown, and it may (like Melville, mentioned below) have been the work of a 'committee'. But James Smith – whom Queensberry had appointed as Surveyor – certainly had a role. In its sophisticated 'naïvety' or antiquarianism it sits alongside Thirlestane and the neo-medievalising Michael Church of 1705 at Gordonstoun (whose patron's family had been clients of James Smith); for Drumlanrig was an up-to-date country seat finished by Dutch sculp-tors and some of Scotland's foremost craftsmen, with a rich state apartment. As at Glamis and Thirlestane, Drumlanrig's builder wanted a castle.

The emphatic display of 'old' castellation combined with classical modernity at both Holy-rood and Drumlanrig, in an almost baroque defiance of established norms, seemed similar in some ways to James Gibbs' venturesome combi-nation at St Martin-in-the-Fields (1722–6) of a classical temple front with an almost Gothic-looking steeple.

Bruce – of more newly landed status – acquired Kinross in 1675, its modernist design advanced from Moncrieffe and Dunkeld. Kinross'

FIGURE 44
Drumlanrig, Dumfriesshire: view from north (© RCAHMS, SC 714472)

profile and interior plan followed 1650s–60s English models such as Coleshill and also recalls Vaux-le-Vicomte, while the giant-pilastered elevations more closely followed those of the *Logis du Rois* and *Logis de la Reine-mère* at Vincennes. A state apartment was intended.

Aligning Kinross House and landscape on Lochleven's abandoned historic castle was a critical decision (the loch has since been partly drained, enlarging the island and altering the view) (Figure 45). The castle had featured in the Wars of Independence, and from there Mary Queen of Scots escaped captivity in 1568. Now, from the new house, views of the obsolete castle

ruins could be enjoyed.

Kinross did three, and possibly four, big things. 'The castle', and all in Scotland that had gone before – including Holyrood Palace – now seemed obsolete due to this exquisite classical model. Second and third: Kinross gave a new meaning to the abandoned castle, or ruin, retrieving it from obsolescence and reviving it for its new function as a thing to view and enjoy – but surely, in addition, a monument to protect for its value not as a residence but as simply a monument? And fourth, it seems that Bruce had a role in the then-nascent cult of Mary Queen of Scots which is with us still.[6]

Proto-Enlightenment and Proto-Romanticism

Mary's role was changing from Catholic martyr (Bruce, an Episcopalian Jacobite, had no interest in nurturing Catholicism) to Romantic heroine. The combination of a ruined castle from where Mary had escaped dramatically, set beautifully on a natural island, brought Bruce and Kinross into the arena of early Romanticism, when emotional reaction to dramatic experiences was a priority. National Romanticism – which demanded a hero(ine), a just but lost cause, and an important thing regrettably lost – is seemingly present here long before Stirling's castellated Wallace Monument of 1859–69 was conceived.

Bruce, the hard-headed proto-Enlightenment intellect whose culture prized raw Newtonian logic, was simultaneously invigorated by the romantic, emotional drama of a lost Scotland. Bruce needed Lochleven Castle, for without it Kinross would be ruined; enemy of 'the oblique' in old architecture, he was also a castle preservationist. Lochleven was a milestone in castle revivalism – revived from obsolescence for new duties – and it helped inaugurate the concept of castles as heritage meriting preservation.

This new value of old castles and ruins as enjoyable to view (and thus, implicitly, to retain) underpinned John Slezer's *Theatrum Scotiae* (1693). Slezer's engravings included some captioned as 'ruins', including St Andrews Castle. Slezer envisaged a market for a book crammed with images, including engraved ruins. He was 'transmitting to Posterity those Venerable Remains of former Ages, and [obliging] other Nations with the Prospects of . . . considerable Places'. His plates of 'ruines' demonstrate interest amongst elites in abandoned historic Scottish architecture. This fondness for ruins became a fundamental element of what in the eighteenth century came to be called the 'Picturesque': the enjoyment of dramatic natural views contrived to be 'picture-like', an exemplar being Raasay House (1740s), facing Skye's wild landscape. And, of course, the concept of enjoying ruins led to preservationism.

Melville House was built 1697–1703 for George, 4th lord and 1st earl of Melville (1636–1707), supporter of William and Mary's new monarchy and Secretary of State from 1689, when his estates were restored. The architect who emerged from an architectural design committee that included Alexander Edward and Bruce was James Smith. Like Kinross, it was symmetrical, with identical opposing fronts, symmetrical interior plan, and it was placed on a new site. It was also in view of a historic castle, the anachronistically named Cardinal Beaton's Tower (dated 1578; Beaton was assassinated in 1546). Contrasting with Kinross, here the associated castle was not a focus, but peripheral in view, and modernised as a cosy tower-house retreat with timber-panelled interior and flat roof for enjoying the view. Part of the family property acquired in 1592, it was also a historical document: relict of the palace of the cardinal who had fought Reformation, now viewed from the perspective of a victorious Presbyterian settlement.

In 1703, Melville petitioned parliament for 'changeing the high way about Melvillhouse in favours of his planting and enclosures'. The country house was becoming an estate – passers-by, like castles, unwanted. The old formula of castle–church–settlement was being broken, as modernisation dispensed with the castle and closeness of the people to their elites in favour of the classical house in its detached grounds. Bruce likewise relocated the town at Kinross, and Hamilton the town at Kinneil, creating Bo'ness as the new settlement. Kinneil parish was suppressed in 1669, Bo'ness church becoming that of the united Bo'ness and Kinneil parish. The old church alone was retained for its new function as a ruin adorning Kinneil's landscape.

At Hopetoun (from 1699), Bruce again stressed the ideal of a new classical house on a new open site. Hopetoun's centralised plan, channelled façade and colonnades made it the antithesis of the castle. But here was developed Bruce's fondness for alignment, the main vista viewing the abandoned island castle of Inchgarvie before terminating at North Berwick Law. Perhaps the dismantling of nearby Staneyhill Tower as an eyecatching ruin was an idea of Bruce's time.

Yet the idea of alignment upon a castle existed by the 1620s, when Baberton's flank was aligned upon Edinburgh Castle; Scotland's mightiest castle whose care was Murray's job. That alignment, though, linked to the separate concept of Edinburgh as a new Rome, a vastly important city and therefore an obvious candidate for viewing.

Designs for classicising Traquair's massive tower were commissioned from James Smith (1695–9) and again, around a half century later, from John Douglas(?–c.1788). On each occasion work was done – Smith built a formal forecourt – but the castle remained. Smith proposed, through duplication, a symmetrical castle. Douglas' scheme, reflecting a new owner's ideals, sought to conceal the old behind a neo-classical façade, as he planned for Blair (Chapter 11).

But castles could only be concealed where funds permitted. Smith and his then partner Alexander McGill produced a re-fronting plan for Cullen (1709) but, like Traquair, it was unexecuted. Classical reconstructions elsewhere, including Hamilton (1693–1701) and Dalkeith (1702–10), were built.

Hamilton's 1590s house was symmetrical. In the 1690s it was rebuilt incrementally, consequently maintaining the sixteenth-century 'footprint' but omitting the south quarter to let more light in and views out. Its deep wings gave it a character like that of Sir Christopher Wren's Chelsea Royal Hospital (1682–92), but the main focus was the centrepiece: a giant Corinthian Order, stepped above the main eaves, giving it added 'punch', its columns freestanding in scooped-out recesses. This was a treatment travellers to Rome would know, but it was unprecedented in Scotland; it was more assertive than Versailles' centrepiece and unparalleled perhaps in contemporary northern Europe. Hamilton, renamed 'Hamilton Palace', illustrated the fullest commitment to academic classicism and the castle's rejection. However, when Hamilton's landscape was developed over the following few decades, vistas were created or planned to take in historic buildings – a question, for example, being whether one vista might take in Bothwell's historic church or the bridge (where a Royalist army had defeated a Covenanter one in 1679). So, again, old buildings, history and politics retained exploitable values for the progressively post-Castle Culture.

Project drawings for Dalkeith Palace show the intention to create it much as it was built: a staggered U-plan in a symmetrical layout. In the event, some pre-existing walling was retained, but concealed, the tower house encapsulated as a fireproof strong room.

At Kelburn (dated 1722), recalling Amisfield or 1660s Craigmillar, a new wing was added. Unlike Kilravock, this was not to blend with the castle, but instead it created a visually independent principal residence, the castle subordinate in function while, of course, visually dominant.

Notwithstanding the increasing fashion for classicism, many ancient castles simply remained ancient-looking, possibly representing their owners' ideals. Places like Blair (Dalry), Castle Leod, or Cawdor, sometimes complied with symmetrical additions, but they maintained prestige for what they were – uncompromising old castles occupied by old families.

The new ideas resulted in a formulaic 'satellite' or laird's house design, such as Ross Mains (1728): centre-doored with unornamented grid-

FIGURE 45
Kinross House, Kinross-shire: Oblique aerial view
centred on Kinross House with Lochleven Castle in
the background, taken from the west-north-west
(© RCAHMS, SC 704832)

ded façades, two storeys, usually five window
bays, maybe raised a half storey, flat-fronted or –
following Newhailes – with pedimented centre
projections. In old burghs, such as Maybole,
Dornoch or Kirkcubright, castellation had
defined the more prestigious buildings. The need
for classicism, though, dictated design in not only
the legion of new towns created from the late

seventeenth century, but also for prestigious new buildings in the old burghs. In Dumfries, for instance, the new Tolbooth (1705–8) was still tower-like but hardly castellated, its parapet modelled on Parliament House; while nearby and later, at 29 Irish Street (?1720s), an exemplar of the new classical town house, the old castle-building skills were applied in creating a stone barrel-vaulted basement extending the building's full length. When Inveraray's new burgh was being built (from 1743), or Edinburgh's New Town (after 1766), all prestigious new buildings were defined by classical modernity.

The Castle's Return?

The new-build castle was perhaps never wholly rejected. In the 1670s–80s, and in parallel with an escalating classicising imperative, castles were, as we have seen, reasserted as a prestigious modern national architecture – reacting, and not giving way, to classicism. As we have also seen, this was the case above all with the Drumlanrig paradox of a giant Corinthian Order on a castle. And a more traditional-looking castle was built in 1677 by Sir Hugh Campbell of Cawdor. This was Islay House: L-plan, crow-stepped and high. This indicates a perceived security risk; for, after all, castles in the 'remote' Highands/ *Gàidhealtachd*, like Duart (Chapter 14), maintained strong external walls enfolding modern apartments long after Caerlaverock's walls had been breached for big domestic windows.

Meanwhile, as we saw, castle revival was already underway at Lochleven. The concept of the old as enjoyable and esteemed was expressed differently in Smith and McGill's 1720 design for a new and classical 'Inveraray Castle'. It envisaged a colossal, two-courtyard mansion, the old castle clasped like a gemstone at the heart of the inner court.

Touch, a multi-phase courtyard castle, was re-fronted in 1757–62 as a new classical house. But (and reminiscent of Bruce's Craighall of 1697–99), recessed on its east side is an equally tall, sixteenth-century parapeted tower, unmissable in frontal views of the house and a clear statement of antiquity. Touch, like Smith and McGill's Inveraray, demonstrated a modernity needing both new classicism and ancient castles.

Another key building on the cusp of castle survival/revival was Alloa. John Erskine, earl of Mar (1675–1732), an important political and cultural figure, inaugurated an ingenious programme of improvements from 1703, continuing until he was exiled for leading the 1715 Jacobite Rising. Like Bruce, Mar exploited views of natural and historic features, including vistas on Clackmannan Tower, Sauchie Tower and the royal castle of Stirling, of which he was hereditary governor. Alloa's ancient tower was reconstructed with a grid-windowed classical front reminiscent of Hamilton's Kinneil, save that Alloa kept more explicitly its castellated form, with turrets, parapets and crow-steps. Mar was a gentleman architect, and advised at Alloa by Smith and McGill. Like Drumlanrig, Alloa's castle design was combined with classicism; and like Dunkeld, bartizans were desirable. Similarly, the ancient Campbell seat of Balloch (Taymouth), originally an L-plan tower, had its jamb duplicated, and when from 1739 William Adam and John Douglas worked there, the house was left as a modified but still symmetrical castle, complete with duplicate crow-stepped gable, bartizans and swept-roofed dormers.

Nonetheless, all Scotland's contemporary leading architectural figures were best known for driving the ideal of the classical house, replacing castles or disguising old fabric where, for practicality, it was retained. Classicism came to represent a unionist political ideology in Britain through another Scottish architect, Colen Campbell, who from 1715 published *Vitruvius Britannicus*, celebrating classicism in Britain and lionising England's Inigo Jones (1573–1652). Queen Anne, the last Stuart monarch, died childless in 1714, raising succession issues that posed a risk to the seven-year-old Britain; and, as we have seen, Lord Mar led a Jacobite army against the new settlement. Classicism was already strong in Scotland and England, so a classical 'British' architectural history and modernity – developed by Scottish architects (Campbell developed ideas that were Smith's) – could be presented to serve unionist rhetoric. Castles were rejected in favour of Jonesian Palladian Classicism.

But Campbell included a plate of Drumlanrig, and it was probably significant that he did. Drumlanrig was the only 'castle' in his first volume (buildings called 'castles' in the third volume, like Mereworth, were classical, except for Drumlanrig, which reappeared there). Campbell described Drumlanrig as the duke's 'ancient seat . . . greatly adorned by the two preceding Dukes', thus presenting as valid the idea of newly built and recently modified 'ancient' castles to both 'ancient' families and a wide, specialist readership which was, soon, anxious to look sometimes beyond classicism and recover or create a dynastic or national history.

Parting is Such Sweet Sorrow

So why, with classicism established, were castles revived? The answer has to be that attitudes toward 'the old' were changing.

Classical antiquity was long considered important, and archaeology was becoming equally so. The orientation of both sixteenth-century Kinneil and Callander Park was dictated by the Roman Wall, and when in 1723 Sir John Clerk of Penicuik (1676–1755) built a classical villa, Mavisbank, he set it against a mount he

believed to be Roman. He complained that he had to prevent Adam from adding a storey to the design, by which it 'wou'd have lookt like a Touer and been quite spoiled'. To Clerk, Thirlestane Castle was 'a great building of a vile Gothick taste'. But, as an antiquarian and proto-preservationist, he explained that:

> It was against my inclination that [Ravensneuk Tower] was pulled down; but as my father . . . wanted stones for the park dyke . . . I submitted. The touer of Pennicuik was pulled down on the same account, but if I had the stones in readiness I would repair them both. Old houses and Touers are, I think, the Honour and pride of a Country.[7]

Europe was entering the phase we call Romanticism. At the heart of Romanticism was the idea of looking back to something valuable which we had lost and should celebrate and retrieve; also that rationalism alone was inadequate, because some things, such as poetry or architecture, were more elevated than simple utility. Such thinking underpinned the 'Scottish Historical Landscape', seen at Bruce's Kinross and still being exploited, say, by William Adam at the so-called 'dogg kennell' of Chatelherault (begun 1731), whose profile might have pleased Romanticists, and where Cadzow's ancient castle was made into an eyecatcher. Bruce's Kinross showed that visual/historic interest alone entitled some castles to be preserved.

Scotland now experienced two great sea-changing events: replacement of the old monarchy in 1689, and parliamentary union with England in 1707. People reacted differently. For Dr Archibald Pitcairne (1652–1713), the death in battle of the Jacobite leader John Graham of Claverhouse in 1689 delivered a farewell to Scotland's existence, her consignment to history. Clerk of Penicuik believed that the union was against popular will, but also believed paternalistically that it served Scotland's best interests. Political opposition coalesced into militarised Jacobitism, bringing a new role for castles, and enormous anti-Jacobite fortifications were built at Stirling Castle in 1708. More modestly, Braemar was made a fort from 1715, partly to further humiliate Lord Mar and the Jacobites, whose rising had failed.

The marquis of Montrose, royalist military leader executed in 1650, was being rebranded as a martyr–hero, his poems published in James Watson's *Choice Collection* in 1706.[8] That was but one of the ingredients now building (Mary Queen of Scots, as we saw, was another), that would create Scotland's national Romanticism. Romanticism needed concepts or slogans like 'the other' (Presbyterians; England); 'the nation martyred' (lost monarchy; union); an 'enemy within' (Presbyterians; unionists); 'attempted liberation / glorious failure' (Montrose; religious wars; Jacobite uprisings). This was all intellectual fodder to the Romantics; intellectual justification to the more prosaic.

Within this polarised new, and to some almost 'post-Scottish', environment of Britishness, people turned to consider the past. In 1719, Elizabeth Wardlaw's historical ballad 'Hardyknute', finding a historical enemy that was not England, celebrated Scots triumph over the Norse in 1263. In 1724, Allan Ramsay (1686–1758), depressed by what he regarded as the treachery of the union, argued that Scottish culture had a legitimate place alongside classicism:

> Readers of the best and most exquisite Discernment frequently complain of our modern Writings, as filled with affected Delicacies and studied Refinements, which they would gladly exchange for that natural Strength of Thought and Simplicity of Stile our Forefathers practised . . . Their Poetry is the Product of their own Country, not pilfered and spoiled in the Transportation from abroad: Their Images are native, and their Landskips domestick; copied from the Fields and Meadows we every day behold.
>
> The Morning rises (in the Poets Description) as she does in the Scottish Horizon. We are not carried to Greece, or Italy, for a shade, a stream, a breeze. The Groves rise in our own valleys; the Rivers flow from our own Fountains, and the Winds blow upon our own hills. I find not fault with those Things, as they are in Greece or Italy: But with a Northern Poet for fetching his Materials from these Places, in a poem, of which his own country is the Scene.[9]

As Bruce had indicated at Kinross, as Slezer believed in 1693, and as Clerk said of Ravensneuk, Scottish national antiquity was intrinsically valuable – but now, to Ramsay, it was under assault.

It took nothing from the paradigms of classicism to say that old Scottish domestic buildings were important. They could be enjoyed as ancient, culturally important things without necessarily being occupied any more than were the antique ruins of landscape painters. For Ramsay, Scots culture was that of the future – even though he was simultaneously collecting or salvaging old material as the European Romantics were soon to be doing; the once-nurturing culture could no longer be relied upon to continue that role.

Meanwhile, William Adam was designing a series of new houses, all classical, such as Arniston (though Duff House has an almost castle-like character); many rich people, such as the 2nd duke of Argyll, stayed in their ancient castles; and abandoned castles were being enjoyed, either through visiting and viewing, or through Slezer's engravings.

This competing duality of Scottish castle / British or European classical house entwined with the great Scottish paradox of the eighteenth century: how it was that, in the age of Enlightenment, writers, artists, musicians, philosophers, architects and intellectuals, nurtured from a much earlier proto-Enlightenment, all combined to make Scotland simultaneously a leading land of Enlightenment and Improvement, yet also an archetypal land of Romanticism. These polarities were exemplified not only by 'castellated classicism' but also by the philosopher David Hume and the Jacobite heroine Flora MacDonald, each of whom shaped critically the culture of the Scotland that was to come. Bruce's Kinross suggested that these polarities might co-exist within the one mind. The same might also be said of the rational yet Romantic castle designs of Robert Adam, as the next chapter shows.

CHAPTER THREE

Inveraray to Abbotsford
Survival and Revival

Ian Gow and Aonghus MacKechnie

In the period covered by this chapter, Scottish secular architecture diverged into two principal strands. First was the continuing classicism of earlier decades seen at, say, Robert Adam's Newliston (1789–90), James MacLeran and Alexander Laing's 1790s Over Rankeillour, or Thomas Hamilton's Edinburgh Royal High School (1825–9). Second was the option of building in a revived castellated style. This chapter examines the latter, new, option: the re-arrival of the castle as a fashionable building type. That fashion, which began with Inveraray in the 1740s and sat within the wider framework of the Gothic Revival, did not immediately catch hold, but from the 1770s it gained popularity. Key to the Gothic Revival was the idea of reviving a national rather than classical antiquity. The spirit was fore-fronted by Robert Adam (1728–1792) who devised his own symmetrical castle formula, an approach continued after his death by followers such as John Paterson (d.1832), until the arrival of a more full-blown revivalism from the 1820s–30s which tilted towards a more organic-looking, as if multi-phase, asymmetry. This new phase was called the 'Scotch Baronial', and is discussed in Chapter 4.

We have seen that from James VI's time, modernising clients, and architects such as Sir William Bruce, James Smith and William Adam, were at the forefront of a determined movement away from castellation towards classicism, and that this was a process begun much earlier with houses such as James Murray's Kilbaberton/Baberton (1622–3). But we saw too that Bruce and Smith had also rebuilt or helped to rebuild castles, at Thirlestane and Drumlanrig respectively, and that a parallel strand of castle fashion clung on – either where the castle was simply retained, as at Cawdor, or was made the dominant element of a refashioned residence, as at Kelburn, whose new wing is dated 1722.

Romanticism

A key driver in the re-arrival of the castle was the developing interest in what our generation calls 'Romanticism': attitudes grounded less in the rationalism of that age of Enlightenment than in emotional reaction, a focus on the past and on the nation or 'race' and, for Scotland, this brought a new focus on the Highlands, wild landscape and Jacobitism. The dashing adventures of Prince Charles Edward Stuart – affectionately, 'Bonnie Prince Charlie' – in 1745–6 conjured up Romantic references, even through his very name; and, from 1760, James MacPherson (1736–1796) published English verse claimed to be translations from a third-century epic by the Gaelic bard Ossian. The cult of Ossianic national-romanticism was born, sweeping soon throughout much of Europe. Thus, when Sir James Clerk commissioned Alexander Runciman to decorate the ceiling of the Saloon at Penicuik, his original proposal for grotesques in the 'Baths of Titus' style was abandoned in favour of a 'Hall of Ossian'. Runciman was to decorate it with Ossianic themes, though still in a classical style. Key to Romanticism was thinking about the past – 'oldness' was becoming increasingly popular, and the long-lost past was inspirational.

Romanticism also threw up new attitudes concerning the value put on old castellated dynastic houses. This inspired another key innovation of the period, namely, the reoccupation of the old; once-abandoned castles were given renewed duties as elite residences, the first such being probably Castle Huntly, from 1776 (Figure 46). There was also a refocusing on clan or family histories and traditions. General William Gordon, laird of Fyvie, for instance, was portrayed in 1766 by Pompeo Batoni in Highland dress. This was the same client who, around 1790, extended Fyvie Castle not with a classical wing but a tower (the Gordon Tower) stylistically correspondent with the 1590s castle.

Revival or Survival?

William Adam's *Vitruvius Scoticus* was so ambitious in its concept, and so long drawn-out in its production, that its plates have something of the character of a topographical gallery, in the tradition of Slezer's *Theatrum Scotiae* of 1693, as much as they are a manual of cutting-edge classical design. The work remained unpublished until 1812, but it tells us much of Adam's architectural vision and that of his clients, and of the paradigms of his generation that were soon to be left behind.

Glancing through the many pages of this outsize volume today, although there are eyecatchingly seductive temple front porticoes proposed for Hamilton and Hopetoun at Plates 11 and 16 respectively, neither of which Adam was to see realised, an undeniable underlying trend emerges from the plates in its record of how a classicising imperative was being imposed on existing piles of castle or tower-house format, through a symmetry, more often than not, achieved by duplication. This was to be Sir William Bruce's forte and is seen on the grandest scale at Holyroodhouse in Plate 3. But while the modern visitor to the palace marvels at his handling of the classical Orders – with a new grammatical suavity, and drawn from Amsterdam's town hall, which he knew – it is impossible to ignore the obvious and rather extraordinary fact that the symmetry of Holyroodhouse from 1671 was achieved through the mirror duplication of James V's massive fortified tower, complete with turreted round corner towers topped by crenellations, with only modish sash windows substituting for King James' securer and massive wrought-iron window grilles.

With this royal imprimatur, which proclaimed at Holyroodhouse that the restored Stuart royal house was firmly grounded in a continuity with an ancient past, hard-up lairds, in more remote corners of the kingdom, must have been relieved that this fashionable symmetry could be achieved without a total and costly rebuilding of the old, at a time when home improvements in Scotland would sometimes be expected to span several generations of family effort, making the choice of style a serious matter. Though not published in *Vitruvius Scoticus*, Bruce provided a model for such lairds in his classicising of his own first seat at Balcaskie from 1668, which combined a modish symmetry with something of the old tower-house glamour. Indeed, a sound tradition of building in intractable stone and lime

FIGURE 46
Castle Huntly, Perthshire (© RCAHMS, SC 1233625)

in Scotland generally meant it was unthinkable to conceive of levelling to the ground and starting from scratch. In plate after plate of *Vitruvius Scoticus*, plans precede the elevations, and several reveal, with an immediacy that could be more skilfully disguised in the latter, the survival of many thick-walled immoveable towers. Only one castle slipped through – Taymouth – but only because it had been refashioned by William Adam (and modified by John Douglas) to be symmetrical on the Balcaskie–Holyrood model, and a bartizaned version of something like Prestonfield (1689) or Cammo (1710), whose gables were curvilinear rather than crow-stepped (Figure 151).

In such a context, Inveraray at Plate 71 of *Vitruvius Scoticus*, whose foundation stone was laid in 1746 and which has the distinction today of being generally regarded as the first major new-built country seat in the Castle Style in the British Isles, inaugurating both a Gothic and a Castle Revival, may be less surprising when seen against these often somewhat hybrid Scottish peers. Inveraray is discussed in Chapter 9.

The complex genesis of Inveraray's design has been traced in great detail by Ian G Lindsay and Mary Cosh in their *Inveraray and the Dukes of Argyll* (1973). The Campbell family was metropolitan in outlook, and the duke's English architect, Roger Morris, brought together ideas and a Gothicism that can be traced back to an initial 1720s proposal seemingly by Sir John Vanbrugh (1664–1726). The novelty of a new-built house, realised in this 'remote' locale by the practical building skills of William Adam, is apparently explained by the hopeless unrepairability of the existing old tower, which was in danger of an imminent collapse; the family had already withdrawn to the safety and comfort of an adjacent detached pavilion. The novelty of its style is perhaps diluted a little by Morris' contemporary Gothic designs for rebuilding the duke's secondary, if rather less remote, seat at Rosneath on the Firth of Clyde, and they are further complemented by the recently discovered Gothic designs by John Douglas for extending this existing tower house.

Jacobite uprisings in the first half of the eighteenth century had given some castles renewed significance as military architecture. During the civil war of 1745–6, the Jacobite army destroyed Fort George, in Inverness, while the victorious Hanoverians installed garrisons at places such as Braemar and Corgarff, with star-shaped defences. Even more 'remote' places like Duart became military bases, sometimes continuing as such into the nineteenth century. The design of Inveraray corresponds with the thinking behind these martial works; though even more directly linked to them was the unexecuted alternative design by Dugal Campbell for Inveraray, its star-shaped plan anticipating the defences at Braemar and Corgarff. Inveraray's design, which combined an up-to-date plan with a soaring verticality in its exterior, crenellations, round corner towers, Gothic-arched windows and even a fosse, was to be widely disseminated in both copy architectural drawings and prints, giving it a contemporary celebrity. Because it was a new-built house, yet also a castle, it certainly deserves its modern celebrity as the exemplar that helped launch the Gothic Revival.

Continuing military presence within the royal castles of Edinburgh and Stirling had a vast impact on their component buildings, as the spirit of Romanticism replaced the fear of Jacobite rebellion. Edinburgh is discussed below by Robert Morris (Chapter 13), but we can note the 'rediscovery' in 1818 of the Honours of Scotland – sealed away in 1707 – and the return in 1829 of Mons Meg from the London foundries, where she had been found too big to melt down. All these items were put on display in the castle, which was already supplementing its role as military base with its new duties as tourist attraction.

Stirling had less to offer tourism and, like Edinburgh, its castle buildings were converted, sometimes quite radically, from royal to military use. James IV's forework gate, once multi-towered and high, had been neglected and its skyline had become ragged through collapse. It was smartened up with a diminutive crenellated external profile, the remaining four towers being demolished and the consequential scarring in the ashlars patched inexpensively with black rubble.

In 1757, the Adam family's close involvement in building Inveraray, with its sophisticated metropolitan design, was to beget the Adam brothers' colossal if not megalomaniacal design for Douglas Castle. The design was by John Adam (1721–1792), who was at the time building classical buildings at Inveraray such as the Town House (1755–7).

Douglas Castle, in Plate 135 of *Vitruvius Scoticus* (Figure 59; the Adams had continued extending their father's project after his death in 1748), has less prominence in Scottish architectural history because it was completely demolished in 1937. Bad press saw it unmourned and unloved, its pasteboard Gothic style had long been out of fashion, and the columns of coal on which it had stood had been extracted. It was exceptionally poorly recorded, is thus difficult to understand today, and the facts of its history are far from clear. The Douglases were one of Scotland's most ancient families, interwoven into the national annals from the time of King Robert Bruce, and to that extent they were in broadly the same league as the Argylls at Inveraray. The Adams' patron, the first and last duke of Douglas, was dead by 1761, leaving no direct heir and causing a sensational inheritance lawsuit. Only one flank of the vast design was ever built, amounting to one third of the project, and more of the irregular old castle (part of which has outlived its successor) had survived than the Adams' plan meant to preserve, for its builder's intention had been to keep and to link both the old and new castles. Douglas was indebted in its detailing at least to Inveraray. It was bulkier if not actually bigger, and if it lacked the suavity of Inveraray's soaring central clerestorey-lit hall, it had a parade of simply enormous rooms, a vast staircase and a gallery wider than that at Holyroodhouse and doubtless also destined for a run of its owner's family portraits.

If its ambitious scale astonishes us today, even contemporaries who found possibly only an isolated fragment of the design extant were curious. The novelty of the duke of Douglas' enterprise in the late 1750s was soon to be the commonplace of such atavistic projects as George IV's rebuilding and purging demodernisation of Windsor but is more understandable in the Scottish context of a Castle Survival, although utterly dependent on Inveraray's Castle Revival concept. Sir William Forbes of Pitsligo, the arbiter of taste in Edinburgh's New Town and a patron of architecture himself, who interfered in most civic building works, thought it 'a most magnificent and princely residence' on a visit in 1795; he sought out an ancient retainer to provide him with an oral history, which he relayed in a letter to Lady Forbes on 7 June:

> The present Castle was meant to form three sides of a square, with a round tower at each corner. Of this plan, only one of the side-fronts, and about one third of the principal front is executed; so that not one half is yet completed: but even this part constitutes an amazing large house; for the Castle is four stories high above the vaults, and the round towers five stories; and on each floor there are 13 rooms, making in all 45 Stately apartments. The form of the Castle is Gothick, with battlements and Church windows, like those of Inveraray Castle; from which George Paterson, who built it, seems to have taken his idea of the plan; only that Douglas Castle infinitely exceeds Inveraray in Grandeur, from the circumstance of Inveraray being only two floors above the level of the ground, whereas that of Douglas is four. The extent of the side that is finished, as near as I could guess by stepping along the ground, may be from 140 to 150 feet including the round towers. The Principal front, as my conductor told me, of which one third only is finished, was meant to have been somewhat more extensive. The Apartments are all large and roomy, and most substantially finished, but there is only one room of any considerable size, the dining-room, which as I guess, is about 42 feet by 30; a drawing-room adjoining is about 30 by 20: and both those apartments are finished in a superior style to the rest; the floors being wainscot, the doors Mahogany, the roofs ornamented with stucco and extremely handsome marble chimney-pieces. Probably the architect meant some larger apartment in the principal front. The House was six years in building, and cost as my conductor told me, £24,000 which I can very well believe; for the whole is of hewn stone. The late Duke never was again at Douglas Castle after the fire; and it is not likely the plan will ever be completed; at

least in the present Lord Douglas's time, who much prefers Bothwell Castle.[1]

At Inveraray, Robert Mylne (1733–1811, and prizeman at the Academy of St Luke in Rome, in 1758), who oversaw its completion, was later to suppress the exterior Gothic window heads into interior classical arches. But, by contrast, photographs of the plasterwork in the drawing room at Douglas Castle do show a Gothic character, and a surviving photographic glimpse of an interior window reveals the charm of its Gothic astragalled glazing, reminiscent of Leixlip Castle outside Dublin, which must have given a markedly Gothic character to the entire interior of the executed wing.

A Wider Interest

In 1761, James Nisbet of Kelso (d.1781) carried out repairs and began additions to Twizel Castle, Northumberland, 'preserving the Gothic form and taste'.[2] It was given Inveraray-type windows, crenellations and quatrefoils but was never completed. By that time, the model of Inveraray and Douglas helped validate the style, where not long before extensions would probably have been more classical.

Commencement of John Baxter's (d.1798) Gordon Castle (1769–82) for the duke of Gordon heralded what was to come: not Gothic, pointed openings, but flat- or round-arched openings, and essentially classical gridded façades (and in that respect like Inveraray, save for the latter's pointed openings), castellated at the wallheads with corbelled and crenellated parapets. Gordon's scale was mammoth, with a 538-foot-long façade – for Charles McKean, 'a tedious quarter mile of two-storeyed crenellated regularity'[3] (Figure 47). It sat on the cusp between traditional mansion and the form of castellation that was to come. On the one

hand, its old six-storey entrance tower was emphasised, for it rose two storeys above the remainder of the main house and retained its duties as main entrance, while its main front was only near-symmetrical – one three-bay end was recessed, the other set forward, presumably indicative to contemporary viewers of organic, multi-phase construction. The overall composition and garden front were symmetrical, and in that sense it anticipated Robert Adam's always symmetrical castles. Within Gordon Castle, however, Baxter's own neo-classical training in Rome, where in 1766 he had been made an honorary member of the Academy of St Luke, was to create a series of refined rooms with superb plaster ceilings that housed the successive Grand Tour collections of the dukes. As at Inveraray, an associated new town was also built. This was Fochabers, also Baxter's design and – also like Inveraray's town – its emphasis was not on castellation but on classicism.

Robert Adam

The Castle Style was to be the forte of Robert Adam, who was to take the family expertise honed at Inveraray and Douglas to new heights and crags. From the commencement of Inveraray in 1745 until 1800, approximately thirty castles were built in Scotland, around thirteen of these by or involving Robert Adam. His castles were of course castellated externally, but they were otherwise essentially classical in window disposition and in plan and, like Inveraray as completed by Mylne, his interior decoration was frequently likewise so.

Much has been written on Adam's Castle Style in an attempt to analyse its complex sources, pointing out that it possibly looked back to Antique Roman military and civil architecture as much to medieval sources. But his motivation,

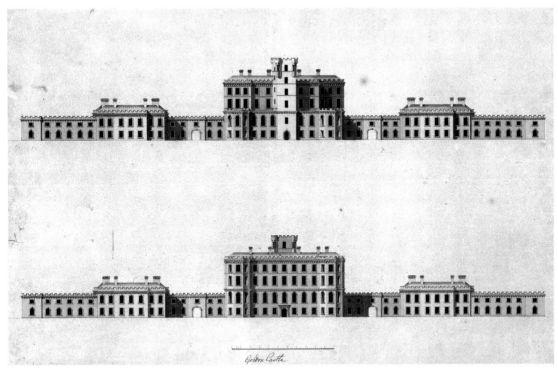

FIGURE 47
Gordon Castle, Morayshire: elevations, John Baxter, c.1769) (© RCAHMS and Duke of Buccleuch, SC 1233616)

with which he was able to enthuse so many of his Scottish patrons, was surely a Picturesque response to the building type that best complemented the often rugged landscape of Scotland. In this context, Mellerstain of 1770 is particularly interesting, because it was a new house for which, like Inveraray, an entire portfolio of previous and classical designs had been accumulated, but only the conventional office wings by William Adam had been realised during the 1720s. For this commanding site, Adam proposed a dramatic simple scenographic crenellated silhouette, dispensing with the ranges of Gothic windows that distinguish Inveraray and Douglas.

Romanticism provided two architectural strands: the castle, and the rustic *cottage orné*, and Adam's castles can be seen in the context of the growth of Ossianic Romanticism, which became an international movement from the closing eighteenth century decades. *The Works of Ossian* was published in several languages, including German, Italian and French, with an impact on these and other cultures receptive to the spirit of Romanticism. Sweden, for example, had two kings Oscar (1799–1859 and 1829–1907), called after an Ossianic hero, while Napoleon carried a copy of the book on his campaigns.

Adam's castles show his, and his clients', interest in pursuing a more assertively Picturesque and Romantic approach, as Adam refocused his interest in Scotland. He set up an Edinburgh office in 1772. Besides the impact in their designs on Romanticism, John, Robert and James Adam had also learned about military architecture at first

FIGURE 48
Above. Wedderburn Castle, Berwickshire
(© RCAHMS, SC 1233576)

FIGURE 49
Opposite. Seton Castle, East Lothian: view from
south-east through entrance arch (© RCAHMS,
SC 823359)

hand, as they took over their father's contracts with the government's Board of Ordnance for building Fort George following his death in 1748.

Adam himself made drawings of castles in sometimes exaggeratedly wild settings, affirming his concept of setting being vital to his castle designs. Mellerstain was followed the next year by Wedderburn, whose rusticated ground floor underlined its still embracing classicism, and the overlap in the two styles that was to continue until the next century (Figure 48). Each of these owed much to Baxter's Gordon Castle, save that they were – as always with Adam – symmetrical. Adam's interpretation of the historic castle was in a sense to classicise it, and not until the next century were new castles to be built asymmetrical. Each interpretation was argued to be valid. James Clerk of Penicuik, Adam's brother-in-law, argued in the 1790s that, whilst Scotland's renais-

sance castles were not built for defence, they still adhered to

> the principal decorations of the old castle; they were still flanked by towers and surmounted with turrets and battlements, and though their regularity and situation deprived them generally of the picturesque contour of the former yet they continued from their grandeur and effect to be pompous and interesting objects. Of this species of building we have a splendid example in the Heriot's Hospital of this city.[4]

For Adam, the archaeological accuracy sought by future Gothic Revivalists took second place to imposing his own style on the genre.

The Adam brothers' houses fell into two main phases, if we exclude the Inveraray model reproduced at Douglas. First, was the Mellerstain/Wedderburn model, described above, which included Caldwell (1773–4); though there, Robert Adam introduced diminutive corner bartizans, elements that were to characterise the next phase, exemplified by Seton (1789) (Figure 49) and Culzean – less 'blocky' designs with everchanging wall planes and a more Gothic language. Adam's stock triumphal arch motif, exemplified by Kedleston (1760) was translated into castle architecture, as at Caldwell (Figure 50), Oxenfoord (1780) and Dalquharran (1785).

Adam and his clients, just like Bruce and his clients a century earlier, were evidently comfortable with the demolition of old work – as at the great palace of Seton – and its replacement with a symbolically ancient though (perhaps entirely) new 'castle'. This attitude to the old is seen at Oxenfoord (built 1780–2), of which the client, Sir John Dalrymple, wrote in 1784 to a friend: 'I have repaired an old castle and by the help of Bob Adams have really made it much older than it was

. . . it would suit you, who are an Antiquary, perfectly.'[5] Ideas taken from the buildings of bygone Scotland were held in sufficiently high regard to warrant being reproduced; the buildings themselves were of lesser importance.

Today, Culzean Castle, in the care of the National Trust for Scotland, is recognised as Adam's canonical masterpiece in his idiosyncratic Castle Style (see Chapter 10). While we might feel that many cannier Scottish patrons, on seeing his designs, asked 'do you have anything cheaper?', David, 10th earl of Cassillis, a bachelor with no family responsibilities, was game for everything that Adam could suggest, and building was to continue up to their deaths in close succession in 1792. The glory of Culzean lies in the drama of its dazzlingly picturesque site on the Firth of Clyde in close proximity to the dramatic, many-peaked silhouette of Arran, with Goatfell, and Ailsa Craig closing the seascape to its south. So comprehensive is the earl and his architect's exploration of pure architectural form and space on the grandest scale, embracing the Home Farm, the rebuilt stables and a ruined 'Roman' bridge of approach, that until recently it was almost forgotten that Adam had moulded his vision from a very real ancient tower house on a defensive site. The first campaign of works in 1777 created a complete new house in the Brucian mode of duplication, but at Culzean the old tower formed the centrepiece and it was flanked by lower pavilion blocks with more modest versions of the Inveraray and Douglas round corner towers providing spiral service staircases and modest closets. The location of the old tower was expressed in the exaggerated verticality of the main rooms (a feature its builder Hugh Cairncross was to transfer to Ardgowan further up the Clyde), and on the roof, where one feels a little as if one is backstage, and the inner faces of old rubble-built tower walls show diagonal lead flashings from earlier roof lines. The neatness of this

FIGURE 50
Caldwell House, Ayrshire (© RCAHMS and Ayrshire Archives, SC 1233615)

elegant rebuilding gives a toy-fort character to the domestically scaled and pre-existing seventeenth-century garden terraces, although there was an asymmetrical dynamic more in tune with 'real' castles in the side entrance, the offset kitchen wing that was to hint at the great expansion – which had no functional imperative whatsoever, as the 1777 house was complete in all particulars – to the sea on the west. It is now clear that there were always lower office buildings, but containing rooms and particularly bedrooms used by the family and guests, that were placed to enjoy the dramatic sea views. Although brilliantly subsumed in the later Wardrop and Reid family wing, Adam's brewhouse was a more complex structure that exploited its picturesque site with a degree of asymmetry. Eventually the round drawing room would replace and rise high above everything and the earlier low buildings on the cliff,

while the oval staircase knits this lifetime's work into an apparent coherence, belying its being an afterthought.

Culzean's interior, to the relief of Adam's biographer, A T Bolton, who was challenged by the unarchaeological character of its Castle Style detailing, is relentlessly classical, if we allow for Eileen Harris' recent suggestion that the long drawing room in the former great hall of the old tower has 'an unusual Jacobean spirit'.

Not just mansions but also public buildings were candidates for castellation. James Adam's octagonal St George's Episcopal Chapel in Edinburgh's York Place (1792–4) was given Inveraray-type windows and castellation. The associated manse next door (No. 7) was an early castellated town house whose presence draws attention to the fact that castellation, while popular for rich rural buildings, was not to be considered suitable for urban terraces. That had to wait until the next century.

James Adam's Barony Church in Glasgow (1793–4) had a steep-pitched crow-stepped gable in addition to its more formulaic castellated turrets. Robert Adam's Edinburgh Bridewell (1791–5) was one of his biggest non-domestic castellated essays – a foil to the 'real' Edinburgh Castle on the hill opposite.

Robert Adam introduced his castellated style elsewhere, notably at Whitehaven (1769), Ugbrooke (c.1763) and The Oaks, Carshalton (c.1777, unfinished), all in England, and Castle Upton in Ireland (1785; his only asymmetrical castle). But critically, in terms of helping redirect the course of Scottish architecture, the ideas he introduced or developed provided a legacy that many were to imitate over the following decades. Interestingly, when Adam met James 'Ossian' MacPherson, Scotland's two foremost Romanticists of their time decided not upon a castellated but a classical house: Belleville, or Balavil, built 1790–6.

In 1753, when the Adam brothers were still establishing their reputations, John Adam designed a remarkably austere classical front on the 'back' of the old Castle Grant, such being the 'modernisation' sought for that old castle; while in 1792, Robert Adam's Barnton converted an old L-plan house, in the old Bruce manner, to a symmetrical twin-gabled front, but with crow-steps, bartizans and parapets (reminiscent almost of the predecessor Taymouth) – the very language Bruce removed from his conversions, a rare exception being Holyrood.

Adam's Contemporaries

This new fluidity in Scottish architectural thinking can be seen in several unrelated projects. At Finlaystone, on a defensive site above the Clyde,

John Douglas' contract proposed the demolition of the existing tower, whose materials were to be refashioned into a small classical villa. This represents one extreme of attitudes to castles at the time – and a possibility perhaps not available to families with larger existing seats that had greater accommodation needs. At Blair Castle, which had been severely damaged during the warfare of 1745–6, the duke of Atholl, with metropolitan taste, had concentrated on classicising the interiors. He merely 'clipped' the towers to create a fairly relaxed modern but also ancient simplified silhouette that was rebranded 'Atholl House', but left the way open, by way of survival, for Bryce's later recrenellating after Queen Victoria's sojourn there (see Chapter 11). A version of Adam's Castle Style, however, was thought suitable for a small villa, Hermitage of Braid of c.1785, possibly by Robert Burn, where Adam's Picturesque thinking came into play in an acknowledged beauty spot (Figure 51).

When Sir William Forbes came to build for himself at Colinton in 1801, the estate had come complete with an old tower, whose rebuilding and improvement he explored in both the castle mode and classicising by duplication. As befitting such an innovator, he had it both ways in that he created both a new built classical villa using an amalgam of advice from different architects while, far from being abandoned, the tower was rendered an even more Picturesque ornament, in an old-fashioned garden of ancient holly hedges, through its partial demolition with gunpowder, on the advice of the artist and landscape architect Alexander Nasmyth in 1804. The old tower at Ardgowan also found a new future as an atavistic eyecatcher in the garden close to the new house.

By the turn of the eighteenth century, this Romantic approach to the distinctive idiosyncrasies of a Scottish past, such as tower houses, was gaining ground: the rage for Improvement, typified by *Vitruvius Scoticus*, was no longer seen

FIGURE 51
Hermitage of Braid, Edinburgh (© RCAHMS, SC 565014)

as the only possible approach for patrons. Just as Robert Burns and Walter Scott were to collect old ballads – and fashion new ones in the character of the 'old' – artists were attracted to both Romantic old towers and new buildings, and they made sets of engraved views to enliven the letterpress of Enlightenment periodicals. This spirit is reflected in such ephemeral suites of plates published as '*Views of . . .*'.

A hybrid Inveraray–Adam composition was Melville Castle (1786–91) by James Playfair (1755–1794) for Henry Dundas, 1st Viscount Melville (nicknamed 'Harry the Ninth, uncrowned King of Scotland') (Figure 52). It occupied the site of its predecessor and comprised a corner-turreted near-square main block and lower flanking wings; most windows were hood-moulded like Adam's castles, the turret windows pointed, and the interior classical with a vast open staircase area – again possibly recalling Inveraray.

FIGURE 52
Above. Melville Castle, Midlothian: view taken
c.1950
(© RCAHMS, SC 1233614)

FIGURE 53
Opposite top. Lanrick, Perthshire: south elevation
(© RCAHMS and Captain Straylan, SC 494694)

FIGURE 54
Opposite bottom. Raehills, Dumfriesshire: view from
east taken in 1968 (© RCAHMS, SC 1233577)

Similar ideas informed Lanrick, which was reportedly re-castellated in 1791 – although another phase of works of unknown scope was done from 1803 by James Gillespie Graham (1776–1855) (Figure 53). There, the tower house was retained and emphasised at the heart of the house, as at Gordon Castle or seventeenth-century predecessors such as Midhope. But, unlike these examples, at Lanrick the design was made symmetrical, with wings of diminishing scale on either flank, rather like Melville.

One building which seems almost to antici-pate Adam's thinking was Raehills, built 1786 for the 3rd earl of Hopetoun to designs by Alexander Stevens the younger (*fl.*1780–1810) (Figure 54). Stevens' father, also Alexander, made his name as a bridge builder, often using castellated elements, as at Glenae Bridge, 1786, and Old Bridge of Dun at Montrose, 1793–6. Raehills followed the estab-

lished model of essentially classically proportioned castellated façades, but here the dramatic
craggy site was exploited with a terraced centre
tower, as at the more dramatically sited Culzean.

This historicising culture, and fondness for
the 'old' and its reproduction, if not retention, was
a factor informing the philosopher David Hume's
statement in 1770: 'I believe this is the historical
age and this the historical nation.'[6]

Historic Landscapes

Besides building new castles as residences, old
castles and new castellation were both used to
convey messages, whether of family antiquity and
legitimacy, or contemporary politics, and often in
the spirit of Romanticism.

In 1750–4 the 2nd earl of Marchmont built
Marchmont House, a classical composition by
Thomas Gibson (*fl.*1750–65). The new site was
near, and on shared orientation with, the predecessor family house of Redbraes. Redbraes was
thereafter partially ruined (the intention in the
1720s had been to upgrade it), and today it
remains an 'eyecatcher'. Instead of regarding the
old building as a problem to erase, or as untidy in
its largely demolished state, it was retained as a
picturesque ruin, an asset to the landscape. On the
one hand, this idea seems hardly new, but
Redbraes was given neither the critical significance assigned the genuinely old Lochleven by
Bruce nor that assigned the new-made Duniquaich at Inverarary, but it was nonetheless a
strong statement of lineal antiquity and of family
advancement. It differed too from the concept we
saw at Douglas, whereby the old and new castles
were to be both retained and linked. The idea of
building a new house whilst leaving the abandoned castle nearby was continued into the nineteenth century and beyond, for instance at
Colinton, mentioned above, or Kirkhill, in

Ayrshire (whose new house dates from c.1845) or
Kilmaronock (whose present house is dated
1901). It was an alternative to repair, and both
Picturesque and Romantic, should the old castle
be made to sit and decay gently as a ruin alongside a new-built mansion.

Castellated Gothic towers or columns dominating the landscape were constructed at Edinburgh's Calton Hill (the Nelson Monument, by
Robert Burn, 1807–14), and Glenfinnan (1815
and 1834), marking where the clans gathered at
the start of the 1745–6 Jacobite Rising (Figure
55). Earlier still, in 1806, was the hilltop Nelson
Monument at Forres (Figure 56), designed by
Charles Stuart, who was then architect at Darnaway. It was octagonal, Gothic-windowed and
crenellated, and its purpose and inspiration was
to document the recent past, unlike Glenfinnan,
where a respectable time lapse was required
before commemorating 'rebels'. But all were
political statements, and castellated.

In 1783, Newhall acquired a new owner,
Thomas Brown. He quickly implemented estate
improvements and added to the house what he
called 'a romantic addition in the Gothic Chapel
style'. Brown also created a Romantic landscape,
which was themed on the popular pastoral drama
The Gentle Shepherd (1725) by the poet, folklorist
and Jacobite Allan Ramsay (1686–1758). Brown
believed Newhall was the setting for the pastoral,
and scenes such as 'Habbie's Howe' and Peggy's
Pool' were pointed out and published on a plan
of 1808.

The story of *The Gentle Shepherd* centres on

FIGURE 55
Opposite left. Glenfinnan Monument, Inverness-shire
(© RCAHMS, SC 1143277)

FIGURE 56
Opposite right. Nelson Monument, Forres,
Morayshire (© RCAHMS, SC 903074)

a laird returned from exile, meaning that everything becomes 'therefore' better. The laird is clearly a metaphor for the exiled Stuart king, the message thus Jacobite. However, these politics could either be ignored or subsumed within Brown's North British politics, for the greater purpose of creating a historically resonant Romantic landscape, and here was a 'Lowland' riposte to the Ossianic landmarks of the Highlands.

Reconstruction and Repair

Meanwhile, this was still the 'age of Improvement', when the entire landscape and the economy were both being transformed. The old was swept away and the expensive, well-built new took its place. But, as we have seen, some people took a more emotional or antiquarian response. Thus, as part of his Harris estate 'Improvements', Rodel Church – within a newly planned fishing village – was rebuilt from ruin in the 1780s by a MacLeod who had purchased that ancient MacLeod estate in 1779. Similar dynastic reasons, combined with an antiquarian emphasis, lay at least partly behind the acquisition of Dryburgh Abbey by the 11th earl of Buchan in 1786, and the re-creation of Hume Castle (Figure 57).

Hume had been wrecked by English soldiers in the 1650s, and left a ruin. But possibly around 1776, it was acquired by the 3rd earl of Marchmont, Hugh Hume-Campbell. On it footings/walling he built a massive curtain wall (completed before 1789), conveying the image of an ancient castle or Borders stronghold, emphasising the importance and antiquity of the Humes, and creating in the process a monumental landscape feature visible for miles. It was above all the image that its builder wanted, and not (in contrast to MacLeod at Rodel) a building with practical function – so nothing was built inside, nothing

roofed. But, like Bruce's ideas a century before, landscape and nature, towers and castles – but supplemented now by lineal imagery – had become interrelated.

Castle Reoccupation

By emphasising the significance of old Scottish castles as residences, Adam's and his clients' new-built castles presaged a new attitude: that of exploitation of the genuinely old, discarded castle as a suitable country seat. This reversal of fashion was perhaps inaugurated at the same Castle Lyon which had been condemned by the earl of Strathmore, builder of Glamis, a century earlier. It was acquired or, his wife might have argued, reacquired in 1776 by a retired East India Company administrator, George Paterson (1734–1817). This was the year of his marriage to Anne, daughter of the 12th Lord Gray, descendent of the Grays of Fowlis who until 1614 had owned the property, then called Castle Huntly. The Patersons restored this name to the castle, and thus now occupied their genuinely ancient (if updated with viewing tower, and so on) dynastic castle.

Another early castle reoccupation was Duntrune (see Figure 58). In 1796, it was acquired by Neil Malcolm of Poltalloch, who repaired it as his main residence. A 'small battlement' was added, and in 1815 it was described as a 'very comfortable residence'.[7] This opinion was wholly at odds with that of the Romantic poet and linguist John Leyden (1775–1811), who visited in 1800: 'It is a clumsy, inelegant structure and has been modernised . . . to very little advantage, as the walls, of seven feet in thickness, resist every attempt to alleviate the prison-like gloom.'[8]

To Leyden, Kinross House had ceased being the keynote or precocious essay in classicism of Bruce's and Clerk's age, being instead dismissed as 'an old Gothic structure'. But he responded

FIGURE 57
Hume Castle, Berwickshire: aerial photograph (© RCAHMS, DP 019843)

more favourably to ancient ruins, which he made it his business to visit on his tour. For example, visiting Oban, he observed that: 'The view of Dunolly Castle, or rather ruins, is eminently picturesque.'[9]

The Contra-flow

More widely, opinions, of course, differed. For example, a view of Craigmillar Castle, as noted above, was important to the builders of Prestonfield House (rebuilt 1680s, but possibly incorporating the shell and therefore orientations of a possibly 1610s–20s house). But at neighbouring Duddingston House (1763–8), the landscape was contrived specifically to exclude views of the castle, as it could be 'seen all over the country' and was thus 'a common prostitute'.[10] The much more prominent and symbolic Edinburgh Castle, by contrast, was important in axiality and views over many centuries, from Aberdour (1570s) and

FIGURE 58
Right. Duntrune, Argyll:
view from south
(© RCAHMS, SC 565370)

FIGURE 59
Opposite. Douglas Castle,
Lanarkshire: plate from
Vitruvius Scoticus
(© RCAHMS,
SC 1233575 CN)

Baberton (1620s), while Edinburgh's Old Town constituted the panoramic main view from Inverleith House (1774). But Edinburgh's was a royal castle, centrepiece of Scotland's capital.

During the late eighteenth and early nineteenth centuries, castles continued being abandoned, demolished or quarried for building materials. By 1803, even the mighty Kildrummy had been recently quarried to build farmhouses.[11] People like Sir Walter Scott and Lord Cockburn, however, valued castles such as Lauriston, whose intended demolition they helped prevent, in the event witnessing it incorporated instead within a new scheme. And while new houses or castles were being built, castle abandonment continued; at Saddell, for instance, where the castle's successor house was built in 1774, the castle of c.1508 was abandoned (and today, once again occupied).

Increasingly, the classicising fashion for ancient castles – as we have seen, an ideal from the seventeenth century until the 1740s and beyond, with examples illustrated in *Vitruvius Scoticus* – was now coming to be vilified. Walter Scott, maybe predictably, contributed to the debate:

> The old castle of Dalhousie – potius Dalwolsey – was mangled by a fellow called, I believe, [presumably John] Douglas, who destroyed, as far as in him lay, its military and baronial character, and roofed it in the fashion of a poor-house. The architect, [William] Burn, is now restoring and repairing it in the old taste, and I think creditably to his own feeling.[12]

Old was good. Castles, for Scott, should not be classicised or have their castellation concealed.

West Front of *DOUGLAS CASTLE* the Seat of
His Grace the Duke of Douglas in the County of Lanark.

Elevation of one end

P. Patton Sculp.

East Front

Adam. Archt.

Architectural Salvage

A separate antiquarian strand was the idea of collecting ancient fabric, and using it as display. Rome's monuments had long been quarried for this purpose, but now, old Scottish stones had become monuments of Old Scotland, to be enjoyed by Romantic-age New Scotland. Portobello Tower, for instance, built in 1785 for a lawyer named John Cunningham, was laced with displays of salvaged sculptured stones. But this was an octagonal garden tower, an ornament, as opposed to a residence. Nonetheless, the idea of building a new tower with inset old stones was rare, and more typically old architectural fragments were set in or seen from gardens/landscapes.

An ornamental garden tunnel at Arniston (dated 1758, and thus presumably designed by a very busy John Adam, then engaged at Arniston, completing the house begun to his father's design) has a sober, neo-classical façade framing its entrance, at whose far end visitors find themselves within a rock-encrusted grotto. The grotto incorporates fragments of the predecessor Arniston, an ancient tower demolished in William Adam's time. There are sculptured fragments, including seventeenth-century rusticated blocks like those reset at Gilmorehill from Glasgow's Old College gateway. Stones salvaged for such features (Wrichtishouses, for example, was another 'quarry' for garden ornaments) might be from any old building, as illustrated by other sculptures at Arniston itself, or the magpie collection at Abbotsford.

Another major castle-like building which had fragments salvaged for display was Edinburgh's 1630s Parliament House, which was re-fronted from 1806 when Robert Reid's new Parliament Close was made. Sculptured fragments were carried to both Arniston and Abbotsford for display. So here was another function of, or attitude to, old castles: as artefactual quarries to be plundered for the decorative and symbolic values assigned to artefacts set in structures otherwise new.

Post-Adam Castles

Chief among the architects to continue Adam's castellated style were Richard Crichton (c.1771–1817) and John Paterson (d.1832). Crichton had once been a draughtsman in the Adams' Edinburgh office, and his most notable work was Rossie Castle (c.1795–1800), which reproduced elements seen at Oxenford and Dalquharran. Paterson had worked with Adam, set up on his own in 1791, and became the foremost practitioner of post-Adam Castle Style. In 1792 he designed an entrance block for the recently reoccupied Castle Huntly. He designed Monzie for Hercules Ross (c.1795–1800), Eglinton Castle (1796–1803) and, in England, he enlarged Brancepeth Castle (1818–19). In 1805, Paterson added a low extension to Winton, in modern castellated style rather than the style of 1620s' Winton itself. The 'mannerist' style of Winton was not yet favoured by castle revivalists, but Winton's dignity was largely retained, standing proud above the additions, in the same way as Melville Castle's design suggested that its main 'castle' was its high tower — as, in the case of Lanrick, it indeed was. Paterson's St Paul's Church in Perth (c.1800–7) followed the octagonal formula seen at St George's in Edinburgh, and it was given characteristic Adam-like diminutive bartizans. Other castellated churches include Edinburgh's Albany Street Chapel of 1816 by David Skae (c.1777–1818), given Gothic-astragalled glazing, and whose flank was cleverly designed to match Albany Street's domestic classicism. And in Tain, for example, the New Parish Church of 1811–16, by James Smith (d. 1845), was given castellated ends. Also in Edinburgh, Lady Yester's Church of 1803, by William Sibbald (d.1809), was given an unusual round-arched style, part-derived/revived from the Canongate Kirk of 1688 but, like St Paul's Perth, it was given Caldwell-like small conical-topped bartizans.

Other castle designers included Alexander Laing (d.1823). His Darnaway (1802–12) for the 9th earl of Moray comprised a new block with a hood-moulded façade with centre and ends all emphasised, re-fronting the carefully retained medieval timber-roofed hall, already regarded as important 'heritage'. Robert Burn's Gillespie's Hospital in Edinburgh (1800–1) adopted the Mellerstain model, but more compactly, with a taller and narrower centre tower. Amongst countless other post-Adam buildings of the period that were less well documented were Cluny (Inverness-shire) (1805, for a kinsman of James Macpherson's) and the contemporary Gelston (which has been attributed to Crichton). And pattern books may have influenced some designers: Charles Ross of Greenlaw (1722–1806) produced designs derived from Batty Langley's publications, notably a farm at Dumbarton (now 20–22 Cardross Road), and lodges to Castle Semple.

Other prominent exemplars of this post-Adam castellation included David Hamilton's Airth (1807–9, refronting an old castle), and Kincaid (1812); James Gillespie Graham's Ross Priory (1810–16); Archibald Elliot's reconstruction of Loudoun Castle (1804–11) and Newbyth (1817). Parallel to this arrived a newly revived English Tudor castellated style, at Dalmeny House (1814–17), by William Wilkins (1778–1839) for the 4th earl of Roseberry.

In the same way as people such as Adam and Paterson carried out work in England so, in turn, English architects carried out castellated commissions in Scotland. We have already encountered William Wilkins, but before his arrival Robert Lugar (c.1773–1855) designed Balloch (1809), a near-symmetrical concave-fronted design encapsulating the predecessor classical house, and a more Picturesque garden front facing Loch Lomond. The more famous Sir Robert Smirke (1780–1867) designed Kinfauns (1820–2). Perhaps the most interesting amongst these was William Atkinson (c.1774–1839) because it was above all he, from a committee-like team, who designed Abbotsford for and with Sir Walter Scott. There, patron and designer together fashioned a composition dripping with explicit allusion to the Scottish past, as we will see below. In 1803–12 Atkinson built Scone Palace, an orthodox post-Adam design. But now new towers – as against castles – were being built for occupation, such as Millburn, from 1806, constructed by Atkinson for the diplomat Sir Robert Liston (Figure 60). 'A beautiful retreat,' observed Sir Walter Scott in 1828. 'The little Gothic tower, embowered amid trees and bushes, surrounded by . . . pleasant gardens, offering many a sunny walk for winter, many a shade for summer, are inexpressibly pleasing.'[13]

By the early nineteenth century, then, there had emerged a range of different strands of castle design, with the crow-stepped and bartizaned option of, say, Adam's Seton developed in time into full-blown castellated as in David Bryce's works; while John Adam's more explicitly Inveraray-derived Douglas Castle was part of a separate strand which developed along more Gothic lines, notably at Taymouth, by Archibald Elliot (1761–1823) and his brother James (1770–1810), from 1806. For with the next generation of architects, such as David Hamilton (1768–1843) and James Gillespie Graham, who each built a castellated Gothic block at Crawford Priory, Adam's innovations in castle-Romanticism were taken in a range of different directions, all with Picturesque asymmetry featuring prominently. Castellation became increasingly popular and appeared in a wide range of building types: Picturesque landscape ruins, like Adam's Caisteal Gòrach at

Tulloch Castle and Alexander Nasmyth's various designs for, say, Inveraray estate; and bridges, notably Thomas Telford's Craigellachie (1812–14), whose modern cast-iron span had castellated stone terminals (Figure 61).

We will trace the development of the mature Scotch Baronial style itself in Chapter 4. All the strands of the Scotch Baronial Revival were, however, fundamentally shaped by the precedent of Abbotsford (Figure 62), where Sir Walter Scott exerted firm control of a committee of architects and craftsmen, including Atkinson and Edward Blore (1781–1879), but gave equal authority to amateurs like James Skene of Rubislaw to realise in three dimensions the sort of architectural romance and fantasy he alone could spin with such distinction and originality in his poetry and novels. So convincingly ancient and resolutely 'Scots' in character is Abbotsford today that one almost has to pinch oneself to realise that it is a brand new house created from a modest modern farmhouse, Cartley Hole (or Clarty Hole), that Scott had purchased in 1811. As its new name of 'Abbotsford' suggested, the inspiration for the new house looked along the Tweed to the richly carved medieval glories of Melrose Abbey. Although an ecclesiastical character informed much of Abbotsford, with the entrance hall fireplace detailing taken from the cloister at Melrose, while the library bay focuses on a cast from a boss at Rosslyn Chapel, the innovative character of Abbotsford came more from its quotations from Scottish castellated architecture in its pepperpot turrets, its central spiral staircase and crow-stepped gables. For most copyists however, Abbotsford was simply inimitable, in that it jigsawed together the choicest elements that only Scott could draw on though his literary fame, a series of close friendships with the great and good as well as more humble neighbours who, along with an ever-growing army of fans including the king, showered on him a treasury

FIGURE 60
Top. Millburn, Midlothian: view from south
(© RCAHMS, SC 687449)

FIGURE 61
Above. Craigellachie Bridge, Morayshire
(© RCAHMS, SC 944773)

FIGURE 62
Opposite. Abbotsford, Roxburghshire: north-east range, view from south (© RCAHMS, SC 665900)

of gifts. The apparent antiquity of Abbotsford derived first from the incorporation of often substantial fragments of genuine old buildings, most famously the door of Edinburgh's Tolbooth, whose skittish placing was to enrage the architectural critic John Ruskin; and second, from its incorporation of casts from celebrated ancient monuments like Rosslyn, to which Scott alone had such privileged access. Third, this character was underlined through its being stocked with antique furniture and artefacts, while Scott's decorator, D R Hay, was asked to give his new paintwork a theatrical character 'to appear somewhat weather beaten and faded' to match the genuine adjacent ancient oak fragments.

With exemplary patience, Scott kept open house to a growing army of Scottish, British and then international tourists, who were excited by his poetry and novels. The house was frequently illustrated, and there were published descriptions to inspire others who could not so readily travel and impose on its laird. A pioneering photographic view of Abbotsford was to be included in 1845 in Fox Talbot's *Sun Pictures in Scotland*. The popular success of Scott's house also, ironically, owed as much to his interest in new technology like gas, and to its practical Regency planning and landscaping, as it did to this arresting foreground of ancient bricolage. As we will see in Chapters 4 and 12, with Queen Victoria's acquisition of the lease of Balmoral in 1848, the revived Scotch Baronial Castle Style became the hegemonic mode of building throughout the Highlands once again, and Billings' *Baronial and Ecclesiastical Antiquities of Scotland*, superbly published by Blackwoods 1848–52, and whose subscription list was headed by the queen and the prince consort, became its Bible.

Conclusion

A new wave of castle building was inaugurated at Inveraray in the 1740s by the 3rd duke of Argyll and his talented architectural team, pre-eminent among whom was his chosen architect, Roger Morris. In the 1770s, the fashion for castle building took hold, driven above all by Robert Adam, and castellation dominated architectural fashion in Scotland for the next century and a half, living on as a separate strand of Scottish architecture. Bound up in the concept of building new castles, the wish emerged to repair or reoccupy old castles, normally family seats; and, again, this idea lives on today, though now governed by state legislation (as discussed in Chapter 5 below). The legacy of this period – with exemplars such as Inveraray, Culzean, Seton, Abbotsford or Duntrune – shaped what was to come and is also a cultural bestowal of enormous significance. The next chapter, concerned with the Baronial, tells us what happened next.

CHAPTER FOUR

'Old Scotch': Victorian and Edwardian High Baronial

David M Walker

To most of us, High Baronial will conjure up images such as David Bryce's The Glen in the mid nineteenth century and Robert Lorimer's Ardkinglas in the early twentieth. Both were designed, albeit very differently, in what they described as 'Old Scotch' and we now refer to as late sixteenth- and early seventeenth-century Scots Renaissance. Such high points in Scottish country house design must be seen in a wider context that will extend to buildings in what is now known as the Court Style of the first half of the seventeenth century, the continental – and particularly French – influences which began to appear in the 1850s, and even houses that might be thought Low Baronial rather than High. The subject has many byways, ranging from the some-times different requirements of industrial and mercantile clients from those of the old gentry in the greater houses, to the development of quite different schools of Scotch Baronial design in Glasgow and the north-east from that of David Bryce and his followers in the Edinburgh main-stream. And over the eighty-four year timespan that this chapter covers, the perception of what houses in the old Scots idiom should be under-went subtle changes: in early and mid Victorian times the plates of Robert William Billings provided a new romantic vocabulary for modern houses with up-to-date plan-forms built in

modern masonry, but towards the end of the century the more sensitive architects began build-ing carefully studied houses which sought to emulate the qualities of original sixteenth- and early seventeenth-century work in both form and material. This was a tendency which had begun in England in the 1860s with George Devey's 'Old English' neo-Elizabethan and neo-Jacobean houses built for bankers, industrialists and old nobility and gentry alike, designed and crafted to look as if they had always been there. It spread to Scotland through the Arts and Crafts movement, but it was also strongly rooted in the field study programmes set by the Edinburgh and Glasgow architectural associations from the mid 1870s.

Although the country houses built in Scot-land between 1840 and 1880 were predominantly Scotch Baronial, or at least Scots vernacular, the style was initially surprisingly slow to develop given the wealth of examples architects and their clients could have drawn upon for inspiration. The English architect George Saunders mastered the Court Style in his unbuilt designs for aggran-dising Scone Palace in 1802 and, as Dr John Frew has shown, John Claudius Loudon identified the defining elements of what he called 'The Turret Style' in his *Treatise on Forming, Improving and Managing Country Residences* in 1806, even if he did not suggest how it should be adapted to

FIGURE 63
Barmore (Stonefield Castle), Argyll, by William Henry Playfair, 1836–40: garden front from south
(© RCAHMS, SC 558838)

modern needs. But despite the popularity of the writings of Sir Walter Scott and the publications of Francis Grose, English manorial and neo-Tudor drawn from John Britton's *Architectural Antiquities* remained the norm: nothing in the Scots idiom was actually built until Scott's own Abbotsford, and it was quite some time before its architecture began to influence other houses. Associated with Edward Blore and William Atkinson at Abbotsford were the three Heiton brothers at nearby Darnick Tower. Francis died building Blore's Alupka in the Crimea and William his Goodrich Court in Herefordshire, but Andrew survived to practise in Perth and seems to have been responsible for the reconstruction and enlargement of Craighall Rattray

(Scott's Tullyveolan in *Waverley*) in the later 1820s for Scott's friend James Clerk-Rattray, a Baron of Exchequer. Like Scott at Abbotsford, Clerk-Rattray made use of sculpture rescued from Edinburgh demolitions. Craighall was a much simpler house, but it did have a variant of Abbotsford's tower overlooking the ravine.

Playfair, Hamilton, Barry and the Revival of the Court Style of the Early Seventeenth Century

Unlike the Gothic and Elizabethan revivals in England, the literate use of Scots sixteenth- and seventeenth-century detail began with alterations to old houses rather than with study books of

94

original examples. Unsurprisingly, the first architect to adopt and develop original details found on site was William Henry Playfair. He remodelled and enlarged Preston Grange for E Grant Suttie and The Grange, Edinburgh, for the antiquary Sir Thomas Dick Lauder, both in 1830–1. The lessons learned from these and from his work at Heriot's Hospital resulted in the completely new Barmore (now Stonefield) in Argyll for John Campbell, where a crenellated tower house containing the main stair formed the dominant element of a mainly two-storey house of conventional late Georgian plan, with a turreted entrance bay and strapwork details (Figure 63). Although now sandwiched between hotel additions, it remains one of the great landmarks in Scottish architectural history, as does the much simpler tower house he built for Lord Cockburn at Bonaly in 1836–8. Also indebted to Heriot's, but with Tudorish hoodmoulds over the windows, was his transformation of William Adam's huge but plain early Georgian Floors from its later eighteenth-century crenellated form to a magnificent Court School palace for the 6th duke of Roxburghe between 1837 and 1845.

Playfair did not, however, found any nationwide school of design. He had only one really successful pupil in David Cousin, whose fragile health prevented him from doing as much as he might have. Cousin's tightly composed enlargement of Newark Castle in Ayrshire of 1852 for the 2nd marquess of Ailsa (Figure 64) had similar details to Stonefield, as had his two huge urban office blocks in Edinburgh: the Free Church and Commissary Offices of 1858–63 and India Buildings of 1864. Both were built in conformity with the Old Scots or Flemish specified in Thomas Hamilton's Improvement Act of 1827 but in a much more picturesque form than George Smith and John Henderson's earlier developments on George IV Bridge of 1836–40. In Glasgow David Hamilton had the strapwork details of the Old

College of Glasgow to draw upon at Dunlop House (1832–4) for Sir John Dunlop, which was as precocious in its use of Scots seventeenth-century detail as Barmore.

In a very similar vein to Newark, but with round towers, battered plinths and bastioned terraces brilliantly exploiting the site, was the dramatic enlargement of Dunrobin in 1844–51 (Figure 65). As John Gifford has shown, the story of its design is complicated. The duke and duchess of Sutherland themselves adapted Sir Charles Barry's design to the site in consultation with their Aberdeen architect–contractor William Leslie, Barry providing the details as work progressed. But an important figure in the project now appears to have been the Aberdonian Peter Kerr, a pupil of Archibald Simpson's who transferred to Barry's office in 1848 and was subsequently architect of the magnificent Roman parliament buildings in Melbourne, Australia.

William Burn, David Bryce and Robert William Billings' Baronial and Ecclesiastical Antiquities of Scotland

Although Playfair and Hamilton were thus the pioneers of the revival of sixteenth- and seventeenth-century Scots forms, the main line of descent was from Playfair's Edinburgh rival William Burn. The sometimes acrimonious differences between them were as much political as personal, Playfair being a Whig and later a Free Churchman, and Burn a Tory like the majority of his landowner clients. Burn was a friend of Scott's at least from the time of the building of Edinburgh's Tanfield gasworks in 1824, but he was not in any way influenced by Abbotsford. He did not visit it until 1830, although he must have been aware of it. Unlike Blore and Playfair, Burn introduced Scottish features only gradually, incorporating conical roofed towers and crow-stepped

FIGURE 64
Above. Newark Castle, Ayrshire, by David Cousin, 1852: photographed in 1860 (© RCAHMS, SC 1232817)

FIGURE 65
Overleaf. Dunrobin, Sutherland, by Sir Charles Barry, William Leslie et al., 1844–51: photographed prior to 1915 (© RCAHMS, SC 1232815)

gables into what were still basically English Jacobean houses from 1829, the first being Faskally in Perthshire, Milton Lockhart in Lanarkshire, the reconstruction and enlargement of Tyninghame in East Lothian, and Auchmacoy in Aberdeenshire. The style of the last of these was taken up by John Smith of Aberdeen at the original Balmoral in 1834 and at Menie in 1836 and was continued by his London-educated son William at Banchory in Kincardineshire, the giant Forglen in Banffshire (both 1839–40) and finally at the new castle at Balmoral, the ultimate if very belated expression of Burn Scots-Tudor.

Burn's first attempts at a purely Scottish vernacular treatment came with his additions to Pitcaple in Aberdeenshire for Hugh Lumsden and Spott in East Lothian for James Sprot in 1830, followed in 1832 by Dawyck in Peeblesshire for John Nasmyth and Auchterarder for James

Hunter, the latter having Court Style strapwork windowheads. In these houses the corbelled turret made a tentative appearance only at Tyninghame and Pitcaple, but full expertise in late sixteenth- and early seventeenth-century detail was achieved in 1836–40 at his enlargement of Stenhouse, Stirlingshire (built 1622) for Sir Michael Bruce (Figure 66) and at Castle Menzies in Perthshire (built 1571–7) for Sir Neil Menzies, both of these having excellent original details to copy, and in his reconstruction of Invergowrie House for Alexander Clayhills in 1837. It was now mainly in the plan-form, proportions and the masonry that Burn's work was recognisably early Victorian rather than original.

A similar mastery of Scots neo-Jacobean, as against the more English forms Burn adopted at Falkland and Whitehill, was acquired at the dramatic reconstruction of the entrance front of Thirlestane for the 9th earl of Lauderdale in 1840–3. How big a hand David Bryce, born 1803 and Burn's assistant from 1825, had in these houses is difficult to say, as their work forms one continuous line of development, but before embarking on Bryce's career we must look at Burn's activities after his increasingly English clientele caused him to move to London in 1844.

Having long recognised that the medieval and early Renaissance architecture of Scotland would never be properly understood at a national level until it had a literature comparable with that available in England, Burn contacted the English antiquarian architect Robert William Billings, who had already done some work for him, joined forces with the Edinburgh publishers John and Robert Blackwood, and advanced £1,000 for the survey work for *The Baronial and Ecclesiastical Antiquities of Scotland*, originally published in their joint names in 1848–52. Almost as soon as his practice was established in London, Burn began introducing the Baronial idiom to England, designing a vast house at Fonthill, Wiltshire, for the second marquess of Westminster in 1847. Surprisingly, it was not much influenced by any of the antiquities Billings had drawn, and in some of its details it was more François Premier than Scottish, anticipating Bryce's work in the 1850s. It was not built, but Burn's smaller, executed design for Fonthill was wholly Scottish in detail, with a circular Castle Fraser-type tower forming the entrance.

Burn did, however, succeed in selling the original Fonthill concept of a long symmetrical-fronted house with a tall entrance tower on its eastern flank to the 4th duke of Montrose at Buchanan in 1851, albeit without the full basement that made the Fonthill design so hugely impressive even if only on paper. Sadly, Buchanan was also not realised as first conceived. As built in 1854–8, it still had the great entrance tower but the mullioned windows were replaced by plate glass, the masonry was hammer-dressed rather than ashlar, and the detail was greatly simplified.

Burn's three further Scottish houses from his London years were rather smaller. These were the mainly symmetrical Dunira of 1851 for Sir David Dundas, which was still in the style of ten years earlier; Balentore of 1859 for David Lyon, rather more original in its tall square-plan form with French-looking circular angle-towers; and Polmaise for Colonel John Murray of 1863. The last of these was more consistent with other Baronial houses at that time and may have been more the work of his wife's nephew, John MacVicar Anderson, who had begun his career in Glasgow as a pupil of William Clarke of Clarke & Bell.

Except at Polmaise, Burn still drew surprisingly little on Billings' *Antiquities* for the detail of these houses, the elevations of which were very much decided by the plan. He withdrew his capital in 1850 before Billings completed the project, apparently as a result of one of his sons running into financial difficulty. Billings himself profited considerably from his book, being employed at

FIGURE 66
Stenhouse, Stirlingshire, enlarged by William Burn, 1836 (© RCAHMS and Carron Company, SC 1232814)

both Edinburgh and Stirling castles and finding a small but wealthy clientele for his hard-edged idiosyncratic version of the Baronial, the sculpture of which he usually cut with his own hands. Castle Wemyss at Wemyss Bay was the main work of his life, built incrementally from 1853 for William Brown and then for the shipowners George Burns and his son Lord Inchcape, work still being in hand at the time of his death in 1874 (Figure 67). He also worked at Dalzell Castle and its terraced gardens, which were radically remodelled from 1857 for Lord Hamilton; and in 1854–6 he introduced very disciplined geometrical

Baronial elevations to the Glasgow street scene at Sir James Campbell's warehouse in Ingram Street.

Amongst the very first to benefit from Billings' activities was the Elgin architect Thomas Mackenzie, born in Perth in 1814 and for a time assistant to Archibald Simpson. He provided Billings with both hospitality and introductions to the north-eastern landowners, and thus gained a preview of Billings' drawings, with results which could be seen as early as 1847 in his extremely elegant remodelling of Ballindalloch in Banffshire and the building of its tower-house lodge and gate for Sir John Macpherson Grant. These were followed by new houses at Desswood (now Dess) on Deeside for the Aberdeen advocate Alexander Davidson; Dall in Perthshire for George Duncan Robertson of Strowan; the now lost entrance wing at Warthill for William Leslie; and the skilful restoration and partial remodelling of Cawdor for the first Earl Cawdor, which was still in hand at the time of his death in 1854. Except for Cawdor, all these houses were harled and at their best so skilfully detailed that it is not always immediately obvious what is old, what is partly new and what is wholly new. Mackenzie's Aberdeen partner James Matthews did not pursue that very sympathetic approach to older houses and took a much less historically based approach to Baronial design, as will be seen later in this chapter.

The main beneficiary of Billings' labours was David Bryce. Like Mackenzie, he had a preview of Billings' drawings. Together with Blackwoods publishing house, the Burn and Bryce office at 131 George Street seems to have been Billings' Edinburgh base, although that is only hinted at in his correspondence with Blackwood. The relationship between Burn and Bryce became increasingly strained after Burn's departure for London in 1844, partly because of problems at the Episcopal chapel at Dalkeith, but mainly because the partnership was coming apart: Bryce was increasingly gaining his own clients, while Burn was designing the Malcolms' neo-Jacobean palace at Poltalloch from London rather than delegating it to Bryce. The partnership was dissolved by July 1850, when Bryce had no fewer than nine new country houses in hand, far more than Burn had in London. Their differences in style and temperament are best seen at Balcarres in Fife, where Burn's tightly controlled and slightly understated Scots Renaissance wing of 1838–43 for Lieutenant-General James Lindsay is overwhelmed by the big scale and bold corner tourelles of Bryce's library and studio wing, built in 1863 for Lindsay's nephew Sir Coutts Lindsay

of Grosvenor Gallery fame with his wife's Rothschild money.

Bryce had arrived at that style only gradually as he gained his independence. His characteristic canted bay corbelled to the square had first appeared in the new entrance wing at Kilconquhar designed in Burn's office for Sir Henry Bethune in 1838, reappearing in a more refined form in 1841 at the remarkably accomplished reconstruction and enlargement of Seacliff for George Sligo, which was designed independently from Burn at Bryce's own house in Castle Street (Figure 68). It had an advanced and turreted entrance bay as at Playfair's Barmore, square angle-turrets as at Stenhouse, and a completely asymmetrical plan with no close relationship to any of the usual Burn plan-types. Still more accomplished was a further reconstruction and enlargement, the giant Inchdairnie for Mrs Aytoun in 1845. This had a full-scale Burn-type north corridor plan, with a symmetrical suite of three big principal rooms and central steps on the garden front, the private family apartments added in 1847 forming a set-back wing on that side, and a two-sided forecourt on the north where the main element was an entrance tower of slimmed-down Pinkie type. This basic plan appeared in a still more sophisticated form at Kimmerghame in 1851 for John Campbell Swinton. Here the private wing was compacted into the main block and the symmetrically arranged principal apartments given an asymmetric elevation (Figure 69).

These larger plan-types were repeated at Maulesden, Angus, in 1853 for the Hon. William Maule; The Glen in Peeblesshire of 1855 with particularly elaborate outworks for the industrialist Sir Charles Tennant (Figure 70); the equally grand Craigends in Renfrewshire for Alexander Cunninghame of 1857; Torosay on Mull for Colonel Campbell of Possil in 1856, Eaglesham for Allan Gilmour; and the tautly composed Fothringham in Angus for Thomas F S Fothring-

FIGURE 67
Above. Castle Wemyss, Renfrewshire by Robert W
Billings, 1853: project perspective (© RCAHMS
and Rev. A A R Torrie, SC 941518)

FIGURE 68
Opposite. Seacliff, East Lothian reconstructed by
David Bryce, 1841 (© RCAHMS, SC 1232154)

ham, both of 1859. Almost all of these houses
stood much taller than their earlier Burn counterparts, being raised on full basements to achieve
greater privacy from callers at principal floor level
and, perhaps more importantly, to achieve a
greater Baronial grandeur. The same formulae
continued into the 1860s at Castlemilk in Dumfriesshire (1864) for Sir Robert Jardine of Jardine
Matheson; the uncomfortably gargantuan Ballikinrain of 1866–9 for the landowner and Glasgow
merchant Sir Archibald Orr-Ewing; Broadstone
at Port Glasgow of 1869 for the manufacturer and
merchant John Birkmyre; Glenapp in Ayrshire of
1871 for James Hunter; and New Gala at
Galashiels of 1872, very close in composition to

Fothringham, for Hugh Scott of Gala.

All these basically similar houses were given remarkable variety by entrance towers drawn from Billings' engravings. The tower house at Maybole was a particular favourite, adopted with many skilful variations of detail at Kimmerghame, at the reconstructed Hartrigge of 1853 for Lord Stratheden and Campbell, at Maulesden, The Glen, Fothringham and New Gala. The circular Castle Fraser-type tower was introduced at Clifton Hall in Midlothian in 1850, becoming an entrance tower at Birkhill in 1855 and at Castle-milk and Ballikinrain, where it was combined with porte-cochères. The linked central towers of Fyvie were adapted as the boldly projecting entrance tower at Craigends, and in a much lower key as the new entrance at Blair Castle, recon-structed to something more like its pre-eigh-teenth-century form for the 7th duke of Atholl in 1869. Nearly all of the larger houses built anew had magnificent neo-Jacobean interiors that drew mainly on English models, particularly at their hall staircases. The finest of all Bryce's interiors seems to have been at Langton of 1862 for the 2nd marquess of Breadalbane, where unusually the hall was double height with a first floor balcony. There the whole house was English Jacobean, and of quite extraordinary magnifi-cence.

Bryce's reconstruction of older houses often

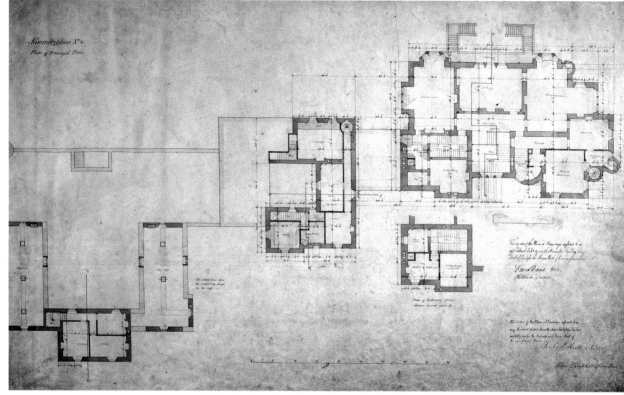

FIGURE 69
Above. Kimmerghame House, Berwickshire,
by David Bryce, 1851: plan of principal floor
(© RCAHMS, SC 1233624)

FIGURE 70
Opposite. Glen House, Peeblesshire, by David Bryce,
1855 (© RCAHMS, SC 1088785)

led to brilliant one-off solutions which did not conform to his usual plan-types. The biggest of these were at Panmure, where the Georgianised 1666 house was remodelled as a great Court School palace for the 2nd Baron Panmure in 1852–5 (Figure 71), and at Cortachy, where a near-symmetrical new house was added for the 5th earl of Airlie in 1870–2, the old castle becoming a set-back wing (Figure 72). At Capenoch, a very substantial house was achieved incrementally from an eighteenth-century core by the addition of a new wing for James Grierson in 1847 and a fine tower house and splendid conservatory for

Thomas Gladstone in 1854–6. Equally skilful were Cringletie, completely reconstructed as an unusually compact house for James Wolfe Murray in 1861, and Keiss, where a big plain Georgian rectangle became a stylish L-plan tower house for the 5th duke of Portland in 1862.

Even before the first parts of Billings' *Antiquities* appeared in 1848, the Baronial houses of Playfair, Burn and Bryce had begun to make the style fashionable. These houses were neither exhibited at the Royal Academy – Bryce did not begin showing his work until 1851 – nor published in the journals, but they clearly inspired

enthusiasm amongst those who saw them. The 68-year-old James Gillespie Graham found he had to adapt to the new Baronial idiom, rising brilliantly to what was required in the commission for the enlargement of Brodick for the 10th duke of Hamilton in 1844–6 – to what extent with the help of Pugin is unclear – and then again at Ayton, built completely anew for William Mitchell Innes of the Royal Bank of Scotland in 1845–51. Likewise the Italian Renaissance master David Rhind, born 1808, abandoned his just slightly eccentric Jacobean of the earlier 1840s for a rumbustiously towered Baronial at Carlowrie, built in 1851–2 for the wine merchant Sir Thomas Hutchison. It was followed by the equally wayward Commercial Bank at Linlithgow in 1859 and the sheriff courts at Dumfries (1863–6) and Selkirk (1868–70) (Figure 73), the latter matched by the adjoining Ettrick Lodge,

FIGURE 71
Opposite top. Panmure, Angus, remodelled by David Bryce, 1852–5 (© RCAHMS, SC 839632)

FIGURE 72
Opposite bottom. Cortachy, Angus, partially remodelled and new main block by David Bryce, 1870–2 (© RCAHMS, SC 1232300)

FIGURE 73
Above. Selkirk sheriff courthouse by David Rhind, 1868–70 (© RCAHMS, SC 1233621)

recast in 1870 with arcaded loggias to the street and the stables. Bold rope mouldings were a particularly characteristic feature of all of Rhind's Baronial buildings. They showed little respect for the sixteenth- and seventeenth-century buildings from which their details were drawn, but they did have panache.

Burn and Bryce's Pupils and Followers

The mid-century Baronial work of Burn and Bryce's Edinburgh pupils, assistants and followers tended to be much more respectful. The oldest of these architects was John Lessels, born 1808 and thus the same age as Rhind. He designed two exceptional Edinburgh houses for the Nelson publishing family, the very refined reconstruction of Salisbury Green House for William Nelson in 1860–7 and the much tougher hammer-dressed St Leonards for Thomas junior in 1869–70. Next in seniority was James Campbell Walker, born 1822, who came of a family of bleachers and solicitors at Auchtermuchty. He designed the giant Blair Drummond, built anew on higher ground in 1868–72 for George Stirling Home-Drummond after proposals for the Alexander McGill house had been abandoned. It was essentially based on Burn's proposals for Fonthill in having a giant entrance tower of the same profile, but on the garden elevations an asymmetrical Bryce-like treatment was adopted.

Still closer in style to Bryce was Charles George Hood Kinnear, born 1830 of a landed banking family and John Dick Peddie's partner from January 1856. He had originally been recruited to provide 'Old Scots' elevations for Peddie's Cockburn Street venture in 1854, and from 1855 he introduced Bryce's country house Baronial to the Edinburgh street scene, the eastern of the towered corners to Market Street drawing inspiration from Bryce's Birkhill to give

a gentlemanly image to the Cockburn Hotel.

As a country house architect, Kinnear closely followed Bryce models in both plan and elevation but in general he preferred to avoid his habit of incorporating large-scale borrowings like the Maybole and Fyvie entrance towers. Sorn on Mull for James Forsyth in 1859 closely followed Kimmerghame on plan, but Crawfordton in Dumfriesshire of 1863 for Major George Gustavus Walker adopted a more Burn-like arrangement, with a towered entrance front at right-angles to the garden front as at Buchanan, the same arrangement being adopted at the plainer Cargen in Kirkcudbright built for the geologist and horticulturalist Patrick Dudgeon in 1870. All of these were for significant landowners. Kinnear excelled particularly in adapting the Baronial concept to smaller houses for merchants and industrialists, beginning in 1861 with the cliff-side Starly Hall in Fife for the shipowner James Taylor, where the principal element was a rectangular tower house with a bartizaned parapet walk at the gable, a feature repeated at the much larger Newtonaird in Dumfriesshire in 1865 and at Dryburgh in 1876. The Binn at Burntisland, built in 1865 for the mining engineer David Landale, was similarly perched on a hillside but had a Burn-type north corridor plan, with the principal rooms looking out over the town towards the sea, a picturesque profile against the woodland being achieved by raising a tower over the library rather than over the entrance. Equally skilful were Kinnettles of 1865 for the Dundee linen manufacturer James Paterson and Glenmayne of 1866 for the Galashiels–Australian wool merchant John Murray, in which the Crawfordton concept was scaled down to a compact villa form without any loss of architectural effect. Threave of 1872 for the Liverpool merchant John Gordon followed the same model, but with a Castle Fraser entrance tower as at Bryce's Birkhill. Kinmonth in Perthshire, built in 1871–8 for J H Pelly Simpson with Hudson Bay money, is still closer to Bryce in general arrangement and perhaps the crispest in composition in this series of smaller houses.

One year younger than Kinnear was David MacGibbon, born 1831 and a pupil of Lessels and of Burn in London, better known to us as an author than an architect. No commission for a major country house ever came his way, but he was quick to follow Rhind's lead in introducing Scots Baronial to branch bank design as an appropriate image for the National Bank of Scotland at Alloa (1861), Falkirk, Forfar (both 1862), Girvan (1863) and Montrose (1864). Alloa and Falkirk both made skilful use of awkwardly angled corner sites, setting a precedent for Peddie & Kinnear, who adopted a similar idiom for their Royal Bank and Bank of Scotland branches from 1870 onwards. It offered greater flexibility in plan and elevation than Peddie's earlier palazzo formats.

James Maitland Wardrop

Perhaps the most thoughtful of all these mid nineteenth-century Baronial architects was James Maitland Wardrop, born the son of George IV's politically radical physician James Wardrop in 1824 and husband of Maria Dundas of Dundas Castle from 1849. Wardrop's more routine houses like Ardwell, a Bryce-derived design of 1869 for Mrs Ommanney McTaggart, did not always have quite the vigour of those of Bryce himself, but his best houses show him to have been an architect who did more than just adhere to successful formulae.

He commenced his career as a pupil of Thomas Brown, architect of Ingliston, a tightly composed Baronial house of 1846 with an effective silhouette for George Mitchell Innes, but whether he gained further experience with Bryce before becoming Brown's partner is uncertain. His earliest really large house was Lochinch,

first planned in 1861 and built mainly in 1864–8 for the 10th earl of Stair and his countess Louisa, daughter of the Duc de Coigny. It was certainly on the scale of the grander French chateaux, but mainly Scottish in style with a giant tower house at one corner and a solitary French-roofed tower on the turreted entrance elevation. In composition it was very picturesque, but it was much less unified than the equally giant Stichill of 1866 for the ironmaster George Baird, where all was concentrated into big simple masses, the entrance front being a masterly variation on Barry's at Dunrobin with a tall pavilion-roofed entrance tower. Still more interesting was Nunraw, where Wardrop's designs for the antiquary Robert Hay were matured between 1863 and 1868 before work commenced (Figure 74). Here the new house was backed onto the original Z-plan house of c.1570, adopting the style of the old with a convincing proportion of wall to window at some cost to the daylighting within, and only the masonry telling us what is new or refaced. Glenternie of 1867–8 for David Kidd of Leyton in Essex was more Bryce-like, and so was Udny of 1874–5 for John Henry Fullarton Udny, which took the old tower house as its dominant element, a treatment which was also to have been adopted at Inverquharity for Leonard Lyell; in the event, Lyell built an almost completely new house at Kinnordy in which Wardrop's son Hew may have had a large hand, as will be seen later. But at Beaufort, built in 1880–6 for the 15th Lord Lovat, the elder Wardrop was clearly still in charge (Figure 75). It had the same big simple masses as Stichill, with a giant entrance tower, bigger and bolder than anything by Bryce, and it also had an English-type great hall, paralleled in Scotland only at Balmoral and at the exactly contemporary Ardross, of which more later. The composition may have been more static than that of Bryce's houses, but it had a serene, commanding presence and refined details.

The French Dimension

Common to all the Edinburgh architects of the Bryce school was a taste for fifteenth- and sixteenth-century French. It appeared first at Bryce's Kinnaird (Figure 76), basically a late seventeenth-century house similar to Panmure, which had been crenellated by James Playfair in 1788–93. Bryce brilliantly remodelled it a second time for the 7th earl of Southesk in 1853–8. It has been described as one of the greatest French chateaux ever reared on British soil, but only the high pavilion roofs, the tall panelled chimneystacks, the dormers and some of the window details, all of François Premier derivation, were French. The other details, both inside and out, were neo-Jacobean as at Panmure and very original and skilful, notably at the magnificent porte-cochère. More consistently French was Eastburgh at Bushey in England – surprisingly absent from the catalogue of Mark Girouard's great book on the Victorian country house – built in 1858–60 for James Carnegie, a Scottish–Swedish trader for whom Bryce had already built the very simple Stronvar in Balquhidder in 1850. It was quickly followed by the reconstruction of Inverardoch at Doune for James Campbell in 1859–61. There a big steep-roofed tower of an earlier French medieval pattern formed the principal feature of the entrance elevation, the garden elevation being more Scottish but with early French Renaissance dormers.

FIGURE 74
Opposite top. Nunraw, East Lothian, reconstructed and enlarged by James Maitland Wardrop, 1868 (© RCAHMS, SC 1232215)

FIGURE 75
Opposite bottom. Beaufort, Inverness-shire, by James Maitland Wardrop, Charles Reid and Hew Montgomerie Wardrop: photographed prior to 1937 (Jim Davidson)

The details of these three houses may well have been drawn from the folios of Victor Pétit and Georges Sauvageot, but they also relate to the development of the design of Fettes College, the commission for which had been given to Bryce when Playfair became too ill to undertake it. Designed in 1862 and built in 1864–70, its symmetrical front was developed from that of Kinnaird but in a more unified late French Gothic form. The sheer quality of the details, down to the lead bees which once made its roof sparkle in the sunlight, leaves little doubt that Bryce must have made a study tour of France, seeing at the very least the Hôtel de Cluny in Paris and the chateau at Blois; it is known that he was a good photographer, although few of his images survive. The details of the interior at Fettes were much simpler than those of the exterior, but they were consistently Gothic and not English Jacobean as at Kinnaird.

Similar in spirit, but much smaller as a result of the long-running litigation over John Morgan's much amended will, was Morgan's Hospital at Dundee designed by Peddie & Kinnear, again with late French details, probably the work of Kinnear as he too had travelled in France with his own pioneer bellows camera from the 1850s. In 1860 they had proposed a relatively economical Baronial design very similar to their Morrison's Academy at Crieff of the previous year, but as fund interest began to accumulate the building was gradually redesigned in a more Fettes-like form from 1862 onwards, the very completely preserved drawings showing that the Douai belfry-like form of the central tower was arrived at quite independently. Designed in parallel between 1862 and 1866 were their Municipal and County Buildings in Aberdeen. Again the drawings show much experiment in composition and plan before the present asymmetrical solution with a corner tower was finalised, the design of the tower itself being achieved rather more

FIGURE 76

Kinnaird, Angus, remodelled by David Bryce, 1853–8. Photographed prior to 1921 (© RCAHMS, AN 1261)

quickly and influencing the final form of that at Morgan's Hospital. As the building was of granite, the details had to be simpler than at Morgan's Hospital, the principal motif being the long semi-elliptically arched ground floor arcade of Flemish late Gothic inspiration.

The Aberdeen–Morgan's Hospital tower quickly became a characteristic feature of Scottish public buildings throughout the 1860s, 1870s and 1880s. Peddie & Kinnear built another at their well-detailed Greenock Sheriff Court, and proposed yet another for the sadly unbuilt Edinburgh University College Hall on Teviot Row, the elevations and perspective of which have not so far been found. It was to have been a taller Morgan's Hospital, with circular angle-towers, a variation on the polygonal one originally proposed for the Broad Street corner in Aberdeen. Both Greenock and the College Hall

dated from 1864. Bryce himself adopted a spired version of the same turreted tower concept for the central administration block of Edinburgh's new Royal Infirmary in 1870, but as built in 1872–9 the early Renaissance columned and pilastered entrance then proposed was simplified in conformity with the austere Scots vernacular elevations of the ward-blocks, very similar to those of his Trumland House in Orkney of 1872. Bryce also designed a large municipal buildings and town hall complex for Langholm in 1873. This was not built at the time, and the drawings do not seem to have survived, but the executed design of 1887 with an Aberdeen-type steeple by the local architect Frank Carruthers was reputedly based on it. Much the finest of these later French-inspired public buildings were the municipal buildings at Dunfermline and Hawick, both designed by James Campbell Walker. Dunferm-

FIGURE 77
Callendar, Stirlingshire, remodelled by James Maitland Wardrop, 1869–77 (© RCAHMS, SC 1224552)

line, built between 1875 and 1879, challenges comparison with Aberdeen, its inventive sculpture as remarkable as that at Fettes; Hawick, won in competition and built in 1883–6, has equally strong but rather more economical detailing.

Like Bryce, Peddie & Kinnear designed a small number of French-influenced houses. The first of these was the impressive Lathallan in Fife of 1864, reconstructed and extended with a forecourt for an old Fife family, the Lumsdaines. There the original plain, late Georgian house was refaced with French early Renaissance detail, corner turrets, dormered pavilion roof and an asymmetrically placed tower that was more Italian than French. Some of these features, though not the tower, reappeared at the much more compact but equally elaborate Brentham Park at Stirling, built new for the local industrialist Robert Smith in 1870, the dome of glazed stars within it remind-

ing us that the division between the Italian Renaissance and neo-classicist Peddie and the Baronialist Kinnear was not always clear-cut. Much grander than either of these would have been their reconstruction of St Martin's Abbey in Perthshire for an ambitious member of parliament, Colonel William McDonald, in 1869, its central feature being a Chambord-type tower, but in the event McDonald spent his money on buying the Bandirran estate. Wardrop and his partner Charles Reid were luckier at Callendar Park, Falkirk, where the north side of an immensely long and plain house of the seventeenth and eighteenth centuries was rationalised on plan and both elevations transformed into a chateau-like appearance, with French pavilion roofs and François Premier tourelles, for William Forbes in 1869–77 (Figure 77).

Baronial Houses by
Architects in Perthshire and Angus

Thus far the story of Baronial has been predominantly centred on the architects who practised in Edinburgh. Perth was very much an architectural outpost of Edinburgh, as its two leading architects, Andrew Heiton junior (born 1823) and David Smart (born 1824), both gained experience in Bryce's office. Heiton's houses were more often Italianate, and in the later 1860s and 1870s sometimes French Gothic, but his early Dunalistair of 1852 for General Sir John Macdonald had good Bryce Baronial details, even if symmetrical on plan with a circular central entrance tower. Much more on the standard Bryce plan was Heiton's Giffen in Ayrshire of 1869 for Henry Gardiner Patrick, and particularly successful were his tall-towered Orchill, Perthshire of 1868 for Samuel Smith MP, the more compact suburban Kinbrae, Newport of 1872 for the Dundee publisher John Leng, and Kilbryde, Perthshire of 1876–7 for Sir James Campbell, built after the old tower house collapsed and incorporating the best of what was left of it. For a period from the mid 1870s he built tall and somewhat brooding houses with Rhenish roofs, but at Fonab, Pitlochry for Colonel George Glas Sandeman and at the new house backed onto the old at Tower of Lethendy for Colonel J H Gammel, both of 1892 and built of red sandstone, he returned to a smooth Baronial orthodoxy that was probably the work of his nephew and successor, Andrew Granger Heiton.

David Smart's domestic practice was undeservedly smaller, his only significant Baronial houses being Balhousie, Perth, rebuilt for the 11th earl of Kinnoull 'to improve the amenity of the adjoining grounds for feuing', and Erigmore, Birnam for Captain Napier Campbell, both of 1862 and loyal to Bryce in composition and detail. Also in Perthshire but based at Meigle was John Carver, son of the late Georgian architect of that name. Information on his early career is lacking, but he was a very competent and sometimes individualistic Gothic and Baronial designer who must have gained experience with Bryce or Rhind, or just possibly Billings himself. Much of his practice was lesser estate work and villa-style banks, but he did design the tall and richly detailed St Mary's Tower at Birnam, built about 1860 as a summer retreat for the Tory statesman Lord John Manners, later the 7th duke of Rutland. Like Erigmore, it owed its existence to the Perth & Dunkeld Railway, opened in 1856, and was leased to others from time to time, Sir John Millais being a tenant of both houses. Carver was also responsible for the large but sparsely detailed Finavon Castle, Angus, built in 1865 for David Greenhill-Gardyne, who had made a substantial fortune in the service of the East India Company.

In Dundee the linen and jute magnates built remarkably little in the Baronial idiom, Charles Wilson's St Helens – of which more later – and the adjoining Taypark of 1863 remaining the only instances of it. Although an assistant of Bryce in the late 1840s, James Maclaren and his Cox clients preferred Italianate or an idiosyncratic neo-Jacobean for their houses, and of Maclaren's contemporaries only Charles Edward and his partner Thomas Saunders Robertson showed much interest in Baronial, their giant asylum at West Green of 1879–82 having crow-stepped gables and a rather sparing distribution of pepper-pot turrets.

Much the most important exponent of the Baronial in the Angus area was the Arbroath painter, antiquary and social and architectural theorist Patrick Allan, who married the widowed Elizabeth Fraser-Baker of Hospitalfield in 1843, added her Fraser surname to his own and sacked his rapacious uncle as the family lawyer. Her house was partly ancient and partly late Georgian and had formed the inspiration for Monkbarns in Scott's novel *The Antiquary*. Fraser began its reconstruction to his own designs in 1849, linking its bow windows together in Fyvie fashion, rebuilding the monastic barn as an orielled great hall and raising a slim five-storey tower house as the pivotal feature of the resulting L-plan composition. Rich in carving in both stone and wood, and still intact with all its pictures and furnishings, the interiors rival those of Abbotsford as the most evocative to survive. Still more picturesque, if plainer inside, was Fraser's reconstruction of Blackcraig in Perthshire in 1856, a very irregular Z-plan house approached over the River Ardle by a tunnel-vaulted bridge with the lodge as its cap-house. At both of these houses Allan-Fraser employed his own workforce.

Baronial Houses by
Architects in Aberdeen and Inverness

Baronial had a much greater vogue in the north-east than it had in Angus. Strangely, Balmoral brought William Smith's career as a country house architect almost to a close, his enlargement of his father's Dunecht as a granite-built Osborne for the 25th earl of Crawford and Balcarres in 1859 being his last house of any importance. Although the English barrister Henry Wolrige Gordon commissioned John Russell Mackenzie to enlarge Esslemont to a mildly Bryce-like form when he and his wife succeeded to the estate in 1864, the market was otherwise completely dominated by Thomas Mackenzie's surviving partner – and Russell Mackenzie's former employer – James Matthews, born 1820, a pupil of Archibald Simpson and briefly an assistant of George Gilbert Scott in London.

Matthews' work followed less scholarly lines than that of Thomas Mackenzie. If resemblance to his subsequent independent work is a reliable guide, his career as a Baronial architect began in 1849 at Brucklay to which he added a near-symmetrical front with a big porte-cochère for Alexander Dingwall-Fordyce, the old house being remodelled in conformity with it. Although some of its features were drawn from Mackenzie's houses, it had the circular towers with boldly corbelled parapets and conical-roofed cap-houses which were to be repeated in 1866 at the still larger Brotherton (now Lathallan, the name transferred from Peddie & Kinnear's house in Fife) for Hercules Scott of the Bengal Civil Service, again with a tall entrance tower and porte-cochère. Like Brucklay, Brotherton was the centre of a very large and prosperous agricultural estate. Not all that much smaller were Roth-ienorman, a remodelling of 1862 for Lieutenant-Colonel Jonathan Forbes Leslie, with an even more exaggerated entrance tower, and the much severer Glack of 1876, built anew for J Macken-zie, which became an outpost of Aberdeen Asylum after the client decided to remain in his old house. More expensively built was Ardoe of 1878, again with a giant porte-cochère, for the soap manufacturer Alexander Ogston. It was suaver in detail than the others, probably because Thomas Mackenzie's son Alexander Marshall Mackenzie was now his partner in the Aberdeen and Elgin offices.

Matthews also had a branch office in Inverness which was run semi-independently by the very able William Lawrie, of whom we know too little. In 1877 Lawrie designed Aigas (Figure 78), very similar in concept to Kinnear's Kinnettles and Glenmayne, and equally refined in detail but less confident in proportion with a slimmer entrance tower. Lawrie's rivals in Inverness were Alexander Ross, born 1834, and John Rhind, born 1836, who were probably slightly older. Ross' major work in the Baronial idiom was Ardross, largely of 1880–1 but incorporating an earlier house by Thomas Mackenzie. It was built for Alexander Matheson of Jardine Matheson and was on a scale that rivalled Maitland Wardrop's

FIGURE 78
Aigas, Inverness-shire, by William Lawrie, 1877 (© RCAHMS, SC 1168082)

exactly contemporary Beaufort in extent if not in mass, with a tall entrance tower reminiscent of that at Stichell. Like Beaufort it had a very large hammer-beam roofed great hall or ballroom, uncommon in Scotland at the time. None of Burn and Bryce's houses had been built with one, although John Bryce had added a sparsely detailed one to Blair Castle in 1876.

Rhind's major work was Ardverikie, rebuilt as a giant shooting lodge for the Yorkshire magnate Sir John Ramsden in 1874–9, again with new money, after a bad fire in 1873. Its principal motifs were tall towers with heavily corbelled parapets and steep-roofed cap-houses, but it was unusual amongst Baronial houses in having broad-eaved roofs to protect its wallheads against the weather. The client and his vexatious litigation were the death of its architect.

*Baronial Architecture in
Glasgow and the West of Scotland*

Although the Glasgow, Lanarkshire and Renfrewshire architects had subscribed to Billings' *Antiquities* like all the others, their Baronial took rather different forms from those of the architects in Edinburgh, Perth and the north-east, at least in part because their clients were almost exclusively industrial or mercantile. Only two houses stand out as having a markedly Bryce-like character. These were Dunselma at Strone, the Coats family's sailing station, built in 1885–7 and designed by a former assistant of Bryce's – Andrew Robb Scott of the Paisley firm Rennison & Scott – and Ross House at Hamilton for Major Thomas Robertson-Aikman, designed by Alexander Cullen in 1891–4. Robertson-Aikman was old gentry and its Bryce-like appearance with a Castle Fraser tower was probably part of Cullen's brief. It is not improbable that Scott was drafted in to help with it, as he was by then a freelance assistant with an unorthodox family life, hiring himself out to whoever had need of him until his second partnership with the Edinburgh architect William Hamilton Beattie.

Both these houses were extremely late examples of their kind, although Ross House was rather more up-to-date within. The story of Baronial in the West of Scotland had begun nearly half a century earlier, in the late 1840s. David Hamilton died in 1843 without any further experiments in the seventeenth-century idiom of Dunlop, and in the following year his practice was sequestrated. His son James did not practise in his own name thereafter, his brother-in-law James Smith inheriting such clients as remained loyal. Smith prospered, designing his own Invergare at Rhu of 1855, a well-sited but not particularly literate house with slim dummy turrets, but at the very end of his career he secured the commission for the giant Overtoun, built in 1859–62 for the

chemical manufacturer James White. Although not particularly imaginative, with conventional canted bays, this was otherwise a well-detailed house with a tall, five-storeyed and cap-house tower, and magnificent Renaissance interiors from the hand of his talented assistant John Moyr Smith, better known to us as a decorative artist.

Hamilton's most gifted assistants, Charles Wilson, born 1810, and John Thomas Rochead, born 1814, had commenced independent practice before Hamilton died and largely succeeded to the position he had occupied. Wilson's reconstruction of Shandon for William Buchanan MP (1849), Pitcullo in Fife for John Pitcairn (1852), St Helens and Dudhope House, both in Dundee and both of 1850, were all somewhat similar in style to the Burn and Bryce idiom of around 1840, albeit with different plan-forms, the last being a very understated and unturreted house. All these commissions in the Dundee area arose from connections within the linen-manufacturing Baxter family, for whom Wilson had built three accomplished Italianate villas. But in 1852 at Lochton for the Dundee merchant Andrew Brown he adopted an L-plan form with a circular Glamis-inspired tower in the re-entrant angle (Figure 79). It was built in rubble masonry, but the proportions of the ground floor windows left no doubt that all was new. At the tall Inverawe in Argyll, reconstructed in the same year for J A Campbell, the proportions were more convincing, partly because of what already existed, and the square turrets gave a fair impression of early seventeenth-century work, at least from a distance. At Largie, built anew in 1857–9 for English MP Augustus Henry Moreton-Macdonald, who had inherited the estate from his wife, the Lochton concept was taken a stage further, the principal rooms being at first floor, and the ground floor small-windowed to ensure a convincingly ancient appearance. In the same years Wilson very sympathetically re-roofed the

FIGURE 79
Lochton, Perthshire, by Charles Wilson, 1852 (© RCAHMS, SC 1232831)

tower house at Duntreath in Stirlingshire for the Edmonstones, partly restoring and partly rebuilding the remainder as the new house. Sadly, this promising line of development was not pursued further, Wester Moffat at Airdrie for William Towers-Clark and the enlargement of Benmore in Argyll for the Scots-American tobacco merchant James Piers Patrick being craggier in detail. Both dated from 1862, and at Benmore the turrets were strangely slim in proportion. The probability must be that these houses were largely the work of David Thomson, who had returned to Wilson's office to help out when Wilson's health began to fail.

Rochead was initially slower to adopt Baro-

nial. His first major house, Minard in Argyll, was Tudor-castellated for an English client H W Askew; and his second, West Shandon of 1852 for the engineer Robert Napier, was more English Jacobean than Scottish. Knock at Largs, built in the same year for the Greenock industrialist Robert Steele, was also Tudor-castellated, despite the substantial remains of a tower house at the site; but around 1850 Rochead built the Baronial Blairvadach at Shandon for Glasgow's Lord Provost James Anderson, a towered and turreted pile in a somewhat similar idiom to Overtoun, and by Edinburgh standards some years out-of-date. It was followed in 1852–3 by the tall and eccentrically detailed Levenford at Dumbarton for the shipbuilder James Denny, and in 1855 by a very large block of warehouses and shops with a corner tower at 74–92 Trongate built for the City of Glasgow Bank, a rapid response to Billings' Ingram Street block of the previous year. The Billings and Rochead experiments in urban Baronial were repeated at Victoria Buildings, 2–8 West Regent Street for Archibald Orr-Ewing, built by Rickman's pupil Jonathan Anderson Bell in 1858. It was a very gentlemanly design, but the vogue for such buildings proved brief.

Like Wilson, Rochead was really an Italian Renaissance designer and would have remained a minor figure in the story of Baronial had it not been for the Reverend Dr Charles Rogers' competition for a colossal shrine to house what had long been believed to be William Wallace's sword. It fired his imagination, and by ignoring both the rules of the competition and the cost limit he came first in the popular vote with a dramatically shadowed crown-towered design 220 feet high, with details that were scaled to be effective from miles around. By the time it was completed, it had cost £18,000 rather than the stipulated £5,000 and brought a gentle but very public rebuke from Thomas Gildard on behalf of the other Glasgow architects. However, as the supreme architectural expression of nationalism anywhere in the world at the time, Rogers' committee may have felt it had been worth the cost, even if they never paid Rochead's fees.

John Burnet senior, also born in 1814 but largely self-taught, showed a similar bravura in his three major houses on the Clyde and on Loch Lomondside. At none of these was Burnet troubled by any thought of making them resemble original sixteenth-century houses, all of them having bold Romanesque detail of early French inspiration at the entrances, but there was nothing formulaic about his planning, each house being an individual response to the brief and to the site. Arden, built in 1868 for Sir James Lumsden, Lord

Provost of Glasgow, was relatively low-profiled two storeys and basement with a slim five-storeyed tower, but the slightly earlier Auchendennan of 1864–6 for the tobacco magnate George Martin was three-storeyed, dominated by a massive five-storeyed tower house, rich in incident with a circular corner tower, a French pavilion roof over the main stair and a conical-roofed bow overlooking its formal garden. As at Salvin's Thoresby, this garden was raised on an elevated terrace to first floor level. Equally grand with its own private loch was Kilmahew for the shipowner John William Burns, symbolically commanding the Clyde from the wooded hillside above Cardross. It was immensely tall three storeys, with an oblong tower house rising a storey and cap-house higher as its salient feature.

Close by Burnet's houses on Loch Lomondside was Auchenheglish, a much simpler house designed in 1865 by John James Stevenson. Born in 1831, Stevenson was a pupil of Bryce who had gone into partnership with Campbell Douglas in 1860. His suave, unturreted elevations at Auchenheglish were an early indication of his views on the revival of 'Old Scotch' architecture, of which more later, but like the Burnet houses it had a Romanesque porch. Campbell Douglas, born 1828, had already shown he was a capable Baronialist at Hartfield House overlooking Cove and Loch Long, which was built for the Glasgow merchant David Richardson in 1859, but from the time of his partnership with Stevenson he had gradually become more a practice manager, with a sharp eye for the most talented draughtsmen on the market. After Stevenson left for London to write *House Architecture* and commence practice there, he was succeeded as Douglas' partner by James Sellars. Sellars, born in 1843, had already designed the tall and slim Cove Castle nearby in 1867, although he was not then in full independent practice. Like Hartfield and the Alexander Thomson villas that adjoined them, Cove Castle

FIGURE 80
Above. Skipness, Argyll, by John Honeyman, 1881: photographed during construction; original house seen on left (© RCAHMS, SC 724599)

FIGURE 81
Opposite. Kinlochmoidart, Inverness-shire, by William Leiper, 1883 (© RCAHMS, SC 765854)

had been made possible by the introduction of a fast and efficient steamer service from Glasgow. So had Knockderry Castle, the original part looking at least partly ancient, but actually entirely Victorian. Its authorship is complicated. The Architectural Publication Society's *Dictionary*, normally completely reliable on Glasgow, as Burnet was its correspondent there, credited it to Alexander Thomson in its biographical notice of him. The original owner of the house, the druggist John Campbell, was indeed already a Thomson client, but it also appears to be the house John Honeyman built there in 1856. Honeyman certainly added to it in 1869 and 1871, and it must be largely to him that it owes its picturesque stepped and turreted profile.

Although his Cardell at Skelmorlie for the shipbuilder William Pearce (1860), The Cliff at Wemyss Bay for the Glasgow merchant Henry Martini (1872) and Roundelwood at Crieff for the warehouseman William Miller (1883) differed from Knockderry in being unmistakably Victorian with Jacobean details and turrets which were mere incidents in the design, Honeyman excelled at Skipness built in 1878–81 for the antiquary Robert Chellas Graham (Figure 80), not of the family which originally owned the estate but old gentry nevertheless, with property in Portugal. Skipness differed completely from the houses of Burnet and of Campbell Douglas and Sellars in consisting of an almost totally convincing rectangular tower house, rubble-built and just slightly

too slim on plan, dominating two-storey wings which gave the impression of being of more than one date. Although it had a rather more conventionally Victorian antiquarian interior, it paralleled Wardrop's Nunraw in marking the earliest beginnings of a sensitive Arts and Crafts approach to Baronial, in which new houses sought to emulate the qualities of ancient ones.

More than any other Scottish architect, William Leiper, born in 1839, bridged the transition from High Victorian to Aesthetic Movement and ultimately to Arts and Crafts. Although Honeyman had had London experience, it had been of a very conservative early Victorian kind with the elderly William Burn. Leiper's experience had been with William White and John

Loughborough Pearson, and somehow he had gained an entrée to the William Burges and Edward William Godwin circle: all of these architects were thirty to forty years younger than Burn and very much the avant-garde of the late 1850s and early 1860s. No other architect in Scotland at the time had such fashionably up-to-date experience as Leiper, particularly in respect of the Anglo-Japanese and indeed the decorative arts generally. He was successful at once, with a clientele that was mainly mercantile, manufacturing and professional but included some old landed gentry as well.

His first large houses were early French of the Burges-Godwin school, but in 1869–70 he built Colearn at Auchterarder for the advocate Alexander Mackintosh, a very compact French-influenced Baronial composition in dark red sandstone with buff dressings, rich in refined sculptured detail and with a very stylish Aesthetic Movement interior featuring stained glass by Daniel Cottier and Anglo-Japanese tiles by W B Simpson & Son. Balgray, Kelvinside, for the printer A D Dean, and the larger version of the same design at Cairndhu, Helensburgh, for Lord Provost Sir John Ure, were both François Premier and of 1872, similar in spirit to Kinnear's unbuilt St Martin's, if much less elaborate in layout. And although Leiper knew France well, the émigré architect Alfred Chastel de Boinville, then in Glasgow working for Campbell Douglas and another unspecified architect, may have had something to do with them. Both of these houses had notable interior work, with Anglo-Japanese ceilings, still visible at Cairndhu. Dalmore at Helensburgh for Robert Little (1873) returned to the Colearn manner in a more disciplined red sandstone form; and at Kinlochmoidart (Figure 81), built as a very lavish shooting lodge for the distiller Robert Stewart of Ingliston in 1883, the same design was reproduced a storey higher by the insertion of a basement, the otherwise close resemblance being varied by its construction in whinstone, with red sandstone dressings and more picturesque outbuildings, which included a hydro-electric plant and a refrigerated game larder. Like Leiper's other houses of the 1870s and 1880s, Kinlochmoidart had a splendid Aesthetic Movement interior, but such was fashion, even in the depth of the worst recession Scotland had then seen, that Leiper's interiors at Dalmore were largely replaced by William Scott Morton as early as 1881.

Very close in style to Leiper's houses at Colearn and Dalmore, but with a segmentally arched entrance seemingly influenced by William Eden Nesfield's Cloverley, was the new castle that Campbell Douglas & Sellars built in 1875–6 within the ruined enceinte of the ancient castle of Mugdock for the insurance broker and historian John Guthrie Smith, who had leased the estate in 1874. The new castle was linked to a surviving tower of the old by a timber gallery carried on a wide archway of Richard Norman Shaw inspiration, the whole forming a remarkably picturesque fantasy which can now be glimpsed only in old photographs.

As author of the classic book on the country houses of the old Glasgow gentry, Smith was an exceptional patron. At Netherhall, Largs, designed concurrently by the same practice for Professor Sir William Thomson, later Lord Kelvin, the priorities were different. Although chateau-like in profile, with conical-roofed corner tourelles and a dormered pavilion roof, the house was otherwise an absolutely plain rectangle. But it had electric light, a lift, patent stoves, an expansive carriage porch and a large conservatory of purely functional design. Only at the boldly arched gatehouse on the roadside was there a hint of the real Campbell Douglas & Sellars. There were few more telling illustrations of the client's significance in dictating the brief than the contrast between Netherhall and Mugdock.

The City of Glasgow Bank failure of 1878, and the severe recession that followed it, severely diminished the demand for such large and expensive houses, particularly in the West of Scotland. Sellars died prematurely in 1888 without building another, but after a brief career break in Paris as a painter, Leiper resumed his Glasgow practice in 1880. When prosperity began to return in the 1890s, he became less concerned with purity of style in his Baronial houses. He concentrated on providing more generous window areas, and on stylish composition, to make them as attractive to clients as his more relaxed Old English houses. This change of direction seems to have been first evident in his largest house, Kelly in Renfrewshire built in 1890–1 for the shipbuilder Alexander Stephen of Linthouse. It still had his characteristic circular and octagonal towers, but the details were much more eclectic than at Kinlochmoidart, with very large neo-Tudor mullioned windows and big crow-steps of Low Countries derivation at its gables and numerous gablets. The same freedom from historical precedent was to be seen at The Red Tower in Helensburgh, built in 1898–1900 for the provision merchant James Allan, where a big circular corner tower was combined with an English Jacobean forebuilding, half-timbered gablets and dormers, and a broad-eaved roof of piended and prismatic forms with no gables. Internally, both Kelly and The Red Tower had straightforward English Jacobean interiors with no Aesthetic Movement elements. Different again was his large addition to Knockderry Castle for the carpet manufacturer John S. Templeton, where the main element was a crenellated tower house with oriels and cap-house. Unusually for Leiper it had a double-height hall and sumptuous decoration carried out by W Scott Morton & Co., a firm with which Templeton's was closely associated.

In 1883 the calico printer William Crum built Danesfield on the seashore at Largs, a compact chateau of banded masonry which is so close in style to Leiper that it has sometimes been assumed to be his work. Crum had spent much of his life in Manchester and his architect was John Douglas of Chester, whose Paddocks at Eccleston for the duke of Westminster must have had particular appeal for him. Leiper seems to have admired Douglas' work too, as the circular corner-tower and two-tier dormer of Danesfield were to be incorporated into his designs for Auchenbothie at Kilmacolm (1898), built for the publisher H B Collins. Unusually for Leiper, it was white-harled with red sandstone dressings. Something akin to the Danesfield tower was also to appear at the rubble-built Glendaruel for the shipowner Lewis Wigan, where the main elevation was, unusually, semi-symmetrical. In these

later houses Leiper was most ably assisted by William Hunter McNab, his assistant from 1881 and his partner from 1899, Leiper becoming more dependent on him after his health was damaged by blood poisoning in January 1903. Although it was not among their largest houses, McNab's Beneffrey in Springkell Avenue, Glasgow (1910) for the building contractor John Anderson was one of their very best houses, sophisticated in composition and scholarly in detail.

From perhaps as early as 1871, Leiper was concurrently designing in what might be described as an 1860s English parsonage manner, as at his own Terpersie in Helensburgh, where the rubble masonry contains narrow horizontal bands of colour, a detail drawn from his former employer William White. By the early 1880s this English strand in his work had become full Old English, either tile-hung or with half-timbered elements, strongly influenced by the work of Richard Norman Shaw. These developments were exactly paralleled on a palatial scale at Campbell Douglas & Sellars' Keil House at Southend in Kintyre (1873–5), the features of which were shamelessly and rather successfully drawn from Shaw's plates of Leyswood, Cragside and Preen in the *Building News*: only the porte-cochère had no precedent in Shaw. Although the client James Nicol Fleming had built it with City of Glasgow Bank money, and his career ended in flight and arrest only three years later, the significance of this now fragmentary house on the direction of domestic architecture in the West of Scotland can hardly be overestimated. The fashion for Baronial rapidly melted away, Thomas Lennox Watson adopting the same Old English idiom on his return from Alfred Waterhouse's office in London in 1874.

The same pattern is to be seen in the work of John Burnet's son John James Burnet (b.1857), their partner John Archibald Campbell (b.1859), and their pupil Alexander Nisbet Paterson

(b. 1862), all products of Jean-Louis Pascal's atelier and of the École des Beaux-Arts in Paris. Burnet adopted Shavian Old English at Corrienessan on Loch Ard from 1886, and in the work of all three there is an element of American influence which, in Burnet and Campbell's case, extended even into their relatively few Baronial houses, notably at Garmoyle, Dumbarton for the shipbuilder Lieutenant-Colonel John M. Denny in 1892. This had a very Scottish garden elevation, with crow-stepped gables, dormerheads and angle-turret, but it also had an English roof of red tiles, which on the entrance side was swept down in Shingle Style fashion over a low polygonal timber porch. More complex in composition and plan was the slightly earlier and much larger Baronald (now Cartland Bridge) at Lanark, built for Alan Farie, who had been driven from his ancestral Farme Castle at Rutherglen by industrial pollution. Constructed of dark reddish-brown stone with buff dressings, it was a house full of original ideas, a three-quarter quadrangle of linked tower house-like blocks around a central stairhall opening into a large conservatory on the entrance front. As at Garmoyle, Baronald is built into a slope so that the garden elevation stands immensely high above the surrounding valley landscape. The same clever use of levels is to be seen at the later Lorimer-influenced Fairnilee, Selkirk, for the mill owner A F Roberts, where the brightly harled new house of 1904–6 enters from a terraced approach high above the formal garden, and is linked to one end of the old house by a magnificent set of gates leading into the woodlands (Figure 82).

Campbell's 1897 scheme for a new house at Dalskairth for the thread manufacturer William A Coats would have been much bigger than any of these, but it was never realised (Figure 83), his best executed house in the Scots vernacular idiom being the simple and unturreted Southwood at Troon (1905). Campbell had, however, already produced an outstanding essay in Scots Renaissance at the Ewing Gilmour Institute, Alexandria (1888–91), where the principal element on the street front was a low, square, bartizaned entrance tower, the roof of the adjoining link-block being swept low in Shingle Style fashion over a dwarf-columned loggia looking into the garden. In the same bartizaned Scots Renaissance idiom was Burnet's baths at Alloa of 1895–8 (Figure 84), but the most impressive expression of their distinctive Scots Renaissance was Campbell's tall and austerely symmetrical Queen Victoria School at Dunblane, won in a competition assessed by Rowand Anderson and built in 1906–10.

Paterson's works in the Scots Renaissance idiom were fewer in number and more modest in scale, the best being his own Longcroft at Helensburgh of 1902, L-plan in form, low in proportion, but turreted and making the same clever use of a falling site as in Burnet's houses. By contrast, his fine Arrochar Hotel of 1911 was relatively simple in its elevational treatment, harled, unturreted and asymmetrically composed on both elevations.

Another outstanding architect in this Beaux-Arts group, although he never attended the École, was Burnet and Campbell's pupil William Kerr, chief draughtsman in the office of the Paisley architect Thomas Graham Abercrombie. He brilliantly exploited the Burnet and Campbell Scots Renaissance idiom in the very large Volunteer (later Territorial) buildings in Paisley's High Street of 1896, as good as anything Burnet and Campbell could do themselves and a testament to the financial might of Paisley's volunteers. Abercrombie's contemporary Royal Alexandra Hospital was in the same idiom, but its design was more compromised by functional considerations.

Of the other leading Glasgow architects, James Miller, born in 1860 and largely self-taught after an apprenticeship with Andrew Heiton in Perth, never built anything which could be

FIGURE 82
Fairnilee, Selkirkshire, by John James Burnet, 1904–6 (© RCAHMS, SC 1224553)

described as Baronial other than the new wing added to Cousin's Newark, although he did sometimes make use of Scots Renaissance details. Neither did Burnet's ex-assistant, the slightly older Henry Edward Clifford, born in 1852, who was the leading domestic architect in the West of Scotland between 1890 and 1914. Both drew on contemporary English work published in the architectural journals and in *The Studio* magazine. Baronial houses thus became the exception rather than the rule. In the Glasgow suburbs, the only houses to stand out are Walter Forsyth McGibbon's two houses in Pollokshields, his own Allerly in Nithsdale Drive (1887) and 48 Dalziel Drive (1892), and nearby John Thomson and Robert Douglas Sandilands' Rhuadsgeir (now Sherbrooke Castle) of 1896 for the builder John Morrison, a toughly detailed symmetrical red sandstone villa with a slimmed-down Balmoral entrance tower on its flank.

The London Scots

Thanks to John James Stevenson, the Glasgow architects also had a strong presence in London, as any really good assistant in Campbell Douglas' office could be sure of finding a place there. Apart from John McKean Brydon, who never built in Scotland, the most gifted were James Marjoribanks MacLaren, born near Doune in 1853; George Washington Browne, also born in 1853, who returned home; and William Flockhart, born in Kilmarnock in 1854. In his early years MacLaren built a couple of Leiper-inspired houses at Grangemouth, Avondhu and Avon Hall (both 1878) for relatives, but in his maturity his main patron was the shipowner Sir Donald Currie. On Currie's Glenlyon estate, he built the farmhouse with its simplified tower house-like profile in 1889, but he died in 1890 when his plans for the enlargement of Glenlyon House and of the hotel at Fortingall were still at sketch-plan stage. These were carried out in 1891 by his assistants and successors William Dunn, a Glaswegian from Duncan McNaughton's office, and Robert Watson, an ex-assistant of Rowand Anderson. Both were masterly essays in a simple unturreted Scots vernacular which provided the inspiration for Lorimer's early Colinton houses and were at least the forerunners of Charles Rennie Mackintosh's Windyhill of 1900–1 and the Hill House of 1902–4, there being as yet no evidence of Mackintosh having seen them other than in the pages of *The Architect* magazine.

FIGURE 83
Opposite top. Dalskairth, Dumfriesshire, by John Archibald Campbell, 1897: project drawing, not built (*Academy Architecture 1897*)

FIGURE 84
Opposite bottom. Alloa Baths, Clackmannanshire, by John James Burnet, 1897 (*Academy Architecture 1897*)

Very different from these simple but sophisticated buildings was William Flockhart's Rosehaugh, built in 1893–1904 for the Peruvian magnate James Douglas Fletcher. Whether this vast towered chateau, asymmetrically composed, with predominantly François Premier and English Jacobean details, tall red-tiled roofs, great formal terraces and sumptuous interiors – partly antique from Duveen Brothers – falls within the scope of this chapter may perhaps be arguable, but it was the first of three great houses designed by London architects. The second was Kincardine House on Deeside, built in 1895–7 for Mrs Mary Umfreville Pickering (*née* Mary Black of Wateridgemuir: her husband was from Yorkshire) (Figure 85). It was designed by David Barclay Niven, a former assistant of the Dundee architect John Murray Robertson and later of Aston Webb, and his partner Henry Hardy Wigglesworth, Aberdonian despite his name and a pupil of Marshall Mackenzie. Kincardine was a reflection of Wigglesworth's subsequent experience with Ernest George and with George B Post in New York. Although shallow on plan, the exterior of the house was on the same huge American scale as Post's houses for Cornelius Vanderbilt and other New York clients, but apart from the canopied Baroque doorpiece, the details were wholly Scottish. Inside the details of the double-height hall and stair were English Jacobean of the George school. The third of these great *fin de siècle* London-designed palaces was Mount Melville (now Craigtoun) built from 1902 for the brewer Sir James Younger. As might be expected from its English architect, Paul Waterhouse, the house was red in colour and less wholeheartedly Scottish than Kincardine, albeit turreted. The sheer scale of it was nevertheless undeniably impressive, particularly on the south front, where it rose from a sunk formal garden; and the Renaissance interiors were of extraordinary magnificence, with much marble work by Farmer & Brindley.

FIGURE 85
Kincardine, Aberdeenshire, by Niven and Wigglesworth, 1895–7 (*Academy Architecture 1895*)

The End of the Baronial Era

At first sight, late Victorian Edinburgh might seem to have remained more loyal to the Baronial than had Glasgow. In Marchmont, the development of which began with David Bryce in 1870 and continued until the late 1880s, the city was unique in having an almost completely Baronial suburb of high-class tenements, even if only a few were designed by architects who were among the leaders of the profession. In MacGibbon and Ross' gargantuan parish council offices on Castle Terrace and Cambridge Street (1886–8), the city had one major public building in that idiom, and in Leith there was another: the equally massive Sailors' Home of 1882–3 designed by Charles Stewart Still Johnston, Orcadian gentry and one

of Bryce's later pupils. Although little remembered now, in his own lifetime Johnston was one of the leaders of the profession in Edinburgh. He had a significant country house practice, which vigorously maintained Bryce's Baronial idiom into the early years of the twentieth century in his major rebuildings at Woodside in Ayrshire (1890), Pollok (also 1890) and Barrochan (1898) in Renfrewshire, and at Ormsary (1905) in Argyll.

Nevertheless, Edinburgh was the epicentre of the reaction against Baronial as practised from the later 1850s. The Aberdonian Londoner Robert Kerr ridiculed it as uncivilised in *The English Gentleman's House* as early as 1864, but few took that seriously at the time. The manifesto for change was set out in Chapter XIV, entitled 'The Renaissance in Scotland', of John James Steven-

FIGURE 86
Kinnordy, Angus, by James Maitland Wardrop, Charles Reid and Hew Montgomerie Wardrop, 1879
(© RCAHMS, SC 1232816)

son's *House Architecture*, published by Macmillan in 1880. There the architecture of Rochead in particular was castigated as 'all mustard with no beef . . . corbelling has run mad in it, making marvellous protruberances where one does not expect them; corners are hacked out of it, and the pieces stuck on somewhere else'. In finding such productions 'not true expressions of national feeling', he advocated the architecture of the seventeenth and earliest eighteenth centuries, and the Old College of Glasgow in particular, as the correct model for a Scottish equivalent to the 'Queen Anne' he was advocating in England, finding it 'well fitted for modern houses. Its details and forms are classic, its use involves no necessity of changing the existing habits of the inmates or the workmen's methods of building.'

Stevenson was based in London, and although his parents and sisters lived in Edinburgh his practice in Scotland consisted only of churches for Free Church congregations. His argument had, however, been anticipated in actual building by at least one year. In 1879 James Maitland Wardrop and his son Hew Montgomerie Wardrop designed the rebuilding of Kinnordy in an unturreted, near-symmetrical early seventeenth-century form, with Pinkie-type mullioned bay windows, for Leonard Lyell, whose wife Mary Stirling was the driving force behind the project (Figure 86). While the Wardrops may well have reached the same conclusion independently, the probability must be that Hew had gained an entrée to Stevenson's circle when working for George Edmund Street in London. More obviously in the younger Wardrop's hand were the 1881 proposals for The Hirsel, where the 12th earl of Home was offered a choice of unturreted Scots vernacular, Stevenson-type Queen Anne and George Devey 'Old English': since Devey never allowed his work to be published, Hew must have had contacts there as well. In parallel, the much older Robert Rowand Anderson, born in 1834 and an ex-assistant of George Gilbert Scott, designed his own Allermuir at Colinton in 1879, the first house in his modern version of old Scots architecture, a simple crow-stepped vernacular with lower ceiling heights, minimal early seventeenth-century detail and small-paned sashes. Anderson himself did not have the opportunity to develop this seventeenth-century idiom on a larger scale until 1895, when he designed The Swallowgate at St Andrews for James Ogilvie Fairlie. In the same year, he also designed the much bigger and very severe granite-built Glencoe House for the Canadian magnate Sir Donald Smith, later Lord Strathcona where, somewhat surprisingly, the original roof was of English red tiles, as at Burnet and Campbell's Garmoyle: these were then believed to have thermal qualities that made houses warmer in winter and cooler in summer.

By the time Glencoe was built, the Wardrop and Anderson practices had merged. Maitland Wardrop died in 1882, and Charles Reid in 1883, compelling Hew Wardrop to find a more experienced, like-minded partner; but he too died in 1887, leaving Anderson on his own. Anderson's Scots-style domestic architecture at Glencoe proved too austere and understated for most clients, and no further commissions in that idiom came his way. Although his palace-like Pearce Institute of 1902–6 for Govan parish was one of the supreme achievements of the revived Scottish Renaissance, Anderson's significance to the later developments in 'Old Scotch' lies more in his role as a teacher. Unlike the younger Peddie – John

More Dick Peddie (b.1853) – and the Glasgow architects Thomas Lennox Watson (b.1850), Henry Clifford (b.1852) and James Miller (b.1860), he did not see Old English or any other form of English vernacular as a solution to contemporary Scottish domestic architecture. Although he had never built anything that could be described as Baronial, he had an intense commitment to Scottish architectural traditions. Very close to Anderson were his one-time chief assistant John Watson, the mainstay of architectural education and field study at the Edinburgh Architectural Association, and, even more importantly, David MacGibbon and his partner Thomas Ross, whose *Castellated and Domestic Architecture of Scotland* published between 1887 and 1892 hugely enlarged the repertoire of Scots Renaissance motifs. These volumes contained almost every building in the land erected before 1650, and demonstrated the possibilities of a far simpler Scots vernacular than the exemplars selected by Billings. Supplementing them were the studybook folios of the Edinburgh Architectural Association, the publication of which had begun much earlier in 1875; and from the mid 1890s there were the folios of Anderson's own National Art Survey, which had its origin in the fellowships for field study at his Edinburgh School of Applied Art, opened in October 1892. These provided the ready source of large-scale details that architects needed to match the robust qualities of original Scots Renaissance work.

Between 1885 and 1887, Wardrop and Anderson rebuilt and greatly extended the ruined Place of Tilliefoure on Donside for Francis Robert Gregson, the youngest son of a Durham landowner and the husband of Mary Grant of nearby Monymusk (Figure 87). The commission was in the hands of Wardrop and closer to Anderson's ideals than anything he built himself. The original building was a diminutive Z-plan house of 1626, and the new wing was matched to it both in its scale and its boulder rubble construction. It was an early Arts and Crafts triumph of sympathy with the original structure, and it had a profound effect on those who knew about it, but as Wardrop died while it was under construction it fell to others to implement his ideas. Of the more successful architects who began their careers in the Wardrop and Anderson circle the oldest was John Kinross, born in 1855, who commenced practice in 1882. His scholarly classical and English Jacobean houses lie outwith the scope of this study, as do his restoration works for the 3rd marquess of Bute. However, the four tall, seventeenth century-style houses he built on Mortonhall Road in Edinburgh, which included one for himself and one for the Scott Mortons, show the same attention to detail as Tilliefoure and have even more studied details, as does his one large Scottish-style country house, the whinstone Peel at Caddonfoot built for William Robert Ovens, a Leith grain merchant. All five of these houses have superb interior work of early to late seventeenth-century character.

Even more successful than John Kinross in terms of the sheer scale of his practice was Arthur George Sydney Mitchell, born in 1856 and a pupil of Anderson, although some of his early work suggests that he may have had London experience. His career got off to a remarkably quick start thanks to the patronage of his father Sir Arthur Mitchell of the Lunacy Board and of the newspaper magnate John Ritchie Findlay. Findlay was his patron for the early seventeenth century-style picturesque fantasy of Well Court (1883–6), which was designed to be seen from Findlay's house, also designed by Mitchell, at 3 Rothesay Terrace. Although superbly composed and detailed, Well Court had very un-Scottish roofs of the newly fashionable red Brosely tiles that Anderson was to use at Glencoe. Late in 1888 Mitchell received the commission for Craig House, a colossal towered and turreted pile step-

ping up Easter Craiglockhart Hill. Built in 1889–94 for the more well-off patients of the Royal Edinburgh Asylum, its turrets had Scottish ogee roofs, but the details were French rather than Scottish and its architecture was picturesquely Romantic rather than Baronial.

Much more Scottish were four major country house commissions. The first was Sauchieburn for Sir James R G Maitland (1890–1), one of the largest Baronial houses ever built, still with echoes of Bryce and Kinnear in its bartizaned main tower and Castle Fraser angle-tower, but quite different on plan and with up-to-date detail. Even more impressive was the new frontal range added in 1889–93 to Charles Wilson's Duntreath for Sir Archibald Edmonstone, who was only twenty-one when work began (Figure 88). The whole house was refitted with palatial interiors and seems to have been intended to receive royalty from the start, although a few years were to elapse before he and his sister Alice Keppel became important figures at Edward VII's court. The new front was clearly inspired by that at Tolquhon, but on a far larger scale, with tower houses at both ends rather than just one. Surprisingly little attempt was made to match the masonry of the original castle, its walling being of coursed hammer-dressed rubble as if to emphasise that all was new. Also of very modern masonry – here bright red sandstone from Annan – was Glenborrodale Castle, a Wagnerian fantasy where the main element was a five-storeyed and cap-house crenellated tower with Scots Renaissance angle oriels, begun in 1898 for the diamond magnate Charles Duneill Rudd. It was far removed from Anderson and Wardrop's strictly rational approach to Old Scots design, but by 1900 Mitchell had followed Wardrop and Lorimer in adopting a more Arts and Crafts approach to work of this kind. At the reconstruction of Glenkindie, where the plain, later eighteenth-century main house was enlarged into an asymmetrical Baronial form

FIGURE 87
Place of Tilliefoure, Aberdeenshire, restored and extended by Hew Montgomery Wardrop, 1885–7, completed by Rowand Anderson with Robert S Lorimer as site agent (© RCAHMS, SC 1224550)

to match the mid seventeenth-century wings, all of the new masonry was as perfectly matched to the original as Wardrop's had been at Tilliefoure.

Also an offshoot from the Wardrop and Anderson practices was the much older James Jerdan, born in 1839, who had set up on his own when the practices merged in 1883–4. His was a much smaller practice, as he had less influential connections, but he had an important role at Heriot-Watt as a teacher. His son John, born in 1875, was to spend five years with Aston Webb before taking over the practice in 1904. Together father and son built Temple Hall in Berwickshire

for the Edinburgh advocate Robert Fitzroy Bell in 1895: three storeys and basement, and very plain, but a place of great charm with convincing, low-ceilinged proportions, one of the happiest expressions of the unturreted seventeenth-century style that Anderson had tried to promote (Figure 89).

Of the same school was the work of Thomas Greenshields Leadbetter (b.1859), of whom we know too little, as he never sought membership of the Royal Institute of British Architects and his death attracted no obituary. He may have been a pupil of Kinnear, as there seems to have been a

FIGURE 88
Duntreath Castle, Stirlingshire, by Arthur George Sydney Mitchell, 1889–93: new frontal range
(© RCAHMS, SC 694747)

Greenshields family connection and, again like Kinnear, he was a landed gentleman himself, married into the Usher family, his clients being mainly relatives, friends and neighbours in the Borders and south-west. He probably had London experience, as he exhibited at the Royal Academy in his early years. He had a stronger commitment to the Scottish vernacular, if not the Baronial, than most of his contemporaries but, like Mitchell, he was happy to work in a Scots Georgian manner or English Arts and Crafts if asked. His practice consisted mainly of additions to old houses, like those at Grandtully in Perthshire and at Cessnock and Blair in Ayrshire, all in an understated but distinctive Anderson-inspired manner that is immediately recognisable once one is familiar with it. His new-build houses are relatively few in number, but in 1904–5 he made designs for an ambitious but fairly reserved Baronial house at Queenshill in Kirkcudbright for the engineer Walter Montgomery Neilson. He also built two modest country houses for himself: Stobieside in Lanarkshire (1907), a low, picturesquely angled house, harled with a very sparing use of turrets; and the rather larger Spital Tower at Denholm (1913), again a low-rise

FIGURE 89
Temple Hall, Coldingham, Berwickshire, by James Jerdan, 1895 (*Academy Architecture 1900*)

composition, but with a towered wing.

In 1885 George Washington Browne withdrew from the Wardrop and Anderson partnership, which he had joined as Anderson's assistant in 1879. The reasons are not known, but there may not have been enough business for three partners in the severe depression of the early to mid 1880s. The competition win for Edinburgh Public Library made his name, but from about 1889 he provided help when required at Kinnear & Peddie, as that practice had become when John Dick Peddie retired and Kinnear became senior partner. The Peddie element was now John More Dick Peddie, who was exactly the same age as Browne and an ex-assistant of George Gilbert Scott. Kinnear was then still at the drawing-board if the commission interested him, as could be seen

at two major Baronial houses the practice built at that time: Cardoness for Sir William Maxwell, which incorporated an older house; and Drygrange, built anew for Edward Sprot of Riddell and further embellished with terraced formal gardens for the mill owner Thomas Roberts from 1904. Drygrange was much the same on plan as Kinnear's Sorn thirty years earlier, but it had an L-plan entrance front with a Castle Fraser entrance tower in the re-entrant angle. What made it quite different from its predecessors was the refined English and Scottish neo-Jacobean detailing which, if not by Browne, was the work of the team Peddie had assembled for Edinburgh's Caledonian Station and the branch-bank building programmes of the 1890s. Peddie himself had no enthusiasm for the Baronial, his houses of those years tending to be Old English with sash windows, superseded in the early 1900s by a more scholarly neo-Tudor or an accomplished Scots Georgian, in which his principal assistant John Wilson probably had a large hand. When Kinnear died in 1894, Browne was taken into partnership. He designed at least one notable Scots seventeenth century-style house in those years: Langlees at Biggar, with features drawn from the Argyll Lodging at Stirling and other early seventeenth-century sources (Figure 90). Johnsburn at Balerno for Hector C Macpherson is said to be his, although primary evidence is lacking – long and low on the Tilliefoure model but with dormerheads. Browne's own house, The Limes in Blackford Road, Edinburgh, also had some Scots Renaissance touches on the entrance front, the mullioned rectangular bays of the garden elevation being English. All three of these houses were built in or about 1899.

By the turn of the century Anderson, Peddie, Browne and Leadbetter were all beginning to be overshadowed as the leading designers of large houses by the fast-growing practice of Robert Stodart Lorimer. Born in 1864, he had observed the business of restoring old houses as a teenager at Kellie, which his father had rescued from near-ruin in 1878, and he gained practical experience as Wardrop and Anderson's site agent at Tilliefoure. That was reinforced by a period in the office of George Frederick Bodley in London, followed by shorter spells with MacLaren, Dunn & Watson. There he became deeply imbued with the principles of the Arts and Crafts movement. On his return to Scotland in 1891, this experience brought him the commission to restore the ruinous castle and gardens at Earlshall for the Perth bleacher R W R Mackenzie. The restoration was achieved without any structural changes or additions and, in sheer sympathy for the original building, far surpassed any previous Scottish work of this kind. A year or two elapsed before

FIGURE 90
Langlees, Lanarkshire, by George Washington Browne, 1899 (*Academy Architecture* 1899)

further similar commissions came his way, his practice then consisting mainly of MacLaren-derived roughcast suburban houses in Colinton, predominantly English Arts and Crafts but with some early seventeenth century-style Scottish features. In 1893 the Edinburgh law lord the Hon. John Trayner gave him the opportunity to develop this style on a larger scale at The Grange, North Berwick, a long and relatively low house somewhat on the Tilliefoure model, with English Arts and Crafts gables, Scots crow-stepped gables and piended roofs. As first built, it was a place of considerable charm but even more successful was the long combined lodge and stable block facing the road, which was in a purer Scots style that at first sight looked like original seventeenth-century work. This plain, low, unturreted style on

FIGURE 91
Hallyards, Peeblesshire, by Robert S Lorimer, 1900: project drawing (*Academy Architecture* 1900)

Anderson and Stevenson principles was developed in a still purer Scots form with straight skews at Stronachullin Lodge in Argyll for John Graham Campbell (1894), and in an unbuilt scheme for a cousin of Lorimer's at Hallyards, Peeblesshire, in 1897 (Figure 91).

These houses set the style for the later granite-built Rhu-na-haven on Deeside for J Herbert Taylor in 1907 and the white-harled Woodhill, Barry for D S Milne, both mid to late seventeenth century in character, with symmetrical garden fronts, piended roofs and dormerheads. Neither of these sought to look old, but in 1899 at Briglands in Kinross-shire, he reconstructed the eastern half of a long and low mid eighteenth-century house as a tall, compact three-storeyed

L-plan Scots Renaissance dwelling for the advocate James Avon Clyde, the western half of the old house becoming a wing of the new. Its concept was drawn from some of the simpler seventeenth-century exemplars illustrated by MacGibbon and Ross.

In the early twentieth century, Lorimer designed and built two really large houses: Rowallan in Ayrshire, begun in 1901, and Ardkinglas in Argyll, begun in 1904 (Figure 92). Both were built on newly acquired estates with relatively new money from industry: the flour millers Brown & Polson, and Shanks earthenware at A Cameron Corbett's Rowallan; and the Armstrong armaments firm at Sir Andrew Noble's Ardkinglas. Noble already had a record of discriminating

FIGURE 92
Ardkinglas, Argyll, by Robert S Lorimer, 1904 (© RCAHMS and the late Dr Peter Savage, SC 714892)

patronage at Jesmond, Newcastle, where his architect had been Richard Norman Shaw. These houses were similar in concept, although quite different in composition, both having tall main blocks entered by low forebuildings which did indeed enclose courts, but with corridors down one side of these courts to link the entrance with the main stair, a plan-type that was without precedent. At Rowallan, the composition was impaired by the omission of half the forecourt buildings when Alice Corbett died in 1902, but at Ardkinglas the scheme was completely realised. Both houses had refined seventeenth-century masonry detail similar to that of Kinross' Morton-hall Road houses and, in accordance with Anderson and Stevenson's principles, angle-turrets were

largely avoided. Ardkinglas was the more success-ful in its less regularly coursed rubble and its more innovative detail – notably the three-arch loggia on the main floor level, apparently inspired by that in Slezer's view of Bog of Gight. Both houses had exceptional interiors with mid to later seven-teenth century-style plasterwork by Sam Wilson and Thomas Beattie, of a quality paralleled only by John Kinross.

Although the 1899 work at Briglands had a convincing seventeenth-century appearance, neither Rowallan nor Ardkinglas was intended to look anything other than an early twentieth-century house, however scholarly the individual features might be. Formakin, Renfrewshire was to be very different, and that was in large part due

FIGURE 93
Formakin House, Renfrewshire, by Robert S Lorimer, 1911–13: entrance front from formal garden
(© RCAHMS, SC 684434)

to the client, the Paisley stockbroker John Augustus Holms, who had begun the project by buying four farms to create an idyllic valley landscape in 1902 (Figure 93). In 1903–4 he and Lorimer laid out the formal gardens, the farmhouse at Gatehead being hurriedly remodelled and extended as a temporary residence. The reconstruction of the mill with a circular angle-tower, the restoration of its late seventeenth-century miller's house, the ogee-roofed lodge houses and the tower house-like bothy followed in 1907–9. Throughout that period the designs for the main house at Formakin continued to mature, much of the plan being determined by Holms' collections. Construction began early in 1911 and ended in the autumn of 1913, the interior being left unfinished as a result of liabilities of over £100,000 arising from illicit trading by Holms' partner in the summer of 1912, but there were no compromises. The L-plan layout of the ancillary buildings formed a highly convincing outer court and inner court with the two walled gardens, and the house itself was a variation on original seventeenth-century Z-plan houses, with both jambs on the north forming an asymmetrical stepped U-plan. Its unturreted elevations were reminiscent of Bruntsfield House, close to the Lorimer family home in Edinburgh's Bruntsfield Crescent, but the details of the dormerheads were drawn from Kellie and Aberdour. Throughout, the masonry was undistinguishable from original seventeenth-century work, Holms having forbidden – as he put it – anything that looked like 'a villa in Camlachie' from the outset. It was, and mercifully still is, an atmospheric place.

Lorimer himself described it as 'the purest Scotch' he had ever done, and indeed it is the purest anyone has done, either then or since. Something of the quality of Formakin was achieved in parallel by Lorimer's close friend

Francis Deas at Braeheads, Newton St Boswells, in 1908, and by Lorimer himself at Laverockdale, Colinton for the chartered accountant J A Ivory in 1912–14. But these houses were much smaller, and Lorimer's proposals of 1915–16 for a second Formakin, costing £40,000, at Sir William Burrell's newly acquired Hutton Castle merely annoyed the client as being over-ambitious.

Highly successful though Lorimer's houses were, by the early twentieth century 'Old Scotch' was not in fact as common as publicity in the pages of *Country Life* seemed to suggest. The work of Lorimer's contemporaries in that vein consists of isolated achievements for clients who wanted something Scottish rather than any consistent line of development. In 1893 George Mackie Watson, born in 1860 and Anderson's long-serving principal assistant from 1884 to 1899, commenced independent practice with Bardrochat in Ayrshire. Built high up on a hillside, this was a low, two-storey house with seventeenth century-style dormerheads on the same general principles as Lorimer's early country houses but more Andersonian in detail. At Castle Lachlan in 1903 Watson remodelled and enlarged a plain Georgian house in a more martial form, with crenellated parapets and a bartizaned entrance tower far removed from Anderson precepts. As clan chief and soldier, his client Major John Maclachlan doubtless had a say in the design. Also within Anderson's circle were John Nicol Scott (b.1863), for a time his assistant, and his partner Alexander Lorne Campbell (b.1871), who was to be Anderson's executor. From 1904 they built Grange at Linlithgow for the landowner, geologist and colliery owner Henry Moubray Cadell, making skilful use of the hillside for the pavilioned formal garden beneath (Figure 94). Similar in size and also built on a hillside with formal balustraded terraces, was Kinpurnie in Angus for the shipowner Sir Charles Cayzer, designed by the very accomplished Dundee partnership of

Patrick Hill Thoms (b.1871), and William Fleming Wilkie (b.1876). Wilkie had worked for Gibson & Russell and for London County Council, and studied at the Royal Academy Schools. His experience there shows. As at Grange, a broad, square outlook tower with a plain corbelled parapet was the dominant element in the composition.

In the west, the most accomplished exponents of Old Scots were James Miller's former assistant Thomas Andrew Millar (b.1880), and the partnership of John Stewart (b.1870) and George Andrew Paterson (b.1876), both of whom had a Beaux-Arts provenance, the former with Burnet and the latter with Alexander Nisbet Paterson. As Millar was rather well-off, he was able to implement his own Arts and Crafts ideals very early at Boghall, Baldernock, built for himself in 1907–8, a small-scale parallel to Formakin in its rubble stonework and convincing seventeenth-century forms. At the slightly later Deasholm (now Silver Glades) at Troon, built for Norman Maclaren in 1911, the concept seems to have been a sixteenth-century tower house which had been modernised and extended in early Georgian times: it even had a screen-walled forecourt with an entrance archway.

Stewart & Paterson's most important Old Scots house within the timeframe of this chapter was the House of Elrig, Wigtonshire, built in 1912–14 for Aymer Maxwell in the simple seventeenth-century vernacular idiom propagated by Rowand Anderson, to whom Stewart had been an assistant in the 1890s. Even simpler in its architecture than Anderson's Glencoe, its two-storey and garret elevations, asymmetrical and mildly Lorimerian on the entrance side and symmetrical H-plan towards the garden, were made more interesting by being constructed of partly cyclopean Arts and Crafts rubble quarried at the site, local slates and ancient-looking chimneystacks, all very much as at Millar's Boghall but on a much larger scale.

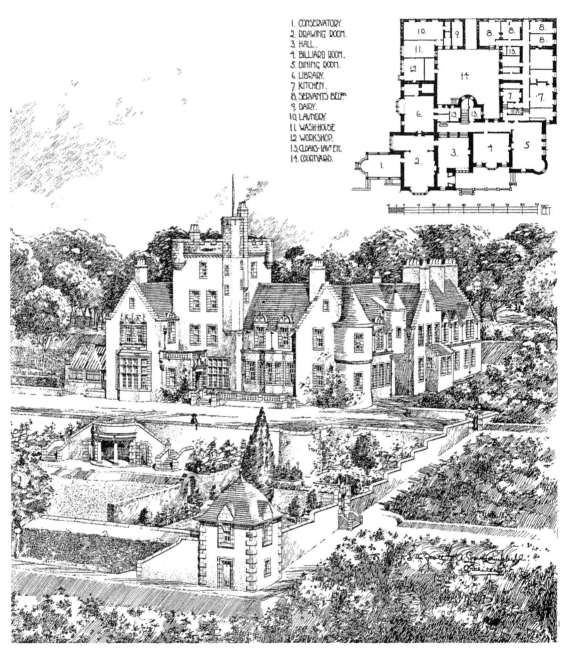

1. CONSERVATORY.
2. DRAWING ROOM.
3. HALL.
4. BILLIARD ROOM.
5. DINING ROOM.
6. LIBRARY.
7. KITCHEN.
8. SERVANTS BEDᵐ.
9. DAIRY.
10. LAVNDRY
11. WASH-HOUSE
12. WORKSHOP.
13. CLOAKS-LAVᵗ ETC
14. COURTYARD.

FIGURE 94

Grange, West Lothian, by John Nicol Scott and Alexander Lorne Campbell, 1904: project drawing
(Nicoll, *Domestic Architecture in Scotland*)

Fornethy in Angus, built in 1914–15 for the Misses Coats by the Largs partnership of Arthur John Fryers and Larmont Douglas Penman, was much grander in scale but even simpler, harled throughout with stonework only at the door-pieces, crow-steps and chimney copes. Although almost on the scale of Lorimer's largest houses, at the clients' own wish this very austere house rose straight from the heather, relying for its effect on skilful massing, clever fenestration and big stacks. Its interiors were plain neo-Georgian, with high quality late eighteenth-century chimneypieces that appear to have been retrieved from Dublin demolitions, only the bolection-moulded chimneypiece being made anew.

Very different from these later houses was Penchrise Peel, designed by the sometimes individualistic Hawick architect James Pearson Alison, born in 1862 and a pupil of Thornton Shiells. Built in 1908 for W Macfarlane Grieve as a harled early seventeenth century-style tower house and extended by a turreted wing in 1912, it was patently new and yet quite convincing in profile. It was unique at the time and is of particular interest now as anticipating the several essays in new-build tower house design of recent years. Experiments like Penchrise were rare, and although suburban villas with Scots Renaissance details were not altogether uncommon, in the city suburbs and in the fashionable golfing resorts English styles prevailed for the larger and more upmarket houses. A vernacular English Tudor from the pages of *Country Life* had a particular vogue amongst the Glasgow magnates who commuted from Ayrshire, James Miller's Kildonan, the grandest country house built in Scotland in the years before the First World War, being the supreme example.

Baronial nevertheless had a late flowering in government and municipal architecture. In 1912 the Office of Works architect William Thomas Oldrieve, a very English Baptist, proposed a great sixteenth century-style Scots Renaissance palace incorporating the fortifications of Archibald Elliot's Calton Prison as the Edinburgh headquarters of the Scottish Office. This exists now only in a dim photograph of a model made to demonstrate its scenic qualities, but the architecture he had in mind can be seen at Aberdeen's former General Post Office in Crown Street of 1907, for which the Aberdonian James Cumming Wyness was job architect, and that at Wick of 1912. In a similar vein was David Barclay's Watt Memorial School at Greenock of 1908, and the ashlar-faced keep that Alexander Nisbet Paterson built as Renfrew's police office in 1910. The finest of these late public buildings was the municipal offices at Stirling, the result of a competition assessed by Leiper in 1908 (Figure 95). It was won by John Gaff Gillespie of Salmon & Gillespie with a magnificent symmetrical Scots Renaissance design inspired by Falkland and Holyrood in its pre-Sir William Bruce form. An ageing workforce slowly built two thirds of it during the First World War but, sadly, the Second World War stalled its completion in 1939 and it survives only as a fragment of what it should have been, degraded by the loss of its cupola and the original slates.

In this chapter an attempt has been made to identify those who commissioned Baronial architecture rather than simply following its stylistic development from Playfair to Lorimer. As Anderson observed in his introductory appreciation to the 1901 reissue of Billings' *Antiquities*, the Baronial country houses built before 1860 owed their existence to a period of great agricultural prosperity. However, as a result of the steep decline in agricultural rents in the 1870s, those built after that date, particularly in the West of Scotland, were – as Stevenson commented in 1880 – more usually 'the mansions of rich modern merchants' who had bought up whatever estates were on the market, in order to establish themselves as country gentlemen. As we have seen, the clientele was in

FIGURE 95
Stirling Municipal Buildings by John Gaff Gillespie, designed 1908, built 1911–18
(© RCAHMS, SC 1224551)

fact considerably wider than that, and many of the houses were built from fortunes made in industry, in banking, in the law, or with money from overseas. But, as a building type, the Baronial house has survived less successfully than any other, whatever its original provenance. All too many of the finest houses discussed above either do not exist today or have been savagely reduced. Partly that is because of their sheer scale, designed for large numbers of guests after rail travel had made that possible, and unsustainable by the mid twentieth century; but it is also because they were increasingly seen, in Anderson's words, as 'sham castles' of negative aesthetic value, a view that persisted until the early 1970s and still has some adherents today. Anderson was, of course, looking at them from a different standpoint from the architects of Bryce's generation. They saw the Scots Renaissance as a rich architectural language, its revival no different in principle from that of the Italian Renaissance, and a lot closer to home.

Acknowledgements

The author of this chapter is deeply indebted to Dr David W Walker for his work on Peddie & Kinnear, research into clients, typing and proof-reading; and to Ian Gow for his research on Billings in the Blackwood archive at the National Library of Scotland.

CHAPTER FIVE

Castle Reoccupation and Conservation in the Twentieth Century

Diane Watters

Introduction

The Scottish castle since the First World War has been dominated by practical and ideological concepts of preservation and heritage control. In contrast, the decades prior to 1914 were characterised by imaginative castle restorations: an estimated eighteen larger Scottish castles were re-roofed and reoccupied as country houses between 1869 and the outbreak of war, to designs by leading architects such as J J Burnet, Sydney Mitchell and Lorimer.[1] Political and economic upheavals following WWI rendered aristocratic castle rebuilding almost obsolete, and no large architect-designed castle restorations were begun in the interwar years. Alongside this, ruinous and occupied castles came under increased scrutiny as ancient monuments designation and protection strengthened the state's controlling legislative role from 1913 onwards. The preservation principles gradually adopted Britain-wide were those advanced by the late nineteenth-century Society for the Preservation of Ancient Buildings (SPAB), with an anti-restoration, 'repair only' approach, and promotion of state guardianship.

Whilst a handful of ancient castles came under state guardianship pre-1914, in the interwar era protection was massively extended, and antiquarian interest flourished. The post-war period was marked by a boom in state grant-aided restoration of derelict and ruined tower houses from the late 1950s through to the 1980s. By the 1980s, the conservation lobby had positioned itself as a key player in built environment affairs, and following a proliferation of international conservation charters, increasingly high standards in conservation practice in the 1990s developed. The high emphasis of state policy on repair as opposed to restoration (policy implemented through the ancient monuments division) was to come into direct opposition with the ambitions of private owners, amidst an economic upturn, to restore derelict castles at the turn of the century.

This broad chapter provides a chronological overview of the shifting nature and structures of this preservation-dominated era of castles: a development reflecting the broader economic, political and cultural climate of twentieth-century Scotland. The overall structure is divided into three spheres of activity: state historic monument 'guardianship' based on the pioneering French monument model; the work of private architectural restorers; and, finally, the state co-ordinated planning protection of historic buildings. Chronologically, the development of these structures can be divided roughly into four time periods (although there is clearly some cross-over within these categories). First, there is the important prehistory of the 1900s up until the outbreak of war, characterised by a cluster of new protective legislation affecting the historic castle, and an architectural high point in castle restoration. Interwar, the focus of politicised preservation campaigning now fixed upon historic burghs threatened directly by municipal slum clearance, but scholarly interest in the castle in no way diminished during these economically stringent years. The nineteenth-century architectural antiquarian tradition of MacGibbon and Ross was pursued enthusiastically by a new generation of heritage-minded historians, and the meticulous state-sponsored research published through Royal Commission on the Ancient and Historical Monuments of Scotland (RCAHMS) *Inventories*.[2]

In the post-war period, the state control of historic buildings in private ownership strengthened with the introduction of 'listing' in 1947. There were now two heritage layers of development control (with often contradictory policies and ideologies) for private owners seeking to restore, reoccupy or demolish their castles, but generous state grants also became available to private restorers from 1954. Ruinous castles and tower houses now became the focus of preservation campaigning and, spurred on by the 1980s economic upturn, private owners could contemplate reoccupying castles and tower houses.[3]

This, at times, quite dramatic programme depended on a supportive ear within the government Scottish Development Department (SDD) Historic Buildings inspectorate, especially on the part of the Chief Inspector of Historic Buildings, David Walker. In the next chapter, he complements this overview account with a more focused recollection of the 1970s–80s boom in castle rebuilding, and the role of the SDD in supporting it. By the late 1980s, however, the stock of potential ruined tower houses for reoccupation was nearly depleted. The repositioning towards castle consolidation in the 1990s (supported by state

grants) in turn led to a turn-of-the-century heritage impasse. Castle and heritage experts debated ad infinitum the pros and cons of repair versus restoration approaches to castles, with both sides claiming their stance as the legitimate continuation of a Scottish traditional approach to ruins and castles. In 2001, at the beginning of a new century, the Historic Scotland policy document *The Conservation of Architectural Ancient Monuments in Scotland, Guidance on Principles* set down clearly and uncompromisingly the current state policy on conservation and the restoration of ancient monuments for reuse, the strong emphasis being on repair and consolidation.

Throughout its chronological run, this chapter will examine two key trends: first, the increasingly dominant legislation and heritage sector (including the guiding conservation theory, and castle scholarship), and second, the ever-decreasing building works and architecture. Up until the 1930s these two strands ran in parallel, but throughout the post-war period it became increasingly difficult to disentangle them, when architecture, as such, was clearly in retreat. Although state control dominated the twentieth century, its role shifted and varied from period to period. Preservation ideologies, although not to the fore in scholarly terms until later in the century, underpinned these trends. The repair and conservation versus restoration debate was a nineteenth-century one which rumbled on and on in the twentieth and twenty-first centuries. The current theoretical framework for conservation and restoration of historic castles, as we will see, was fundamentally constructed in the nineteenth century. To understand these ideologies, this chapter will also attempt to examine how that debate had an impact at different stages on castle preservation and restoration in the twentieth century.

Castles in Parallel: State Guardianship, Antiquarianism and Private Restorations, 1900–1914

In the years prior to the outbreak of WWI, two parallel trends affected the historic castle. A cluster of new protective legislation spread tentatively over medieval secular buildings, alongside related events, such as the formation of RCAHMS in 1908, which corresponded, on the other hand, with a new high in castle reoccupation. In turn, imaginative re-creations developed from a flurry of influential late nineteenth-century castle restorations.[4]

Protective legislation was introduced in the United Kingdom through the private bill of Sir John Lubbock. The 1882 Ancient Monuments Protection Act enabled ancient monuments to be purchased or gifted from willing private owners and transferred into the care of the state, which under the Commissioners of Works (in Scotland, the Boards of Trustees for Manufacturers in Scotland), would be maintained and cared for at the expense of the state.[5] Properties were detailed in a list. 'Guardianship' was entirely voluntary and respected the absolute rights of private property. The Scottish list of monuments, compiled by the Society of Antiquaries of Scotland, consisted of prehistoric sites that had lost their original function and were, of course, unoccupied, and its character reflected contemporary advances in archaeology. Monuments of like character could be added to the schedule, and brochs, standing stones and early Christian crosses were brought into guardianship following 1882. The leading archaeologist Augustus H L Pitt-Rivers was the first appointed Inspector of Ancient Monuments, and soon toured Scotland. These were tentative beginnings, and in comparison to other Western European trends, UK protective legislation was late and relatively weak. It was not until the Ancient Monuments Protection Acts of 1900 and 1913 that preservation of secular monuments, like medieval castles, crystallised into a characteristic type of protection that we can recognise today. A complex range of factors, with their origins in the eighteenth and nineteenth centuries, shaped the theoretical basis of this cluster of British legislation. Key to this development was the emerging late eighteenth-century antiquarianism, and the associated broader cultural concepts of Romanticism and the Picturesque. Old buildings, admired for their irregular appearance and patina of age in their own right, became an inspiration for new architecture. The founding of the Society of Antiquaries of Scotland in 1780, in reaction against 'demolition of ancient buildings and destruction of public archives and private documents', developed into serious nineteenth-century antiquarian recording, but the associational and visual Romantic antiquarianism of Walter Scott was equally as important in establishing the place of old buildings (often ruins) in their landscape.[6]

More central to state preservation was the emergence of a small number of pioneering and highly influential mid and late nineteenth-century English architects and polemicists, most notably A W N Pugin, John Ruskin and William Morris. In summary, these men put forward in their various works the ideal that old, essentially medieval ecclesiastical buildings were symbols of a past 'wholeness' that contrasted with the chaos and alienation of the post-Industrial Revolution modern world, and that old buildings were collective rather than individual property.[7] In 1849, Ruskin first put forward the idea that old buildings 'are not ours . . . They belong partly to those that built them, and partly to all the generations of mankind who are to follow us.'[8] These ideas were translated into preservation action, with a moral forcefulness, in 1877 with the founding of the SPAB by William Morris. SPAB argued that because old buildings were 'living pieces of history on which each succeeding generation had left its mark', and were bearers of meaning and knowledge of something lost in their modern world, the 'scrape' restoration of the type carried out by Georgian architects was to be abhorred.[9] For Ruskin, restoration was a lie and a destruction: 'The old building is destroyed, and that more totally and mercilessly than if it had sunk into a heap of dust, or melted into a mass of clay.' SPAB called for repair only and was nick-named 'anti-scrape'. The basic principles for British state preservation were in turn set: the concept of trusteeship or guardianship of a shared heritage; ancient monuments as documents to be read; and anti-scrape, repair-only practice. Amongst the first SPAB committee members was Sir John Lubbock. But these concepts would take some time to evolve, especially in Scotland.

In Scotland there was a long tradition of official repair work on ancient buildings, with works being carried out at Dunkeld Cathedral and St Rule's, St Andrews, in the late eighteenth century. The post-Reformation condition of a number of Scotland's ruined abbeys and cathedrals had become a state responsibility in the eighteenth and nineteenth centuries, and between 1827 and 1839 the Scottish Office of Works was established under architect Robert Reid, who was charged with maintenance of state-owned buildings.[10] The restraint practiced by Reid in a number of his ecclesiastical repairs, where he aimed to restore and not embellish the monuments under his charge, has been high-lighted as potentially progressive within an early nineteenth-century context. Whilst this may be the case, Reid's practices were not consistently restrained, particularly in schemes of the early 1800s. For example, when he oversaw the refacing of Edinburgh's historic Parliament House (1803–38), elements of the discarded 1630s sculpture was, thankfully, salvaged by Dundas of Arniston and Walter Scott.[11] The state's ownership respon-

sibility, and involvement in historic buildings, pre-dates the 1882 legislation, but Reid's work became a forerunner for the more methodical system of guardianship established. Numbered amongst these pre-1882 crown properties were, of course, the ruinous St Andrews Castle (in state ownership from 1870), Linlithgow Palace, and properties in military use, such as Edinburgh Castle (in ownership from 1871), and Blackness Castle, which came under monument guardian-ship in 1912.

It was not until the aftermath of the 1900 Act that preservation had an impact on the historic castle. The Act was still voluntary, and still concerned unoccupied structures, but extended the breadth of 'scheduling' to any monument of 'historic, traditional, or artistic interest'.[12] In that first decade, only two ruined secular buildings were scheduled and brought into guardianship: the sixteenth-century Scalloway Castle in Shet-land in 1908, and the multi-phase fifteenth- and late sixteenth-century Newark Castle, Port Glas-gow, in 1909 (Figure 96).

In 1882, the architect George Washington Browne published notes on Newark in the proceedings of the Society of Antiquaries urging a 'much-needed renovation'.[13] The impact of antiquarian scholarship on the development of preservation of castles was great. The force of anti-quarian studies of the castle had broken though with the major publication of MacGibbon and Ross' five-volume survey *The Castellated and Domestic Architecture of Scotland from the Twelfth to the Eighteenth Centuries* (1887–92). MacGibbon and Ross were the founders of modern 'castelol-logy' in Scotland, and the publications' influence on the preservation-dominated era of castles was immense. The antiquarian-recording tradition was further strengthened in 1908, with the estab-lishment of RCAHMS.[14] For the first time government recognition was given to the concerns and interest for both inhabited and

FIGURE 96

Newark Castle, Renfrewshire, photographed in the late nineteenth century (© Edinburgh Public Library, SC 1232916)

ruinous structures, and it further broadened monument scope with a pre-union 1707 cut-off date – although it wasn't until the 1947 Act that in-use buildings were given protection. RCAHMS was also entrusted to 'specify those which seem most worthy of preservation', but the 1913 Act, as we will see, superseded this role.

The parallel architect-cum-antiquarian strand of activity was led chiefly by architect Robert Rowand Anderson. He established the National Art Survey in 1893, and was the friend of the influential art historian G Baldwin-Brown, who campaigned for greater statutory preservation powers, and for the formation of RCAHMS.[15] It was through the work of Anderson that SPAB principles gradually began to influence the archi-

tectural treatments of old buildings in Scotland. In the 1901 new edition of R W Billings' *Baronial & Ecclesiastical Antiquities of Scotland*, Anderson wrote an appreciation attacking the Baronial 'sham castles'. One of his earliest works was the rebuilding of the late fifteenth-century Broughty Castle as a coastal defensive fort in 1860–1. His intervention was far from SPAB-compliant, and highlighted Anderson's pragmatic approach. Roofless from the mid eighteenth century, Anderson cleared away all original enclosures surrounding the castle, transformed the tower by adding another tower to the angle, and added a small courtyard with a single-storey range of offices to the west. Broughty initially came into state guardianship in 1935, but it was under mili-

FIGURE 97
Threave, Kirkcudbrightshire: photographed in 1923 (© RCAHMS, SC 1197025)

tary control until 1946. The development and adaptation of Broughty Castle reflected the changing defence requirements in the first half of the twentieth century.[16] Anderson also carried out the influential restoration of Dunblane Cathedral nave in 1889–93, but this was not characterised by SPAB restraint. The most notable architect–restorers of the late nineteenth and early twentieth centuries – Robert S Lorimer, R Weir Schultz, George Mackie Watson, and George Washington Browne – were all closely related to Anderson, and were based in the east. In the west, John Honeyman and Peter Macgregor Chalmers led the way.

In terms of state preservation activity, over twenty monuments were brought into guardianship in 1911–13, and eight of these were historic castles. In retrospect, the selection doesn't appear to have been guided by firm criteria. Outwith the crown properties of Stirling and Dumbarton castles, those brought into state care were chiefly fifteenth- and sixteenth-century castles in the Galloway & Kircudbrightshire area, including MacLellan's Castle and Carsluith Castle. But in 1913, two monuments of perceived national significance, Threave (Figure 97) and the thirteenth-century Urquhart, were included in the schedule and brought into guardianship. This increasing focus on secular monuments has been attributed to the appointment in 1910 of the English Commissioners of Works' Inspector of Ancient Monuments, Charles Peers, regarded as the pioneer of the analytical method in architectural history, who became Chief Inspector in 1913. The focus on Galloway & Kirkudbrightshire was possibly linked to the new research by

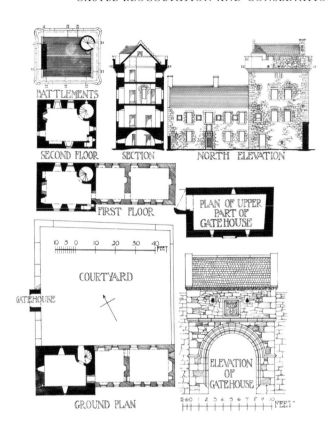

FIGURE 98

Hills Castle (Hills Tower), Kirkcudbrightshire:
*Inventory of Monuments and Constructions in
Galloway, Vol. II: County of the Stewartry of
Kirkcudbright* (1914), p.174 (© RCAHMS
SC 1233937)

RCAHMS for the two *Inventories* covering those areas in 1912 and 1914 (Figure 98) – although by the time of publication, Threave was already in guardianship. Peers established a new works organisation to deal with guardianship monuments, and in Scotland responsibility lay with the architect J Wilson Paterson, who joined the Office of Works in 1909 as Assistant Architect, and became Chief Architect in 1913.

So, increasing home-grown and state-supported antiquarianism in the first decade of the century, amidst growing pressure from influential individuals to widen and strengthen protective legislation, and the push for more not less state intervention, led to the important 1913 Act. The voluntary nature of existing legislation was toughened up. A system of advance notification and, in the case of local authority-funded works,

pre-approval of proposed works or demolition to a 'scheduled monument' were put into place, and lists of schedules were to be published. Ancient Monuments Boards for each country were to be established to oversee the work of the Ancient Monuments inspectors, who were now able to give advice. For some, the legislation was too restrictive: it still concerned only unoccupied buildings, and excluded churches. However, this Act remained the foundation of ancient monument legislation until 1979. The functions of the new Act clearly duplicated those of RCAHMS, which effectively withdrew from its preservation role to concentrate on the antiquarian research and survey side of its work.

The Scottish section of the first Inspector of Monuments' report following the 1913 Act, authored by J Wilson Paterson, was not a riveting read. The report on the works carried out at Huntingtower Castle, Perthshire (remodelled in the seventeenth century, but consisting chiefly of two linked late-medieval tower houses), typically focused on fabric details, not the overarching conservation approach: 'In the east tower the chimney heads were very loose, and the cope-stones were therefore lifted and rebedded, the joints raked out and repointed in Arden lime mortar, and the whole grouted, the flues being first packed with sawdust to prevent waste grout.' (Figure 99) Under the direction of the Office of Works, the wooden ceiling of the first floor hall early sixteenth-century decoration was restored in 1913 and the 1930s, but in the search for early painted schemes seventeenth-century panelling was stripped out.[17] But, in the instructions to the foremen in charge of works at the end of the 1913 report, detailed by Wilson's equivalent in England, repair-only SPAB principles were encapsulated:

> The foreman must understand quite clearly that the work carried out upon the ancient buildings in charge of the board is to be that of preservation only . . . Pulling down any part of original work, or restoration as commonly understood will only be permitted upon the personal instructions of the Architect in charge, in those cases where the safety of the building absolutely demands such treatment. And although the new work shall in all cases be designed so as to be in harmony with the old work, no attempt should be made to give it the appearance of other than modern origin.[18]

Free from state preservation control were the patron- and architect-led castle reoccupations, re-creations and restorations that began in earnest

around 1900 – some embedded in the architectural pursuit of a perceived national essence.[19] Architecturally, the years around 1890 were dominated, particularly in the east, by prominent traditionalist-inspired architects and the Arts and Crafts preoccupation with the elite home. In rural Scotland the historic castle was central to national perceptions of tradition. Scottish rubble, and the late nineteenth-century revival of harl, was brought to the fore most notably by Lorimer, who developed his own individualistic and imaginative 'Scotch' style.[20]

Diversity and inconsistency characterised the castle projects until the outbreak of war. Some turn-of-the-century schemes anticipated the SPAB-inspired small post-war restorations. The early seventeenth-century L-plan Barcaldine Castle, Argyll, was re-roofed in 1897–1911 by Alexander Butter and, crucially, accommodation was limited to what could fit within the existing walls (Figure 100). At Wester Kames, architect Weir Schultz restored the ruinous tower (less than half of it survived) for the 3rd marquess of Bute in 1897–1902 (Figures 101 and 102). Schultz speculated on what had been there, a line of red tile-work distinguishing the new from the rebuilt old. Neither of these schemes attempted to reinstate the original interior. One particular scheme at Barra Castle, Aberdeenshire, attracted the praise of the English SPAB-oriented heritage press. The castle was 'judiciously repaired' inside and out by George Bennett Mitchell in 1909–11. Following restoration in 1912, Lawrence Weaver, architectural editor of *Country Life*, claimed: 'So many Scottish castles have suffered havoc beyond repair at the hands of careless or ignorant 'restorers' that it is the more pleasant to emphasise a case where one has been made fit for modern life without any loss of its historical quality.'[21]

Lorimer's late nineteenth- and early twentieth-century restorations typically aimed for modern comfort and were, on the whole, less

FIGURE 99
Huntingtower Castle, Perthshire: photographed in 1966 (© RCAHMS, SC 1233863)

mindful of previous functions or planning. The Picturesque restoration of Dunderave, Argyll, 1911–21, also added a range of new buildings to provide twentieth-century home comforts; and adopted domestic detailing, such as its casement windows, were not generally accepted as indigenous Scottish forms.[22] In 1929, following Lorimer's death, Leslie Grahame Thomson outlined Lorimer's 'idea' for Dunderave: "'Let the old building stand out and tell its own story" and the additions, whilst carried out with similar materials and detail to the old work and so generally harmonising with it, stand confessed as the work of a different age.'[23] The restoration of the decayed Kellie Castle in 1878, carried out by John Currie of Elie for Professor James Lorimer, Lorimer's father – may have inspired Lorimer's

own restoration at Earlshall in the 1890s, when reinstatement of original interiors was attempted. But Lorimer apparently grew impatient of the 'demure quietness' of his own earlier, more restrained (including cash-restrained) castle restorations.[24]

But two other reoccupations marked the highpoint in castle restoration pre-1914. The thirteenth- and fourteenth-century Duart Castle was restored by J J Burnet, 1911–16, on lines suggested by MacGibbon and Ross, and by mid eighteenth-century Board of Ordnance views. Alfred Lightly MacGibbon (David MacGibbon's son) gave advice on behalf of RCAHMS when it was still able to carry out that role. Duart had been bought back by Sir Fitzroy Donald MacLean with the intention of restoring it as the

FIGURE 100
Left. Barcaldine, Argyll: view from south-east photographed in 1969 (© RCAHMS, SC 71504)

FIGURE 101
Above. Wester Kames, Buteshire: photographed in 1895 (© A B Waters, SC 1232918)

FIGURE 102
Opposite. Wester Kames, Buteshire: photographed in 1905 (© A B Waters, SC 1232917)

house of the Clan MacLean. This act was part of a growing late nineteenth-century fashion in neo-Celticism, which promoted clan heritage. In the 1854 MacLean clan history, historian the Rev. John Mackechnie says: 'Night had fallen on the House of Duart, and the dawn did not come till in our own day the castle was restored by Sir Fitzroy Maclean, who took procession of it and made it his home.'[25] From 1913 to 1932 Eilean Donan was rebuilt from a ruined stump by George Mackie Watson for Colonel Macrae Gilstrap, and exemplified the exuberant individualism of castle patrons in this era.

The restoration of the fire-damaged and unoccupied Dean Castle, Kilmarnock as a monument rather than a comfortable home introduced another imaginative layer to the diverse, early twentieth-century Castle Culture (Figures 103 and 104). The ambitious long-drawn-out (almost forty years) restoration initiated by the 8th Lord Howard de Walden entailed the rebuilding of the fourteenth- and early fifteenth-century tower, and the fifteenth-century palace block and courtyard range. It began in 1905 under the architectural direction of Ingram & Brown and was continued, from the mid 1930s, by J S Richardson, Inspector of Ancient Monuments, and senior partner in Richardson & McKay. He was responsible for the new sixteenth century-style gatehouse (1935–6) and timber fighting platform on the courtyard block. Historian David Walker thought that it 'came near to being the Scottish Pierrefonds'. Lord Howard lived in the adjoining nineteenth-century Dower House, and entertained in the

FIGURE 103
Dean Castle, Ayrshire: photographed in 1881 (© South Ayrshire Libraries, SC 1232920)

restored palace. In 1975, the family generously donated the castle and its medieval cultural collections to the town of Kilmarnock.[26]

Castle as Monument:
The Interwar Expansion of Preservation

Following the First World War, significant aristocratic castle restoration became almost obsolete. From the 1870s onwards, country estates came under severe economic pressure, and with the up-

ending of the old social order post-1914, the role of the private owner–restorer faded to vanishing point. Economic pressures slashed the number of stonemasons from 10,000 in 1914 to virtually none in 1939.[27] Now fewer tower houses were kept in repair by landowning estates – a common practice pre-1914 – and the consolidation of ruins was probably viewed as economically unviable. Tower houses were viewed as no longer suitable for modern living, and between the wars few restorations took place, and only modest additions were attempted. The last of Lorimer's MacGib-

FIGURE 104
Dean Castle, Ayrshire: view of wing from south, photographed in the 1960s (© RCAHMS, SC 1232894)

bon and Ross-inspired restorations was the seven-teenth-century Balmanno, Perthshire (1916–21) (Figure 105), and a few proposed schemes fell by the wayside.

A new generation of architect–restorers emerged, despite inactivity in built work. Fore-most amongst these was Ian Lindsay, whose restoration of the sixteenth-century tower of Aldie Castle, Perthshire, was begun just before that war but not completed until 1957. The plight of Aldie was reported by architectural writer George Scott-Moncrieff in his 1938 *Stones of Scot-* *land*: 'Perfectly situated on the edge of the Cleish hills . . . well within living memory it was intact, and even now it could be turned into the most delightful modern home.'[28] It was subsequently bought by Hope Dixon, who commissioned Lindsay, a contributor to the 1938 book. Aldie set a new standard for post-war work; it retained its original form and was not augmented by new accommodation. In the mid 1990s David Walker hailed it as 'the most respectful restoration ever done and remains exemplary even today'.[29] Birse Castle, Aberdeenshire, restored by George

Bennett Mitchell in 1905–7, had a three-storey east wing added and fenestration reinstated in 1930 to designs by the historian–architect Dr William Kelly.

Historic castles and tower houses increasingly became a state concern in the interwar era. Pressure mounted to increase the role of the state and local authorities in the preservation of the broader built environment. Amidst a background of growing public acceptance of the state's increasing role in architecture and homebuilding in the 1920s, campaigning to expand preservation beyond the narrow confines of unoccupied ancient monuments began in earnest.

The focus of politicised preservation campaigning now fixed upon the 'humble' historic burgh houses threatened directly by municipal slum clearance under the 1930 and 1935 Housing Acts.[30] A vocal and influential group of private individuals, led by the powerful 4th marquess of Bute, launched a 'national crusade' to 'save' these threatened houses. The general preservationist aims of almost all of these voluntary organisations and projects, with their frequently overlapping personalities, were diverse, but at their core was the notion that the 'humble' historic burgh houses could symbolise the organic community embracing all Scots, 'rich and poor alike'.[31] And like the romantic late nineteenth-century vision of 'Old Edinburgh' and the civic reformism of Patrick Geddes, these voluntary organisations were concerned with public amenity values rather than narrower fabric SPAB-inspired concerns. These initiatives included the formation of the Council for the Preservation of Rural Scotland in 1927 (CPRS, driven by the planner–architect Frank Mears, Geddes' son-in-law who carried out early urban restorations at

FIGURE 105
Opposite. Balmanno Castle, Perthshire: photographed in 1961 (© Scottish Field, SC 1232913)

Huntly House, 1927–32, and Gladstone's Land, Edinburgh, 1934–6). The founding of the National Trust for Scotland (NTS) in 1931 was a direct result of lobbying by the CPRS, Sir John Stirling Maxwell and Mears, and heralded the beginning of the pioneering Little Houses scheme at Culross. The first property gifted to NTS was Stirling Maxwell's Crookston Castle in 1931. The publication of the 1936 pamphlet *A Plea for Scotland's Architectural Heritage*, by Bute, and the compilation of a basic inventory of old burgh houses, carried out at Bute's instigation by Ian Lindsay in 1937–9, marked a turning point in the campaign. Lindsay, an architect, historian and preservation campaigner, was a leading figure in the 1930s. The formation of the state-funded Scottish National Buildings Record (SNBR) in 1941, with Bute as chairman and George Scott-Moncrieff as secretary until 1945, anticipated greater state control in the post-war period. The SNBR aimed, amongst other things, to 'record the modest homes of the people', and Bute tried but failed to link it to his preservation cause. It remained, like RCAHMS, independent from preservation concerns, and in 1966 the two organisations merged.[32]

In parallel with this broader ideological inter-war preservation movement, ancient monument protection was massively extended. The war may have interrupted the momentum of guardianship and scheduling, but the interwar economic and political climate proved highly advantageous for its expansion. Just over 100 buildings and sites were brought into state guardianship in the 1920s and 1930s, one quarter of these being historic castles. These included: Tantallon in 1924; Huntly in 1925 (Figure 106); Claypotts and Crichton in 1926; Hermitage in 1930; Carnasserie in 1932; Castle Sween in 1933; Bothwell Castle in 1935; and Lochleven in 1939. The mid 1930s were peak years for guardianship. Anticipating its post-war boom, scheduling for the first time expanded

FIGURE 106
Huntly Castle, Aberdeenshire: photographed by George Washington Wilson in the late nineteenth century
(© RCAHMS, SC 1232949)

beyond the confines of guardianship, and over 115 castles were added to the schedule in the interwar years. The 1931 Ancient Monuments Act strengthened the 1913 Act, by requiring that a minimum of three months' notice of any works to a scheduled monument in private ownership be given to the government department responsible – the Office of Works. J S Richardson, former pupil of Lorimer, became a part-time Inspector of Ancient Monuments in 1914, and by 1920 he was working full-time, whilst also lecturing in architectural history at Edinburgh College of Art. Consolidation and repair, as detailed in the 1913 report, continued along similar lines, but now at an increased pace. This appears to have formed the bulk of Office of Works activity. In his populist, preservation-slanted publication *Shrines and Homes of Scotland* (1937), John Stirling Maxwell, former chairman of the Ancient Monuments Board, heaped praise on Richardson's office, claiming that it was 'wholly admirable and that its staff has brought the technique of strengthening and preserving old masonry to the level of a fine art . . . nowhere so well or with so firm a grasp of the fact that a copy is not the same thing as an authentic document'.[33]

The major programme of works at Blackness Castle, West Lothian, during 1926–35 illustrates that a pragmatic, architect-led, rather than ideologically restrictive, approach to preservation was adopted in the interwar years. Works at Blackness went beyond the simple 'repair-only' model. The multi-phase castle had fabric dating back to the fifteenth century, but it was chiefly sixteenth- and seventeenth-century in form. In 1870–4, the War Office had altered the castle's superstructure of three towers, covered the courtyard with concrete and iron roof, and built new barracks, in order to use it as a central ammunition depot. Following WWI, the Office of Works (under Richardson) undertook restoration: most of the late nineteenth-century fabric was cleared away and, most notably, the upper part of the central prison tower was rebuilt and castellated. Because the castle was in military use in the late nineteenth century, it had not been surveyed by MacGibbon and Ross, so an authoritative template for conservation was not available. In the early 1980s (amidst the strengthening repair-only policies on ancient monuments) Iain McIvor, then Chief Inspector of Ancient Monuments, criticised the imprecise nature of Richardson's earlier work: 'The upper parts of the tower were rebuilt to something resembling their ancient form.'[34]

Richardson was also central to debatably the most significant architectural project of the interwar years: Lorimer's Scottish National War Memorial at Edinburgh Castle of 1924–7. The 'great controversy' of the war memorial stretched over four years from 1919 to 1923. It highlights the fact that the state approach to monuments in use (as distinct from unoccupied), was still fundamentally fluid but starting to become more stringent. Richardson, who possibly had some score to settle with Lorimer, was at the forefront of the building-related objections to the initial schemes, which involved the demolition of the eighteenth-century barrack blocks (reconstructed by the antiquarian–architect Billings in 1863). The Office of Works won through: it did not object to the demolition of the Billings building itself, but insisted that the replacement must adhere in bulk and silhouette to the existing structure. Richardson forced Lorimer to construct scaffolding to illustrate the height and bulk of the proposed shrine. The Office of Works argument was similar to the general amenity campaigns led by other interwar preservation campaigners, and did not reflect the fabric concerns promoted by SPAB.[35]

Integral to the development of ancient monuments in state protection, and the growth of scheduling, was the continued scholarly and antiquarian interest in the historic castle. The late nineteenth-century antiquarian survey tradition of MacGibbon and Ross, published at the height of late Victorian eclectic revivalism in Scotland, was carried forward by a new generation of historians and the RCAHMS *Inventories* – most notably, the work of William Douglas Simpson and William Mackay Mackenzie. Distinct from the more general preservation-oriented 1930s books on Scottish architecture that prominently featured castles, such as Stirling Maxwell's 1937 *Shrines and Homes of Scotland* ('a handy book on Scottish architecture'), a new wave of state-sponsored research and survey came to dominate scholarly castle publication from the interwar period onwards. This dominance was really only challenged in the early to late 1980s with the decision to abandon the traditional RCAHMS *Inventories*, the emergence of a new wave of independent, revisionist castle scholars, and more preservation-focused work on tower houses.

In the interwar era, the ongoing historicising impact of MacGibbon and Ross was also strengthened by the absence of a Scottish critical architectural press, and the effect was felt well into the twentieth century. A new generation of castle scholars developed the traditional interpretation

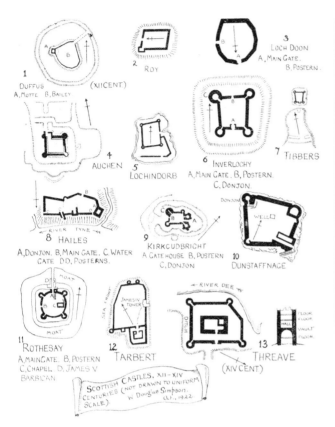

from the South

FIGURE 107
Above left. 'Scottish Castles, XII–XIV Centuries',
drawing by W D Simpson dated October 1922,
from *The Scottish Castle* (1924), p.10

FIGURE 108
Above right. Craigievar Castle, Aberdeenshire:
illustration by George Mackie from *Craigievar
Castle*, the National Trust for Scotland guidebook
to the property written by W D Simpson, p.16
(© NTS and George Mackie)

FIGURE 109
Opposite. Portrait of William Mackay Mackenzie by
J Cowie (© RCAHMS, SC 1233806)

of the Scottish castle and fortified house, which
held that these were products of a society where
defence and security was paramount, and that
their evolution depended on their military functions. The decline in the later Middle Ages was
linked to the type's inability to adapt to gunpowder artillery. W D Simpson, an Aberdonian and
prolific castle scholar, was the key proponent of
the interpretation of castles as defence structures
from the 1920s onwards. According to historian
Geoffrey Stell, Simpson was a product of post-
WWI military consciousness in British society.[36]
Simpson left a legacy of over 400 publications and
had a significant bearing on the post-war understanding of the castle. He began publishing in
1919, with detailed accounts of individual castle
histories, and developing a regional analysis of
castle history. In 1924, he published his first

national overview, *The Scottish Castle*: an illustrated leaflet that charted castles from the 'earliest military structure' to the early seventeenth century when 'all defensive features had been dropped . . . and the laird's house was now a castle only in name' (Figure 107). Simpson wrote many of the state guardianship castle guides from the 1940s onwards (Figure 108), and co-authored the general survey of buildings and sites in care of the Ministry of Works in 1952.[37] In 1954, he became the first chairman of the reconfigured Ancient Monuments Board. Simpson was enormously influential and attracted many defence devotees (see below).

Simpson's contemporary, Cromarty-born William Mackay Mackenzie, was the exception to the defence-evolved castle rule, and he was amongst the first to emphasise the domestic influence on castle design (Figure 109). Secretary of RCAHMS from 1913–35, he edited the *Inventories* series, in particular the volume covering the Outer Hebrides, Skye and the Small Islands in 1928. He wrote *The Medieval Castle in Scotland* in 1928. The topographical survey approach was adopted by the independent novelist and castle historian Nigel Tranter in his 1934 *The Fortalices and Early Mansions of Southern Scotland*, which contained a foreword by Mackay Mackenzie praising his exploration of castles' 'intimate relation with social life that makes these houses so instructive historically'. But there were clearly divisions between the two state-supported publishing strands. John Dunbar's history of RCAHMS explains that, in the interwar period, the relationship between the Office of Works and RCAHMS became strained: there were 'skirmishes' between Mackay Mackenzie and Wilson Paterson and Richardson over the sharing of research. Compounded by the effective cutting-off of the advisory role of RCAHMS through the 1913 Act, a 'legacy of mistrust' between the two bodies embedded itself.[38]

Fragmented Castle Ideologies: Tower House Revival and Government Control: 1945–2000

Between 1945 and 2000 a series of parallel preservation, restoration and academic activities developed in distinctive ways. The overriding trend was towards more state and local authority control, and by the end of this period the conservation movement held a key role in built environment affairs at a local and national level. Although there were significant shifts in the approach to castle and tower house restorations (privately owned and, to a lesser extent, public works), it was the time-honoured conservation ideology of 'repair-only' and the consolidation of ruins that dominated state control of ancient monuments from the late 1980s onwards. Castle architecture and building and conservation control had of course existed in parallel up until the 1930s, but throughout the post-war period architecture as such was firmly in retreat, with only a few rare examples of new castle building beginning amidst a Postmodern historicist revival in the late 1980s. Developments in state preservation and control in relation to ancient castles and tower houses dominated. Whilst the post-war period was marked by a boom in state grant-aided restoration of threatened derelict and ruined tower houses from the late 1950s through to the 1980s, guardianship was halted and the scope of scheduled monuments greatly expanded from the 1970s onwards. Within the related field of castle studies, the field was still dominated in the 1960s and 1970s by state employees who were archaeologists, but a new generation of 'Castle Revisionists', from an architectural and historical background, challenged this dominance from the late 1980s onwards.

It was the shifting legislative context that drove the two heritage-focused trends. The early post-war period marked a watershed in the protection of historic buildings in general. A comprehensive system for protection was introduced under a succession of Town and Country Planning Acts from 1945 onwards, which strengthened control of historic buildings in private ownership with the introduction of exhaustive 'listing' in 1947 – overseen then by Ian Lindsay within the Scottish Department of Health. This legislation contrasted with that of monument guardianship and scheduling because its scope was extensive: the lists (made statutory in 1968, and coming into force in 1971) covered all buildings of given standards of significance. These methods were ultimately founded on the systematic recording of RCAHMS, though it was not invited to undertake the task. The cumbersome guardianship procedures were simply sidestepped by making owners of protected buildings (listed or scheduled) rather than the state responsible for the financial consequences of repair or restoration. There were now two levels of heritage control for private owners seeking to restore, reoccupy or demolish their homes: scheduled monuments and listed buildings, and these often, as we will see, had contradictory policies.

Initially, the thrust of ancient monument activity continued along similar lines to that in the interwar era. Guardianship continued apace in the 1950s: Castle Campbell and Smailholm Tower were brought into guardianship in 1950, and the fifteenth-century Kilchurn in 1953. Because skilled masons were difficult to find, post-war consolidation works were costlier and slower. New post-war legislation highlighted the fact that the state wanted preservation solutions that did not rely so heavily on the public purse. The Ancient Monuments Board in 1954, aware of increasing financial constraints, argued that in Scotland there was 'room for considerable expansion' of guardianship, insisting that guardianship for monuments should not be declined on economic grounds.[39] It drew up a list of primary monuments – twenty secular and seven ecclesiastical – and strongly recommended that guardianship should cover 'all castles which ante-date the Wars of Independence and of which there are substantial remains worthy of preservation'. But only three castles (including Dunstaffnage in 1962) came under guardianship in the 1960s, and between 1960 and 2000 only a handful of castles were taken into guardianship, including Doune in 1984. But by the 1960s, the guardianship estate in terms of castles was very strong, with over sixty castles. Crucially, guardianship expanded its scope in the late 1970s to include industrial and vernacular monument types, and by the early 1980s, 328 monuments were in guardianship; a significantly large number of monuments were in state care in comparison to England and Wales.

Post-war scheduling, on the other hand, started slowly but was greatly expanded from the

1970s onwards. In the 1950s the Ancient Monuments Board reported that no longer was 'a casual word sufficient to persuade an owner of a scheduled monument to spend money on its repair'. It was through the Ancient Monuments and Archaeological Areas Act of 1979 that the control of scheduling was strengthened. Unlike listed buildings, which always had a great measure of delegation to local authority level, scheduled monument consent was received through the unified Ancient Monuments and Historic Buildings division of the Scottish Development Department, which in turn became Historic Scotland (HS) in 1991. The professional and legislative distinctions between the ancient monuments and historic buildings divisions were retained under HS.

The most significant post-war development in castle and tower house restoration came with the Historic Buildings and Ancient Monuments Act of 1953. Generous state grants became available to private restorers for repair and maintenance through the newly formed Historic Buildings Council for Scotland (HBC). Whereas the impetus behind the formation of a state grant system had been growing concern over the scale of country house demolition in the post-war period, the fate of Scotland's sixteenth- and seventeenth-century tower houses was directly affected by this piece of legislation, as was the future health of Scotland's urban and ecclesiastical architecture. The Gowers Committee, and the 1950 *Report of the Committee on Houses of Outstanding Historic or Architectural Interest*, overwhelmingly focused on English country houses and drew on aristocratic and academic views to promote urgent preservation. 'The English country house is the greatest contribution made by England to the visual arts,' the report said; and it remained as such – 'a living element in the social fabric of the nation, uniting visibly the present and national history'.[40]

As a result of this British legislation, the Historic Buildings Council for Scotland was established in 1953 as an independent advisory body to the Minister of Works and Secretary of State for Scotland. When founded, it included amongst its eight members architects Ian Lindsay and Robert Matthew, as well as 'assessors' Stewart Cruden from the Ministry of Works and D M MacPhail, from the Department of Health, representing the Secretary of State's interests (Figure 110).[41] Despite its focus on the country house, this legislation heralded a revival in tower house restoration. David Walker, who had joined the Department of Health in 1961, worked with Lindsay, and became principal investigator from 1976 (the post had lain open since Ian Lindsay's death), and in turn became the HBC's advisor from 1978. Walker remained the main government expert representative until he retired in 1993.[42] He later claimed that prior to the grant-aid system of listed buildings, 'it seemed inevitable that a very high proportion of the finest Scottish houses of the fifteenth, sixteenth and seventeenth centuries would be lost'. He legitimised the post-war restoration of tower houses as gentlemen's residences, and claimed it as a late nineteenth- and early twentieth-century tradition that had only in 'recent' times lapsed.[43] (Figure 111) From the late 1950s to the early 1990s, HBC's grant-aiding brought about over seventy tower house restorations. As we will see, this more than matched the number of castles brought into guardianship during the entire twentieth century.[44]

But, prior to the implementation of this historic buildings grant aid, some early important post-war tower house restoration had begun. As outlined, by the late nineteenth century those tall towers that had not been incorporated into larger houses were either roofless or falling out of use as farm servants' accommodation. On the whole, tower houses were not subjected to the same

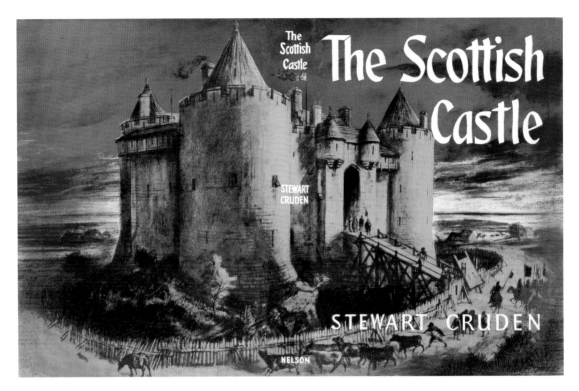

threats and pressures as country houses in the interwar and post-war eras, but there had been some demolitions. David Walker later recalled that the demolition of the fifteenth-century Elphinstone tower in early 1960s 'concentrated the mind' of the preservationist campaigner.[45] In the early 1950s, two events had an impact on tower house restoration and marked a turning point: Oliver Hill's lavishly illustrated *Scottish Castles* (1953); and the trend-setting 'modest restoration' of Castle of Mey.[47] Restoration of the mid sixteenth- to nineteenth-century Castle of Mey for the Queen Mother was carried out in 1952 by local architect Sinclair Macdonald, with J S Richardson being consulted. A spate of romantically led restorations followed 'in the Queen mother's footsteps by private individuals'. The two-part *Country Life* articles of 1974 by Walker & Rowan focused on the appeal of the tower house for restorers, with the 'gentry retrenching to an historic but manageable property and pruning properties back to earlier origins'.[47] Amongst these restorers were Scots returning from exile, and Americans falling 'under the spell of most seductive building types'. Throughout the disparate published and unpublished accounts of this post-war era of tower house restoration, an underlying distinction between the families who originally built the houses carrying out restoration, and those who purchased with the aim of restoring, can be identified. This undercurrent

identifies the fact that established aristocratic owners appear to have had more noble intentions in terms of conservation approach than newcomers, but this area of castle historiography has not yet been examined in detail.

But it was not until the late 1950s that the groundbreaking reclamation of derelict and ruined tower houses really got under way. The HBC accepted the principle of grant-aiding the restoration of roofless castles as early as 1958. In the 1970s, twenty-five castle properties received grants. Its peak period was the decade between the mid 1970s and mid 1980s, when two thirds of tower house restorations nationwide were funded by HBC grants.[48] Given the scale of this programme lasting over forty years, it is difficult to summarise its key aims and objectives, as well as its governing restoration policy, but at its core was a pragmatic approach to save and repair a declining stock of tower houses. Unlike the historic and set ideologies of the guardianship and scheduling policies, the nature of post-war tower house restoration appears to have shifted in reaction to developing external conservation forces and, ultimately, targeted professional criticism of its work.

Structurally, the programme developed in roughly five stages. The early grants of the 1950s reflected a public amenity ethos, such as Menstrie, which was restored partly as a museum and social housing in 1957; and Merchiston, Edinburgh, which received grants in 1958 and 1961, and was incorporated into the modern Napier College (Figures 112 and 113). By the second phase in the 1960s, it was characteristically aristocratic and landed families, who had originally built the houses, who received grant aid: such as the two restoration schemes by the Aberdeenshire architect John Lamb at mid sixteenth-century Abergeldie in 1963 and 1969–70; and Drumminor in 1958, which started off as a Lindsay project but was completed for the Forbes Sempill family under

FIGURE 110

Opposite top. Front cover of Stewart Cruden's *The Scottish Castle* (1960); the cover was based on a conjectural restoration drawing of Dirleton Castle, East Lothian, which was made by Alan Sorrell for the Ministry of Works (© HMSO)

FIGURE 111

Opposite bottom. Castle Menzies, Perthshire, view from south-east photographed in 2003 (© RCAHMS, SC 1232909)

another architect's supervision. By the 1970s, the third phase, private non-aristocratic reoccupation and restoration, dominated demand. Saddell, Argyll, was grant-aided in 1975, and was the first Scottish project for the Landmark Trust, by architect Stewart Tod. The restoration of the long-unoccupied castle was undertaken by the clan society in the first half of the 1970s, and the largest grant awarded to date was given to restore Rossend, Burntisland, in 1976 amidst a backdrop of late 1970s' rising building costs.

By the early 1980s, as the programme entered its fourth phase, the wider conservation climate was changing. From its inception until the mid 1980s, the ideological and fabric approach to tower house restoration had been pragmatic, and shifted over time, but there was an increasing awareness of improvements in conservation and antiquarian standards from the late 1970s under the direction of David Walker and his colleagues. Difficult fabric compromises were made, in order to keep costs low, and state funding was kept to a minimum. With the benefit of hindsight, of course, many of the projects simply didn't conform to current conservation practices. Up until the late 1980s, conservation and fabric approach focused on four key areas. First, the decision had to be made whether the tower was complete enough for restoration to be a viable option. Kisimul in Barra was the first roofless grant case in 1958, and although it was fairly complete to the wallheads, its fabric restoration, even at that early stage, was seen as crude. In the late 1970s, the late sixteenth-century Z-plan Pitfichie Castle, whose north-east back wall had collapsed in 1936, was not judged as 'too far gone'. W D Simpson had made a detailed recording of the castle and fallen masonry beginning in the 1920s, and subsequently it was grant-aided in 1977–8.[49] This 'brave decision' was inspired by the 1971 restoration of the ruinous Inchdrewer Castle, whose courtyard was filled with fallen

masonry by the mid 1960s. It was one of a small number of influential tower house and castle restorations carried out without grant aid, and Inchdrewer was rebuilt with carefully matched rubble. At Pitfichie, blockwork was used for reasons of cost.

Second, archaeological and documentary evidence was the ideal basis for proposed restoration, and MacGibbon and Ross' work was the key historical source. From the 1970s onwards conjectural restoration was kept to a bare minimum if documentary evidence could not be found: for example, at the ambitious restoration of Fawside from 1978 to 1985, where the parapets were left plain because the original form was not known. The ancient monuments inspectors were in essence against conjectural restoration from the beginning, but it was not until the grant-aiding of Fawside that it 'became an issue'.[50] Third, the removal of later additions to historic towers was common in the 1960s and 1970s, primarily to reduce the scale and cost of the restoration work. The grant-aided restoration of the 1594 tower house at Kinkell in 1969–70 involved the demolition of an eighteenth-century wing to cut costs. These schemes set some sort of precedent, according to David Walker, and were followed by the restoration of the roofless Balgonie (1973–4) and Rusco (1974–9), but the later houses were left as roofless shells. In the 1990s, Walker recognised that these pragmatic decisions 'might cause more heart-searching now', yet it was the demolition of William Adam's derelict 1740 wing and its interiors – to reduce costs and save the tower house at Carnousie in 1977–80 – that proved the most 'painful' decision. The fourth fabric approach concerned the use of preferred rubble, against harled brickwork or blockwork with stone dressings. Although recognised as not ideal, up until the early 1980s the latter was ultimately used as the usual method for reasons of cost. This compromise started with Kisimul in 1958, but by

FIGURE 114
Hillslap Tower, Roxburghshire: photographed c.1940
(© RCAHMS, SC 1232888)

FIGURE 115
Hillslap Tower, Roxburghshire: photographed in
2002 (© RCAHMS, SC 1232911)

the late 1970s it was still an option – at the
fifteenth- and sixteenth-century towers at Hillslap in 1978–84, blockwork was used to complete
the crumbled wallheads (Figures 114 and 115).
Yet, at the large-scale restoration of Leslie Castle
from 1983, the replacement of extensive rubble
masonry was grant-aided at a cost of £700 a
square metre.[51]

The 1980s marked a fundamental shift for the
grant-aided tower house restoration programme.
In 1981 and 1985, the programme was reviewed

on a number of levels under pressure from its crit-
ics, and amidst a climate of increasingly rigorous
conservation practice. The chief concerns were:
vastly increased costs, and over-commitment by
the Historic Buildings Council; limited public
access to private properties that had received
grants; and the question of whether restoration of
substantial ruins constituted repairs. But the
underlying criticism was from the anti-tower
house restoration lobby, who objected to its non-
purist programme in principle. The potentially

contradictory policies of repair versus restoration that existed within the two legislative sectors and two heritage divisions of Historic Buildings and Ancient Monuments were increasingly acting in direct opposition to one another. On a broader conservation level, the early 1980s witnessed the beginnings of critical debates about current pragmatic conservation practices in Scotland, following a proliferation of international conservation charters. The most notable of these was the Burra Charter of 1979, which combined greater strictness in restoration procedure and a demand for reversibility. These conservation standards, by the 1990s, were fundamentally shaped by the nineteenth-century SPAB anti-restoration ideology of minimum intervention.

In 1985 there was a suspension of grants, with recommendations that there be a greater emphasis on consolidation (the grant aid policy for scheduled monuments) rather than restoration, with a requirement to tighten up the selection criteria. Defenders of the programme argued that consolidation, and the weighing up of risk to existing building fabric, had always been a central consideration: of the fifty-three grant-aided towers completed up to 1985, only eight had lost significant masonry. The consolidation versus restoration policy was ever central: it had been argued by prospective restorers and their architects, in fact, that a number of still-roofed castles brought into guardianship in the course of the twentieth century were straightforward candidates for reoccupation. Claypotts was cited as just such an instance, and others could have been re-roofed and made habitable through restoration, such as MacLellan's Castle, Huntly, Greenknowe and Tolquhon.[52] Yet the grant-aiding scheme viewed its restorations of a significant number of threatened tower houses as supplementing, and indeed providing an alternative to, expensive state guardianship.

Despite a 1985 HBC report highlighting seventy-two potential listed and scheduled candidates for future restoration, from that time tower house grant-aided restorations reduced to a trickle. But in reality, and as a direct result of its success, restorers were running out of potential tower houses; and, of those remaining, most were, on the whole, not complete enough for restoration to be an option. When restoration schemes resumed under scrutiny in 1987–8, conservation standards were consistently more stringent, and returned to the public/community amenity ethos of the original late 1950s' schemes, such as restorations of the fifteenth-century tower Alloa Tower of 1989–96 in partnership with the local council and Alloa Preservation Trust, under the architectural control of Bob Heath and Martin Hadlington. In 1986, Maurice Lindsay, member of the HBC for nearly ten years, happily recalled how he and his colleagues had 'the wherewithal to bring about more or less complete restoration' of these valuable cultural assets. Between 1954 and the early 1990s, over sixty restorations were undertaken with HBC grant aid and, as David Walker has pointed out, this more than matched in numbers those held in the guardianship estate.[53]

Adding fuel to the anti-tower house restoration lobby were a number of late 1970s' and 1980s' private restorations carried out without grant aid. Earlier private schemes – such as Castle Stalker, Argyll, 1965–75, and Breachacha Castle, Coll, from 1965, where owners met all the costs of restoration alone – were criticised for apparently lacking expert architectural input; Ian Lindsay was only initially involved with both projects. Amongst heritage professionals, these set a poor conservation precedent. The dismantling and rebuilding of the fifteenth- to eighteenth-century tower house of Aiket in 1976–9 led to the castle being demoted from Category B to C in 1978, although there were calls to delist it completely. These private restorations were highlighted in the 1991 Architectural Heritage Society of Scotland's annual conference, 'Restoring Scotland's Castles', which included a number of Aiket-style 'do it yourself restoration projects', studies of which were included in its associated publication.[54]

But it was the formation of the unified government heritage agency Historic Scotland in 1991, at the height of the conservation movement ascendancy, which established the dominant conservation ideology for the repair and restoration of castles in the last decade of the twentieth century. With this change also came greater autonomous financial responsibility. The repositioning towards castle consolidation in the late 1980s resulted in architectural works on castles slowly grinding to a halt in the 1990s but, as in previous periods, there was still potential for significantly different approaches. Although grant aid was still essentially central government funds, the 1990s witnessed a gradual shift in accountability from the HBC and AMB to Historic Scotland. The HBC and AMB were disbanded in 2003, and the unified heritage agency became the main advisors to the Scottish Executive. There were three key areas in which this shift affected castle heritage: repair grants; 'consent' for proposed works on historic castles; and, to a lesser extent, guardianship policy.

Since the late 1950s, repair and restoration grants for historic castles had been operated independently by the AMB (for repair-only works for scheduled ruins), and the HBC for listed structures. The two boards met together for the first time in 1986, to discuss the development of industrial heritage. Despite a moratorium on grants in 1994–6, by the late 1990s Historic Scotland was running its own HS Repair Scheme for 'outstanding' monuments, in parallel with the HBC. By 1998, HS had taken over the oversight of grant awards. Grants for castles were rare, and grant-aiding was now dominated by an urban renewal agenda and strict building fabric concerns, backed by minimum-intervention

SPAB ideology. Yet a very small number of repair schemes were authorised in the mid to late 1990s, and reflected the broader, increasingly high standards in conservation practice at the end of the century. These were carried out by leading specialist conservation architects, with restoration based on meticulous documentary research, and the towers were extensively recorded prior to works beginning. These included the restoration of the late sixteenth-century Z-plan castle of Ballone, by and for architect Lachlan Stewart. Its grant-aided restoration from 1998 to 2000 aimed at providing a more joined-up approach of HS control, as it was both listed and scheduled. Because it was restored for residential use it was, of course (in line with the Act), de-scheduled. The four-storey sixteenth-century L-plan ruin of Melgund Castle, Angus was upgraded to Category A listing in 1995, prior to its grant-aided partial restoration and consolidation by Ben Tindall Architects in 1998–9; and Liberton Tower, Edinburgh, was restored by Simpson & Brown for the Castles of Scotland Preservation Trust in 1996–7, and de-scheduled a decade later in 2008.

In 1998, HS restated its overall policy for grant-aiding the restoration of tower houses. Ancient monuments grants were not available for restoration for domestic use, but 'in certain cases, however, a degree of restoration might be considered grant-eligible if it were to be non-intrusive, appropriate and reversible', and historic building repair grants were confined to assisting the repair of the internal and external historic fabric of the building. Perhaps with an undercurrent of righting the wrongs done by earlier HBC grant-aiding, restorations, it claimed, were to be evidence-based, and to result in 'no undue loss or masking of the original fabric'. (Grants were not, of course, given towards the cost of providing services or otherwise for 'inhabitants' comfort'.[55]) In terms of approval for non-grant aided works on scheduled or listed historic castles, ambitious castle restoration was firmly in decline. As one castle owner recalled in 2009, 'the days of gung-ho were almost certainly over'.[56] The strict control over fabric repair of scheduled monuments led to a number of high-profile cases in the 1990s , such as Dairsie Castle, where owners were taken to task for unauthorised or 'inappropriate' conservation works, which were common practice in the 1970s and 1980s.[57]

As outlined, by the 1960s a very large number of castles – over sixty – were in guardianship. The interwar pragmatic approach to repairs, as witnessed at Blackness Castle, was gradually developed in the post-war years into a strict conservation ideology: monuments were to be preserved 'in the state in which they have come down to us'.[58] These policies were strengthened, as we have seen, post-1991. Yet improvement programmes at key guardianship monuments in the 1990s – at Stirling Castle and, to a lesser extent Edinburgh Castle – appear to have contradicted its own uncompromising policy on conservation and the restoration of monuments. The building of new restaurant and visitor facilities at both locations caused the AMB and HBC concern. Stirling Castle highlights the shifting attitudes to guardianship monuments in the post-war period, and in particular the long-running ambition to restore its great hall. The idea of the restored hall as a memorial to the dead of the Second World War was first pursued in 1945 by J S Richardson, former Inspector of Ancient Monuments. But it was not until it came out of military use in the mid 1960s that the restoration programme began. Following its completion in 1999 'to something like its original state', and mindful of criticism arguing an inconsistency of conservation principle, a number of heritage professionals defended the decision. David Breeze, then Chief Inspector of Ancient Monuments, stated: 'While Historic Scotland still adheres to the long-held attitude to ruins in the care of the state, that is "conserve as found" it has always accepted that Stirling Castle is a special case'; it was also defensible because it was 'a faithful copy, [and] not intended to deceive'. Iain McIvor, former Inspector and latterly Chief Inspector of Ancient Monuments from 1955 to 1989, later admitted that the restoration of the great hall 'sits rather awkwardly alongside the stern principles of non-restoration'.[59]

Fuelling a growing criticism of Historic Scotland's broader cultural approach to castles in guardianship in the 1990s, and challenging the 1960s' and 1970s' dominance and accepted authority of its state-employed experts in the area of castle studies, was a new generation of 'castle revisionist' scholars. From the late 1980s, a number of writers challenged the traditional military interpretation of castles with a more rounded social-economic and cultural one. This was, to a certain extent, a natural progression from Mackay Mackenzie's interwar analysis of castle architecture. In 1967, G Scott-Moncrieff, in his introduction to *Scottish Country Houses and Castles*, recalled how Mackay Mackenzie had expressed his 'irritation with writers who too freely bandied the word 'functional' when describing Scottish tower houses . . . much of their detailing was not strictly functional but carried out with a keen eye to decorative detail'.[60] In the 1990s, a number of scholars drew particular attention to the international cultural context of castle architecture.[61] These broader contexts had been little heeded in the traditional Ministry of Works guardianship monument guidebooks, which employed 'the usually sterile . . . field of castles and the dreary taxonomy of gunloops'.[62] In his 2001 *The Scottish Chateau*, Charles McKean attempted to 'remove the warlike overcoat of theses great houses'. Some of these 'castle revisionist' academics were to be drawn into the heated repair-versus-restoration castle debate that dominated the first decade of the twenty-first century.

In conclusion, by the end of the twentieth century the ideological and heritage debate concerning the pros and cons of castle restoration was quickly gathering force. In 2001, a government heritage policy document, *The Conservation of Architectural Ancient Monuments in Scotland: Guidance on Principles*, written by Richard Fawcett, was published by Historic Scotland. It set down clearly and uncompromisingly the current state policy on conservation and the restoration of monuments for reuse, emphasising the resurgence of the prestige of SPAB orthodoxy amongst some within Historic Scotland, in striking contrast to the flexibility once possible under Walker's regime at SDD. State and local government heritage control of castles continued to be strong, with an estimated 800–1,000 castles and fortified houses under legislative protection in Scotland.[63] The controversial application for the restoration and reoccupation of the thirteenth- and fourteenth-century ruined Castle Tioram, Argyll, in 1999, witnessed the beginning of a new episode in castle heritage in Scotland – the impact of which is not yet known.

Acknowledgements

Thank you to David Walker (who was 'in the thick' of much of this story from the late 1960s onwards), for his continued guidance, and for kindly allowing me to utilise his research. Thanks also to Geoffrey Stell, Aonghus Mackechnie, Miles Glendinning and, finally, Scottish Centre for Conservation Studies students T R Revella and Neeraj Bhagat, who carried out research into this subject during a placement at RCAHMS in 2008.

CHAPTER SIX

Radical Restorations of the Late Twentieth Century
Recollections from the Front Line

David M Walker

In the previous chapter, Diane Watters traced the broad currents of castle restoration during the twentieth century, including the role of state and private agencies. This chapter aims to complement that overview at a more personal level. It recalls the realpolitik of the situations which confronted the Historic Buildings Council and its advisers in both facilitating and regulating the sudden torrent of castle restorations inaugurated by the pioneer reconstruction and reoccupation of the ruined or semi-ruined castles of Inchdrewer, Balfluig, Kinkell, Inverquharity and Pitcullo in the later 1960s. The council's advisers included the present writer, who was area inspector for Renfrewshire, Perthshire, Aberdeenshire and Banffshire from 1962, and (under four different titles) Chief Inspector of Historic Buildings from 1975 to 1993.

Forter Castle:
A Microcosm of 'Re-roofing' Controversy

This chapter begins with the rebuilding of Forter Castle, as it encapsulated the philosophical issue in its most extreme form (Figures 116 and 117). It cannot be said that the writer was particularly conscious of it at the time: consideration of the case centred narrowly on its architectural merits,

the feasibility of accurate reconstruction and, of course, cost. The scheme was implemented in 1989–92 with the aid of a £220,000 Historic Scotland grant, one of the latest and boldest schemes in the restoration programme. This project highlighted a range of complex and fascinating issues of authenticity and integrity, not least because of the castle's extraordinarily short period of active occupation and intact structure. Built from the 1580s and completed only in 1608, it was burnt in 1640 by the earl of Argyll's forces, acting on a commission from the Estates (government). Argyll mounted a comprehensive attack on Lord Ogilvie's Airlie estates, including Alyth, Glen Isla, Forter and 'the bonnie Hoose o' Airlie'; reportedly, Argyll himself contributed to the demolitions with a sledgehammer. Dougall Campbell of Inverawe was despatched to destroy Forter Castle, his orders stating: 'Ye shall not faill to stay and demolische my lord Ogilbies hous of Forthar. Sie how ye can cast off the iron yeattis and windowis; and tak doun the roof: and if ye find it be longsome, ye shall fyre it weill, that so it may be destroyed.'[1] Following that, the castle seems to have been left roofless for 362 years: in other words, 92 per cent of its existence since the date of completion. In financing Forter's radical 'restoration' to a state that it had only fleetingly enjoyed in the first place, had Historic Scotland

FIGURE 116

Top. Forter, Angus: photographed during works
(© Historic Scotland)

FIGURE 117

Above. Forter, Angus: photographed during works
(© Historic Scotland)

and the Historic Buildings Council (as advisory body) acted outwith the provisions of the governing legislation, the Historic Buildings and Ancient Monuments Act of 1953?

On the positive side of the equation, the walls had stood complete to the chimneyheads until about 1880, when the top of the west wall was blown down, and it could hardly be denied that the completed restoration of Forter Castle looked superb, and enhanced the landscape of the glen in which it stood. The work had been supremely well carried out under the supervision of Nicholas Groves-Raines, the external walls were at least 80 per cent undisturbed original masonry, the vaults were rebuilt in part with the original stones, and the other stonework had largely been retrieved from the buildings and dykes nearby. A mid Victorian photograph had informed the rebuilding of what had fallen and, apart from the loss of the adjacent courtyard and most of its outbuildings (as with many other castles, ruined or not), we were confident that it looked as it had when completed in 1608. Personal gain was not an issue, as the owner had put some £700,000 of his own money into the project, significantly more than its market value at the time.

But there were also more challenging aspects to the project, not least the radical character of the transformation from its condition in the 1980s. At that stage, the building seemed a complete wreck, with trees growing out of it. When in 1981, and again in 1985, the Historic Buildings Council instructed our department (at that stage, the Historic Buildings and Monuments Division of the Scottish Development Department, or SDD) to prepare a complete catalogue of tower houses that might be the subject of future applications, the writer himself had discounted Forter, on grounds not of architectural quality but of feasibility, owing to its apparently comprehensive ruination. It was only after an acquiring owner, Robert Pooley, had the trees and other vegetation cleared out in 1988 that the late William Murray Jack, Historic Scotland's long-serving part-time inspector for Fife and Angus (and an eminent conservation architect), was able to report that the trees had not affected the stability of the walls, and that Forter was in fact capable of being rebuilt and re-roofed. This assessment was subsequently confirmed by SDD colleague Chris Macgregor when he and the writer visited the site before reporting to the council.

The case for supporting the restoration was primarily architectural, although the house also had an element of historic interest, as a victim of the Covenanting civil strife of the mid seventeenth century. Forter was the largest, although not the best preserved, of a group of Angus tower houses of similar L-plan design built from 1581 onwards, the others being Braikie and Fleming-

ton – neither of which was likely to survive – together with the now-vanished Boysack. The failure to secure the future of Braikie when grant was offered in 1974–5 had been a considerable disappointment to the council and its advisors. Rebuilding Forter ensured that at least one of these houses would survive. And, very exceptionally, the building of Forter was at least partially documented: its completion, or perhaps its reconstruction after a fire, is recorded in a contract in the Airlie Muniments held at the National Archives of Scotland.

However, the central issue of criticism was, of course, not the architectural and historic interest of Forter but what constituted 'repair' under the 1953 Act: did it matter if the roof had been burned off only months before, or 300 years previously? The issue had first arisen at Pitcullo in 1969, and the conclusion then had been that it did not matter, a decision strongly influenced by the quality of the entrance jamb, which had retained its roof. Earlier Scottish shell-reconstructions, such as that of Dunderave and Duart; the more speculative stump-rebuilding of Eilean Donan; or the internationally renowned work of Viollet-le-Duc the previous century at Pierrefonds and Carcassonne, had provided ample precedent for the latter approach. But those who had drafted the 1953 legislation did not seem to have considered that issue, and provided no guidance. There was only the context of the Gowers Report to suggest that grant aid was primarily intended to apply to buildings which were still occupied. Although, to the best of the writer's knowledge, the principle of grant-aiding roofless houses was never formally raised with the Scottish Office, Brian Anthony and other English colleagues did express reservations on the subject. They did say that it was not something they would ever have done, although they have since done so at Lulworth and (in part) Appuldurcombe; only a few years earlier, before acid rain became an issue, they had seriously considered deconstructing the 1858 re-roofing of Brinkburn Priory church to return it to 'pure' medieval fabric.

Our response was that we were facing a very different set of circumstances in relation to houses of this vintage, and that we had to take a more pragmatic view. England's Elizabethan and Jacobean houses had always proved adaptable to modern living and had remained in continuous occupation. Scottish houses in the same time-frame, particularly the smaller ones, had not been regarded as suitable gentry houses since the late seventeenth and early eighteenth centuries, and far too many were in imminent danger of being lost. Since so many were already part of the monuments-in-care estate, and in some cases not regularly shown to the public because of staffing constraints, more innovative solutions to their survival and future maintenance thus had to be sought. In terms of authenticity, it was further argued that houses such as Forter, which had long been abandoned or had become bothies for farm servants, were, paradoxically, on the whole much better preserved in terms of plan and window openings than those which had been continu-ously adapted and extended in Georgian and Victorian times, and that not all of the latter had their original roofs. It has to be said that at the time the problems we faced were understood rather than accepted by our English colleagues. We had to agree to differ.

Consolidation versus Restoration: Issues of Principle, Practice and Legislative Powers

The specific case of Forter leads to a range of more general questions, all essentially concerned with the issue of why the Ministry of Public Buildings and Works, the Property Services Agency of the Department of the Environment that succeeded it, and the Scottish Office and its advisory bodies and advisers, all took the deci-sions they did thirty to forty years ago. These have to be looked at not through the lens of present-day attitudes but in a proper historical perspective, in the light of the circumstances and factors prevailing at that time.

The most obvious of those factors was the issue of constructional methods, especially the tendency to make use of blockwork and brick-work in restorations of the late 1970s and early 1980s. Why was this ever accepted by the Historic Buildings Council and its advisers? The issue first arose in 1977 at Pitfichie, where the fallen stonework was still largely on site, although some of it was broken (Figures 118 and 119). When it was agreed that Pitfichie was such an outstanding and well-recorded tower house that its rebuilding could be grant-aided, it was initially assumed that this would be done in rubble, as at Inchdrewer. But in 1977 there were few masons experienced in building in boulder rubble on such a large scale, and it was a correspondingly high-cost option. The transfer of the small Z-plan Benholm Lodging from Aberdeen's Netherkirkgate to Tillydrone Road in 1964 had been the only other recent contract of that kind, and here cost had hardly been an issue, as the move of the Benholm Lodging was paid for by Lord Marks to facilitate

FIGURE 118
Opposite top. Pitfichie, Aberdeenshire: view from north-west photographed in 1936 (© RCAHMS, SC 1200089)

FIGURE 119
Opposite bottom left. Pitfichie, Aberdeenshire: photographed in 1996 (© RCAHMS and Ian Shepherd, SC 990549)

FIGURE 120
Opposite bottom right. Benholm's Lodging, Aberdeen: photographed in 1940 (© RCAHMS, SC 1232299)

FIGURE 121
Opposite. Benholm's Lodging: rebuilt in Tillydrone housing estate in 1964, photographed in 1996 (© RCAHMS, SC 1232298)

FIGURE 122
Above. Fawside, East Lothian: aerial photograph taken in 1978 (© RCAHMS, SC 1232295)

the expansion of the adjoining Marks and Spencer store. In both cases the rubble-work had been left exposed (Figures 120 and 121).

By the 1970s, however, there was an increasing awareness of the role of harl as the universal finish in sixteenth- and seventeenth-century Scottish building, recently reinforced by the discoveries at Castle Menzies. There, demolition of a mid eighteenth-century rear building had revealed a thin coat of harl that had extended over the dressings and the corbelling of the turrets to produce a completely unified appearance. Thus both the Ancient Monuments and the Historic Buildings Inspectorates required Pitfichie to be harled, as it had been originally; but, as the council's architect, the late William Boal, ruefully observed, it was impossible to persuade grant applicants to stretch far beyond their means on rubble-work they would not actually see. In the event, William Cowie's skilful rebuilding produced a visually satisfactory result, both externally and internally. The dressed stonework was retrieved from the debris and reused as far as possible, and the junctions between the original rubble and the blockwork were only just discernible under the harl, and even then only in small areas.

But in the major project at Fawside, where far less rebuilding was required and carried out in brick, the result was less satisfactory (Figures 122 and 123). The contrast between the rugged surface of the harl, where it covered original rubble, and its smoothness over brick, was all too obvious, and the joints in the brickwork tended to show through in very wet weather. Yet no one should assume that these imperfections arose from a slapdash or headstrong attitude to the project. The late Tom Craig, as acquiring owner, was an engineer who took the job very seriously, with an architect engaged on it virtually full-time and with Ted Ruddock as his consultant structural engineer; but, as he acknowledged in a 1991

Architectural Heritage Society of Scotland (AHSS) lecture, the rapid increase in building prices in the late 1970s tested his commitment almost to breaking point. Fawside still stands proudly on its hilltop, and further work has been done there since. In 1977, by contrast, it had been in imminent danger of total demolition under building control procedures as a danger to children and, as will be seen later in this chapter, at that point there was little that could have been done to prevent such an outcome, other than the intervention of a restoring owner.

In the event, these unavoidably 'impure' tendencies in conservation practice were superseded in the later 1980s, not so much through any diktat of international charters as by the arrival of a new and enthusiastic generation of specialist contractors. This process began with Ian Cumming and his team, initially at Tillycairn, where relatively little rebuilding was required, and then in the major works at Hatton in Angus in 1987–9. To the writer they seemed an intrepid lot, fearlessly unpicking the nineteenth-century consolidation of partly fallen mural stairs to reinstate the original plan. And during the years that followed, beginning with the work at Leslie in 1982, the leading conservation practices and the Scottish Office's inspectors and architects addressed the 'blockwork problem' head on, by seeking higher standards of rebuilding in compatible materials: in effect, the dominance of blockwork lasted little more than five years. In its place, this new generation of contractors developed a distinctive philosophy, the outline of which is to be found in Ian Cumming's chapter in the book *Restoring Scotland's Castles*, originally written in 1991 and published in 2000.

The second, much wider issue of those years was that of conservation principle. Given that the 'conserve as found' philosophy, from the days of John Ruskin and William Morris, had been the guiding principle for ancient monuments in care

FIGURE 123
Fawside, East Lothian: aerial photograph taken in 1997 (© RCAHMS, SC 1232296)

from the beginning, why were the normally vocif-
erous defenders of 'anti-scrape' so slow to react to
Scotland's castle restoration boom? Only from
1985, after all, was there a greater official emphasis
on consolidation rather than restoration for those
castles in private hands, and only from 1998
(revised in 2001) was there a formalised policy on
reconstruction and consolidation. Why was such
a wide window of opportunity left open to the
restorers? One explanation may have been the
very 'Englishness', and inactivity in Scotland, of

SPAB itself up until the 1980s – a situation partly
addressed by the formation of a 'SPAB in Scotland' in the 1990s. Thus, although the Historic
Buildings Council's recommendations were
reported in the press and in the annual reports,
there never was any concerted criticism of its
policy on re-roofing tower houses. The anti-
restorationist viewpoint in Scotland was solely
reliant on individual members of council – most
notably Englishman Sir Harry Jefferson Barnes –
and on the government's own ancient monu-

ments inspectorate, which enjoyed only a partial influence within the fragmented government regulatory apparatus. This fragmention arose partly from the way in which the ancient monuments and historic buildings legislation had developed. In 1944–7, responsibility for buildings still in occupation was, quite correctly, allocated to the Ministry of Housing and Local Government in England, and to the Scottish Office (or Department of Health for Scotland (DHS)) in Scotland, the primary responsibility resting with the planning authorities, as listed building consent was, for all practical purposes, inseparable from planning permission. Policy on listing and consent was at first derived mainly from the English Maclagan (later Holford) Committee. As only about two thirds of Scotland's unoccupied castles were statutorily protected through scheduling, it was left to DHS listing to cover the remainder; and, as a precaution against de-scheduling or any careless misunderstanding on the part of the planning authority, DHS chief investigator Ian Lindsay also instructed that all scheduled castles should be listed as well. Thus, although the Ancient Monuments Acts were the 'senior' legislation, the ancient monuments inspectors were left with a much more circumscribed authority in relation to castles than their Historic Buildings counterparts. This was a situation that led to occasional 'turf wars' between the two, particularly in 1969–71 when the planning authorities – quite unnecessarily – sent notices of statutory listing to custodians of castles that were in state care.

The 1953 Historic Buildings and Ancient Monuments Act, which was implemented by the UK Ministry of Works, introduced grant aid for repairs to buildings which, in general, were either occupied or about to be reoccupied (the Act was not in fact explicit on that point, only requiring them to be of 'outstanding' interest) and set up the Historic Buildings Councils, under the aegis of the Ministry of Works. The Scottish Council also took over the role of the Maclagan Committee as the Secretary of State for Scotland's statutory adviser on listing. The 1950s and 1960s were not a happy period for the built heritage in Scotland but, at an administrative level, these fragmented arrangements worked better than might have been expected, primarily because there was a good working relationship between the professional staffs and Ian Lindsay. He was the essential link-man in the entire system, being a member of both the Ancient Monuments Board and the Historic Buildings Council as well as Chief Investigator of Historic Buildings. The main defect of the 1953 Act was that, in the difficult economic circumstances after the Second World War, it did not make corresponding provision for the consolidation and maintenance of ruins and archaeological sites in private hands. Whether there would have been much take-up of ancient monuments grants at that time may be doubted: in the high tax regime that prevailed after the war, only a very few large estates were prepared to spend money on buildings that were of no beneficial use.

By the 1960s, then, as financial stringency had ruled out unlimited expansion of the monuments-in-care estate, grant aid for reconstruction and reoccupation became the only option for the survival of tower houses at risk. This was a pragmatic approach, aimed at stabilising and, where possible, revitalising a declining stock, through an arrangement in which most of the capital cost and all future maintenance became the responsibility of private individuals rather than the state. Contradictory philosophies there may have been, but the writer does not recall any serious disagreement between the Ancient Monuments and Historic Buildings Inspectorates. Many of the castles which were re-roofed and reoccupied had already been scheduled: consent for the works could theoretically have been blocked. However, in those days, scheduling meant no more than one month's notice of proposed works in which to secure a preservation order, a troublesome process usually requiring ministerial approval and that could imply a commitment to taking the site into state care. As the Scottish Works secretary, Graham Patrick, put it to the writer fifty years ago, inspectors had to remember that they were only bluffing: there was little prospect of any support if their bluff was called. The inspectorates had greater influence at Historic Buildings Council level, as they could have advised against recommending grant, but that course of action carried the risk of a poor and damaging scheme, or even demolition. In practice, therefore, they tended to recommend the awarding of grant, in order to secure control, unless the site was too archaeologically sensitive to be disturbed by reconstruction works. Such few cases as there were of that kind never reached council consideration.

The first step towards a unified policy on ancient monuments and historic buildings came in July 1966. The Historic Buildings Council was transferred to the Scottish Office's Historic Buildings Branch at St Andrew's House, but the professional advice at both inspector and architect level remained with the Ministry of Public Building and Works at Argyle House, into which the Branch was ultimately squeezed in 1970 after a short period when it was out-stationed in Hill Street. In the first year of the new arrangements, 1966–7, there were some serious teething problems, as the Historic Buildings Branch's secretariat grappled with the higher standards required for grant work. Some of the staff had not been accustomed to accepting professional advice, and it came as a humbling shock when they discovered that what was acceptable for grant was not within their personal discretion, as it had been with listed building consent work. The one immediate advantage of the change was that it removed tower houses and such distinctively Scottish architecture in general from the oversight of

English ministers and select committees. These were largely composed of English members of parliament, some of whom found Scottish tower houses small, plain, 'not real castles' and perhaps even a bit foreign-looking – not at all like English castles and country houses of the same vintage. Full integration, in the form of the Historic Buildings and Monuments Division of SDD, was not achieved until 1978, and even then the two elements were still housed in separate buildings, in Drumsheugh Gardens and Melville Street.

A much more significant development was the long-sought Ancient Monuments and Archaeological Areas Act of 1979. This put scheduling on a similar basis to that for listing and listed building consent from 1968, but without any planning authority involvement: the Ancient Monuments Inspectorate could at last refuse consent if necessary.[2] The 1979 Act also introduced grant aid for consolidation, making that a viable option if the owner of the site was willing to co-operate and find the balance of the cost. But in the first few years of the new Act, there was neither the opportunity nor the money to develop a policy in the matter. The incoming Conservative government changed the grant system from an annual allocation of funds for grant offers, which could be taken up at any time over the next few years, to cash limits on grants actually taken up. The council and its secretariat then had to calculate how much commitment they had to have to ensure that their cash limit was fully used, as an underspend would have led to a reduction in future years. Although careful projections were made from past cases, in the event the take-up was faster than predicted, leading to an overspend and a moratorium on all grants in 1981, and again in 1985. Expenditure on tower houses was reviewed in both years, and in the second of these reviews there was a greater emphasis on consolidation, as was made possible by the Act of 1979. This policy was refined and formalised in 2001, and is illustrated in *Renewed Life for Scottish Castles* by Richard Fawcett and Allan Rutherford, published in 2011. In practice, ancient monuments grant aid has been used to consolidate major castles that were too incomplete to be suitable subjects for reoccupation, rather than as an alternative solution to the survival of those that might have been re-roofed. Although reduced, the problem of persuading owners to contribute substantial sums towards the consolidation of buildings of no beneficial use still remains, and in some cases matching funding has had to be cobbled together from charitable trusts and, more recently, the Heritage Lottery Fund.

Castle Re-roofing: A Formula for the Future?

This chapter is not in any way intended as a mere apologia for what has been done. Legislation and international charters have never given Historic Scotland and its predecessors absolute rights over other people's property or authority to spend their money in pursuit of a purist ideal. Negotiations with applicants for listed building or scheduled monument consent, and for grant aid, have always had to aim at securing the best possible outcome for the long-term future of an individual building, operating under the circumstances prevailing at any one point of time. There were nevertheless strict criteria. Grant applicants had to confine their requirements within what existed or was known to have existed; and they had to respect the historic plan, door and window openings and any internal finishes that had survived. In the more radical reconstructions, the greater part of the original structure had to survive, and there had to be clear evidence for the reinstatement of any element which had fallen. Where the proposals were more conjectural, or where there was too little left, as at Dairsie, listed building or scheduled monument consent might be given

but grant aid had to be refused. The grants might seem generous now, but several of those who undertook work on the more ruined structures suffered serious financial and personal stress and were unable to retain their castles.

Looking back, the writer has regrets: Elphinstone, which should have been taken into care; Jerviston, where British Steel's argument that it had no statutory power to spend money on it, other than for demolition, was too readily accepted; Braikie, where the Historic Buildings Council's secretariat might have tried harder to secure agreement; the magically complete and unaltered Faichfield, where the owners could not be persuaded to apply for a grant; and Carnousie, where the owners were neither able nor really willing to save the William Adam wing as well as the Z-plan tower. The relatively few do-it-yourself cases where the detail could have been better, some as a result of the unavailability of grants in 1981–2 and 1985–7, were fortunately not major houses.

All in all, the great restoration drive of the 1970s and 1980s conferred substantial benefits on Scotland's architectural heritage, both in the present and for posterity. While the Historic Buildings Council for Scotland (or at least the majority of its members, as there always was at least one dissident) was primarily concerned with ensuring the survival of the best tower houses of all periods, Scotland's later sixteenth- and early seventeenth-century castellated houses proved to be particular beneficiaries of the re-roofing policy. So much of the architectural beauty of these houses, as originally constructed, lay in the geometry of their roofs, and at Ballone (Figures 124 and 125), Fenton, Forter and Spedlins that has been recovered. In Aberdeenshire, Harthill, Pitfichie and Tillycairn again rival Midmar in picturesqueness of outline, even if they lack the original woodwork and plasterwork within.

What, then, of the future? Is castle re-roofing

FIGURE 124
Ballone, Ross and Cromarty: photograph taken before restoration (© Lachlan Stewart)

a discredited idea whose time has passed? Certainly, to judge from the current upsurge in facsimile reconstructions in Germany and elsewhere in the wake of the Frauenkirche restoration in Dresden (1994–2005), the fortunes of architectural re-creation schemes in general are rising rather than declining in the twenty-first century, whatever the misgivings of anti-scrapers. Should Scotland's castles be insulated from that international trend – or can the restorations of the 1970s and 1980s provide a viable precedent?

Looking at John Claude Nattes' sketch of Huntly when it was still as grand as a Loire chateau, it is impossible not to regret what has been lost and to wonder if, like the Stirling great hall and palace interiors, it might not be possible to re-create it, when there is so much evidence as to what we should have in the surviving fabric. The magnificent chimneypieces within would be protected from further erosion by the weather and by the harsher winters we are currently experiencing. The issue is not just one of abstract conservation

FIGURE 125
Ballone, Ross and Cromarty: photograph
taken after restoration (© Lachlan Stewart)

principles or ideals, or, conversely, a narrowly
practical, short-term matter of money; it is also a
question of the wider social role of these buildings, now and in the future – a question of what
we intend to pass on, in palpable form, to the
generations to come.

Acknowledgements

The writer is grateful to Dr Aonghus MacKechnie for factual assistance and to Dr Miles Glendinning for editorial comment.

PART 2

Landmarks of Castle Culture:
Ten Case Studies

CHAPTER SEVEN

'That stalwart toure'
Bothwell Castle in the Thirteenth and Early Fourteenth Centuries

Allan Rutherford and John Malcolm

Bothwell Castle, located on a loop of the Clyde, has been rightly identified by William Douglas Simpson as one of the 'foremost secular structures of the Middle Ages in Scotland'. The impressive late thirteenth-century circular donjon usually known as the Valence Tower stands at the eastern end of a subrectangular enclosure, which is itself a truncation of a larger enceinte. This larger enclosure was apparently not completed before the outbreak of hostilities with England in 1296, and the current form is largely that created during or after the Wars of Independence (Figure 126).

The purpose of this chapter is to explore the thirteenth- and fourteenth-century context of the castle as it then stood, in order to situate fully its archaeological and architectural importance. The accepted interpretations of Bothwell will be explored in the light of both recent research in castle studies and a reassessment of the masonry remains. In particular, the social context of the Bothwell donjon will be assessed against the cultural milieu of which its builders were part; while formal architectural parallels will be explored, the chief focus will be on the ideology of castle building in the Anglo-French world. By looking closely at the masonry remains, it is also hoped to demonstrate that early Bothwell was more extensive and more sophisticated than hitherto suspected.

Bothwell and its Historical Context

The earliest parts of the castle were constructed by Walter de Moray, lord of Petty (to the east of Inverness), where a modest motte represents his family's castle. De Moray also held lands at Smailholm on the border with England, and at Lilford in Northamptonshire, and he probably had additional holdings in Lincolnshire. Nevertheless, Bothwell Castle represents Walter's entrée into the higher nobility of the Scottish realm, and would have befitted an aspirant to an earldom. It stands comparison with the de Vaux castle at Dirleton or the earl of Mar's castle at Kildrummy. The donjon and the adjoining Prison Tower were completed by either Walter or his son William (known as le Riche or 'the Rich'), who inherited the earldom of Bothwell in 1278. Conventionally, it has been understood that by the outbreak of Scottish hostilities with Edward I in 1296, the only completed parts of the castle were the donjon, the Prison Tower and the short stretch of curtain walling in between, as well as the lowest courses of the rest of the large enceinte. This enceinte represented the largest castle in Scotland at the time, and stands comparison with the castles of similarly wealthy English lords.

Bothwell fell (without any apparent military action) to the English in the early stages of the

FIGURE 126
Bothwell, Lanarkshire: aerial view (© Historic Scotland)

English incursion in 1296, and was successfully besieged by the Scots two years later. The celebrated account of the month-long English siege in the summer of 1301 involved the use of a wooden siege tower, or 'belfry', taken overland from Glasgow at great expense, after which the castle became the *caput* of the Scottish barony of the earl of Pembroke, Aymer de Valence. The castle was surrendered to Edward Bruce in the aftermath of the Battle of Bannockburn in June 1314, after which it was slighted and appears subsequently to have remained unoccupied. It was seized as a suitable stronghold by the English in late 1336, during which time there appears to have been some rebuilding. The final eviction of the English in the spring of 1337 by Andrew de Moray, the lineal descendant of William de Moray, represents a significant turning point in the history of the site.

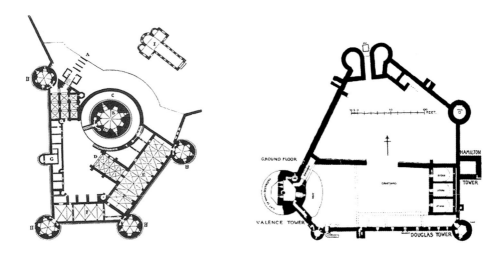

FIGURE 127

Comparative plans of Coucy-le-Château, Picardy, France after Viollet-le-Duc, *An Essay on the Military Architecture of the Middle Ages* (1860) (l); and Bothwell, Lanarkshire after W D Simpson, 'The Architectural History of Bothwell Castle', *Proceedings of the Society of Antiquaries of Scotland*, 59 (1925) (r)

Bothwell and its Place in Castle Studies

Bothwell castle represents *the* truncated exemplar of Scottish castle building in the thirteenth century. Since the excavation of the unfinished enceinte in 1888, most interpretations of the castle have focused on this unfinished archetype. This has been in some ways justifiable, as the circular donjon known popularly as the Valence Tower and the adjoining masonry enceinte represent the finest piece of Scottish secular architecture from the period before the Wars of Independence.

In one sense, the history and architectural development of the castle are well understood, sketched out firstly by MacGibbon and Ross before and after the nineteenth-century excavations, and then more fully detailed in a study by William Douglas Simpson. Simpson's understanding of the castle evolved considerably following the excavations carried out in 1937–8

after the castle passed into the guardianship of the Ministry of Works. It is Simpson's modelling of Bothwell's evolution that has prevailed in subsequent studies of the site.

MacGibbon and Ross had noted the formal parallels of the donjon with that of Coucy-le-Chateau in Picardy, and they closely linked the design with the arrival of Marie de Coucy (granddaughter of Coucy's founder) as wife of Alexander II in 1239 (Figure 127). Apart from the similar plans, both towers dominate the rest of their castle complexes and are separated from them by an inner moat. Internally, the tower's spaces were multangular and the principal chambers were vaulted. There are a number of significant differences, most obviously in terms of scale: Bothwell's donjon is 20 metres across and almost 35 metres high, whereas Coucy is 31 metres in diameter and around 55 metres high. Moreover, Coucy's internal spaces featured particularly elaborate double-height arcading.

In terms of formal parallels, Bothwell's donjon would therefore appear to be a poor copy of Coucy. However, simple familial connections were far from the only means by which architectural ideas could be transmitted. For example, the de Morays' possession of lands on both sides of the border would have lent a broader perspective on castle building than a purely Franco-Scottish one. Moreover, it is exceedingly rare to find a castle that represents a slavish imitation of an earlier one – more usually, certain architectural elements are repeatedly emulated, but avoiding reproduction of every detail.

Rather than being an apparently mediocre emulation of one particular tower, Bothwell is equally likely to have drawn on contemporary aristocratic ideas of how a donjon should look. From around 1200, the French monarch Philippe Augustus constructed a series of circular donjons of a scale and complexity similar to that of Bothwell, the best preserved examples being found at Gisors (Figure 128), Falaise and Dourdan. These towers had a noticeable effect on architectural trends in the French realms. Nesles en Dole in Picardy was built in the 1220s by Roland de Dreux, whose great-granddaughter Yolande was to marry Alexander III in 1285. Such towers were relatively rarer in England and its French and Irish dominions, although the de Balliol seat at Castle Barnard in County Durham represents an example which would have been known to many who travelled between England and Scotland. From the exterior, Barnard's donjon appears to sit apart from the rest of the castle, although inspection from within the enclosure shows that it is well integrated with the other ranges. These examples demonstrate that there were a number of potential influences upon which the builders of the Bothwell donjon could have drawn. However, it is worth considering that lords such as the de Morays could have utilised these potential exemplars and added something of their own.

The Donjon of the de Morays and its Relationship with the Castle

The Bothwell donjon dominates the perceptive experience of the site, due to its massive scale relative to the other towers of the castle. Marked off from the rest of the complex by an inner moat, the tower represents an apparent strongpoint in the defensive circuit.

The naming of the donjon for an English earl, Aymer de Valence, is at first glance a puzzling one, and does not appear to greatly pre-date the eighteenth century. As already noted, the architectural and historical evidence point strongly to either Walter or William de Moray as the most likely patrons of the work. De Valence would almost certainly have used the tower as a residence, and this occupation will have inevitably had associative as well as practical intent – seizing the donjon implied a concomitant seizure of the most visible exhibition of *dominium*. Indeed, de Valence may have spent more time living at Bothwell than those who built the castle. Nevertheless, there is much to be said for re-identifying the tower with the de Morays, given their role as creators. It is argued here that the donjon should be more correctly identified as the Moray Tower (Figure 129).

What, then, were the roles and functions of the Moray Tower? Most interpretations of these aspects of Bothwell have focused primarily on the defensive display inherent in its features. The wide inner moat would have been water-filled, as the drains through the curtain wall at either end of the moat demonstrate. Access to the tower appears to have been solely via a drawbridge which passed over an enclosed pit lying within the moat. The drawbridge pivoted from a beaked projection from the rounded face of the tower, through which a doorway granted access to the first floor. Four stone corbels projecting from the wallhead over this doorway would have supported either a stone machicolation or a timber hoarding. Within, the beaked entry facilitated an entrance passage into the lobby which zig-zagged from the door. In the upper level of the beak, a plunging arrowloop would have allowed an archer to cover movement over the drawbridge. This approach would certainly have been an intimidating one for an attacker, and it would have required either considerable sacrifice or considered tactical versatility to overcome. Bothwell has no parallels for this in a Scottish or northern English context, and the approach would have appeared genuinely innovative even when set against the French examples considered above. It is no surprise that the tower has been seen as the apogee of thirteenth-century Scottish military architecture, but it is worth emphasising its wider significance.

There is inevitably a social context to architectural expression, and that was most certainly the case at Bothwell. The relative novelty of the access arrangements are key to a fuller appreciation of the importance of how the tower was entered. There was a strong element of theatricality in the way in which many great towers were approached and entered, as has been shown in a number of recent studies of English examples. The key elements in these arrangements include the use of non-linear approaches, a surplus of defensive features beyond that which was strictly necessary, and the use of a lobby as a form of 'waiting room', further limiting access to the great chamber beyond. From a phenomenological perspective, these arrangements were designed to impress and overawe visitors of all social classes accessing the tower. Put simply, these access paths constituted a deliberately designed approach intended to put visitors into a suitably deferential frame of mind before being received into the inner sanctum of the tower.

Looking at the Bothwell arrangements from this perspective, the defensive elements actually appear to be a form of 'overkill'. This appears to derive from the same mindset that saw many of Edward I's great Welsh castles possess a multiplicity of portcullises within the same gate passage. The entry to the tower at Bothwell meant that the discerning visitor would rapidly identify the de Moray family as being concerned not only with the immediately visible display of power inherent in the construction of a castle and great tower, but also with the finer detail associated with state-of-the-art knowledge of military architecture. In this sense, the Moray Tower would clearly have been highly unusual within the Scottish kingdom, and a clear statement of social intent by the de Morays.

Many other Anglo-French round towers had interior spaces of circular plan, with either simple timber floors or rounded stone vaults. These presented challenges not only in practical terms such as flooring and roofing wide circular spaces (particularly where such spaces adjoined rectilinear ones), but also in terms of how that space was used. Flooring arrangements had implications in terms of aesthetics, structural stability and cost. In Scotland, round mural towers were relatively common in thirteenth-century castles, so the problems were not unprecedented at Bothwell. The builders of the de Moray donjon utilised an octagonal plan for the inner spaces, which at least partly overcame some of these difficulties. A stone pillar carried up from the basement directly supported the vaulting of the first floor hall. The mural arcading within this space includes the mouldings for wall ribs, indicating that a stone vault could have been used. However, the springing of these ribs is not in solid masonry but instead forms a recessed support for the ribs. These moulded forms clearly were intended to support a timber vault, with timber ribs inserted into the springers. The second and third floor chambers have substantial vertical channels cut into the wall faces, again indicating that these spaces were also vaulted in timber rather than stone. It can reasonably be assumed that this vaulting was plastered and painted throughout, and its final appearance would have been very similar in appearance to stone vaulting. Timber vaulting was not common in British medieval buildings, and survivals are almost entirely ecclesiastical. Given the expense taken with the entry arrangements to the Bothwell donjon, such vaulting is unlikely to have been a cost-saving measure. The rarity of this form in Scottish secular architecture suggests that this form was a deliberate choice by the de Morays.

The currently accepted interpretation of the castle's development is that by the outbreak of the Wars of Independence in 1296, the masonry elements of the castle consisted of the Moray Tower and a short stretch of the wing wall to its north, as well as a stretch of curtain wall leading from the Moray Tower to the Prison Tower and the adjacent postern gate. This is derived largely from Simpson's studies and his published plans (Figure 130). However, the interpretation is not borne out by close study of the masonry remains, and the thirteenth-century elements of the castle also include much of the southern curtain running to a junction with the later south-east tower (Figure 131). Simpson posited the idea that there was a masonry junction immediately to the east of the postern gate, and that this represents the joint between thirteenth-century and early fifteenth-century work. There is indeed a projecting frame around the gate which superficially indicates a vertical joint in places, but there are a number of quoins which knit this element of the masonry into the curtain wall to the east. Higher up in the wall, the loss and delamination of facing stones has resulted in the obscuring of this relationship.

Following the curtain wall eastwards, the latrine tower is also bonded into the thirteenth-century masonry and continues to a vaguely

FIGURE 128
Above. Gisors, Normandy, France: Tours Philpienne

FIGURE 129
Opposite. Bothwell, Lanarkshire: the Moray Tower from the courtyard (© Historic Scotland)

defined junction within the lower courses of the south-east tower. The size, shape and bedding of stone is consistent throughout. There are clear differences in the size and shape of individual stones in the upper masonry of the south curtain, consistent with those found in the upper levels of the south-east tower, suggesting that this wall and the south-east tower were rebuilt and heightened in the early fifteenth century. The plaque over the postern containing the Douglas arms has been previously cited as evidence that the underlying walling is of a date later than 1362, when the castle was granted to Archibald the Grim.

However, the snecking of the masonry surrounding the plaque (particularly above the top right corner) and its uneven bedding clearly point to this being an insertion.

Elsewhere in the enclosure, the foundation courses and basal plinth of the square north-east tower underlie masonry of fifteenth-century date. Simpson correctly identified the earlier masonry as consistent with that used in the de Moray Tower. The 1937–8 excavations revealed no destruction debris of medieval date around the north-east tower, suggesting that the thirteenth century did not see it completed above founda-

tion height. The lower courses of the wing wall leading northwards from the Moray Tower are also of thirteenth-century date.

This leaves a question: how much of the intended plan had been built in masonry before 1296? Simpson noted that the large outer enclosure was never built beyond foundation levels, as there were no layers of demolition rubble found during the clearance excavations. However, the probability that these foundations served as a basis for timber defences has never been fully explored. The evidence for these could easily have been missed, as timber defences frequently leave

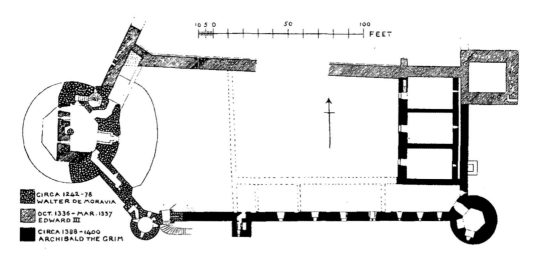

FIGURE 130

Bothwell, Lanarkshire: Simpson's phased plan (after W D Simpson, 'Bothwell Castle Reconsidered', *Transactions of the Glasgow Archaeological Society*, 11 (1947))

ephemeral traces that would have proved difficult to detect by the archaeological methods employed. More to the point, the 1937–8 excavation of fourteenth- or fifteenth-century pottery from the well in the north-east tower of the unfinished thirteenth-century enceinte strongly suggests that the early castle was more extensive than is immediately apparent. The habitation associated with this pottery may represent use of a timber enclosure, or possibly a settlement immediately outside such defences. The more extensive thirteenth-century south curtain described above implies that these probable timber defences must have replicated either the plan of the intended enceinte, or at least those of the late medieval castle.

In terms of the use of space, it is unclear how the Moray Tower related to the rest of the thirteenth-century castle. The first floor hall would not have been a suitable venue for the entire household of the castle, let alone for the substantial numbers of retainers who would accompany visiting nobility, so there must have been a great hall elsewhere in the enclosure. However, there is no evidence of this on the ground. Such a structure may have been either of timber or stone, and it is perhaps likely to have been located closer to the tower than the fifteenth-century hall at the other end of the enclosure. The undated structure adjacent to the postern partly excavated by John Lewis may represent part of such a building, although there is the possibility that this relates to the rebuilding of the south range in the sixteenth century.

Bothwell Castle in the Later Wars of Independence

The reoccupations of the castle by the Scots between 1298 and 1337 appears to have included some demolition works, particularly in the aftermath of its capture by the Bruce party after Bannockburn. It is unclear which elements of the castle would have been breached or felled so as to render it defenceless in line with Bruce's standing orders, but it probably meant the demolition of at least short lengths of curtain wall.

During the prolonged English occupations of Bothwell, it has been widely assumed that repairs and small-scale building works were made to the castle, none of which are documented in detail. The *Lanercost Chronicle* notes that the castle had been repaired for Edward III in late 1336. The English king's mason, John de Kilburn, was based at the castle that December. However, the remains of the castle do not lend themselves to a close chronological analysis. In the eastern section of the north curtain wall, Simpson identified the remains of a shoulder-headed fireplace of being a type potentially English in origin. It certainly has no known Scottish parallels. This feature is set within a short stretch of the curtain, which can be distinguished from the remainder of the north curtain by the lack of a basal plinth (Figure 131). Simpson argued that this represented a freestanding hall built by John de Kilburn, which is consistent with the visible evidence. On the east, this masonry abuts the later east curtain, while the relationship with the rest of the north curtain is obscured externally by a square buttress of later date. There are no accounts of significant expenditure at Bothwell, although it is possible that any such spending was rolled up into accounts of monies spent at other English-occupied sites, given that de Kilburn accounted for works at Stirling while based at the Lanarkshire castle. This construction is unusual in that the majority of works carried out by the English in Scotland were of earth and timber rather than masonry – although Kildrummy also saw extensive rebuilding in stone by the English. It is probable that this construction work postdated the erection of a timber enclosure.

The final eviction of the English in the spring of 1337 by Andrew de Moray led to the partial demolition of the Moray Tower, according to Fordun and others. Apart from being militarily necessary, this was a highly symbolic act by a man who had the most pressing claim to possession of the castle and its lordship. In casting down half of this most visible manifestation of his patrimony, he was demonstrating his commitment to the Bruce cause. It is interesting to note that de Moray used a timber 'belfry' like that seen in the English siege of 1301, which will inevitably have had a practical justification; but it also potentially had a further symbolic element.

Archibald the Grim and the Reconstruction of Bothwell

Following his marriage to Joanna de Moray, heiress to the Moray earldom of Bothwell in 1362, Archibald Douglas, Archibald 'the Grim', began to re-edify the castle, which may have lain unoccupied since 1337. He has been credited with the completion of the south curtain which adjoins the Prison Tower and with the rebuilding of the donjon, and he may also have commenced construction of the circular south-east tower and the completion of the north-east tower on old foundations.

The reconstruction of the Moray Tower involved the building of a cross-wall enclosing the exposed internal space, recycling stone that must have remained on site after the demolition. The surviving round heads of the window embrasure, garderobe and cupboard are all fully consistent with a late fourteenth-century date, and similar to forms seen at Archibald the Grim's tower at Threave. The roof was flat, supported on putlogs driven into the surviving masonry of the great donjon. A basement and two upper storeys lay within this space, with the upper floors supported

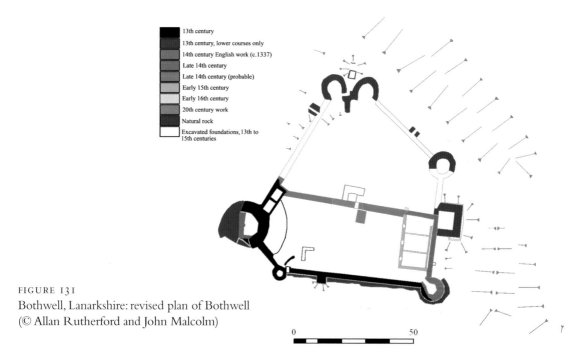

13th century
13th century, lower courses only
14th century English work (c.1337)
Late 14th century
Late 14th century (probable)
Early 15th century
Early 16th century
20th century work
Natural rock
Excavated foundations, 13th to 15th centuries

FIGURE 131
Bothwell, Lanarkshire: revised plan of Bothwell
(© Allan Rutherford and John Malcolm)

0   50

on timbers set in relatively small and shallow putlogs. These new floors were at a completely different level to those of the donjon as first built, and would have rendered unusable the earlier window embrasures overlooking the courtyard. The windows in the cross-wall all have provision for iron bars to prevent access. The overall impression is of relatively crude work, conducted with an eye to minimising expenditure. On the basis of the window bars, Simpson argued that the re-edified tower served as a prison. While this is possible, it seems somewhat unnecessary, given that there was provision for prison accommodation in the adjacent (and tellingly named) Prison Tower. Instead, the remains strongly suggest that they were to serve as residential accommodation, of reasonably high standard but most certainly not on a par with that of the donjon. It is unlikely that the repaired tower would have been deemed an appropriate personal residence for Archibald, and is more likely to have housed elements of his household.

Going beyond merely practical considerations, this rebuilding must be regarded as the symbolic counterpart to earlier actions by the de Morays; just as Walter or William le Riche had completed it, and Andrew destroyed it, Archibald brought it back to life. For a man who had designs on something more than a mere lordship, this was an action intended to stake an obvious claim to an illustrious ancestry. Moreover, the strong likelihood that Archibald was behind the building-up of the north-east tower from its extant foundations would have accentuated this claim, particularly because this new donjon had a sophisticated drawbridge setting it apart from the rest of the castle, just as with the Moray Tower. In his work at Bothwell, Archibald both revitalised an ancient past and showed how his expanding *dominium* could be literally and figuratively built on old foundations.

CHAPTER EIGHT

Pioneer of Scottish Baroque?
The Refashioning of Glamis, 1668–1684

Charles McKean

I arriv'd at the Noble Palace of Glamis belonging to Lion, Earl of Strathmore.
This palace, as you approach it, strikes you with Awe and Admiration, by the many Turrets
and Balustrades at top: It stands in the middle of a well planted Park with Avenues cut through
every way to the House. The great Avenue, thickly planted on each side, at the entrance of which
is a great Stone Gate, with offices on each side of free-stone, like a little Town, leads you in half
a mile to the Outer Court, which has a statue on each side of the Top of the Gate as
big as the Life . . . The House is the highest I ever Saw.[1]

Introduction

For all that Glamis (Figure 132) must be one of the most obvious buildings of Scotland, as John Macky observed in 1723, its rightful place in Scottish cultural history has been concealed by the way that Scottish architectural history has been constructed over the last two centuries. For the transformation of Glamis between 1668[2] and 1684 by Patrick, 1st earl of Strathmore, has been presented as throwback architecture, if not actually recidivist, when assessed against the story of the belated triumph of Palladian architecture in Scotland – which has been the dominant post-Enlightenment take on Scottish architectural history. This case study suggests that such a 'Palladian perspective' is a nonsense approach to understanding Scottish architectural culture of the century between 1650 and 1750 (and earlier). It

fails to appreciate the extent to which a national architecture remained the favoured expression of the Scottish aristocracy; or how Earl Patrick's work at Glamis, far from being the last gasp of a *retardaire* medievalism, was instead probably the earliest, noblest and *most Scottish* expression of Scottish Baroque. Glamis therefore encapsulates perfectly a central problem of Scottish architectural history.

Understanding the Scottish Cultural Context

Naturally, MacGibbon and Ross conceived of Glamis as a modified fortress (for that was how they thought)[3] based on a great tower of the late fourteenth century with the staircase within the wall thickness of the two wings.[4] Despite the evident indefensibility of the site – save a few

FIGURE 132
Glamis, Angus: view from the entrance avenue. Note its low-lying setting. The original avenue, with its sequence of gates/ thresholds, was designed to accentuate the visitor's perception of height. (© Charles McKean)

bogs – a fortress was also the perspective of the monograph *Glamis Castle* (2000), albeit it accepted the work undertaken by Earl Patrick as 'the apotheosis of Scotland's most distinctive and highly developed architectural style'.[5] The implication, however, was that this was not just its finest but its *final* expression. The *History of Scottish Architecture* (1996) goes further, in describing Glamis as 'a startling and for Scotland an unprecedented solution . . . [that] had no immediate followers'; i.e., it was an aberrational one-off. The *History's* standpoint is, instead, that between 1660 and 1760 Scotland underwent a 'fundamental change . . . from a north-west European country preoccupied with religious and dynastic issues to a secular oriented society increasingly committed to world-wide British imperialism'.[6] Viewing the century after 1660 through the narrow prism of Sir William Bruce and the supposed triumph of classicism, it concluded that there was 'a full establishment in Scotland, for the first time, of a mainstream European classicism' – whatever that was meant to imply.[7]

This appears to be an uncritical acceptance of the thesis originally put forward by Sir Howard Colvin, the doyen of British architectural historians who, back in 1986, stated that the function of Sir William Bruce was 'to design unfortified houses for the first generation of Scots lairds to realise that the tower house was an anachronism, and to persuade them to abandon corbel and crowstep in favour of cornice and pediment'.[8] Given the lamentable state of Scottish architectural history at the time, and that this was written as part of an overview from an English perspective, such a conclusion was understandable. We now know it to be wholly misconceived. However, the suggestion that Earl Patrick 'may well have taken Bruce's advice' in pursuing an elusive symmetry at Glamis shows the pervasiveness of this Bruce hagiography:[9] and it could not be wider of the mark. Earl Patrick *detested* Bruce, whom he regarded as an upstart – 'a contentious and tough lawyer' who had cheated him out of a reversion of the lands of Kinross.[10] Moreover, he never once mentioned any aspiration to make his house classical; and his essential concept was never exactly symmetrical. As had been the case throughout the Renaissance, what he and his peers strove to achieve was *balance*.[11] Earl Patrick was proud to take personal responsibility for the redesign of his ancient paternal seat and estate; and in his *Book of Record* (written for the private edification of his son), he recorded both his ambitions and his achievements, as well as his views on Bruce and 'Publick Architecturs'.

To view the advancement of architecture solely in terms of the inevitable triumph of the civilising nature of Palladianism is a particularly British – predominantly English – art historical perspective, somewhat outdated now in European circles. New research has revealed the glories of the Scottish Baroque great house, of which Glamis forms such an outstanding example, and the seventeenth-century Scottish aristocratic mindset that created it.[12] The principal preoccupations of Scottish peers remained rank, lineage and kinship, as had been the case for centuries. In his *Book of Record*, Earl Patrick recorded how much he was motivated by 'the memorie of my familie';[13] and when the earl of Mar proposed doubling his ancestral tower at Alloa, its parapet was to have been embellished with enormous letters stating: 'Thus hath a lord cultivated the monuments of his forebears.'[14] Consider, therefore, the numerous proposals to classicise ancient paternal seats throughout Scotland in the later seventeenth century. The fact that these plans remained abortive has usually been ascribed to lack of resources – national poverty, if you like – whereas the opposite was the case, particularly if one could gain a government appointment. As Earl Patrick observed: 'Improvements have been more since the time of the King's happie restauration than has been a hundred years before'.[15] So there must have been another reason for not building them. It is much more likely that members of the Scottish nobility had no taste for living in a house that resembled a merchant's – worse! a merchant of Venice's house – for such were Palladian villas. Such buildings may have been perfectly understandable for the 'new men'

– the *noblesse de la robe* – such as the tax gatherer– architect William Bruce; but they were quite unacceptable for the Scottish *noblesse d'epee*, just as they were for their French peers. Thus Palladian villas remained rare in Scotland before 1750, and the only pediment in the country, before the arrival of bourgeois King Billy in 1688, was inside Holyrood's courtyard.

Country houses combined the need to emphasise rank and lineage with the particular Scottish tendency to rebuild on site, tenaciously retaining existing structures; above all, they incorporated the ancestral tower into the composition, just as the French equally tenaciously preserved their donjons. The revived Franco-Scots architecture of the reign of James VI had contrived a new mode of emphasising rank by enhancing an already flamboyant skyline through increasing a building's height, raising it from the standard three to four-and-a-half storeys up to six or seven storeys, decorated by attenuated studies intended to resemble warlike turrets, and capped by a belvedere. These 'tall houses', as they have been christened,[16] are exemplified by twenty-four that are mostly within comfortable reach of Inverurie, including Craigievar (see Chapter 15), Castle Fraser, Crathes and Craigston – probably with Glamis as an outlier. As the century wore on and other methods were found to celebrate the ancestral tower, however, buildings quite as tall as that became rarer. Height as the premier signifier of nobility gave way to new expressions as Scottish Baroque developed in what has been described as 'the Scottish feeling for spendour combined with romantic conservatism'.[17] Primarily, it accentuated medievalism – rebuilding the parapets of Cawdor, Glenbervie and Elcho, for example, to make them appear even more martial – just as the Earl Marischal adorned his great gallery at Dunottar with carved monuments from the Antonine Wall. Then bastions – round or rectangular corner towers – were added to frame the

FIGURE 133
Hatton, West Lothian (now demolished). The western entrance façade as remodelled with bastions, a lowered tower and a belvedere, by Lauderdale's brother Charles Maitland c.1670. (© Charles McKean)

vista and convey the simulacrum of ancient lineage. This feature appeared first at Panmure in the 1650s, followed by Dudhope and Hatton for Lord Hatton, Glenbervie, Brechin and Kinnaird, inter alia. (Figure 133)

Next, the Renaissance pattern of approaching a house first through an outer then an inner court was replaced by a much more dynamic and dramatic approach. The functions of the outer court were transferred to distant barnyards and mains, and those of the inner court moved to a back court, thus permitting the visitor to enter directly into the heart of the establishment. Finally, the broader setting of the house was changed in line with European practice to signal the extension of the power of the landowner over the surrounding countryside. It has been suggested that this approach represents a 'Scottish Historical Landscape' embodying Roman values, characterised by the way in which landscape, politics, nationhood and identity are embedded in the design, and the way in which the principal axis passes through the centre of the house to distant totemic monuments or landscape features. Although Kinross House, which is aligned upon the tower of Lochleven castle, is often cited as the inspiration, there has been much research on the much larger and more

flamboyant later design by the earl of Mar for his enormous garden at Alloa.[18] Finally, it has also been suggested that the Scots habit of designing landscapes with overt and obvious historical references reveals something particular about the Scottish relationship with the past.[19]

However, some interesting points emerge from this notion of a particularly Scottish historical landscape when applied to Glamis. First, Glamis' concept preceded both Kinross and Alloa. Second, Bruce's axis at Kinross was not focused upon features associated with his *own* lineage (he being a new man), whereas those selected as vista closers for the great houses appear to have been selected specifically for the emphasis that they gave to the family's history; as indeed was the case with the earl of Mar in Alloa, and Earl Patrick at Glamis. Third, the axial anchor of the Glamis redesign – a Pictish cross-slab – was more or less invisible from the house, implying that this emphasis on lineage was more of a psychological issue for the great aristocrats: it did not have to be made manifest. Finally, whereas Bruce's landscape at Kinross was essentially rectangular, those of Glamis and Alloa were broader and infinitely more subtle, and probably far more complex in inspiration than being merely 'kite-shaped'.[20]

One of the most intriguing approaches to incorporating an ancient seat within a modern but not classical concept was James Smith's design for Traquair House which, probably by virtue of lack of funds (the earl having no public office during the period) remains half complete. (Figure 134) It is evident from the floor plan that a large ancestral tower lay to the south-east, and that there was a much smaller secondary tower to the north-east, joined by a Renaissance 'main house' (or *corps de logis*).[21] Smith's concept was to retain the original tower but decapitate its western projection, making it subservient to the main house – rather resembling a rectangular bastion – and then adding a balancing one on the north-west. The original tower was duly shrunk but, although the inner court was reformatted and the axial entrance drive completed, the balancing north-west tower was never built. Smith's design for Traquair was for a thoroughly modern and modernised house that paid homage to the past and recognised the present. At the same time, for himself, Smith recast the manor of Whitehills in the form of a pedimented classical villa, as befitted a new man.

Thus the only way in which to interpret Earl Patrick's work between 1668 and 1684 is within the context of an almost mythical accentuation of the expression of aristocratic rank, lineage and kinship, in which nobility was conveyed not through the demure horizontal expressions of Palladianism but in a tall, nobly caparisoned Baroque that would last until the 1750s. It would eventually embrace such gems as Inveraray, Douglas and many designs by William Adam, including his last one, Duff House, in 1748.

The Transformation of Glamis

Rich though they are, the sources for Glamis are incomplete. Apart from building contracts between Earl Patrick and his various craftsmen –

notably the mason Alexander (Sanders) Nisbet, the wright Andrew Wright, the painter Jacob de Wit, and the extraordinary wright/main contractor/occasional architect James Baine[22] – there is only his 1684 memoir *The Book of Record*. Thus whilst there is much (often contradictory) construction information, his architectural or design intentions have to be inferred. His dynastic objectives, however, were absolutely clear. At the age of seventeen, he inherited two fundamentally unmodernised houses badly damaged by military occupation: his ancient paternal seat of Glamis, and his jointure or summer house of Castle Huntly (which he renamed Castle Lyon after his family), as well as a grievously indebted and bankrupt estate. 'Inflam'd stronglie with a great desyre to continue the memorie of my familie,'[23] he set about restoring family fortunes, paying off debts principally through pioneering agricultural improvement,[24] modernising Castle Lyon, and refashioning Glamis as an ancient paternal seat worthy of both his family and of the new age. It took enormous effort, but Earl Patrick, who 'looked upon nothing as too hard', was ultimately successful in all he set out to do.

Glamis itself was in such a state that the Strathmores had to live in Castle Lyon for the first decade of their married life. It had, effectively, been trashed by the English garrison, who 'spoyled and damnified the house and all about it verie much', while 'some of the worst furniture' that even the soldiers had left behind was purloined by Earl Patrick's wicked stepfather[25] (Figure 135). Although his grandfather had undertaken significant works in the early seventeenth century (probably with the Bels[26]), Glamis remained otherwise fundamentally unchanged from its Renaissance form. It comprised the typical outer and inner courts, encompassing a structure whose origins probably lay in a late fourteenth-century 'great tower' extended eastwards with a fore-entry, wing and 'great round'

FIGURE 134a and 134b
Above and opposite. Traquair, Peeblesshire: James Smith's only partly realised plan for the remodelling of Traquair House. The avenue, entrance court and right hand side were realised: the left was not (© RCAHMS and Traquair House archives, SC 1232803 and SC 1232809).

tower. The remainder of the inner court comprised offices, brewhouse, bakehouse and an 'old hall' with chamber of dais and stables, mostly in ruins, environed by 'chatter'd and decay'd trees'. The approach, about 40 degrees to the east of the present one, was from the south-east on the line of the parish kirk, where a later aerial survey has identified foundations under the ground.[27]

Although all the building contracts can be seen as specific and sometimes ad hoc, there is no doubt that, from the very start, Strathmore had a design, an overall concept, to which he adhered for over sixteen years, so that, as he wrote, he could restore his family 'to some condition of living'.[28] Indeed, he had quite a lot to say about the need for such a comprehensive plan: 'I did

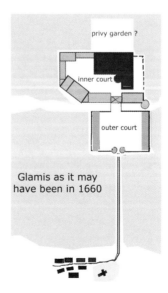

FIGURE 135
Glamis, Angus: conjectural plan of Glamis as inherited by Earl Patrick, based on the *Book of Record* (© Charles McKean)

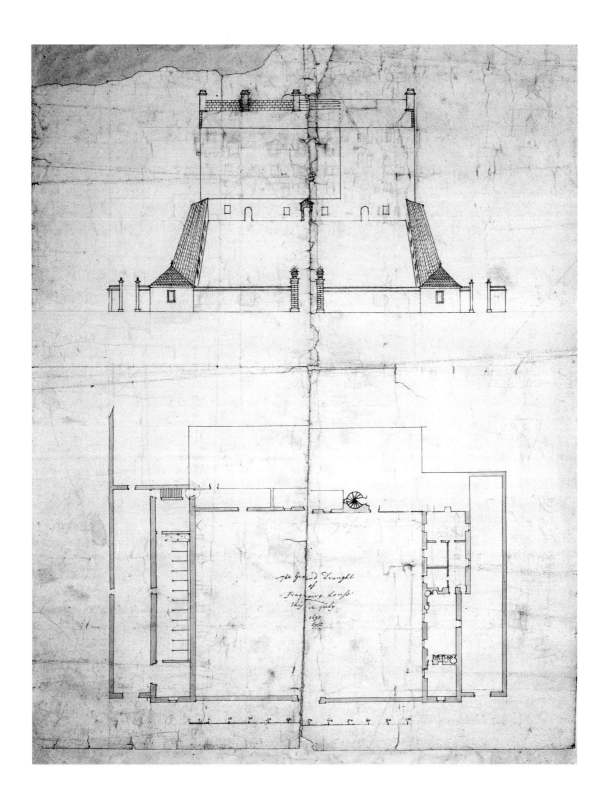

The Ground Draught
of
Prestoune house
this in july
1695
9/3

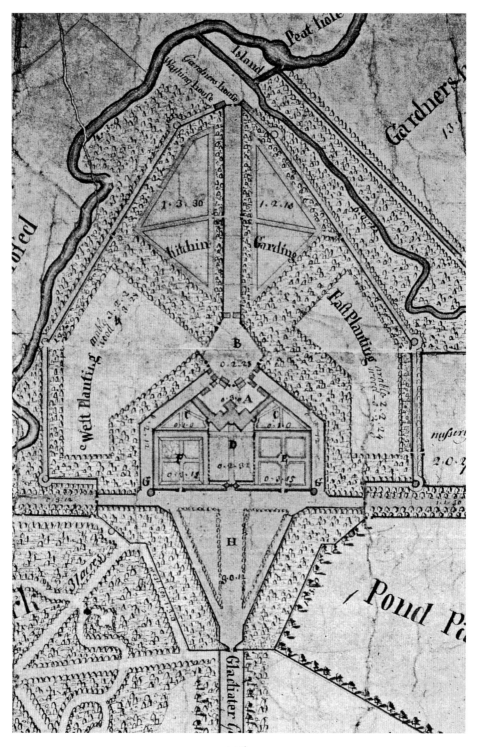

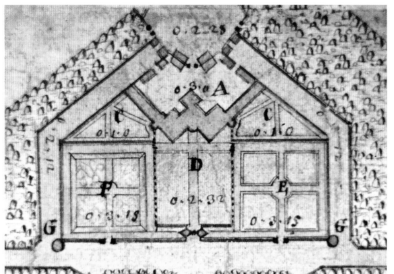

upon my first resolution [i.e., 1668 or earlier] . . . make a skame and draught of my whole project, for unless men so doe, they will infallibly fall into some mistake, do that wch they will repent ymselves aftr . . . Therefore necessarie it is for a man to desyne all at once.'[29] He observed wryly that when resources allowed only partial, periodic and piecemeal implementation, as had been the case at Glamis, he had needed to be 'extremely tempered with patience' (Figure 136).

Whilst it is entirely possible that Earl Patrick might have been influenced by John Reid – whose book *The Scots Gardn'r* was published in 1683 – in that the house lay as the epicentre of a large design,[30] his concept came at least fifteen years earlier and its geometries were very complex, so it is quite likely that the influence went the other way. At the core of Earl Patrick's design was the reorientation of the entire policies from a south-east axis to one marginally off south-west, so that the new one ran like an arrow between the original site of the Glamis Pictish cross-slab[31] and the great stairtower in the angle of the house. That angle would determine the plan of the new back court, inner court, west

wing, chapel tower and the walled policies as a whole in a rigorous manner completely unlike, for example, Versailles. As was the case in nearby Kinnaird, the perimeter wall, over several miles long, was punctuated by small circular bastions at each change of orientation; and running along the entirety of its outside was a walk, which was bounded by a gurgling burn to enhance the experience.

The outer and inner courts were replaced by a back court at the rear, allowing the metamorphosis of the approach. He then balanced the composition by adding a new west wing and bastion to match the restored and heightened sixteenth-century east wing. A new inner court was created to complete the diamond begun by the house; and that diamond shape formed the dominating motif of the entire concept. At the apex of the diamond, he added a square tower on edge (thus also in the form of a diamond), in which Earl Patrick's two crucial chambers – his charter room and his chapel – were stacked above a new kitchen. He appears to have referred to this structure as his 'mounthoolie', implying that it may have been the spiritual core of his concept.[32]

FIGURE 138
Glamis, Angus: Captain John Slezer's 1686 drawing of Glamis. The wing on the left is not entirely as constructed: it was instead, capped by a balustraded belvedere. (© Charles McKean)

It was certainly at the epicentre of the design.

The diamond form even extended to the gatehouse of the inner court, which was flanked by twin diamond-shaped summer houses, 'verie convenient and refreshful roumes' with black and white marble floors, marble table and cane chairs. One opened onto the bowling green, and the other onto the garden. At each far end of the inner court wall was a 'round' or circular bastion, the one containing a still house and the other a dairy (Figure 137).

The back court was also in the form of a diamond; and this same conceit governed the walled policies to the north, containing the kitchen garden and tree nursery, albeit modified by scale. A much broader-scaled diamond design

embraced the entrance axis; and it is from this axis that Strathmore's design agenda might be surmised.

In contradistinction to the great Baroque gardens then being prepared or soon to be prepared for Drumlanrig, Kinnaird, Hamilton and Alloa, Strathmore conceived of a quasi-mystical approach to Glamis, whereby the perceptions of visitors were manipulated not just by the rise and fall of the entrance drive (for that can be seen at Brechin) but by having to pass through a sequence of thresholds: the outer gate, the Barns – or Satyr – Gate, the Gladiator Gate, and finally the inner court gate flanked by its triangular, horizontally proportioned balustraded lodges. Each threshold appears to have been designed to

FIGURE 139

Glamis, Angus: view in the eighteenth century, showing the entrance to the inner court. Some of the compression of the approach avenue between the Barns and the Gladiator Gates, as painted by de Wit in the portrait of Earl Patrick, had been removed and replaced by vistos. (© Charles McKean)

accentuate the scale of the tower upon arrival. A possible source for his concept is the masonic diagram 'The Tree of Life', in which the celebrant passes through thresholds to higher levels of purity.[33] The geometry is very similar, and the Strathmores – particularly Earl Patrick's son – were prominent masons.

As for the house, all Earl Patrick retained was 'the great old house' itself. Everything else was swept away – to 'great censure in the cuntrie – especially amongst my owne people'.[34] He had three principal ambitions. The first was to achieve balance: 'to order my building so as the frontispiece might have a resemblance on both sides,' which he achieved by constructing the new west wing to replace his father's brewhouse and bake-

house, to match the heightened east wing. 'The old house stands now in the middle with two wings whereof that upon east syde coast me a new roof, the other on the west side was founded and furnished by myselfe'[35] (Figure 138). However, contrary to the Slezer 1685 engraving – which shows both wings as identical – the west wing was given a flat lead platform or belvedere for a roof instead of the spicily roofed eastern wing. Earl Patrick observed with satisfaction that the lead flat was 'of great convenience and use to us who live in this side of the house'[36] (Figure 139).

The new wing also allowed him to create what he called 'a following' to his great hall ('a rowme that I ever lov'd'[37]), by which he meant

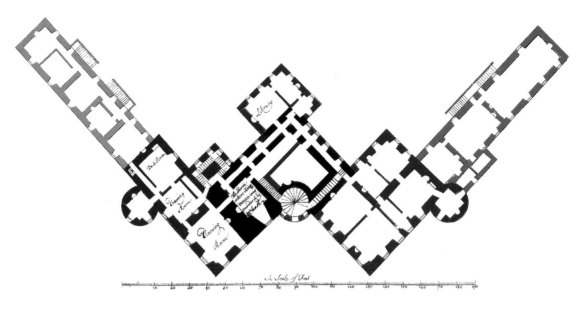

FIGURE 140
Glamis, Angus: plan in the 1740s, and probably as realised by Earl Patrick. Note the corridors linking east west wings, the new west stair, and what had by now become the library (charter room) at the centre. (© Countess of Strathmore).

the required sequence of increasingly private chambers of a state apartment. He then reorganised the internal sequence so that the women and children occupied the east wing, and he the west. The 'mounthoolie' or chapel tower was at the centre of the new plan. (Figure 140) The new wing needed a new rear staircase similar to that added to the east wing, and the cutting of new corridors through the thick walls of the original tower to provide communication between the two wings without going through the principal chambers. Finally, to cap it all, he created a new belvedere or viewing platform above the gallery on the roof, designing special ironwork, which he commissioned from the Edinburgh smith, John Walker,[38] and probably the two delightful stone gazebos on the gables, capped by carved lions who command the countryside for miles around.[39]

Earl Patrick, Architects and Design

In his *Book of Record*, Earl Patrick explained why – beyond despising Bruce who, at this time, had quit Balcaskie to begin the layout of Kinross – he had taken control of the design himself rather than employ 'publick Architecturs'. Although he had never been able to go abroad because of the wars and the Cromwellian occupation, he visited Edinburgh and London frequently, where he had observed 'things weell ordered and contrived att other mens dwellings'. Moreover, he was very close to his benefactor, his uncle Panmure, and it is probable that he met Panmure's fine architect John Mylne, who was to die only in 1668, by which time Earl Patrick had almost completed his transformation of Castle Lyon and just begun to realise his design for Glamis. He might well have learnt subtleties of planning from Mylne, but

Glamis is so different from Panmure and Mylne's other buildings as to imply a totally different design inspiration.

Despite acknowledging the value of 'taking counsell' from those 'known and reput to be the best judges and contrivers' (i.e., people like Mylne), Earl Patrick produced his own work: 'I have prosecut my designe,' he wrote, 'every yeare.' From his reference to the walls of the west wing as having been erected 'according to my draught', one may infer that, in addition to conceiving the overall 'skame', he had also produced detailed elevations. He gave three reasons why he had not employed 'publick Architecturs'. First, his project was too complex – embracing architecture, interior decoration, structure, gardening and estate layout – for the skills of a single individual. Second, there was modesty; the resolution to proceed with 'little noice and by degrees'. The third reason was the crucial one: he had acted as he had more 'to pleas and divert myself then out of any ostentation'.[40] *He wanted to design it himself.* The only possible conclusion is that Earl Patrick, like the earl of Mar some forty years later, was a

FIGURE 141
Top. Glamis, Angus: view from the south drawn by John Elphinstone. Note not only the Quellin statues, but the fact that the lettering on the stairtower has been changed to 'Countes of Strathmore'.
(© British Library, Maps.K.Top.49.23.a.5)

FIGURE 142
Above. Glamis, Angus: the view from the belvedere
(© Charles McKean)

keen architect. His *Book of Record* is littered with references to other plans for further improvements and his designs to improve the barns his father had built, to design an additional gate for the avenue, to design the fountain, to continue laying out the parkland and, by planting trees, to make 'the seat of the house verie glorious as invi-ron'd with a wood'. In his patronage, he was absolutely up to the sophisticated mark. He purchased paintings in Holland, highly fashion-able and expensive fashionable furnishings in London, and commissioned four larger-than-life statues for the inner court, 'adopting what was very much the current fashion in London, and employing one of the most fashionable sculptors [Arnold Quellin] of the period'[41] (Figure 141).

On the other hand, the building accounts also reveal that whatever his skills on the large scale (and they were many), he lacked the architectural ability of imagining space and volume. Only during construction on site did he realise that his plans for both the west wing and the chapel tower were too narrow; and the instructions to widen them to an appropriate volume caused disputes with his workmen, who had already supplied the narrower-dimensioned timber and sought additional payment for supplying the wider spans.[42] Indeed, a number of the great building disputes can probably be attributed to problems caused by Earl Patrick's 'learning by doing'. Whether or not he also used John Slezer as architect as well as perspectivist (as did many, such as the duke of Lauderdale and the earl of Southesk at nearby Kinnaird) is unknown, but it is worth observing that Slezer had first been in

the neighbourhood in 1678, and that his later elevation of Glamis did not show the west wing as finally executed.

Conclusion

This examination of Glamis implies that the approach to Scottish architectural history bet-ween 1650 and 1750 requires a radical overhaul (Figure 142). Glamis was neither the last nor the only great house to be conceived of in terms of the Scottish Baroque that formed its context. Many of its key features were later to be found in other houses – although none, so far as can be discerned, to a comparable geometry with a comparable inspiration. Earl Patrick's sophisti-cated work at Glamis was almost certainly the progenitor of the flamboyant Scottish Baroque houses and landscapes that characterised the period 1660–1750; and the architect was Earl Patrick himself.

Acknowledgements

This case study is dedicated to the late Dr Mary Young, who first introduced me to the fascinating character of Earl Patrick. I am particularly indebted to the researches and insights of Charles Wemyss, Kate Newland, Sue Hewer and Christo-pher Dingwall in the preparation of this chapter. I am also very grateful to Dundee University Archives and the countess of Strathmore.

CHAPTER NINE

Caisteal Inbhir-Aora /
Inveraray Castle

Aonghus MacKechnie

Introduction

Inveraray was reconstructed from 1743 by Archibald Campbell, 3rd duke of Argyll, who inherited the dukedom from his brother in that year. Campbell's programme embraced a new castle, new town and consolidated estate (Figure 143).

A context for these developments was Scotland's 'Age of Improvement': the century and a half or so from around 1700. This was an incredibly energetic nationwide programme of social, economic and architectural reconstruction, on an unprecedented scale. Rural townships were erased to create modern farms and consolidated estates, and the displaced populations were settled in new-made towns, which were commercial and, in addition, often newly industrial centres, containing places of worship, education, government and justice. Scotland's most famous new town was possibly Edinburgh's (albeit really an extension to the city), commenced in the 1760s, but it could be argued that in an architectural context Scotland's Age of Improvement was exemplified by the key developments begun two decades earlier at Inveraray for the 3rd duke.

This study proposes another context within which Inveraray Castle might be set: that of the myth-making surrounding the new concept of an ancient Britain. This myth-making arose from the new political context of fragile union, and an ideology that sought to elide the differences between England and Britain by creating a new history — a history that was simultaneously English and British, and within which Scotland was placed.

Early Inveraray

Inveraray was a long-established settlement. Sites such as this, at the rivermouth intersection of two waters, were often settled early, as the legion of 'Inver'/'*Inbhir*' or (Pictish) '*Aber*' placenames, denoting such sites, shows. Here at Inveraray was fresh water, a crossing place and a navigable transport route: the River Aray and Loch Fyne.

A key moment in Inveraray's development came around 1440 with the decision by Sir Duncan Campbell (d.1453) to relocate the primary Campbell seat from inland Lochawe to the more fertile and accessible Inveraray. There he built a massive tower, mainstream contemporary Scots in design (and resembling the same client's Kilchurn), with the town and church alongside, each serving the other in the standard arrangement of medieval settlement.

One route to the main Lowland/eastern

FIGURE 143
Inveraray Castle Argyll: view from south (© RCAHMS, SC 457768)

centres was partly overland, optionally along Loch Eck, which resulted in Campbell bases being established at Carrick Castle, near Lochgoilhead (?fourteenth century) and Rosneath (a tower house), and a collegiate church endowed at Kilmun in 1442, containing the family sepulchre.

Inveraray 1650–1743

By the time of the Restoration of the old order in 1660, architecture was a standard intellectual interest amongst Scottish elites, exemplified by the 'gentleman architect'; albeit there was a tradition, too, of architects – such as Sir Anthony Alexander (d.1637), Charles I's joint master of works – being

from the landowning class. This 'hands-on' aristocratic interest in architecture within the Argyll family is known from 1669, when a plan of, or for, Kilmun Church was drawn by the 9th earl (1629–1685), while in 1666 another aristrocrat, Sir Robert Moray, was advising the earl on a new house and classical landscape.

Seventeenth-century interventions at Inveraray seem to have focused on the gardens and landscape rather than on the castle. Both the Beech Avenue (incorporated within, and helping dictate the orientation of, the new town) and the Lime Avenue, for example, seem to have been planted for Gilleasbuig Gruamach, Archibald Campbell, marquis of Argyll (1607–1661). The marquis led the Covenanter government army which in the 1640s had opposed the royalist army under the marquis of Montrose.

Montrose's army had sacked Inveraray when the estate was savaged, and for the first time since the Reformation mass was witnessed in the town. Argyll was the technical winner, seeing Montrose to execution and placing the crown on Charles II's head in 1651, only to himself be executed by the Restoration government in 1661 for his compliance with the regicidal Cromwellian regime of the 1650s. Montrose and Argyll, famous in martial history, had a place too in wider cultural history: Montrose wrote poetry, but less well known was Argyll's close interest in architecture and garden design. Inveraray was again attacked in 1685, in reaction to the 9th duke's crusading anti-Catholic invasion of that year.

An Unbuilt Project

At the old castle, symmetrical and detached pavilion blocks, flanking the Lime Avenue, were added for the 1st duke by or around 1720, emphasising the concept of a formal classical arrangement (as was seen too at, say, Killochan, where the asymmetrical tower was given a symmetrical setting). But around 1720, a remarkable and colossal house was designed by Alexander McGill (d.1734) (Figure 144). The pavilion blocks – one a stables, the other domestic – seem to have been built in different phases, and perhaps both were also designed by McGill. These pavilions were now intended to be incorporated as terminals to the outer court of the McGill mansion. A second, enclosed courtyard was to be the heart of the house. It would have three great stairs, the centre and main stair leading to the state apartment and salon/main public room above. The outer stairs were private ones, leading to either the duke's or duchess' apartment set on either side. In having paired apartments the building was orthodox,

based on the great palaces of Europe and ultimately Versailles, but its scale was colossal for a Scottish house. It was never built, but it does illustrate some ideas of the time. Remarkably, the ancient castle was to be clasped, unaltered, at the heart of the inner courtyard, but not accessed from the new work. The castle door would be its only entrance, perhaps suggesting a wish to retain the tower as a security in case of attack, or perhaps simply to keep it intact. Nonetheless, it was ultimately the ancient tower that dictated the intended new building's location and orientation, and as it was to be emphasised rather than concealed, the castle was presumably esteemed for its antiquity.

The Third Duke and Inveraray

Above all it was Archibald Campbell (1682–1761), second son of the 1st duke of Argyll and, from 1706, earl of Ilay (Islay); who was responsible for creating the Inveraray of today. His patronage brought a sequence of major architects, designers and craftsmen.

Campbell had been educated at Eton and the universities of Glasgow and Utrecht, becoming first a lawyer, then a soldier, and then a politician. He worked closely in his political career with his brother, John (1678–1743), who succeeded as 2nd duke in 1703. Although the brothers oscillated in and out of royal favour for decades, they were ultimately two of the most prominent politicians of their time in Scotland – or, in the 2nd duke's case, Britain. Archibald was nominated by Queen Anne as one of the commissioners for union, and both he and his brother had a key role in bringing about the union with England of 1707.

Although the two saw Scotland was a low priority in the context of the new Britain, they accepted this, because of their overriding commitment to what was for them the much

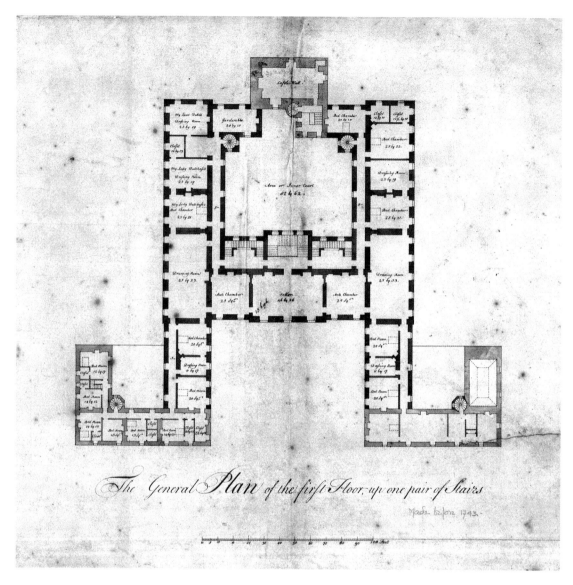

FIGURE 144
Inveraray, Argyll: first floor plan for unbuilt scheme
by Alexander McGill of 1720 (© RCAHMS,
SC 1233582)

greater issue, or prize, of union and Protestant
Britain's interests. They supported the appointment in 1714 of the genetically distant but
Protestant Elector of Hanover as King George I,
as opposed to reinstating the ancient dynastic
Stewart monarchy: that is, the two brothers were
anti-Jacobite. Archibald was wounded at the
Battle of Sheriffmuir during the Jacobite Rising
of 1715. He had also a major role in creating what

became the Royal Bank of Scotland in 1727. In 1743, aged sixty-one, he became one the greatest territorial magnates in Scotland and began a new life, becoming the richer with treasury compensation from the government's abolition of heritable jurisdictions in 1747. This abolition followed defeat of the Jacobite Rising of 1745–6, crushed by the government army on the battlefield of Culloden and through follow-up reprisals. He had lots to spend, and he was – as we see so clearly today – at the forefront of the new generation of Scottish elites determined to modernise their country and reconstruct its entire landscape and economy.

Aside from politics, Campbell was an intellectual, classicist, scientist, botanist, mathematician, patron, trustee from 1753 of the British Museum, and he amassed 'one of the largest private libraries in western Europe'.[1]

Inveraray Rebuilt

With the 3rd duke's programme for change at Inveraray, the town was relocated to a nearby site and built totally anew, thereby creating a private estate landscape. This was a process begun in the previous century, when the parkland was extended northwards by absorbing townships such as Kilmalieu, giving the castle more privacy and a stronger presence.

A litany of major architects and designers was to be involved, including William Adam (Scotland's foremost architect from about the 1720s until his death in 1748), John Adam (William's son, brother of Robert), and Robert Mylne (1733–1811; prizeman at the Academy of St Luke in Rome. Mylne was present in 1744 when what may be the earliest known, although seemingly unexecuted, design for an iron bridge in the western world was made for Inveraray.). The duke's architect was Roger Morris (1695–1749), while

William Adam (1689–1748) had a visiting, superintending role. Another architect, John Douglas (d. 1778?) was also connected to the project in some way, having produced a drawing of the castle.

In 1740s Scotland, the 'castle' formula was widely seen as out of date, and new architecture was classical. The 3rd duke reversed this by choosing Gothic for both Inveraray Castle and Rosneath, which he also reconstructed.

Rosneath was by then an L-plan tower. Morris' 1744 project envisaged something similar to Inveraray. The tower would be incorporated, its single angle-turret duplicated, the main façade a classical grid but with Gothic pointed openings, precisely as built at Inveraray. Rosneath was ready for the duke's occupation by 1757, but how far this particular project was followed through is unclear.

Partly driving this creation of new Gothic castles were changing attitudes towards the 'old'. Sir William Bruce's Kinross House (begun late 1670s), a sparklingly modern palazzo set in a formalised estate, was aligned upon the ancient and historic Lochleven Castle. The castle was revived from obsolescence by Bruce as an object no longer to inhabit, but to view.

The 3rd duke's new Inveraray Castle contrasted with this (Figure 145). It was not an up-to-the-moment piece of neo-classicism, but instead an 'ancient' and simultaneously modern dynastic castle. At the same time, a new architectural landscape feature was built: the rustic Gothic tower on Dun na Cuaiche/Duniquaich, high above the castle (Figures 146, 147 and 148). As an unmissable, critically important and dominant eyecatcher, it had a 'satellite' function akin to that of Lochleven to Kinross; here, though, not terminating a vista, but instead set as a picturesque, rubbly, intriguing and castle-like 'ornament', placed as if randomly on a hilltop skyline. Thus both Kinross and Inveraray were touchstones of

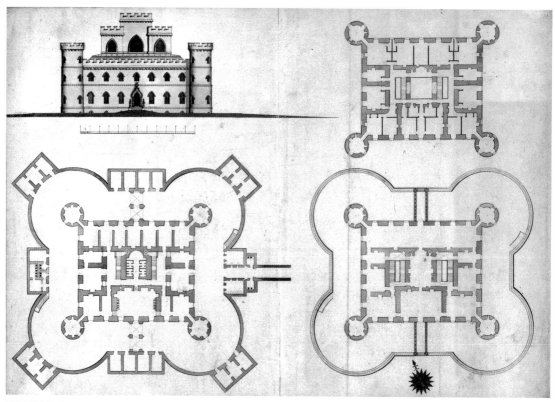

FIGURE 145
Inveraray, Argyll: plans and elevation by Roger Morris of 1744–5 (© RCAHMS, SC 1233622)

FIGURE 146
Inveraray, Argyll: perspective elevation for addition to Duniquaich of c.1747 (© RCAHMS, SC 1233581)

FIGURE 147
Inveraray, Argyll: view showing Inveraray Castle and Duniquaich before 1877 (© RCAHMS, SC 1233617)

FIGURE 148
Inveraray, Argyll: view of Duniquaich Tower, Castle and town from north-east (© RCAHMS, SC 457808)

new fashion, and each was significant in the wider terms of British architectural history, or beyond.

Campbell's Unexecuted Scheme

Before the final decision to build Inveraray as he did, the duke explored options. He considered retaining the old castle, but was advised against this in 1744 by the mason William Douglas, as its condition was so poor that it made repair unviable. So a new residence was necessary. Another option explored was a project for a new 'house . . . in the castle stile', made by Dugal Campbell (d.1757); an early neo-castle, but hybrid, in being also clearly domestic (Figure 149).

Campbell, besides being a kinsman of the duke, was a military engineer from 1734 or so. He fought at Culloden and died in 1757, the same year he was appointed chief engineer in North America, where he was on service, having served previously in Flanders and elsewhere. His best-known work was the Governor's House at Edinburgh Castle (1742), which still exists. His Inveraray design was for a 'house', 'defended with a fosse and covered way', and a drawbridge, all 'to defend the house'. Client and designer were both alive to the political opposition of many neighbouring clans to the Campbells, and were attuned to the risk of Jacobite attack. After all, Atholl's sack of Inveraray in 1685 had taken place during the 3rd duke's lifetime.

Campbell's design is undated, but it must date from around 1743–45 if it was intended for the 3rd duke's consideration. Its obsessive symmetry in plan ties it firmly to its period, its balustraded wings to the precedent of Glamis, but it lacks key fundamentals of an eighteenth-century elite house such as a big saloon/gallery and grand staircase, these sacrificed in favour of other priorities. Its star-shaped 'footprint', developed from Renaissance fortifications such as Rocroi, was stan-

dard in military work. Castellated flat roofs, dome-topped turrets and towers were all martial-looking, too. On the other hand, the house had standard-sized windows, like any other mansion of the time. Campbell sought to straddle the division between martial and domestic, while the design that was executed employed some of the same vocabulary, notably the moat or fosse, bridged entrances and casemates, and crenellated circular corner towers.

Campbell's domestic block had a symmetrical splay-plan, a formula dating from at least the 1620s, and used over a century after then by William Adam at Minto (1738–43) for Sir Gilbert Elliot (1693–1766), a friend of Argyll's. Here we see it planned for Inveraray at almost exactly the same time.

The Castle's Final Design

In the event, and as we have seen, the architect appointed by the duke was an Englishman, Roger Morris, who had worked for him previously and had also been an employee of another of the duke's Campbell kinsmen, the architect Colen Campbell (1676–1729). Morris produced a classical design whose plan was similar to the one that was built and that in turn was based on a design seemingly by Sir John Vanbrugh (1664–1726) of possibly the 1720s, when the 2nd duke was – as McGill's above-mentioned scheme demonstrates – clearly thinking of building. Vanbrugh's scheme (if it was his) was for a much smaller house than was eventually built – while McGill's was for one much larger – but the design was castellated.

There are several strands that possibly influenced the 3rd duke's final choice of design. As the interior is classical and the exterior, by contrast, Gothic, we can consider these aspects in turn.

Internally, the plan was symmetrical in layout, all composed around the central lantern tower and twinned staircases. It consisted of two apartments (one presumably a state apartment) flanking a T-plan suite of public rooms which comprised entrance hall – saloon – and full-width gallery designed to impress visitors such as Argyll's tacksmen, tenants and so on, the gallery's function being for grand entertainment. The duke was Highland clan chief while at Inveraray in his 'ancient' castle, in contrast to his more anglicised persona in London.

The Inveraray arrangement of a top-lit square centre tribune flanked by twinned staircases around which the rooms were disposed was not new. This was the formula at Broomlands (unexecuted c.1719 project, possibly designed by James Smith), for instance, William Adam's project for Newliston (c.1730?), and Dugal Campbell's scheme itself, but the mammoth scale of Inveraray's tower sets it apart from these. Inveraray could be compared too with Campbell's own Mereworth Castle (c.1720–5), the colossal centre dome here substituted by a Gothic square tower. The castle's original entrance was on the south. On either side of the entrance hall were identical apartments: three rooms of diminishing scale extending so far as the gallery, with a fourth smaller room beside each stair and thus unwindowed. This twinned three-room arrangement, comprising drawing room/parlour, bedroom and dressing room/closet (the fourth rooms evidently for servants), was an established Scottish formula, seen at Melville House (c.1697–1702, which was included in Colen Campbell's *Vitruvius Britannicus*), where one such apartment was a state apartment. John Gifford discusses state apartments in Chapter 11. These were built in hope of a royal visit, but the fashion was ending precisely when Inveraray was being built, and he has suggested that the idea may at Inveraray have been to create a state apartment at concept but not completion stage – particularly as the duke required the southmost drawing room/parlour to have a Corinthian

Order. The corresponding north-west apartment was plainer, and contained the duke's bed. As fitted out, after the death of the two key architects – Roger Morris, the designer, in 1749 and William Adam in 1748 – John Adam was in charge.

Turning to the exterior, the façades are gridded and symmetrical as on a classical design; but the design is Gothic. The windows are pointed, while the classical balusters favoured on platform roofs since the 1660s (for instance, at Drumlanrig) were substituted by crenellations like the work of the 1620s or earlier. It was this decision to choose Gothic that set Inveraray apart from contemporary architecture, and that made it so innovative.

What were the reasons for building a Gothic castle, and what were the signals this arresting new design were intended to convey? There are numerous possibilities. The obvious point is simply to suggest that because revived Gothic was new, it was thus attractively fashionable. But was there more?

As we have seen, *Vitruvius Britannicus* was the work of a Campbell kinsman who was Morris's one-time master. Its production was supported disproportionately by Scots (around a quarter of volume 1's subscribers), including seventeen of the Clan Campbell, showing strong family or clan support. Amongst these were both the 2nd duke and the future 3rd duke, each of whom had a design dedicated to them. The design for Lord Ilay was unbuilt, but elements – the twinned stairs flanking a tribune – were to reappear at the castle, as if Colen Campbell's ideas retained duke Archibald's favour.

Vitruvius Britannicus volume 1 included one ducal seat from Scotland. This was Drumlanrig (spelled 'Drumlenrig', as the name was then pronounced by the Scottish elite), the only named castle included in that volume, and (save for Hampton Court) the only castellated building in the entire three-volume work. It was not a Gothic castle but a classical one, with giant Corinthian

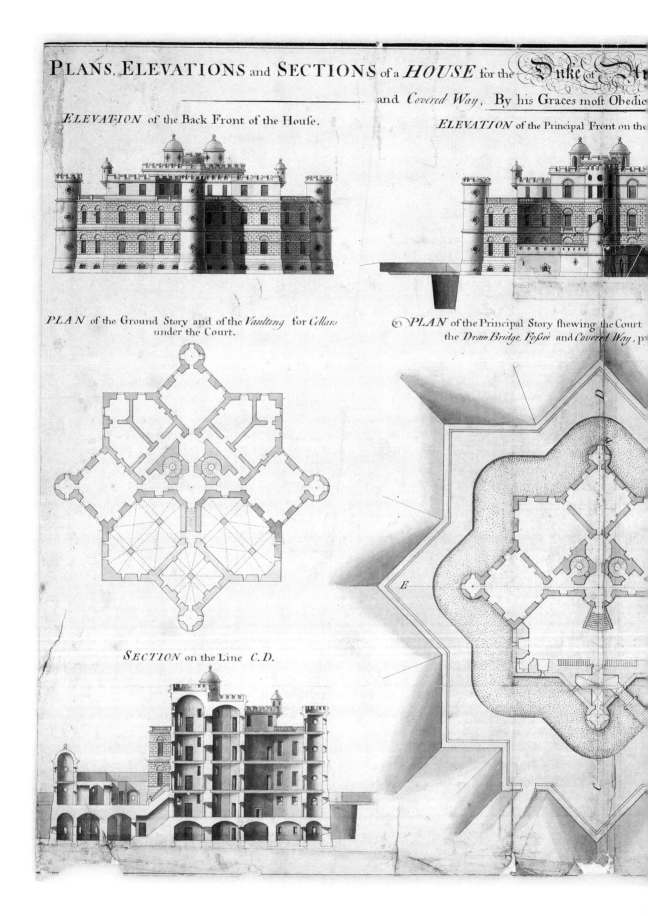

PLANS, ELEVATIONS and SECTIONS of a *HOUSE* for the *Duke of* ...

and *Covered Way*, By his Graces most Obedie ...

ELEVATION of the Back Front of the House.

ELEVATION of the Principal Front on the ...

PLAN of the Ground Story and of the *Vaulting* for *Cellars* under the Court.

PLAN of the Principal Story shewing the Court ... the *Draw Bridge*, *Fossee* and *Covered Way*, p ...

SECTION on the Line *C.D.*

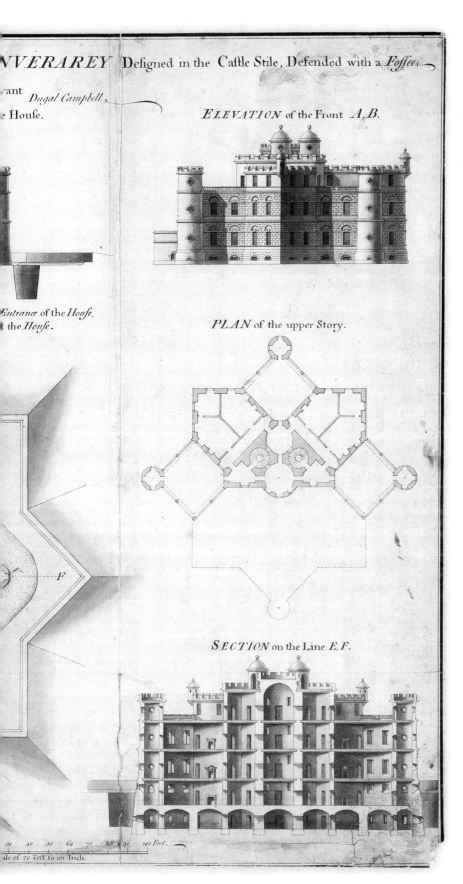

NVERAREY Defigned in the *Caftle* Stile, Defended with a *Foffee.*

vant *Dugal Campbell*

e Houfe.

ELEVATION of the Front *A,B.*

Entrance of the *Houfe,*
the Houfe.

PLAN of the upper Story.

F

SECTION on the Line *E,F.*

30   40   50   60   70   80   90   100 Feet.

ale of 20 Feet to an Inch.

FIGURE 149
Inveraray, Argyll: plans,
elevations and sections
for unbuilt scheme by
Dugal Campbell of
1743–45 (© RCAHMS
and the Duke of Argyll,
SC 1233583)

Order. Drumlanrig's significance was that it was a modern castle, rebuilt for the Queensberrys, one of Scotland's most prestigious 'ancient' families. The 2nd duke of Queensberry played, together with the two Campbell brothers, a critical role in the Act of Union. Drumlanrig's inclusion indicated that an 'ancient' ducal castle was appropriate for a modern (Protestant and unionist) Scottish duke.

Another strand of thinking might have been the significance that Gothic had to English elites. For antiquarians, from the early eighteenth century or earlier, it was the most valued ancient national style, to be protected, and then revived. This assigned Gothic a patriotic, political value, and that in a time when sophisticated political landscapes were being created – the most famous examples including Stowe, and the 'Temple of Liberty' of 1741, by James Gibbs for Lord Cobham, a Gothic structure created as a defiance of continental absolutism and Catholicism.

To some modernising English architects and clients, revived Gothic became therefore both excitingly novel and patriotic. These values were broadcast by Batty Langley, famous as the introducer of 'pretty' Gothic (soon termed 'Gothick' by those interested in more archaeological revivalism) for garden structures, and whose publications promoted the Gothic style. Langley (with Thomas Langley), set out his position in his 1742 publication *Ancient Architecture, Restored, and Improved, by a Great Variety of Grand and Usefull Designs, Entirely New in the Gothick Mode for the Ornamenting of Buildings and Gardens*. To Langley, England's great ancient Gothic buildings were really Saxon (i.e., English):

> As it is very reasonable to believe that the Modes in which all these buildings have been erected, the Banquetting House excepted, were taken from Fragments, found among the Saxon ruins, they may

therefore be called Saxon buildings; but why they have been called Gothic, I cannot account for.

The book's patrons were termed 'Encouragers to the Restoring of the Saxon Architecture', the 2nd duke of Argyll being amongst them.

Langley's bombastic nationalism was evident earlier when, in 1736, he attacked the Rome-trained James Gibbs (1682–1754), a Catholic crypto-Jacobite whose politics Langley opposed but whose talents he respected. He criticised Gibbs for his 'Scotch Mode of Speech', and undertook for his readers:

> I will make all these [i.e., Gibbs' Scots] easy to your Understanding, and his Terms also; you must not critically read this master, nor be angry if his Terms be a little aukward, as indeed they are in many Places in his New Rules of Drawing, as he only can call them . . . when he says cross-wise, he means (tho' he had not Sense enough to say) at Right Angles'[2]

As for Gibbs' rule for drawing the 'Scotch volute' to the Ionic capital, the reader was warned it 'hath a very disagreeable and clumsy Diminution, not to be practised by any'. Gibbs' Scottishness was presented as a problem; and this was a time when Scottishness seemed too closely aligned with Jacobitism and the threat of invasion from the north. On the other hand, Langley devised 'The English Order of my own Composition'. He had found his task a problem because there were so many existing versions of the Orders. It was

> to the immortal shame of ourselves, they are all either the Inventions of Foreigners, or Monkey imitations of them; nor has any one Englishman, that I know of, ever yet attempted to compose an Order in

Honour of his Country, as the Greeks, Latins, Romans, French and Spaniards have done'[3]

The English Order had a star and garter and symbolic oak leaves ('a glorious oak preserved the sacred person of Charles II', whilst the mighty navy – 'the strength of the Nation' – and ships of trade used the oak).[4] Langley's plates included technical details of arches, including Gothic ones (Plates ccclvi–ccclxiii).

Revived Gothic had been considered or used frequently in England before the 1740s, for instance by Vanbrugh, but the style was still innovative. Maybe more important than all else was the nationalist political value placed on Gothic in England by people such as Langley, for these values could be translated into British ideologies. The distinction of what constituted British as against English culture and history was elided – as seen at Stowe's 'Monument of the British Worthies', who were all English, including King William, given his English numeral of William III (he was William II of Scotland and of the United Kingdom). Back in union-age Scotland, Scots such as the philosopher David Hume were busily 'Englishing' their writing and speech, giving thus an at least tacit approval to this elision.

The earliest known account of an ancient Scottish building being restored or repaired simply for its intrinsic value as a monument was not a castle in the national style, but a Gothic one.[5] This was Rosslyn's collegiate church, and the work was the consequence of pressure on the owner by Sir John Clerk of Penicuik, union politician and antiquary, who also oversaw the work, recognising it to be specialist. It was repaired in 1739, to the approval of Roger Gale, one of Clerk's English antiquarian friends.

However, Scotland seems not to have built Gothic Revival monuments before the 1740s. Here, the authority of antique classicism was unchallenged. But the use of monuments to tell political stories was far from novel, and Scotland's old national ideologies were now replaced by those promoting the new, fragile Britain.

An excellent opportunity for commemoration was provided by the Battle of Dettingen, in Bavaria, in 1743.[6] An alliance of British, Hanoverian and Hessian troops (the 'Pragmatic Army') overcame a French army, and present was King George II, whose safe deliverance was celebrated extravagantly. Georg Friedrich Handel, for example, composed a celebratory Anthem and thanksgivings.[7]

The British army at Dettingen had been commanded by a Scotsman, Field Marshal John Dalrymple (1673–1747), 2nd earl of Stair, and the victory was commemorated in Scotland. At Carnell House, for example, lime plantations were created to replicate the two Scottish squares at the battle, and similarly inspired landscaping at Dumfries House included a 'Mount Stair'.[8] A monument was erected at Newhailes: it was classical, but here we see Scottish architecture called into the service of both Scottish pride and British unionism. The key point for us in all this is that these Dettingen commemorations show that precisely when Inveraray was being built, unionist British politics was being celebrated in Scotland through estate architecture and landscaping.

We have already noticed the 3rd duke's own politics as likewise strongly unionist and anti-Jacobite – like the mainstream of English thought. Yet, while heritable jurisdictions – where Highland landowners were empowered to implement local justice – were gone, the mentality continued nonetheless in the 3rd duke's mind. He manipulated the outcome of the 'kangaroo court' trial of James of the Glens, a Jacobite, hanged ostentatiously in 1752 as the alleged murderer of Colin Campbell of Glenure, a kinsman of the duke but, maybe more significantly, a government man.

Fear of Jacobitism and Catholicism, and solidarity with England in opposing both, also helped align Scottish elites not with the bulk of their own Highland countrymen but with England. The 3rd duke's grandfather, the 9th earl, had been executed by the Catholic King James VII/II for his invasion, which he had hoped would make the united kingdoms Protestant. Argyll's heir, General John Campbell of Mamore (1693–1770), the future 4th duke, was aide-de-camp to the 2nd duke at Sheriffmuir, while his son served with the Argyll Militia at Culloden under the duke of Cumberland, one of many of the 3rd duke's kinsmen present at the battle. (Furthermore, the duke's advocacy of new roads to 'open up' the Highlands brought him the personal advantage of a new military road from Dumbarton over the Rest And Be Thankful to his own front door.) The victors of Culloden tended not to build physical monuments to themselves, but inscribed on Inveraray's foundation stone was one such piece of triumphalism, a homage to the duke of Cumberland for his role in extinguishing militarised Jacobitism. The stone was laid in William Adam's presence on 1 October 1746, five and a half months after Culloden.[9]

It seems therefore fair to suggest that the 3rd duke's strong anglophile/British politics – which meant close alignment with England – possibly helped influence his choice of building style. After all, architecture was being used during this period for political purposes. Furthermore, Gothic showed allegiance to the values that the duke had helped create through his part in union, and had helped defend on the field at the Battle of Sheriffmuir: values that were manifest otherwise through his strident, undying anti-Jacobitism.

Postscript

Work on Inveraray Castle continued into the 1750s and beyond. Regarding its architectural legacy, this took perhaps two immediate strands. First, the idea of a symmetrical design with Gothic-pointed windows was reproduced by the brothers John and (probably) James Adam at Douglas (from 1757); and, closer to Inveraray's design, with centre tower, at Taymouth, in 1801, for the Breadalbane Campbells (Figures 150 and 151). But such designs were few, for, as set out in Chapter 3, the next generation of castles were not Gothic, but were arguably more akin to Dugal Campbell's scheme. Campbell's design was not built, but its splay-plan formula lived on. It is possible that Robert Adam, who knew Inveraray and knew extremely well what was going on there, had Campbell's scheme in mind when composing his plans for Beauly and Beaufort, each being splay-planned, or for Wedderburn, which was similarly part-rusticated. After Inveraray – maybe an aberrational design for unsettled times in an unsettled region – Scotland in the main returned rapidly to a more orthodox castellated formula, brought to the fore at first by Robert Adam and followed by William Burn (1789–1870), David Bryce (1803–1876), and many others; for Gothic, of course, continued into the early nineteenth century as one strand of design.

The 3rd duke died in 1761, his programme only partly complete (Figure 152). The new town continued being built to completion, as well as the new corner-towered offices at Cherry Park, all in classical style, with John Adam initially in charge after Morris and William Adam were dead. Robert Mylne oversaw the castle's completion, with the plasterer Thomas Clayton undertaking some of the more sophisticated decoration, but its character changed from Gothic back/forward to classical. The estate was embellished, with contributions from, for instance, artist–designer Alexander Nasmyth (1758–1840), best known for his much-reproduced portrait of Robert Burns and for participating with Burns

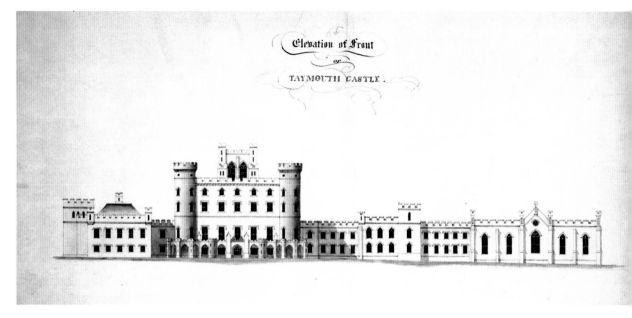

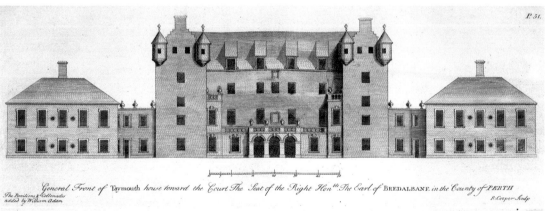

and William Symington in, reputedly, the world's first steam-powered boat ride, at Dalswinton Loch in Dumfriesshire in 1788. Thus the castle remained until 1877, when it was damaged by fire. It was repaired under the supervision of Anthony Salvin (1799–1881), when the present dormered attic was added, plus the fairytale pointed roofs over the turrets. It was renovated in the 1950s by the architect Ian Lindsay (1906–1966), who was so seduced by the place that he co-wrote, with the historian Mary Cosh, an

FIGURE 150
Top. Taymouth, Perthshire: front elevation of the nineteenth-century castle (© RCAHMS, SL 887109)

Figure 151
Above. Taymouth, Perthshire: the courtyard front as modified by William Adam c.1733 and illustrated in *Vitruvius Scoticus* (© RCAHMS, SC 761027)

227

FIGURE 152

Inveraray, Argyll: pen drawing showing the view of the castle from the south from *A Tour in Scotland* (1772), vol. 2 (3rd edition, 1774) (© Historic Scotland)

exemplar architectural history of Inveraray. Lastly, the castle was again restored by Lindsay's old firm, subsidised by an international appeal to the clan, following another fire in 1975.

Conclusion

Inveraray, like Blair, had early been a 'castle'. McGill and the 2nd duke intended to supersede it with a 'house', and Dugal Campbell – presumably exploring an option with approval from the 3rd duke – with a house in the castle style, while the duke settled on his new house being called 'Inveraray Castle'. Ultimately, it may be that Inveraray Castle – to James MacAuley 'the first major Gothic revival building in Britain' and for

Howard Colvin 'the progenitor of a whole sequence of symmetrical Georgian castles' – should be considered as having a meaning beyond that of innovative artistic design. It seems that Inveraray, like many of England's Gothic creations of the wider period, was built not simply to be fashionable but also to convey a political message. Sometimes, politicians do things for political reasons. Not simply would the duke of Argyll's seat exemplify what a Highland duke might build in the bulwark between 'Jacobite Highlands' and 'Lowland unionism', but it would signify too an absolute commitment to the recently made and more recently threatened state that was Protestant Britain, the alignment with English culture and the myth of a single 'national' history which this demanded.

CHAPTER TEN

Culzean Castle

Michael Moss

Culzean Castle in Ayrshire, formerly the home of the marquesses of Ailsa, is the most visited property of the National Trust for Scotland (Figure 153). The castle sits in a commanding position on the cliffs overlooking the Firth of Clyde and is surrounded by a remarkable designed landscape studded with intriguing buildings. It is often described as one of Robert Adam's finest domestic compositions, although many of the buildings that form the castle complex date from well before his time. Culzean Castle has its origins in the sixteenth century when Sir Thomas Kennedy, the brother of the 4th earl of Cassilis, was granted a charter over the lands of Cullen, a huge tract of land extending from Ayr to Girvan and as far inland as Loch Doon. He presumably either began building or enlarging the castle, then known as Cove. Given the size and wealth of the estate, it was a large building, possibly not dissimilar to the family's principal stronghold at Castle Kennedy, near Stranraer, the ruins of which are still standing. The first records that survive of the castle are from the early eighteenth century when Sir Archibald 'the Wicked' Kennedy, so called because of his pursuit of Covenanters, broke through the barmkin wall that surrounded the building and constructed the terrace gardens that survive to this day. Impoverished by their political support for the Jacobite cause, the family took to smuggling on a large scale in the North Channel, and to slave trading with the American and Caribbean colonies. For much of the time they lived in Ayr, only occasionally visiting Culzean in the summer months.

In 1744 Sir Thomas Kennedy, who at the time was serving in the Netherlands with the Hanoverian army, inherited the estate on the unexpected death of his older brother Sir John. In the army Sir Thomas made friends with young aristocrats who were enthused by the ideas of the enlightenment and by classical antiquity. Returning to Scotland in 1746 to help put down the Jacobite Rising, he was so outraged by the behaviour of the duke of Cumberland's forces that he espoused the Jacobite cause. He left Scotland in 1748 for an extended Grand Tour that was to last for seven years and took in France and a long stay in Rome, where he moved in the circles of the aesthete the 1st earl of Charlemont. He appeared playing the bass-viol in Joshua Reynolds' well-known painting 'Parody of the School of Athens'. While he was away he sent instructions in 1750 for improvements to be made to the castle, including a new dining room on the ground floor overlooking the terraces, a new kitchen and a drawing room in place of the great hall on the first floor. At the same time, the entrance to the castle courtyard was dignified with a classical

FIGURE 153
Above. Culzean, Ayrshire: general view to the south-east. The terraces created by Sir Archibald 'the Wicked' are in the foreground. Photograph taken by the 3rd marquess of Ailsa.

FIGURE 154
Opposite. Culzean, Ayrshire: view of the tower gate and stables taken from the castle to the west. This was the main entrance until Adam created the new archway on the right. Photograph taken by the 3rd marquess of Ailsa.

tower and stables added to accommodate Sir Thomas' racehorses (Figure 154).

On his return in 1755 he built a Palladian villa for himself in the neighbouring town of Maybole, which today does duty as a branch of the Royal Bank of Scotland. During the remainder of the decade Sir Thomas continued to make minor improvements to the castle and the estate. The 8th earl of Cassillis died childless in 1759, and Sir Thomas claimed the title; but he was not officially recognised as 9th earl until 1762. He was back in Italy in 1764, when he commissioned a portrait from the fashionable painter Pompeo Batoni. Returning home, his mind turned once more to improvements. The castle was re-roofed

and the walls razed to their present height. In September 1766 the foundation stone was laid for a new block overlooking the sea called the 'office houses of Culzean' attached by a corridor to the castle. Apart from the offices, it included three bedrooms and a billiard room. It took two years to build. All that survives of this building are piles of masonry at the foot of the cliffs. To fund these ambitious projects, the earl borrowed heavily, to the concern of his agent. He died in Edinburgh in 1755, leaving debts of over £30,000, and was succeeded by his brother David.

David, an Edinburgh advocate, lived when in Ayrshire a short distance from Culzean, at the charming Newark Castle. At first he thought of

moving the family seat there, but he quickly changed his mind and decided to remodel Culzean, possibly as a memorial to his brother. He invited Robert Adam to give him advice. The first project was to build a new kitchen and an east wing adjoining the office houses of Culzean to serve his brother's new eating room. This was a major undertaking, involving the removal of huge quantities of rock. The next operation was to fill in the 'L' of the old castle to form a rectangular house with turrets at each corner. At the same time the tower gate was to be heightened and crenellated, and all the retaining walls and terraces were to be embellished with battlements and mock fortifications (Figure 155). The walled

garden was also removed from its site beneath the terraces to its present site. This phase of the building work was completed in 1783.

Before further work could be carried out on the castle, the estate offices had to be moved to a new location. Earl David instructed Adam to design 'an extensive and very commodious plan of offices' along with a home farm steading. Built on the promontory half a mile to the north of the castle in about 1787/8, the buildings arranged around an open courtyard contained everything a land steward could want, including a house, dairy, dairyman's house, stables, poultry sheds and barns. It is now the visitors' centre for the country

park. It was not until the offices had been removed that Adam could persuade Earl David to demolish his brother's extension and commence building the saloon, great circular staircase and adjoining rooms, including a replacement billiard room.

Work began on this massive operation, which almost doubled the size of the castle, in 1788, rendering it almost uninhabitable. At the same time, extensive alterations were to be made to the grounds by the landscape gardener Thomas White that probably included proposals to flood the old Cow Park to form the Swan Pond (Figure 156). The approach to the castle was altered by Adam

to include a massive new entrance gate to the courtyard and the ruined arch leading to the battlemented causeway (Figure 155). In the midst of these extravagant building works, the earl became strapped for cash and was forced to ask his bankers to meet the interest payments on his debts. He became seriously ill in February 1790 and, with no heirs, he had to decide who should inherit the estate. Providing no other claimant came forward, the next heir to the title was a distant cousin, Captain Archibald Kennedy, who was born in New York and now lived in London. He was immensely rich, having made a fortune in prize money during the Seven Years War. This

FIGURE 155
Opposite. Culzean, Ayrshire: view along the viaduct towards the old tower gate in the 1880s. Photograph taken by the 3rd marquess of Ailsa.

FIGURE 156
Above. Culzean, Ayrshire: the lawns in what is now Fountain Court with the conservatory behind, which was conceived by Thomas White. This was previously the vegetable garden and orchard. Photograph taken by the 3rd marquess of Ailsa.

was just as well, as Earl David's debts were now some £60,000 and the rental income of the estate about £4,000. No doubt aware that Captain Kennedy could afford to shoulder the burden, Earl David entailed all his property to him.

It is difficult to know how much of the final phase of building work was completed by 1790. A drawing of Culzean in 1791 shows the drum tower roofless, with a considerable amount of work to be done. It is very likely that the earl's creditors would not have allowed any more work to proceed other than to make the building wind- and water-tight. Adam died suddenly in March 1792, and the earl followed him to the grave in December. All the evidence suggests that the new building work was unfinished and, more seriously, no attempt had been made to control costs. With the estate so burdened with debt, the creditors insisted that it must remain in trust until they were repaid. In these circumstances, no further investment on the property could be made. Moreover, Sir Andrew Cathcart, whose mother was Earl David's sister, challenged his will in the courts, claiming the estate through the female line. Such cases were invariably long, costly and heavily influenced by the political allegiances of the contestants. Cathcart was a Tory, while Captain Kennedy had Whig sympathies.

The 11th earl visited Culzean in 1793, when he ordered furniture for the castle. His wife died in Edinburgh in December of that year, and he died exactly a year later. His eldest son, also Archibald, became the 12th earl. He was an irascible character with a fiery temper, who did not like to be thwarted. He also had ambitions to cut a figure in London society and in the House of Lords. At first his attitude towards Culzean was ambivalent. He was mired in a protracted lawsuit whose outcome was by no means certain. He made some modest improvements to the grounds and built a new coach house behind the old tower gate that now does duty as a shop. Even

when he emerged victorious in the House of Lords in 1810, he toyed with the idea of selling the whole estate and moving to a more convenient property near Edinburgh. This intention was frustrated by further legal action by Sir Andrew Cathcart. Making the best of a bad job, the earl resolved to improve the management of Culzean by taking a number of the farms in hand and appointing his cousin Captain John Shaw as his factor. Nevertheless, he took a keen interest in the smallest details of husbandry, issuing a stream of instructions every time he was at Culzean.

By the summer of 1812 any idea of selling Culzean had passed. The earl purchased a veritable armoury of obsolete weapons from the Tower of London to decorate the hall, which can still be seen at Culzean. It is the largest collection of eighteenth-century hand guns in the United Kingdom outside the Royal Armoury. It would seem that the internal finishing of the great oval staircase and saloon finally began at this time. The grounds were improved (Figure 157). The old public road that had passed in front of the castle was diverted to the line of the present A719, and three Gothic lodges were built to guard access to the estate. The Swan Pond was finally created and the park embellished with a number of new buildings. An ornamental battery was built on the cliff top to the south of the castle; an orangery (known as the Camellia house) between the walled garden and the castle; an aviary or bird house, including an aquarium, near the Swan Pond; and a pagoda to house a menagerie. This work was entrusted to a variety of architects and engineers, with the earl endlessly interfering.

Work on the castle progressed more slowly, as the earl was unable to decide whether he wished all these projects in the grounds to take priority. Most of the work in the grounds was finished by 1815 and the castle was finally completed more or less to Adam's design at about the same time. A year later, the sea-bathing

FIGURE 157
Culzean, Ayrshire: the path from the Swan Pond to Piper's Brae. Photograph taken by the
3rd marquess of Ailsa.

changing room was built on the beach, along with the extraordinary rustic bath house behind it, which is now used as a store house. The lawsuit with Sir Andrew was not finally settled until 1825, by which time the creditors of the 10th earl were becoming very impatient. Part of the estate was sold, and the 12th earl could now take full possession. However, by then the earl had decided to spend most of his time in London, either in his grand town house in Privy Gardens facing the river opposite Horse Guards Parade in Whitehall, or at his new country seat at St Margaret's in Twickenham Park, which he began rebuilding in 1823.

Culzean was simply to become a summer retreat. Although the walled garden was greatly enlarged, the bird house extended and water closets installed in the castle in 1820, no further building work was undertaken for much of the remainder of the decade, presumably because the earl was preoccupied at St Margaret's. In 1829 the mortar battery was constructed in the castle courtyard and an opening made in the perimeter wall to afford spectacular views out to sea (Figure

FIGURE 158
Culzean, Ayrshire: a liveried coachman holds a horse in front of the mortar battery in the 1880s.
Photograph taken by the 3rd marquess of Ailsa.

158). Two years later the earl was created marquess of Ailsa by King William IV. They had been boyhood friends in New York, and the king's illegitimate daughter Lady Augusta was married to John Erskine-Kennedy, the new marquess' second son. John Erskine-Kennedy died of tuberculosis in 1831, followed a year later by his elder brother Lord Kennedy, a spendthrift and notorious gambler, and his wife Eleanor Allardyce. The marquess was left with nine young children to bring up. To cope with the added washing, a new laundry was built alongside the bath house at Culzean in 1839, now known as the Dolphin House and used as an educational centre. Two years earlier, St Enoch's lodge was built to provide access to the carriageway up Mochrum Hill. Unlike previous buildings undertaken by the 12th earl, the design of these projects was a self-conscious attempt to replicate Adam's designs.

In 1842 disaster struck when the marquess' grandson, the titular 14th earl of Cassillis, and his brothers lost somewhere in the region of £100,000 on the racecourse at Bogside in Irvine. Urgent action was taken by the marquess' agent to prevent disaster, and expenditure was reduced to a minimum. Overwhelmed by these troubles, the marquess died at St Margaret's in 1846. His heir, now the 2nd marquess, did not care much for Culzean and preferred to indulge his passion for hunting by renting the Priory in Reigate, while his trustees struggled to clear his gambling debts. Alarmed at his improvidence, his agent and factor called for restraint and retrenchment. It was not until 1852 that they compelled him to leave Reigate and move to Culzean, where he was to remain for much of the rest of his life. His debts were colossal and the only solution was strict economy. He and his wife spent their time at Culzean hunting, shooting and curling in the winter months, and in the summer fishing and sailing. With the finances more firmly under control by 1855, his trustees allowed him to buy a small cutter and to begin to make an annual visit to London. Only essential building work took place on the estate, including in 1859 a new vinery to replace its predecessor, which was in danger of collapse, and a new stables (now a shop) opposite Adam's office and farm buildings in 1863, to replace the old stables that had been gutted by fire.

In March 1870 the 2nd marquess was thrown from his horse while out hunting with the Eglinton hounds, and died a few days later. This tragedy was also a stroke of fortune for others, as the proceeds from his life assurance policies cleared much of his debts. As a result his eldest son, the 3rd marquess, was able to indulge his passion for sailing in a way that his father had not been able to. At the time of his father's death he had just married Lady Evelyn, the daughter of Lord Blantyre and granddaughter of the fabulously wealthy duke of Sutherland. She insisted that Culzean should be refashioned for comfortable modern living. In 1877 the Edinburgh architects Wardrop & Reid were commissioned to make substantial alterations to the castle while at the same time respecting the integrity of the Adam design. The brewery wing was converted into a new nursery

wing connected on three floors to the existing house. The hall was to be enlarged with a new portico. The dining room was to become a sitting room with views over the garden. The library and the old dressing room were to be knocked into one to form a new dining room with a magnificent papier-mâché ceiling in the Adam style by Jackson & Sons of London. On either side of the new portico, offices and model rooms were to be fitted up for the marquess to pursue his interest in ship design. The whole house was to be redecorated from top to bottom. Building work began in the autumn and was not completed until the spring of 1880. In the garden below the terrace, a huge fountain was fitted up, and the long-neglected deer park restored to provide a home for exotic animals.

The marquess began boat building at Culzean in 1880 in a shed put up on the shore below the castle, which still stands. With a rapid growth of orders, the business was moved in 1883 down the coast to Maidens. By then, due to his extravagant indulgence in owning and sailing yachts, coupled with a decline in his rental income as the agricultural depression began to bite, the marquess was in serious financial difficulties. Despite abundant warnings, he did little or nothing to reduce expenditure. In fact it went up. Lady Evelyn, the marchioness, became ill with consumption in 1885 and in 1886 her youngest daughter Lady Evie died at Culzean of diphtheria. In her memory, a convalescent home was built at Ardlochan, which now serves as the reception centre and offices of the caravan site. At the same time the estate workers built the charming thatched summer house in the walled garden for her brother Lord Charles. These were the last buildings to be constructed in the grounds by the Ailsa family.

Lady Evelyn died in July 1888. Her distraught husband could not bear to be at Culzean without her. He abandoned his children to their evangelical governess and went off to his shooting lodge above Loch Doon. The castle was shut up, and the marquess was only occasionally there for the next three years. On his visits his agent and his factor tried in vain to persuade him to face up to his increasing financial problems as debts mounted. He remarried in 1891 and it was hoped he might settle down. Instead, he took to spending much of the summer fishing and shooting in Scandinavia, staying in a modest shooting lodge near Gunnarvatinet that he built with his cousin Admiral Sir John Baird. The winter months were spent in London. This, in some ways, was a relief to his agent, as it was much less expensive than summer yachting expeditions or heating Culzean during the winter. Nevertheless, household expenditure was consistently greater than the income from rents could support.

In 1898 Lord and Lady Ailsa retreated to Pau in the south of France, which had become a sanctuary for impoverished and bankrupt members of the nobility. He quickly became bored, and to while away the days he took up golf. Much to his alarm the factor was soon bombarded with letters proposing that a golf course be laid out in the old deer park. This was completed by October, when a greenkeeper was appointed. Since the family was, unusually, to spend the winter at Culzean, the marquess ordered a new curling pond to be fitted up nearby at Morriston. The golf course was relocated to Turnberry in 1903 and is the origin of what is now the world-renowned hotel and international course. On the death of his mother in 1899, the marquess no longer had to pay her £3,000 annuity, and this allowed him to begin a major restoration of the grounds, particularly the cleaning and repairing of the Swan Pond and making the elaborate rockery in the walled garden.

Nothing, however, could disguise the pressing financial problems. To avoid the enormous cost of running Culzean, the family spent much of the time when they were in Scotland at the shooting lodge above Loch Doon. The site is now marked by a monument on top of a pile of rubble in the woods above the Stinchar bridge in the Galloway Forest Park, near Straiton. In 1904 crisis struck. Culzean was shut up and the family were forced to live modestly in a rented house in Yorkshire. When the crisis had passed, the marquess, true to form, returned to his passion for sailing, which he financed out of his interest in his boat-building business, now called the Ailsa Shipbuilding Co., with a yard in Troon. The election of the Liberal government in 1905 with a mandate for social and educational reform resulted in a massive increase in the tax burden on landed property. At Culzean, it climbed from 13 per cent of revenue in 1900 to 21 per cent by 1914. Although it was now essential to sell property to make ends meet, the marquess and his wife embarked on a most extraordinary project to refurbish the castle in the style they imagined Adam had intended, if it had been completed in his lifetime, which of course it had not. This involved selling off surplus furniture and fittings and using the proceeds to redecorate and refurnish the principal rooms. The best eighteenth-century furniture was sent to be restored in Bath. The work included new hangings and the rebuilding of the chimneypieces in the dining room and the first drawing room. Additional eighteenth-century furnishings and fittings were purchased, in a conscious attempt to re-create the Adam interiors.

On the eve of the First World War the estate was running at a loss even before the household expenditure was added. The outlook was bleak. By 1921 the factor's overdraft had climbed to £28,000–£3,000 more than the credit limit. There was pressure for even greater economy. As the world slid into depression and then slumped, the situation became even more serious; but the marquess and his wife were quite incapable of addressing the future of the castle and the estate.

With the marquess in his eightieth year in 1926, there was alarm about the possible death duty liabilities that could easily have bankrupted the property. By the early 1930s the estate was in arrears with both the Inland Revenue and the local authorities, which were threatening legal proceedings. At the eleventh hour the marquess agreed to disentail the estate, which was transferred to a new limited company. He died in April 1938, in his ninety-first year.

Like many other great houses, Culzean was now much too expensive for the family to maintain, and the 4th marquess and his wife urgently began to seek a solution to secure its future. Their efforts were interrupted by the war and the 4th marquess' death in 1944. However, his widow was determined to ensure that the castle passed into the safe keeping of the National Trust for Scotland, which had been formed in 1931. Agreement was finally reached in October 1945 for the Trust to acquire the castle, garden, policies and the home farm. Although Lord Charles, who had succeeded his brother as the 5th marquess, warned that the castle was not all by Adam, the Trust was deceived by his father's restoration into thinking that the work had been completed by 1792.

Thanks to the Trust and the foresight of the 4th marquess, Culzean has survived, unlike the homes of two other Ayrshire earls, Eglinton Castle and Loudon, both now nothing but ruins. The family still lives in and farms the surrounding estate. There are, though, many unanswered puzzles about the castle, particularly what motivated the 10th earl to build it and amass such enormous debts in the process. He had no children, and at the outset only a distant heir whom he did not even know. Why did the 1st marquess lavish so much expenditure on it when he was only there in the summer months, and what could have induced the 2nd marquess and his brothers to wager their inheritance on a horse race at Bogside in Irvine, of all places? These questions will never be answered; but what is true is that, thanks to the extravagance of several generations of the family, and the huge fundraising initiatives of the National Trust for Scotland, Culzean is a place of rare beauty that can be characterised as one of Robert Adam's greatest achievements.

CHAPTER ELEVEN

From Blair Castle to Atholl House to Blair Castle

John Gifford

Between c.1680 and 1750 there was scarcely a nobleman's or gentleman's house built in Scotland which was not designed to include a state apartment. After 1750 the state apartment no longer featured in new houses. The mid eighteenth-century schemes for remodelling Blair castle exemplified this change, a change perhaps linked to a change in the way the social and political order was viewed by Scots of the same years.

In 1755 James, 2nd duke of Atholl, erected a rubble obelisk with a gilded ball finial (the 'Balvenie Pillar') on the hillock of Tom na Cròiche (the 'Gallows Knowe') just outside but visible from the parkland of Blair Castle.[1] This commemorated the former place of execution within the regality of Atholl, an area covering about 200,000 acres of Perthshire in which successive earls, marquesses and dukes of Atholl had exercised jurisdiction, effectively as sub-kings, over all criminal cases excepting only high treason. After the 1745 Jacobite Rising, regalian jurisdictions were abolished by the Heritable Jurisdictions (Scotland) Act of 1747, which brought all cases under the direct jurisdiction of the crown.[2] It may not be an entirely accidental coincidence that 1747 was also the year in which the 2nd duke of Atholl began a massive programme of remodelling of Blair Castle along lines radically different to what he had contemplated only a few years earlier.[3]

This converted the castle, renamed Atholl House, to a wholly pacific and externally unambitious domestic structure, although containing state rooms of a magnificence with few parallels in Scotland. Did this also mark a change in the duke's self-awareness from seeing himself as part of a feudal hierarchy ultimately dependent on the monarchy to a member of a Whig oligarchy by whose permission the King reigned? In his earlier schemes for remodelling the house the duke had intended, as its architectural climax, a state apartment, a processional suite of rooms, theoretically for occupation by the king or his deputy. In the executed design the state rooms served to glorify the dukes of Atholl, and the king's apartment became an appendage.

Blair Castle in the Early Eighteenth Century

When Lord James Murray succeeded his father as 2nd duke of Atholl in 1724,[4] he inherited vast properties in Perthshire, including the sizeable late seventeenth-century mansion of Dunkeld House. Blair Castle seems to have been neglected except as a fortification which had been garrisoned during the Jacobite Risings of 1689 and 1715.[5] Although in the 1720s it was described by Daniel Defoe as the duke's 'ordinary Residence, and

FIGURE 159
Blair Castle, Perthshire: view of east front by C Frederick, 1736 (© RCAHMS and Blair Charitable Trust, SC 1232872)

where I say he keeps his Court like a Prince',[6] it was a ramshackle agglomeration stretching south from a thirteenth-century tower to an uncompleted seventeenth-century block, its irregularly turreted and towered appearance of a description which was not to be fashionable for another century.

The house inherited by the 2nd duke was still apparently recognisable as the west range of a castle of enclosure begun in 1269.[7] This had contained at its north-west corner a small stone keep ('Cumming's Tower'). Perhaps in consequence of a visit to Blair Castle by James V in 1529, when a wooden hall had been erected for the reception of the king, this keep was heightened to a five-storey tower with turreted corners and a sizeable block added to its south. The new block contained cellars on the ground floor. At

the south-east corner a bowed tower, surmounted by a two-storey rectangular and corner-turreted top, contained a comfortable turnpike stair to the two principal upper floors. On each of these was a 15-metre long hall entered from the turnpike and probably with a screens passage at its south end. From the hall's north end opened an inner chamber in the remodelled keep. This layout, with two sets of apartments or suites of rooms, each consisting of a hall or outer chamber and an inner chamber, seems to have been derived from contemporary royal palaces. One of these sets of rooms, probably the upper, was intended, at least in theory, for the king's occupation, the other for the earl of Atholl's.

About 1630 John, first of the Murray earls of Atholl, began a further extension of the house. At the north end of the sixteenth-century hall

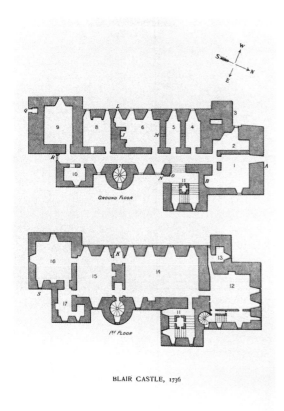

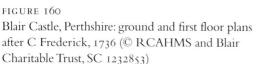

FIGURE 160
Blair Castle, Perthshire: ground and first floor plans after C Frederick, 1736 (© RCAHMS and Blair Charitable Trust, SC 1232853)

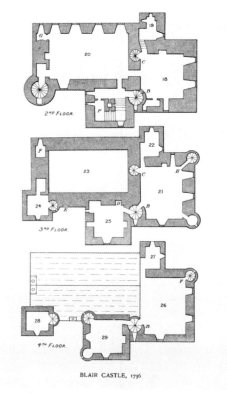

FIGURE 161
Blair Castle, Perthshire: second, third and fourth floor plans after C Frederick, 1736 (© RCAHMS and Blair Charitable Trust, SC 1232864)

block's east side he added a rectangular tower, also with a corner turret, which contained a large scale-and-platt stair to serve as a new principal access to that block's lower and upper halls; these were presumably given new screens passages at their north end and had the position of their high tables moved to the south. South of the main block the earl began the construction of an addition containing a first floor inner chamber or drawing room, bedchamber and closet. A similar set of rooms was presumably intended for the floor above, thus providing a suite of rooms for the earl on one floor and a state apartment, at least

theoretically for the king's occupation, on the other. The former inner chambers on the first and second floors of Cumming's Tower were relegated perhaps to bedchambers for less important guests or members of the earl's retinue. The civil wars of 1638–50 brought work to a halt before the second floor had been begun. After the Restoration of 1660 the attention of the earls (later marquesses and dukes of Atholl) turned to the building of Dunkeld House, and Blair Castle remained unhappily incomplete and antiquated (Figures 159, 160 and 161).

The East Front of an Addition to the Castle *of* Blair

one of the SEATS of

His Grace The Duke of Atholl

By Mr Douglas 1736

FIGURE 162

Blair Castle, Perthshire: view of east front in John Douglas' scheme, 1736 (© RCAHMS and Blair Charitable Trust, SC 1232871)

John Douglas' Proposals of 1736

In 1736, twelve years after his succession, the 2nd duke of Atholl at last obtained designs for the extension and remodelling of Blair Castle from John Douglas,[8] an architect who was to be described accurately enough ten years later as 'next in character [as an architect] to Mr. Adams [William Adam]'.[9] (Figures 162, 163 and 164) Externally, Douglas proposed to recast the house by thickening it to the east and removing all overt 'castle' references. For the new front he designed a three-storey façade of classical swagger with an advanced and pedimented centre and ends. The first floor was to be approached by an external double stair, the wallhead's parapet crowned by a

procession of urns. The relatively small windows of the ground floor denoted its humble function as containing service and servants' rooms, the taller first floor windows disclosing the presence of the ducal family's room behind and the yet taller round-headed openings at the second floor acting as an expression of that floor's status as the home of the castle's state apartment.

Douglas' proposed interior would have been one of the grandest and most clearly laid out examples of the early eighteenth-century planning of country houses to contain both a family apartment or set of rooms and also a state apartment. For Blair Castle, Douglas proposed that the first floor be reserved for the occupation of the duke and his family. The outside stair would have

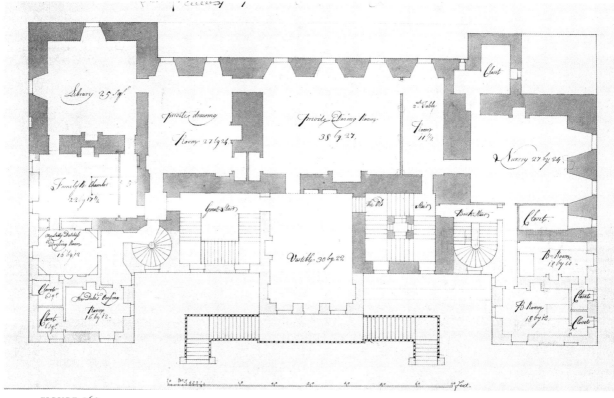

FIGURE 163
Blair Castle, Perthshire: plan of first floor in John Douglas' scheme, 1736 (© RCAHMS and Blair Charitable Trust, SC 1232869)

opened onto a large entrance hall of 30 x 22 feet. Either side of this were to be staircases, the north being the existing seventeenth-century stair, perhaps remodelled, rising from the ground floor the full height of the house, the south (the 'Great Stair') only from the first to the second floor. West of the entrance hall was to be the private or family dining room (38 x 27 feet) with, to its north, a smaller 'second table' room where the upper servants ate, these two formed from the house's sixteenth-century lower hall. This L-plan ducal apartment would have continued from the south end of the private dining room into the private drawing room (27 x 24 feet) formed from the seventeenth-century inner chamber. At the

house's south-west corner would have been a 25-foot square library, a remodelling of the seventeenth-century bedchamber. East of the library was to have been the family bedchamber (22 x 17½ feet) formed from the seventeenth-century dressing room and closet and an extension to the south. Wholly new and contained in Douglas' south-east wing were to be dressing rooms for the duke and duchess, each with a closet. The north end of the first floor (Cumming's Tower and Douglas' addition to its east) would have been less formally arranged and held a virtually self-contained group of a nursery and two bedrooms, all with closets.

Douglas planned a state apartment for the

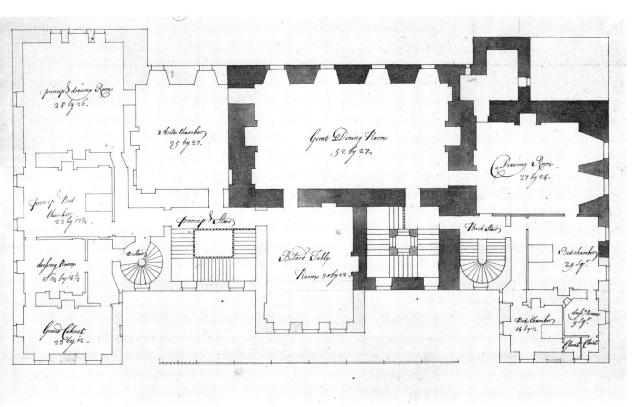

FIGURE 164
Blair Castle, Perthshire: plan of second floor in John Douglas' scheme, 1736 (© RCAHMS and Blair
Charitable Trust, SC 1232868)

second floor, generally similar to the ducal apartment below and reached by the Great Stair on
the south of the first floor entrance hall. At the
centre of the east front, above the entrance hall,
would have been a billiard room serving as an
ante-room to the state rooms. These would have
begun with the Great Dining Room, the remodelled sixteenth-century upper hall, a magnificent
space of 52 x 27 feet with a fireplace at each end.
South of this were to be new rooms, some occupying the place of intended rooms in the uncompleted seventeenth-century extension and others
in Douglas' south-east wing. First would have
come an ante-room above the ducal apartment's
private drawing room. Off this would have

opened the state drawing room above the ducal
apartment's library in the house's south-west
corner. East of this drawing room, above the
family bedchamber, would have been the state
bedchamber. Beyond this would have been the
state dressing room above the duchess' dressing
room and, at the house's south-east corner, above
the duke's dressing room and a pair of small closets, the 23 x 12-foot Grand Closet. At this floor's
north end, off the Great Dining Room and occupying Cumming's Tower and part of the new
north-east wing, would have been a smartly
planned suite of rooms, perhaps intended for a
visitor of some importance, consisting of a drawing room, bedchamber, dressing room and small

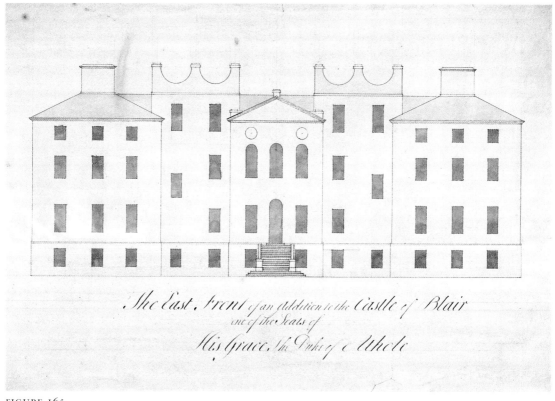

The East Front of an addition to the Castle of Blair one of the Seats of His Grace the Duke of Atholl

FIGURE 165
Blair Castle, Perthshire: view of east front in James Winter's scheme, 1743 (© RCAHMS and Blair Charitable Trust, SC 1232865)

closet. The south side of the new wing would have been occupied by another bedchamber and closet.

In the event, Douglas' grandiose proposals remained unexecuted. Although the duke received an estimate of almost £1,800 as the cost of completing the intended seventeenth-century scheme by adding a second floor state drawing room and bedchamber south of the sixteenth-century upper hall and with attic rooms above,[10] this too seems not to have been carried out. Had it been, Blair Castle would have been provided with a state apartment appropriate to a seventeenth-century house of pretension but one which, lacking either dressing room or closet,

would have seemed mean to the eighteenth century.

James Winter's Scheme of 1743

In 1743 the 2nd duke of Atholl again considered the remodelling and enlargement of Blair Castle. He commissioned the mason–architect James Winter, employed at that time in the construction of a new stable block at the castle, to prepare a design for the work[11] (Figures 165, 166 and 167). Like Douglas seven years before, Winter proposed to reduce the house to a uniform height and thicken it to the east. Here would have been a

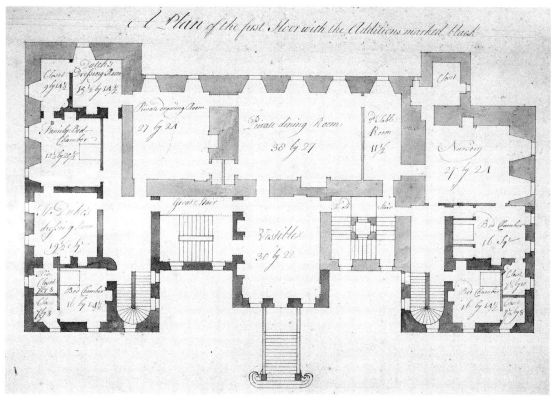

FIGURE 166
Blair Castle, Perthshire: plan of first floor in James Winter's scheme, 1743 (© RCAHMS and Blair
Charitable Trust, SC 1232867)

symmetrical E-plan façade, although with more
economically designed classical elements (a pedimented centre and piend-roofed end wings)
linked not very happily by taller sections containing the two main stairs and surmounted by scal-
loped parapets of faintly Vanbrughian inspiration.
The principal entrance, placed, as Douglas had
proposed, in the centre of the first floor, would
have been approached by a less assertive and
smaller straight flight of steps. The entrance itself
would have been a relatively narrow round-
headed door, not Douglas' Venetian; the centrepiece's second floor openings would have been
round-headed windows and, although taller than
those below, without the panache of Douglas'

intended Venetian. Only at the centrepiece would
have been expressed the hierarchical primacy of
the second floor *piano nobile* containing the state
apartment. At the ends, the second floor openings
are lower than those of the first floor so as to
allow for an additional storey above.

Winter's proposed planning of the interior is
a variant of Douglas', more economical and less
architecturally assured. In the centre of the first
floor, the principal entrance opened onto a hall
flanked by staircases, just as Douglas had
proposed. Also in accordance with Douglas'
scheme was the remodelling of the sixteenth-
century lower hall behind the new entrance hall
to provide a private dining room with a second

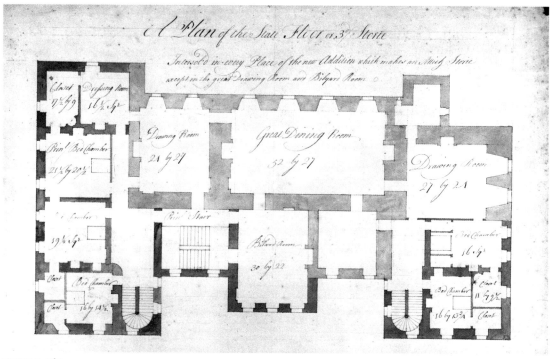

FIGURE 167
Blair Castle, Perthshire: plan of second floor in James Winter's scheme, 1743 (© RCAHMS and Blair Charitable Trust, SC 1232866)

table room to its north and the private drawing room (the seventeenth-century inner chamber) to its south. However, Winter omitted Douglas' library at the hinge of the L-plan family apartment. In its place he designed a dressing room and closet for the duchess. This was followed, to the east, by the family bedchamber and the duke's dressing room with a closet in the house's new south-east wing, most of which was to be occupied by a separate bedchamber, closet and subsidiary stair. Following Douglas, Winter proposed that the house's north end (Cumming's Tower and the new north-east wing) should be given over to a nursery, bedchambers and closets.

For the second floor, Winter again produced a cut-price version of Douglas' scheme. From a new billiard room above the entrance hall were

to be entered the Great Dining Room (the sixteenth-century upper hall) with, to its south, the state apartment's drawing room in place of an ante-room, presumably omitted on grounds of cost. However, instead of the drawing room opening to the state bedchamber – according to the usual usage of Scottish lairds' and noblemen's houses of the earlier eighteenth century – there now followed, as at the floor below, a dressing room and closet, off whose east end was entered the state bedchamber. The south-east wing would have been occupied by two more bedchambers and closets. At the house's north end, in Cumming's Tower and the new north-east wing, would have been a smart set of rooms (drawing, bedchamber and closet), and a second bedchamber and closet, all much as Douglas had proposed but with the omission of a dressing room.

Like Douglas' proposals, Winter's scheme seems to have been unexecuted. However, at about this time the main block's southmost second floor and attic rooms may eventually have been completed to the seventeenth-century design and in accordance with the specifications prepared in 1736.

The 'New House' of 1743–1744

Despite Douglas' and Winter's schemes for remodelling the castle's main block, the duke of Atholl began the construction of a new house in 1743. This was sited on lower ground just south of the existing castle, and it seems clear that the intention was that it should supersede the old building which, presumably, was intended for demolition. Only one wing was built in 1743–4, and it seems clear that this was designed as a family wing.[12] It is of two storeys, a piend-roofed projection housing the stair at the centre of the east front the only external architectural embellishment. On the ground floor there was a kitchen and associated service rooms (bakehouse, brewhouse, etc.) and, in the centre, the parlour or principal family room, whose west window may have been intended as an exit to the garden. On the first floor were the main rooms, consisting of four bedrooms with closets, a dining room and a drawing room. A door at the west end of each room's north wall provided a full-length enfilade whilst, on the wing's east side, a narrow vaulted passage stretched the full length, serving each room.

There can be little doubt that the new house was intended also to contain a state apartment, probably in a balancing wing, the two perhaps joined by a great entrance hall or saloon from which the wings were to stretch out. The planning of the house would thus have been similar to that of Hopetoun House as remodelled and enlarged by William Adam in 1721–36, although the two wings may have been intended to form a V-shape as at the near-contemporary Minto House. On completion of the shell of the family wing, work may have been suspended temporarily awaiting the arrival of joiners and plasterers to finish the interior. However, the Jacobite Rising of 1745–6 enforced a longer delay, and it was not until 1747–8[13] that the rooms were fitted out. The stucco work (by Thomas Clayton) was all in the best domestic manner of the time, very similar in character to the contemporary work in the superior Edinburgh tenement of Chessels Buildings. One ceiling, that of the Star Chamber, probably originally intended as the ducal bedchamber, had as its centrepiece the badge of the Order of the Thistle, of which the 2nd duke of Atholl had been appointed a knight in 1734. Even before the completion of this wing, however, the duke seems to have been changing his mind as to the desirability of erecting a completely new house.

The Transformation of Blair Castle to Atholl House, 1747–1758

During the rising of 1745–6, Blair Castle was held for the Hanoverian dynasty against a Jacobite force commanded by the duke of Atholl's younger brother, Lord George Murray, just as it had been held for James VII against Lord George's Williamite father, Lord John Murray (later 1st duke of Atholl) in 1689.[14] Not surprisingly, perhaps, in September 1746, after the failure of the last Jacobite Rising, the duke of Atholl minuted his 'Resolution to take down the castle of Blair' – lest, were it to be repaired, there be 'a danger of making it a garrison again' – and also his resolve to continue with building 'the new house'.[15] However, by February 1748 the duke had again changed his mind and given up the idea

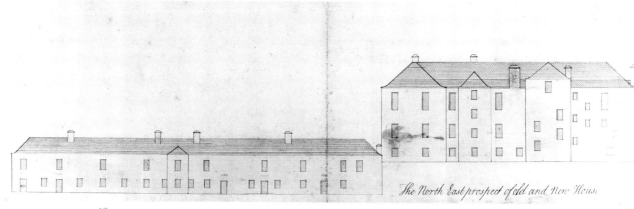

The North East prospect of old and New House

FIGURE 168

Above. Blair Castle, Perthshire: view of east front in John Douglas' scheme, 1748 (© RCAHMS and Blair Charitable Trust, SC 1232852)

FIGURE 169

Opposite. Blair Castle, Perthshire: reconstructed plans of c.1760 (© RCAHMS, GV 004759)

of completing the new house. Instead, he began the construction of a short west wing to join the north end of the new family wing's first floor to the south end of the old castle's ground floor. At the same time as building the new west wing, the duke began a thoroughgoing remodelling of the old Blair Castle, now renamed Atholl House.[16] It was ruthlessly recast as a barracks-like, roughly oblong, harled structure of three and four storeys and an attic, which was shorn of turrets, parapets and, indeed, almost all architectural display. John Douglas was the principal architect for the work, with James Winter acting as executant architect or master of works.[17] (Figures 168 and 169)

The new wing, joining the family wing of 1743–4 to the old castle, had its own entrance through a north porch. This opened onto a hall at the wing's east end. West of that were a new family dining room and ducal dressing room and bedchamber, presumably replacing those that had just been finished at the north end of the 1740s family wing. From a passage outside these rooms was a door to the foot of a new stair (the Picture Staircase), formed in the place of two former ground floor rooms, and the first floor dressing

room of the seventeenth-century ducal apartment. The stair began at the level of the first floor of the new wing, a few steps below the ground floor level of the old castle, and rose to the castle's first floor. When completed in 1751, it was of exceptional grandeur, with woodwork by Archibald Chessels and plasterwork by Thomas Clayton.[18] The walls were divided into panels, in which were hung portraits, and adorned with festoons of trophies hung from ducal coronets; the enriched ceiling had a shallow central dome. Dominating all was a great, late seventeenth-century portrait of the first marquess of Atholl in Roman dress, with a scene of the Battle of Bothwell Brig behind. For a stair that was part of a family apartment of rooms, not intended for viewing by the general public, this was a staggering display of self-pride. Off the head of the stair, in place of the seventeenth-century earl of Atholl's bedchamber, was the small drawing room, its decoration of the 1750s: it had panelled walls and a marble chimneypiece supplied by Thomas Carter, its pedimented overmantel carved by Charles Ross from a design by Abraham Swan, author of numerous books of archi-

250

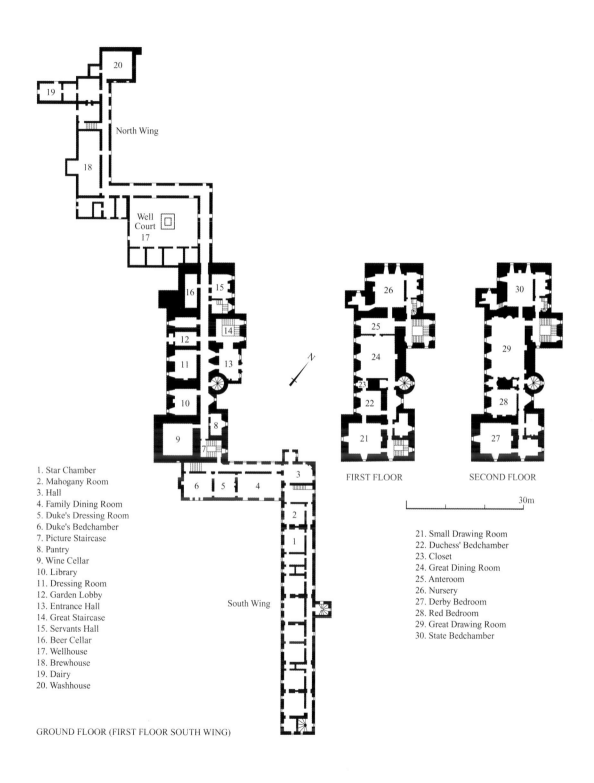

20

19

North Wing

18

Well
Court
17

16   15

14

12

11   13

10

8

9   7

3

6   5   4

2

1

South Wing

26

25

24

23

22

21

FIRST FLOOR

30

29

28

27

SECOND FLOOR

N

30m

1. Star Chamber
2. Mahogany Room
3. Hall
4. Family Dining Room
5. Duke's Dressing Room
6. Duke's Bedchamber
7. Picture Staircase
8. Pantry
9. Wine Cellar
10. Library
11. Dressing Room
12. Garden Lobby
13. Entrance Hall
14. Great Staircase
15. Servants Hall
16. Beer Cellar
17. Wellhouse
18. Brewhouse
19. Dairy
20. Washhouse

21. Small Drawing Room
22. Duchess' Bedchamber
23. Closet
24. Great Dining Room
25. Anteroom
26. Nursery
27. Derby Bedroom
28. Red Bedroom
29. Great Drawing Room
30. State Bedchamber

GROUND FLOOR (FIRST FLOOR SOUTH WING)

tectural designs. This served as an ante-room to the similarly finished Duchess' Bedchamber, its tiny cove-ceilinged closet in the thickness of the north wall providing an entry from the ducal apartment to one end of the Great Dining Room, the first of the house's new state rooms.

The public access to the Great Dining Room was from the main block's principal entrance at the centre of the ground floor of the east front, a pedimented Doric aedicular surround its only embellishment. This opened into a hall, its north side with a segmental arch opening to the Great Staircase, constructed in 1753–8 to replace the seventeenth-century stair in this position. Designed by Abraham Swan with a richly carved mahogany stair, stucco-panelled walls, pedimented staircases and a boldly ornamented plaster ceiling by Thomas Clayton,[19] it was designed to overawe the visitor. From the Great Staircase's first floor landing, a door opened into an ante-room formed from what had been the screens end of the sixteenth-century lower hall as recast in the seventeenth century, the proposed second table room in the 1736 and 1743 schemes of John Douglas and James Winter. As first finished in 1750, its walls were studded with antlers and pegs on which visitors were to hang their cloaks,[20] an economical form of decoration when the state rooms were in use for receptions. From here was entered the south end of the Great Dining Room.

The Great Dining Room occupied the place of the northern three-quarters of the castle's sixteenth- and seventeenth-century lower hall, the first of the suite of rooms that had been designed to lead to the earl of Atholl's Bedchamber, the inner sanctum of the first floor apartment. In its 1750s transformation, the Great Dining Room swapped this processional quality for one designed to make the visitor stop to gawp in admiration at this visible expression of the power and wealth of the duke of Atholl. Although

the walls' huge landscapes of local scenes were not executed until 1766–78,[21] most of the decoration is of the early 1750s, the lavishly enriched rococo ceiling again by Thomas Clayton.[22] Also by Clayton is the overmantel above the chimneypiece in the centre of the east wall.[23] This is a huge stucco trophy, one of its standards bearing a ducal coronet, the other the three-legged armorial device of the lordship of the Isle of Man held by the dukes of Atholl from 1736 to 1765, all an unequivocal celebration of the position of Blair Castle's owner. Although the pair of segmental-pedimented doors at the room's south end are smartly finished, suitable for the appearance of the duke and his family from their private rooms, they do not promise a way forward for the public. Instead, that is provided by the great northern doorway, its grandeur only noticed by the visitor when turned to leave through the ante-room. This is framed by a Doric aedicule whose columns are carved with a swirl of oak leaves, the metopes with military and naval emblems, and the pediment's tympanum with a helmet, its sides supporting the figures of reclining ladies.

The processional route back through the ante-room returns via the Great Staircase to the second floor. From the staircase's top landing a door opens into the Great Drawing Room, created in 1754–8[24] and occupying the position of the sixteenth- and seventeenth-century upper hall and the intended Great Dining Room of the state apartment in the schemes of 1736 and 1743. It is even more grandly finished than the 1750s Great Dining Room below, given added dignity by its greater height and coved ceiling, also by Clayton,[25] the head of Apollo in a sunburst its principal feature. At the centre of the east wall stands the white marble chimneypiece supplied by Thomas Carter[26] and surmounted by a Corinthian-columned aedicular overmantel, again designed by Abraham Swan.[27] At each end of the room a central round-headed niche is framed by a

FIGURE 170
Blair Castle, Perthshire: watercolour perspective of David Bryce scheme, 1869 (© RCAHMS, DP 035164)

Corinthian-columned and swan neck-pedimented aedicule, its design a narrower version of the overmantel. Even more strongly than in the Great Dining Room, the room's character is static, with no suggestion of progress to more exclusive delights beyond. The further rooms of a state apartment were provided, but these lay not at the south end of the Great Drawing Room as a goal to be reached after walking the full length of that room, but off its north end. From there a door gave access directly to the State Bedchamber in Cumming's Tower, off which were a closet and dressing room. All of these were well finished, with smartly executed woodwork and plasterwork, the bedchamber hung with late seventeenth-century tapestries and containing a state bed of 1700; but after the glories of the Great Dining Room and Great Drawing Room, they seem an anticlimax, an appendage to these rooms' celebration of the wealth and status of the dukes of Atholl. The dukes might have lost their regalian jurisdiction, but that freed them to assert themselves as part of an oligarchy on whose goodwill the dynastic monarchy depended for its continuance.

The Re-creation of Atholl House as Blair Castle

The utilitarian outer dress that Blair Castle donned on its transformation to Atholl House after 1747 must have seemed unworthy of its owners by the early nineteenth century. In 1840–1 the 5th duke of Atholl commissioned designs from R & R Dickson for reclothing it in castellated finery,[28] and in 1845 the recently formed ducal bodyguard of the Atholl Highlanders received formal recognition from the crown when presented with colours on behalf of Queen Victoria. However, it was not until 1869 that the 7th duke employed David Bryce to carry out a wholehearted remodelling of the exterior, the extension to be in keeping with the pageantry of its kilted private army[29] (Figure 170). Bryce's principal alteration to the form of the building was to heighten it so as to provide extensive attic accommodation for Victorian shooting parties. However he also recast the elevations, giving them conical-roofed turrets and battlements and, at the east front, a new entrance tower, its design copied from seventeenth-century work at Fyvie Castle. Internally, however, except for a new neo-Jacobean hall, Bryce left the eighteenth-century decoration of the state rooms and principal bedrooms untouched. Behind the Baronial garb and the reversion to the name of Blair Castle still stands the Georgian Atholl House, the product of the 2nd duke of Atholl's changing view of what architectural setting he should occupy but also, perhaps, of the political and social order in which he was placed.

Acknowledgements

I am grateful to the Blair Charitable Trust for allowing me to study papers in the Atholl Muniments at Blair Castle, Perthshire, and for permission to reproduce drawings in that collection to illustrate this chapter.

CHAPTER TWELVE

Balmoral

Simon Green

In the creation, or re-creation, of Balmoral Castle – the epitome of a grandly 'Baronial' appearance expressing a peaceful, modern purpose – the second, Victorian, phase of Scotland's Castle Culture reached its climax (Figure 171). Far from being the redoubt of a 'Scotch baron', the new Balmoral was the creation of a German prince, Albert, consort of Britain's Queen Victoria. And far from an 'ancient keep', Albert's creation, with its massive, dominating tower, was a new complex built in the place of an 'authentic old castle', an extended fifteenth-century tower house that was simply pulled down to obtain for the royal couple better views west of the Cairngorms. The new Balmoral mingled evocations of 'Scottishness', as formulated in Sir Walter Scott's writings and anti-quarian villa of Abbotsford, with ideas of comfort, practical planning and recreational escape in the Highlands. Prince Albert's two great private building projects, Osborne (Isle of Wight) and Balmoral, were built almost concurrently, and although their architectural styles are very differ-ent, the basic premise was the same – to provide a comfortable family home in a recreational, healthy setting. Neither was designed for state occasions or large-scale civic events (the Durbar Hall at Osborne was added in 1893): instead they were visualised as an attempt to remove the family from the rigours of royal protocol and,

perhaps, allow Albert to be the master of the house.

The first recorded appearance of the name 'Balmorain' or 'Balmoral' appears in the fifteenth century, when the Gordon family acquired Abergeldie Castle.[1] The core of the old castle seems from surviving illustrations to be of this date, consisting of a relatively modest three-storey tower which in 1746 was described as 'a long steep roofed high gabled house, with narrow windows high in the walls'. The estate passed to the Farquharsons of Inverey in the seventeenth century; they forfeited it in 1715, and then it passed to the earl of Fife, who bought the free-hold for £7,020. Sir Robert Gordon leased the estate in 1830 and in 1834–9 employed John ('Tudor Johnny') Smith (1781–1852) to extend Old Balmoral Castle to create a comfortable family home with a spectacular lyre-shaped winter garden (Figure 172).[2] The scheme involved the creation of a new suite of reception rooms and bedrooms attached to the earlier castle. An exceptional record of this building survives in the royal archives, both photographically and in a series of watercolours by James Giles.

To understand the subsequent project for a 'new' Balmoral Castle, we have to trace the love affair between Victoria and Albert and the Scot-tish Highlands. In the autumn of 1842 Victoria

FIGURE 171
Balmoral, Aberdeenshire: photograph of the castle from the south taken by Thomas Polson Lugton c.1900
(© RCAHMS, SC 1115651)

and Albert made their first trip to Scotland, which was arranged to replace a cancelled trip to Belgium. The royal party arrived at Granton harbour, and since the Palace of Holyroodhouse was not considered habitable, Dalkeith Palace, a residence of the duke of Buccleuch, was used. They then travelled to Taymouth as guests of the marquess of Breadalbane. It was here that Albert was introduced to stalking and the couple's romance with the Highlands was kindled.

Scott's novels had introduced the young Victoria to the idea of the Highlands and this vision was now put into reality at Taymouth. The house had been transformed and enlarged into a vast fairy-tale castle from the more modest Balloch Castle. This programme of transforming the old structure had possibly begun with William Adam in the 1730s and continued under Archibald Elliot in the early nineteenth century, culminating in additions by James Gillespie Graham and A W N Pugin, perhaps specifically for the visit. One of the social highlights of the visit was a ghillie's ball, held in the Banner Hall. A lavishly decorated ballroom with a vast Gothic-traceried window and delicately fan-vaulted ceiling, this was far removed from a 'real' Highland ceilidh hall. This event was captured in a romantic engraving which reflects the royal couple's growing passion for the Highlands. The role of the art and the artist became an important part of this

FIGURE 172

Balmoral, Aberdeenshire: lithograph by P C Auld of old Balmoral Castle with shepherd and sheep in foreground, c.1850 (© RCAHMS, DP 004956)

love affair. They both commissioned artists and photographers throughout their lives to capture their excitement, but Victoria's sketchbooks are also a clear testimony of this growing fascination.

Their second Scottish visit was in 1844, this time because of a cancelled trip to Ireland. The couple stayed at Blair Castle as the guests of Lord and Lady Glenlyon. One of the highlights of the trip was that Prince Albert was able to shoot a stag from his window, an act frowned upon by certain sportsmen. Blair at this time was not as we see it today, having been transformed since John Douglas' 1747–58 classicising scheme into 'Atholl House' (see Chapter 11). Later, in 1869–71, David Bryce would 'return' the building to its previous

name and transform it architecturally into the Baronial 'stronghold' seen today. In 1844, though, 'Atholl House' was still a rambling agglomeration, with Georgian sash windows and hipped roofs politely hiding or disguising its Baronial past. Their next trip north of the border was in 1847. This was a very important holiday in that it confirmed the royal couple's love of this wild part of the kingdom. One of the highlights was a cruise aboard the royal yacht around Kintyre, the Sound of Mull, the small Isles and Staffa, with the obligatory nineteenth-century experience of a visit to Fingal's Cave. The tour included a visit to the dramatic eighteenth-century Inveraray Castle on the shores of Loch Fyne, seat of the dukes of

Argyll (see Chapter 9). Ardverike,[3] a shooting lodge on the shore of Loch Laggan, was rented from the marquis of Abercorn, Prince Albert's Groom of the Stole. Abercorn had leased the Ardverikie estate from Cluny Macpherson, chief of Clan Macpherson, and had begun building a shooting lodge in 1844, which had grown as the need required. It was described later in the century as 'A plain unostentatious building, rather irregular in its construction, the windows, roof and chimney stalks a good deal in the cottage style, and the whole fitting pretty closely one's ideas of what quarters for the accommodation of a large shooting party ought to be.'[4] This is a far cry from the sophisticated splendour of Taymouth or the ancient seat of Blair. Each of the front windows was surmounted with a deer's head and antlers, a form of decoration that survives, for example, at Berriedale Smiddy, Sutherland, and is recorded in a perspective by J J Burnet of Dougarie Lodge, Arran. The Ardverikie we see today was designed by John Rhind for Sir John Ramsden in 1874–9, after a fire of 1871, but incorporating the low west wing that had been added to the earlier house for Victoria's visit.

The royal party arrived by carriage from Fort William on 21 August, and the royal couple were determined to enjoy the wild scenery; as ever, Albert was keen to examine technological marvels such as the Caledonian Canal. The scenery of the Highlands reminded Albert favourably of Thuringia.[5] Edwin Landseer accompanied the royal party, providing drawing and watercolour advice, and recording the royal progress. The weather was so poor that Landseer decided to sketch versions of some of his most famous works onto the bare walls of two of the reception rooms.[6] Victoria summed up the visit in a sentence: 'There is little to say of our stay at Ardverikie: the country is very fine, but the weather most dreadful.'[7] The courtier Baron Stockmar wrote: 'Whenever we stir out we come

home almost frozen and always wet to the skin.' How to resolve the dilemma of their passion for the Highlands but disdain for the weather became a problem that needed a solution. This came through the queen's doctor, Sir James Clark. His son John had been recuperating at Balmoral Castle on Deeside, home of Sir Robert Gordon, and had written to his father about the lovely dry weather he was enjoying on the other side of the Cairngorms whilst the royal party were being drenched at Ardverikie. Although the royal couple had not visited the area, they were intrigued, and the ever-pragmatic Albert commissioned a meteorological report on Upper Deeside which appeared very favourable. By an unfortunate but ultimately fortuitous coincidence, whilst the research was being undertaken Sir Robert Gordon choked to death on a fish bone on 8 October 1847. He had leased the Balmoral estate from the earl of Fife's trustees in 1833, and on his death the lease passed to his brother, the earl of Aberdeen, the prime minister. Aberdeen suggested that Victoria should take up the unexpired twenty-seven years of the lease. The three views of Balmoral Castle painted by James Giles in 1835 for Sir Robert were dispatched to London so that the royal couple could get an idea of what they were acquiring. In early 1848 Victoria instructed her solicitor to acquire the lease on behalf of Albert, and on 20 May 1848 the lease was agreed and completed.

The Balmoral Castle they acquired comprised, at its core, a relatively modest fifteenth-century tower to which additions had been made in the seventeenth and eighteenth centuries. The estate appears to have been let at various periods, having being rented by the earl of Wemyss in the late eighteenth century, for example.[8] Between 1834 and 1839 John Smith of Aberdeen – 'Tudor Johnny' – extended the castle for Gordon, adding a suite of reception rooms and a large conservatory, all facing south, away from the public road that separated the castle from the River Dee. The extensions were in the architect's favoured eclectic style, with a picturesque mixture of crow-steps, bartizan turrets, curly gables, castellations and bay windows. It created a modern comfortable home in the Highlands for a successful diplomat. The lease included the furniture, and many of Sir Robert's staff, and consisted initially of 10,000 acres. A further 14,000 acres were added in 1849 when the lease of Abergeldie Castle was acquired from another branch of the Gordon family; and still later the 6,000-acre Birkhall Estate was bought for the Prince of Wales.

On 5 September 1848, the royal family set sail for their new Highland home, landing at Aberdeen and then making a royal progress up Deeside. Yet again, the all-important parallels with Albert's homeland were recorded, with Victoria agreeing that Deeside 'reminded us very much of Thuringerwald'.⁹

The royal family enjoyed their Highland home, but the relatively modest castle was far too small. Charles Greville wrote that the party retired after dinner 'to the only other room there is besides the dining room, which serves for billiards, library and drawing room'.¹⁰ The first floor drawing room, designed by Smith for Sir Robert, was used by Victoria and Albert as their private sitting room. The cramped conditions were hated by the court, with a number of staff being lodged on neighbouring farms. In 1848, Albert began discussions with John Smith, designer of the castle's extensions during the 1830s, and his son and partner William, and in 1849 a large new service courtyard was added to the north-east at a cost of £2,047 12s 5d, almost doubling the castle's size. At the same time, William Smith was proposing a large extension to the south containing more reception rooms and bedroom accommodation.¹¹ This was recorded in a watercolour by James Giles dated 28 July 1849. By 1852 a dressing room for Prince

Albert and three 'wooden' rooms for Princess Helena and her governess had been added as the agglomerative process continued.

Whilst the development of their Highland home was ongoing, Albert was also designing another private retreat on the Isle of Wight. In 1845, Old Osborne House was bought, overlooking the Solent that Albert thought looked like the Bay of Naples, along with its 1,000-acre estate. To fund the purchase price of £28,000, Victoria sold off the contents of the Brighton Pavilion, that monument to the excess of her paternal uncle. On 23 June 1845 Victoria and Albert laid the foundation stone of the new Italianate Osborne. It was designed by Albert with the assistance of the builder–developer Thomas Cubitt. The burgeoning architectural profession was dismayed by their collective exclusion from such an exciting commission. The design consisted of a pavilion containing all the accommodation for the royal family, completed by September 1846, linked to a larger block containing accommodation for guests and the household, which was not completed until 1850. The Durbar Hall was not added until 1893, a marquee being used for large functions before then. In 1850 Victoria proposed the demolition of the Brighton Pavilion and the sale of the site, but she was persuaded to sell the building to Brighton council. This added £60,000 to her personal finances, and presumably helped with the completion of Osborne.

In 1851, with Osborne barely completed, Albert began to contemplate building a new Balmoral Castle with William Smith. The choice of a local rather than a nationally famous architect probably provided Albert with the opportunity to have detailed control over the design whilst not offending the architectural profession. Albert's boundless energy was exemplified by the fact that he was heavily involved with that monument of the Victorian age, the Great Exhibition, whilst both these major building projects were ongoing.

FIGURE 173
Above. Balmoral, Aberdeenshire: photograph of
the castle from the hillside to the south taken in
2001 (© RCAHMS, SC 1201458)

FIGURE 174
Opposite. Balmoral, Aberdeenshire: photograph of the
castle from the formal garden to the south taken in
2001 (© RCAHMS, SC 1201465)

Albert was heavily involved with every aspect of
Balmoral's design, from the disposition of the
rooms to the size and type of windows. He had a
belief that he was designing something distinctively 'Highland' and had a 'great horror of an
influx of London improvements', and was 'afraid
of getting out of the rough character of a Highland residence'.[12]

How the new Balmoral was to be financed
was at first uncertain, but a totally unexpected
bequest solved the problem. John Camden Neild,
the epitome of an eccentric miser, died at 5

Cheyne Walk, Chelsea on 30 August 1852, aged 72, and was buried in the chancel of North Marston church on 9 September. By his will, after bequeathing a few trifling legacies, he left the whole of his property, estimated at £500,000, to 'Her Most Gracious Majesty Queen Victoria, begging Her Majesty's most gracious acceptance of the same for her sole use and benefit'. Two caveats were entered against the will, but were subsequently withdrawn. Queen Victoria increased Neild's bequests to the three executors from £100 to £1,000 each; she provided for his

servants, for whom he had made no provision; and she secured an annuity of £1,000 to Mrs Neale, the wife of one of his tenants, who had frustrated Neild's attempt at suicide. In 1855, Queen Victoria restored the chancel of North Marston church and inserted a window to Neild's memory. The legacy had given the royal couple the means to transform their new Highland home.

With this fortuitous influx of capital, a large, new palace could have been constructed. There is in the royal collection a perspective for such a building by an unknown hand.[13] However, a

FIGURE 175
Balmoral, Aberdeenshire: photograph of the castle from the north taken in 1860 (© RCAHMS, SC 775929)

more modest scheme was proposed, although it is impossible to determine whether the scheme changed dramatically when the Neild bequest was received, which appears to have enabled Prince Albert to buy the estate's freehold in 1852. James Giles was commissioned again in 1853 to produce another series of watercolours, but this time of the envisaged new castle. The images conform almost exactly to what was eventually built and have often been mistaken as views of the castle on completion.

A new site was chosen north of the old castle, which meant that the latter could still be used whilst the new castle was being built. The public road had to be diverted, with a new bridge

constructed to take the public road over the Dee. Balmoral's foundation stone was laid in 1853 and the family moved into the new castle in the autumn of 1855, whilst the staff remained in the old castle. There is a George Washington Wilson photograph in the royal collection showing both castles. Victoria also commissioned James Giles to record the interiors of the old castle in 1855, just prior to its demolition, an early such example of antiquarian recording.

The design for the new Balmoral consists of two courtyards with a linking block dominated by a magnificent tower.[14] The castle is designed with the principal rooms looking westwards to the Cairngorm Mountains and north to the

River Dee, both views not possible from the reception rooms of the old castle. Although the south, or entrance, front is the view most often published of the new castle (see Figures 173 and 174), it is the west front that is most accomplished, implying that is a two-storey shooting lodge incorporating a tower, the whole making a much more effective composition (Figure 176). This also reflects, perhaps deliberately, the form of the original castle. The new castle provided comfortable, spacious accommodation, but it was not designed for state occasions or civic functions. A large porte-cochère provides covered access to a spacious entrance hall that leads into a gallery, off which lead all the reception rooms. Along the west front is the library, connecting through to the drawing room and on to the billiard room, which in turn leads along the north front through the garden vestibule to the dining room. The south and east sides of the courtyard provided accommodation for visitors and principal courtiers, including a dedicated prime ministerial suite. The grand staircase rises from the gallery, and there are two secondary staircases. The west front of the first floor contained Victoria and Albert's suite, centred on a large sitting room directly above the drawing room. The royal nurseries and family bedrooms were also on this floor, along with further guest accommodation.

The smaller second floor included accommodation for the royal family's personal servants. The largest room in the castle, the ballroom, although attached to the kitchen block, was originally only accessible from the garden terrace or the kitchen yard. The link building contained the dinner service rooms, including the butler's pantry, the plate room and the gun room, whilst the base of the tower held the wine cellar and the luggage entrance. This area was soon doubled in size, with further service accommodation including another corridor, so that the servants and the members of the family could move about freely

without accidentally coming across each other – a segregated pattern that was normal in most large country houses. The service or kitchen wing contained a large enclosed courtyard where all the outdoor activities of the household could be carried out unseen. The kitchen was top-lit with attendant sculleries, pantry and larders, and there was a servants' hall and stewards room, along with accommodation for the housekeeper and other servants.

Although it may appear at first glance a large, rambling structure, it was very well designed and, uniquely, still functions as intended: as a royal residence used in the autumn of each year. Architecturally, the building is not revolutionary, yet the combination of a comfortable and practical layout with the rhetorical 'signature' element of a massive tower sets it strikingly apart from the somewhat anonymous products of the William Burn school of well-planned country houses. It is built of pale grey granite from Glen Gelder on the estate, with sculptural panels by John Thomas RA. Victoria and Albert's passion for the Highlands is expressed in the interior, not only through the liberal use of numerous tartans but also the commissioning of a wide variety of paintings relating to their life in the Highlands. An amazing suite of decorative silverware figures was made for the table that celebrated Highland life, including such disparate activities as tossing the caber and the transportation of dead stags off the hill on a pony. Highland figures of Parian ware held up flaming torches (or, really, candelabra) in the drawing room. Stags' heads adorned the gallery and the hallways, but did not appear in the rooms. There is nothing of the later excesses of Victorian shooting-lodge chic, such as deerskin panelling or antler door handles. It was Albert who decided that the original paintings commissioned from the likes of Landseer and Winterhalter would be hung at Osborne, whereas engravings of them would be hung at Balmoral. This appears to have

FIGURE 176

Balmoral, Aberdeenshire: photograph of the castle, ballroom and stone staircase from the west taken in 2001 (© RCAHMS, SC 1016873)

led the fashion for decorating shooting lodges with engravings. After Edward VII gave up Osborne, many of the original Scottish paintings made their way to Balmoral, where one can now often see both original and engraving on different walls. In 1857, James Roberts made a series of watercolours of the interiors, held in the royal collection, which show the relatively plain, largely classical interiors. In 1864, William Kerr put it succinctly that Balmoral contrasted the

medievalism of its style with its planning, which displayed an obvious desire to

provide that regular disposition of thoroughfare lines which is so important a means of convenience and . . . that simple rectangularity of partionment which belongs to good plain modern rooms.[15]

The ballroom is mildly baronial, with a few stags' heads and crossed swords, closer to the 'Metropolitan Baronial' of Taymouth than to the almost macabre celebration of the stag at Mar Lodge, or to the ballroom at Glen Tanar, with its enormous fireplace and great wooden roof studded with stags' heads.

For the monarchy, the essence of Balmoral was, and has always been, the landscape and the estate. Carl Haag produced thirty-four views of Balmoral and the estate, which were bound into a volume titled 'Original Studies from Nature in the Highlands',[16] providing Victoria and Albert with a constant reminder of their Highland retreat. Balmoral has always been about getting away from the pressures of a very public life. Outdoor pursuits were an important part of the daily routine, including spending the occasional night away from the castle in wild and romantic locations such as the Glas Allt Shiel on the shore of Loch Muick, and at Allt-na-guibhsaich in Glen Muick. Closer to the castle, the Garden Cottage was built so that Victoria could remove herself from the hubbub of the castle itself. Its construction could almost be interpreted as a political act by Victoria and Albert, removing her ministers as far as possible from their comfort zones and the safety of London.

A comprehensive campaign of tree planting was undertaken, along with new drives, rides and paths, enabling the estate to be enjoyed and to work as a shooting estate. The landscape was studded with monuments and statues in commemoration of important events and personages. After the lease was taken up, in every one of the first few years new projects were completed in time for the annual autumn visit, including new estate cottages, a model farm, stables and game larders. In 1851 Albert ordered a prefabricated ballroom from Edward T Bellhouse of Manchester; it still survives, having been moved at least twice, and now serves as a joiners' workshop. Although other buildings were added throughout Victoria's reign, and subsequently, the estate remains and is used much in the way Victoria and Albert intended that it should.

Balmoral's place in Scotland's Castle Culture is a curious one. Its creation involved the complete destruction of a historic tower house at a time when most rebuilding projects retained and incorporated old houses, and its architecture was not at the cutting edge of innovation. Relatively few Scotch Baronial castles or mansions were directly influenced by Balmoral, unlike the plethora of Italianate villas that Osborne spawned. Balmoral, architecturally, stood at the end of the early nineteenth-century William Burn school of practical homes in Baronial clothes, rather than the exuberant castellar confections that came later. Yet, through the image created by the rhetorical gesture of its dominating tower, it was able to shake off the stodginess of the Burn tradition and play the 'instrumental' role intended for it by Victoria and Albert, embedding the monarchy in the Highlands while, at the same time, putting the Highlands at the heart of the popular and elite discourses of Victorian 'unionist nationalism'. We should bear in mind that Braemar Castle, further up the Dee, had been garrisoned until 1820, and so the area had been regarded as unruly in living memory. Although shooting in the Highlands as a largely male pastime had been popular before Balmoral, it now became a fixture in the elite social calendar. Highland estates were rented, new shooting lodges were constructed and the whole economy of the Highlands was transformed. Roads were improved and the railway system expanded: the Inverness sleeper remains a symbol of this phenomenon. Ardverikie, the rambling shooting lodge that the royal family rented in 1847, was transformed into a magnificent Baronial edifice in the 1870s, reflecting the social and cultural significance of Balmoral rather than any direct architectural influence.

Thus the creation of the royal retreat of Balmoral, in its fusion of 'old' and 'new', and 'Highland' and 'cosmopolitan', lay at the heart of Scotland's modernisation in the Victorian age.

CHAPTER THIRTEEN

Edinburgh Castle and the Remaking of Medieval Edinburgh

Robert Morris

Edinburgh Castle is one of the most spectacular nineteenth-century buildings in Edinburgh. Settlement and fortification on the site has a long history, but the dominant visual impact was created between 1880 and 1930. Engravings and photographs show the importance of these years.

The 1822 engraving (Figure 177) showed the castle substantially as it had been rebuilt after the 'lang siege' of 1571–3 and the palace reconstruction of 1615–17, together with the addition of a variety of utilitarian buildings required by its function as a garrison. The esplanade created in the eighteenth century was put to the use for which it was intended, as a promenade and display area.

George Washington Wilson must have taken his picture of soldiers on the castle esplanade in the late 1880s, for it showed the transformation of the castle from barracks to monument (Figure 178). This process was already under way when the Honours of Scotland were unearthed by Walter Scott in 1818 and Mons Meg returned from London in 1829, but it was given new momentum with the reconstruction of the Argyle Tower.[1]

When Valentine took his photograph of the castle in the early 1900s (Figure 179), the War Office had completed the ceremonial entrance, which confirmed the castle's status as a national monument.

Three buildings, St Margaret's Chapel, the Great Hall and Argyle Tower, were key to the remaking of the castle. This chapter looks at the processes, the individuals and the motivations involved.

Francis Napier, 10th Lord Napier of Merchistoun and first Baron Ettrick, had made his name as a skilful diplomat and much valued governor of Madras. He is best known in Scottish history for his leadership of the Crofters Commission. He was relevant in the castle story as an active member of the ruling class whose views were a little more radical than most of his fellow landowners.[2] On 10 December 1883, he wrote from Thirlestane Castle in the Ettrick Valley to the editor of the *Scotsman*. It was a letter which displayed the notion of a distinctive identity for Scotland and a view of the manner in which this

FIGURE 177
Opposite top. Edinburgh Castle, Midlothian: sketch made at the time of George IV's visit in 1822 and published by W Lizars (© Trevor Griffiths)

FIGURE 178
Opposite bottom. Edinburgh Castle, Midlothian: photograph of soldiers on esplanade with castle behind taken by George Washington Wilson, c.1880s (© RCAHMS, SC 1129310)

FIGURE 179
Edinburgh Castle, Midlothian: photograph taken c.1900–7 (*Bonnie Scotland, Leng's Portfolio of the Scenic Beauties of Scotland* (1907))

related to historic buildings. The letter involved a description of the condition and uses of various spaces in the castle at the start of the 1880s.

Sir, – At a time when public attention is particularly attracted to the restoration of buildings in Edinburgh connected with our national history, it may, perhaps, interest your readers to know that researches have recently been made into the condition of a portion of the castle which has a high claim on the curiosity and affection of Scotsmen.

It has long been known that the great hall of the castle – the 'Aula Castri' of our ancient records, the Parliament House and place of State of the Stewart Kings – exists, though concealed, disfigured and converted to an uncongenial use. Forming the greater part of the southern side of the Palace quadrangle – which, alas, was once bounded on the north by a noble Norman church – the great hall, 80 feet long by 33 feet wide, still stands in its fair proportions, but divided internally by floors and partitions into two storeys and several rooms, used as an hospital, with its offices and dependencies. On the higher floor, the carved timbers of the ancient roof are apparent, descending through the modern ceiling, and resting probably, on their proper supports below the level of the floor. Only one of these supports is at present visible. It is shown on the stair-case, to which the floor does not extend – a stone bracket sculptured with a fine female head, and adorned on the side with thistles boldly wrought. I do not know whether any preceding explorer had ever inspected the roof above the ceilings of the upper wards. I find no traces of it in our popular books.

Gore Booth, the officer of the Royal Engineers on duty in the castle, and who takes a lively interest in its historical features, has now done so: and I have been kindly permitted to accompany him and Colonel White, commanding the 92nd regiment, into the dark recesses which have been so long sequestered from human sight. Preceded by a sergeant of the Sappers with a lantern, we crept up by ladder through a trap door, and found ourselves in a maze of mighty beams, on which the dust of centuries lay thick and soft. From end to end the converging rafters and cross pieces stand in their orig-inal positions – a rude but impressive structure. Having wiped a portion of the woodwork, we found the surface of a clear yellow tint, finely veined.

The men decided that the timbers were chestnut rather than oak, and that the original walls and roof were in position.[3] The letter continued:

> The windows can be identified by refer-ence to ancient prints and traces in the masonry; which have been carefully compared by Major Gore Booth. Now this is the hall in which the parliament of Scotland sat before it was transferred to the Tolbooth, and afterwards to the Parliament House on the High Street. It is the hall in which Chancellor Crichton

set the bull's head before the Earl of Douglas (if we may credit the gloomy legend of the Scottish Chronicle), where Knox conferred with Grange and Lethington, where Charles I held his coronation banquets, where Argyll feasted Cromwell.[4]

So far, this long letter had introduced several aspects of the ideology and ideas behind the rebuilding that was to take place. It was to be a part of the remaking of Scottish identity in the last half of the nineteenth century.[5] The letter introduced James Gore-Booth as an important personality in the process. Gore-Booth was a younger son of a younger son of an Irish landed family from Sligo.[6] Napier introduced a notion we would now call 'authenticity'. The search to reconstruct something as it had been in the past was important because the building was a stage set for telling stories of the past – a paradox of modernity is the constant need to relive the past in the present.[7] The stories Napier told in the Great Hall did two things. They confirmed the independent national history, and hence exis-tence, of Scotland; and they outlined a history of progress from a legendary and violent past.

The letter finished with a list of grievances against English government for their assaults on Scottish culture exemplified by the treatment of Scottish castles and palaces.

> The English government has been unlucky with our Scottish Palaces. The soldiers of Cromwell burned old Holy-rood by accident; but Cromwell had a sort of honesty – he repaired the damage. The soldiers of King George II burned Linlithgow by accident; the English government have left it a ruin ever since.

In his view, Holyrood Chapel had been wrecked

and left 'a corpse linked to a living creature [the Palace] – desolate, desecrated, dead'. The beautiful Renaissance buildings of Stirling Castle were 'sordid and neglected'.

The English government pulled down piecemeal the great Chapel of the castle of Edinburgh, and they have turned the great hall into a hospital. Who did these things? No one can tell me. They did anything in those days, and were without understanding. Some Cope or Hawley did them. There were no Gore Booths and Whites in the army then. I do not say that the Hall is disgraced. After all, it is inhabited by Highland soldiers, and nothing is too good for the 92nd. But the sick are not in the right place; they would be better off in other quarters, which could be easily arranged.

Is it too much to expect that the Government in London will now make us kindly reparation, and gives us back a monument of antiquity which time and fortune have spared so long? If they have no money to restore this venerable relic of the ancestors of our gracious Sovereign, they might at least give the soldiers a decent hospital, and turn over the empty fabric to the Society of Scottish Antiquaries, or the Cockburn Association. There seems to be a Providence for lovers of the past, and in time some Chambers would be raised up who would give us back the 'Aula' and 'Magna Camera' of Scotland, in its pristine integrity and beauty.[8]

The following year the castle was visited by the members of the Edinburgh Architectural Association. They were shown around by Major Gore-Booth. They had a lecture from David Mac-Gibbon, their president, who used the tour to give an account of Scottish history from David I onwards. Baldwin Brown, Professor of Fine Art at Edinburgh University was by now involved and gave a vote of thanks, asking that pressure be put on the government, acknowledging Gore-Booth's 'scientific acumen'. The group included the dungeons in their visit and found them used as the beer cellar. The immediate object was the restoration of the Great Hall, as 'a unique and interesting national monument . . . a military museum or as a place of recreation . . . the public would have the opportunity, under proper regulations, of seeing one of the ancient residences of the old Scottish Kings and the hall in which parliament met'. MacGibbon called this 'the plan which Major Gore-Booth had so wisely devised'. Gore-Booth gave a cautious reply, saying 'he hoped something might be done towards the object he had in view, but he was not over sanguine. He had been lucky enough to get a great deal of solid help from various quarters, and Lord Napier, who was a very powerful nobleman, had taken up the matter most warmly.'[9] Napier was a major Selkirkshire landowner with distinctive views. He wrote his letter as he was making preparations to take the final evidence and compile his report on the Inquiry into the Condition of the Crofters and Cottars in the Highlands and Islands of Scotland.[10] Historians have seen his contribution to the Crofters Commission as a 'historicist recreation of an idealized version of the communal pre-clearance Highland Township'[11] His letter to the *Scotsman* showed an approach to the assertion and remaking of Scottish identity which was based on a subtle and at times contradictory version of Scotland. Cromwell gained some praise, as suited a Presbyterian nation; Cromwell also had some status as a radical hero in the nineteenth century.[12] Hawley and Cope were invoked to indicate the destructive nature of Scotland's relationship with

England. These soldiers were remembered not only for their defeat by the Jacobite army of 1745 but also for their participation in the assault on Highland society after Culloden.

There was a flurry of activity in the months which followed Napier's letter. The relevant institutions of civic and civil society were mobilised. Key personalities were in competition for attention in the public sphere. At the end of December, the *Scotsman* set Napier's letter in a broader context, quoting a recent report of Major-General Sir Andrew Clarke, Inspector General of Fortifications. This had attacked 'the miserable and incommodious way in which the troops are lodged in the existing barracks . . . the thriftless and injudicious appropriation of certain buildings within the castle as a Commissariat . . . [and] strong disgust at the mean and hideous erections which have from time to time been added to the grand old fabric.'[13] By January 1884, the castle was on the agenda of the town council, and the Lord Provost's committee prepared a memorial to the House of Commons, where it was presented by Mr Dick Peddie in March. Shaw Lefevre replied that the matters were 'under consideration'.[14] At the same time, the Cockburn Association had prepared and sent a memorial to the marquis of Hartington, Secretary of State for War. The Society of Antiquaries of Scotland sent their memorial to Gladstone, the prime minister. All of them gave priority to the Great Hall; and reflected the growing sense of Scottish national identity as one based on a distinct history and a parity of esteem with England, to be reflected by the restoration of the castle. An editorial in the *Scotsman* noted: 'Under the present government much has been done to make the Tower of London a credit instead of a disgrace to this generation and Edinburgh Castle has quite as strong a claim to attention.'[15]

Professor Baldwin Brown joined in. He gave a documented history of the Great Hall, suggesting that little remained that was really old. He

then proposed, given 'the comparative plainness' of the hall, that 'the young artists who are showing such promise in our midst should be employed, at a moderate remuneration'. He wanted carved heads of kings for the roof, and mural paintings inspired by 'the legends and ballads of Scotland' by Burns and Scott. His letter to the *Scotsman* suggested that: 'Our artists might throw upon the walls, the spell of a romantic past . . . which might make the restoration of Edinburgh Castle the starting point in a new development of the national art.'[16] He was promptly attacked by 'W', who repeated the views of the Architectural Association and the Antiquaries: 'Let it be restored as nearly as possible to its original condition'. 'W' noted: 'The great failures of nearly all the restorations of ancient buildings in the early part of the century were caused by loading the structures with, what were considered at the time, architectural improvements, which, as a rule, are looked upon nowadays with disgust.' He drew attention to the work done on St Giles by William Burn in 1829–33.[17]

Those involved knew they inherited a very recent change in the taste and politics of the built environment. Burn's remodelling of St Giles had destroyed much. The Cockburn Association might take Lord Cockburn's pro-conservation 1849 letter – 'A Letter to the Lord Provost on the Best Ways of Spoiling the Beauty of Edinburgh' – as a founding document, but that letter had done little to prevent another high-profile anti-conservation intervention from continuing, namely, the dismembering of Trinity College Church by the North British Railway, who acquired the building in 1848. The work at the castle in the 1880s took place in the shadow of an earlier attempt to restore St Margaret's Chapel inspired by Daniel Wilson, then secretary of the Antiquarian Society.[18] The *Scotsman* claimed that 'the taste and public feeling of today are better and more wisely directed than they were some years ago'.[19]

Running through the debate was the growing self-awareness of Scotland as a nation with a distinctive history, leading to an equal claim for partnership with England and a grievance that this was not fully recognised. The castle was becoming a focus for these sentiments. John Grant the antiquarian blamed 'the want of any local administration in Scotland' for the 'hideous buildings which have so long disfigured the splendid site they occupy on the castle Rock'. The participants talked in terms of 'Scottish history', 'Edinburgh and Scotland have a right to expect' and 'pride and honour . . . to Edinburgh and Scotland'.[20]

The exchanges of 1883–4 brought into the public domain several issues relating to the politics of the castle. The castle asserted its place in the distinctive and developing Scottish sense of self as a nation with its own history and a demand for equality within the union. Changing tastes meant that restoration now required a return to an 'original condition', even if that condition was ill-defined. Accompanying this was a growing concern for soldiers' welfare and the condition of the physical fabric of the castle. Discussion was dominated by the Great Hall as the embodiment of Scotland's distinctive history of statehood. These issues were established in the public sphere of town council, newspapers and the relevant associations of Scottish civil society.[21] There matters might have remained 'under consideration' by a government preoccupied with Ireland, franchise extension and Highland discontent. Change in the intensity and direction of the debate, as well as very real changes in the fabric of the castle, was brought about by the intervention of William Nelson. Nelson's firm was one of the largest of the Edinburgh printer–publishers in the second half of the nineteenth century; W & R Chambers was the major competitor for industrial leadership. William brought his reformed Presbyterian faith to his interest in the castle and to his sense of Scottishness. He was nearing the end of his life and wanted to make an impact on the landscape of his city. Above all he brought money. The fragmentary surviving records of the company show that he withdrew over £46,000 from the company in 1885–6, instead of his normal £5,000 to £10,000 a year.[22]

His offer to finance the restoration of three key buildings in the castle – the Portcullis Gate or Argyle Tower, St Margaret's Chapel and the Great Hall – brought a complex response. In August 1885, the War Office told him: 'Your generous and patriotic offer will receive every consideration by the Secretary of State for War.'[23] The castle was the property of the War Office, and was an active and rather scruffy barracks. There were already some aspects of the castle as monument. The Palace building on the east side of Crown Square contained a 'regalia room' for the crown jewels famously unlocked by Walter Scott early in the century. St Margaret's Chapel was managed by the Office of Works, although W W Robertson from the office warned that the keeper of the chapel was 'an old woman who may have no clear idea of the duties of her office'.[24] The chapel was a place for 'the sale of photographs and other miscellaneous objects'.[25]

Nelson worked with the patience, determination and clear sense of purpose which had brought him business success. By September he had already persuaded the authorities to appoint his choice of architect, Hippolyte Blanc, an Edinburgh architect with offices on George Street, who had been employed by the Office of Works between 1864 and 1878. The surviving plans show the progress that had already been made by James Gore-Booth and his considerable input to the initial planning of the restoration. Gore-Booth had made detailed plans of the existing buildings, showing the clutter of buildings criticised by the Inspector General of Fortifications. The major had also prepared plans for the restora-

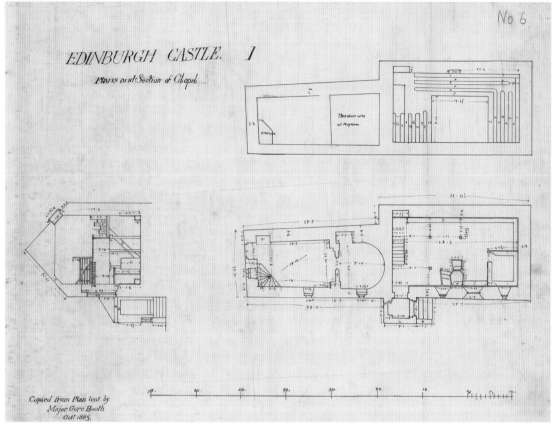

FIGURE 180

Edinburgh Castle, Midlothian: plans and section of the chapel copied from a plan lent by Major Gore-Booth, October 1885 (© National Library of Scotland, 1739/6)

tion of St Margaret's.[26] These had all been copied by October 1885 (Figure 180).

With the arrival of William Nelson and his money, both the War Office and the Office of Works realised that the question of Edinburgh Castle had a new urgency. Although they readily accepted Nelson's recommendation of an architect, their dominant instinct was to slow things down. R S Gowland of the Board of Works wanted to see detailed plans before responding 'to your public spirited offer'.[27] In February 1886, they wanted the plans to be submitted to Rowand Anderson, Architect to the Board of

Manufactures in Scotland.[28] After prompting by Napier, the plans were submitted to a committee, which reported in April. Nelson's friend Daniel Wilson was angered by this: 'Government Officials are most irritating in their red tape formalities. One would have thought they would jump at the liberal offer of Mr Nelson to do what they should have done long ago themselves.'[29]

Nelson himself was patient and persistent. He turned attention away from the Great Hall to the other buildings, partly because of his own interests in the religious substance of Scottish history and identity, and partly to give the War Office time to sort out new hospital accommodation. He and Blanc worked steadily around the principle of restoring the castle to its 'original condition'. The methodology developed in several stages. First they looked for documentary evidence. Here they had some help from Ingress Bell at the War Office:

> My researcher at the British Museum had no reference to St Margaret's Chapel or the Old Parliament Hall at the castle. The Museum is very rich in drawings of Edinburgh and contains several which throw a light on the earlier aspect of the older portions of the fortress ... [but] ... mostly general views.[30]

These drawings had been consulted by Daniel Wilson for his *Memorials of Edinburgh*.[31] The problem was that they had no interiors and little before 1600, although Colonel Malcolm claimed he had found a sketch dating from the early sixteenth century.[32] Blanc himself visited the British Museum, but was no more successful.[33]

They then proceeded by analogy and looked for other buildings in Scotland from the period they wanted to mimic. St Oran's Chapel in Iona was frequently mentioned in the debate over St Margaret's Chapel. Borthwick Castle, Seton and Corstorphine churches were also quoted.[34] Other evidence was gathered from the remains themselves. Gore-Booth was especially useful here. He clearly had a detailed knowledge of his building. Early on in proceedings, he had shown Nelson 'a heap of old stones that were taken from some old building that was near St Margaret's Chapel and among them is the old stoop of the Chapel'.[35] His drawings also included detailed information on old window and door openings that were blocked up but still evident from existing stone.

The debate over the appropriate roof for the chapel and the Argyle Tower showed the prob-

lems of getting back to the 'original state of things'. Nelson looked at the Sandby sketch of the 1750s as it had been redrawn by Wilson for his *Memorials* and asked for a flat roof: 'There can be no doubt that this existed before the roof was altered to its present state and the restoration of it therefore to the sketch as made by Major Gore-Booth would have been an absurdity.'[36] Colonel Malcolm's sketch showed 'the Argyle Tower finished with a tall roof', 'a high pitched roof' and, being the oldest, it had the greater claim on Blanc's attention. As the debate proceeded they drew on the authority of Daniel Wilson, childhood friend of Nelson and by the 1880s a leading anthropologist and academic in Toronto. Blanc explained his ideas to Wilson in November 1885. He thought the idea of thatch for St Margaret's was unlikely because of the exposed situation, and suggested stone. He had found some artistically pleasing stone from Dumfriesshire, but 'its introduction would be criticised by those wishing to preserve the characteristics of the "Old Grey Castle"'[37] (Figure 181).

Argument over what was involved in seeking the 'original state' was central to the power struggle between the various agencies and personalities. As far as the Portcullis Gate was concerned this seemed quite easy. Ingress Bell suggested: 'An upper storey – that now existed – was reared about 100 years ago, but architecturally it is entirely out of harmony with its surroundings, having nothing to distinguish itself from an ordinary dwelling ... It is now proposed to remove the modern upper storey and reconstruct it, as nearly as possible, in accordance with the appearance as built by David II.'[38] What Nelson wanted was a room that recreated the state prison in which the Presbyterian hero the earl of Argyle had been confined the night before his execution.[39] St Margaret's Chapel proved more difficult. When the committee for the restoration of St Margaret's reported in April 1886, they

Edinburgh Castle, Midlothian: extract from Georg Braun and Franz Hogenberg, *Edenburgum, Scotiae Metropolis* (c.1582) (© National Library of Scotland, EMS.s.653)

wanted to keep much of the restoration work which had been done in mid century, especially 'the modern Norman Gate . . . as being the first example of modern Norman restoration in Scotland'.[40] Napier summed up the situation:

> I have heard from Mr Nelson of the difficulties that have occurred about the Chapel. I do not at all agree with the views of the London Office . . . I consider it quite legitimate to remove every portion of the external building of the seventeenth and eighteenth century, to replace that building with ecclesiastical work of the earliest and rudest Norman type, subject to the condition that not one stone of the primitive structure now in situ is concealed or removed.[41]

Blanc disliked what had been done on the earlier restoration: 'The new face however given to it about 30 years ago seems in very bad feeling and in its projection unlike the treatment which is usually found in Chapels of that period.'[42] Wilson was thoughtful in his reply and set out some of

the principles for 'restoration': 'What is wanted is not a fine building, but the original, or a facsimile of it . . . It is a memorial of some former condition of things which may not be wholly irrecoverable.'[43] As a result of this debate, and the power plays within it, the doorway was modified and the clutter of buildings around the chapel removed. Doorways that had been made for access when the building had been a powder store were 'obliterated', although some of their shadows remain on the reconstructed walls. Blanc noted that the corners of the buildings had been especially affected by the variety of buildings attached to the chapel. His restoration involved the use of some of the old stones that Gore-Booth had found. The tooling on many of these still reflected stone tooling familiar on late eighteenth- and early nineteenth-century work in Edinburgh and its region. There were similar issues in restoring the floor of the chapel, and Wilson provided practical advice suggesting the use of existing paving. Even if it was 30 years as opposed to 800 years old, it looked worn.

The principles behind these re-creations fell somewhere between the purist position of a Ruskin and the creative imagination of Viollet-le-Duc. References to the work of both remain in the correspondence collected around the castle restoration.[44] The outcome satisfied the ambitions of many participants by creating places and spaces for telling key moments in the story of Scotland. Daniel Wilson wrote: 'What you have to do is to create as far as possible the actual ancient chapel in which Queen Margaret worshipped and where its genuine ancient features have disappeared . . . to restore it as far as possible to the actual condition in which it was when the sainted Queen worshipped there for the last time in AD 1093.'[45] Nelson himself was especially keen that the remade Portcullis Gate should be the place to remember the marquis of Argyle. Wilson again expressed this view with great clarity, 'It will of

FIGURE 182

Above. Edinburgh Castle, Midlothian: recent photograph of the roof of the Argyle Tower. No effort was made to conceal the fact that this was a modern reconstruction using machine-cut stone and the code book of the Scotch Baronial. (© Robert Morris)

FIGURE 183

Opposite. Edinburgh Castle, Midlothian: drawing by Hippolyte Blanc showing the Argyle Tower, proposed restoration, December 1885. (© National Library of Scotland, 1739/31)

course be an indispensable condition in any restoration that the chamber in which Argyle passed his last hours be preserved intact.'

The outcome was a distinctive statement of the remaking of Scottish national consciousness as well as a reflection of wider changes in attitudes to historic buildings. Those involved were aware of the work that had been done in the Tower of London in the 1860s and 1870s, and at one level they followed the re-medievalistion and the desire to achieve 'its original appearance'. They recognised the symbolic value of the castle as a monument, representing a specific version of the nation. In London the tourist had to compete with the utilitarian functions of the Tower as an armory, powder store and public record office, just as Edinburgh remained a working barracks. The Tower represented English progress from the torture and executions embodied in the dungeons, all outcomes of tyranny and religious intolerance.

By 1900 the Tower was imbued with solidly English – or was it British? – virtues of duty and courage.[46] In Edinburgh, the castle was an assertion of Scottish difference. The renewed Argyle Tower shouted 'Scotland is different' with every

EDINBURGH CASTLE RESTORATIONS.

ARGYLL TOWER. (PROPOSED RESTORATION)

East Elevation.

Hippolyte J. Blanc.

73 George Street Edinburgh

Dec. 1885.

FIGURE 184
Edinburgh Castle, Midlothian: drawing of St Margaret's Chapel after the reconstruction of 1849 from James Grant, *Old and New Edinburgh*, vol. 1 (1880) p.20

architectural motif (Figures 182 and 183). The story of Argyle was a reminder of a Presbyterian nation and its virtues. The chapel, a plain and rather thrawn little barn, and tales of the queen's simple faith, recruited Margaret to Protestant virtues (Figures 184, 185 and 186), whilst the Great Hall was a reminder of the history of kingship that made Scotland a separate and distinctive nation. The accounts of destructive sieges were another reminder of difference but also of progress from the conflicts of the past. Edinburgh

Castle was remade as a symbol of Scotland as a religious and distinct nation, an equal partner in the union, the true counterpoint to the remade Tower in London.

Acknowledgements

My thanks to Trevor Griffiths for permission to use his copy of the engraving of Edinburgh Castle that appears as Figure 177.

FIGURE 185
Left. Edinburgh Castle, Midlothian: recent photograph of the reconstructed north-east corner of St Margaret's Chapel. The dressed corner stones are reused ashlars of differing character. Their tooling – such as horizontal 'droved' lines – mean they were not dressed until the late eighteenth century or later.
(© Robert Morris)

FIGURE 186
Below. Edinburgh Castle, Midlothian: photograph of St Margaret's Chapel with plain doorway and marks of older openings from its powder store days
(© Robert Morris)

CHAPTER FOURTEEN

Duart and
Eilean Donan Castles

Iain Anderson

Today, the restored castles of Duart and Eilean Donan are amongst the most picturesque and iconic castles of Scotland (Figure 187). They are both strategically placed seaboard fortresses in the heart of Gaeldom: Duart Castle sits on the east coast of the Isle of Mull, at the meeting point of the Sound of Lorn, the Sound of Mull and Loch Linnhe; whilst Eilean Donan sits near the Kyle of Lochalsh, at the meeting point of Lochs Alsh, Duich and Long. Both castles carry strong clan associations (at Duart, the MacLeans; and at Eilean Donan, the MacKenzies and the MacRaes) and share similar historical backgrounds: both are ancient settlements, with the present buildings first dating from the thirteenth century, and both played prominent roles in the Jacobite uprisings of the late seventeenth and early eighteenth centuries. As a result of this involvement, both castles lay abandoned and largely ruinous until the early twentieth century. So, moving into the era of 'modern architecture', a new chapter was opened in both the history of Duart and Eilean Donan, and in Scotland's Castle Culture.

Development and Ruin

The MacLeans were one of the most powerful and influential clans in the West Highlands, and were to be found at the heart of the politics and localised conflict of later medieval Gaelic Scotland. Duart Castle was their principal seat from around 1390 when it was granted to Lachlan MacLean by his father-in-law, the Lord of the Isles.[1] It remained in MacLean hands until 1691, when it was forfeited to the Campbells.[2] Despite the loss of their clan seat, the MacLeans proved to have longevity, and during the post-1745 Jacobite repressions, the clan septs retained lands, titles and influence. The chief was imprisoned for only two years for his role in the rebellions and, once free, he fled to France. Despite ending his days in Paris, he retained the baronetcy, which continues to be passed through the family today.

Duart Castle was an enclosure castle built by the MacDougalls of Lorn in the thirteenth century. The MacLeans added a four-storey tower in the late fourteenth century, and a lower south-east range in the mid sixteenth century. Finally, another range of buildings was added to the north-east in the late sixteenth century, the façade of which was again remodelled in 1673.[3] Although these buildings existed only as roofless shells by the mid eighteenth century, they formed what was reworked as the modern Duart.

Eilean Donan was a seat of the Mackenzies of Kintail and Seaforth from the late thirteenth century. The Clan MacRae, who formed the

FIGURE 187A
Eilean Donan, Ross and Cromarty: general view from south-east (© RCAHMS, SC 707300)

FIGURE 187B
Duart Castle, Argyll: view from east (© RCAHMS, SC 581222)

FIGURE 188A
Eilean Donan, Ross and
Cromarty: Board of Ordnance
drawing of Eilean Donan by
Lewis Petit (© National
Library of Scotland, MS.1648
Z.03/26a)

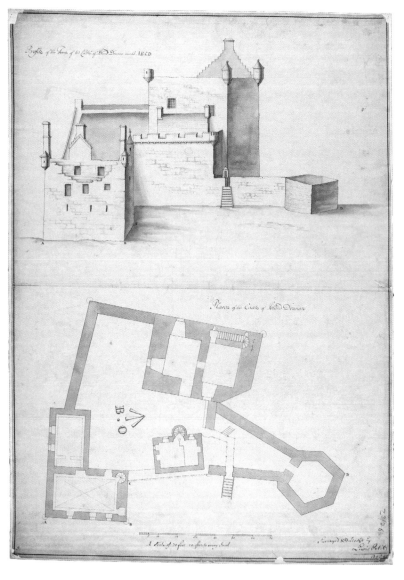

Chief of Kintail's bodyguard, were Constables of Eilean Donan from 1509, intermittently resident there until the mid seventeenth century, without ever owning the castle. The first habitation of the 'Eilean Donan' is thought to have been an ecclesiastical cell,[4] but the first recognisable built remains belong to an early thirteenth century enceinte castle. This castle, with a much larger footprint covering most of the island's habitable surface, established the position of the principal building, which later became the keep, or tower. In the fifteenth century the footprint of the castle was significantly reduced, an L-plan building was added to the south-west and a smaller gatehouse located to the east. Finally, in the late sixteenth century a hornwork was built across the existing entrance and a hexagonal bastion placed at the end. There is no precedent or contemporary for

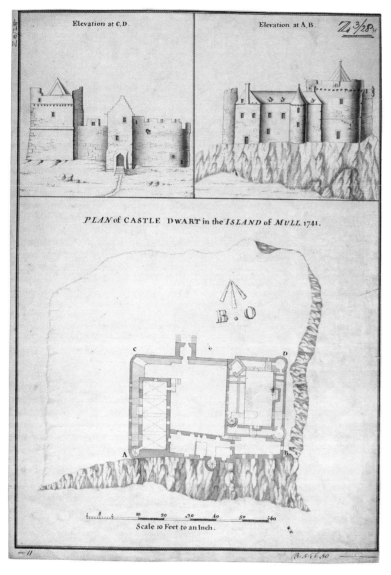

Duart Castle, Argyll: Board of
Ordnance drawing of Duart
Castle by Lewis Petit (©
National Library of Scotland,
MS.1648 Z.03/28b)

this structure in Scottish architecture, thought to
serve as both a new entrance and protection to a
well inside. Later still, in the early seventeenth
century, another new entrance was positioned on
the south wall of the hornwork.[5]

The clans related to both castles were Jacobites and, as important strongholds in the late
seventeenth and eighteenth centuries, both castles
were targeted. Duart, after being ceded to the

Campbells, was used for a short time as a
Hanoverian garrison. In 1748, a Board of
Ordnance survey shows that the castle's roof was
'quite ruinous', and only a small amount of
accommodation remained usable (Figure 188b).[6]
Duart declined slowly into ruin, but the fall of
Eilean Donan was more spectacular. In spring
1719, whilst being used to garrison Spanish
soldiers involved in a new Jacobite uprising, the

castle was blown up by three Royal Navy frigates. Many were killed or imprisoned, and others who escaped went on to participate shortly afterwards in the Battle of Glenshiel. The castle was damaged beyond use and abandoned. Like Duart, Eilean Donan was recorded in 1714 by the Board of Ordnance (Figure 188a).[7] However, that drawing was lost until after the restoration and was never able to inform the works.

The Twentieth Century

By the twentieth century, both castles had been abandoned for nearly 200 years; Duart was a roofless shell and Eilean Donan a fragmentary ruin. However, the political and cultural climate of Scotland had changed drastically in this 200-year period. The clan and Gaelic cultures that had previously been suppressed had come full circle and, in the later nineteenth century, Scotland was rediscovering its Celtic past. Scotland's ancient buildings were the subject of academic study, and the Romantic movement had great influence upon attitudes to Scotland's past. In this context, neither castle lacked charm when etched or photographed as a ruin. The rich were again living in 'castle-style' buildings, often regardless of Scottish lineage or political allegiance. By the early twentieth century, being Scottish, and Scottishness itself, was fashionable.

In the midst of this revival, several individuals who *were* descended from clans that had lost property and identity saw the opportunity to reacquire their patrimony. The Stewarts of Appin reoccupied Castle Stalker and, later still, Kisimul Castle was purchased by the Chief of the MacNeils, the title having passed to an American architect. The clan or clan-inspired re-acquisition and restoration of Eilean Donan and Duart Castles are undoubtedly the most complete examples of this trend.

The Restoration of Duart

Duart Castle was bought in 1911 by Sir Fitzroy Donald MacLean, 10th Baronet of Dowart and Moraven, and 26th Chief of the Clan MacLean. Sir Fitzroy, a lieutenant-colonel in the army, was seventy-six when he bought Duart. Until then, he had resided in the south of England, with houses in Kent, Folkestone and London. He served as President of the Highland Society of London; with such societies influential in spreading 'Scottishness' amongst the upper echelons of British society, and as Clan Chief, Sir Fitzroy was active in reviving the Clan MacLean on a worldwide scale.

An article of January 1934 in the American magazine *Time* reveals Sir Fitzroy's motivation for purchasing Duart:

> Eighty years ago Sir Fitzroy, then a beardless youngster, sailed out from the mainland on a yachting cruise with his father. They passed Mull. On a headland jutting into the water were a few tumbled walls – all that remained of his ancestors' castle . . . Twenty-two years ago, already an old man, he returned to Mull to fulfill his dream. Masons and workmen went to work and soon the towers of Duart Castle were standing again.[8]

An architectural competition was held for the job of restoring Duart Castle. The entry from the office of J J Burnet, developed with advice from Thomas Ross (co-author of *Castellated and Domestic Architecture of Scotland* (1887–92)), was chosen. Charles Cleland Harvey, an assistant within Burnet's Glasgow office, was job architect.

Burnet's architecture practice at this time was one of the best and most influential in Britain. Whilst his office worked in many architectural styles, Burnet's use of traditional Scottish archi-

FIGURE 189
Duart Castle, Argyll: postcard showing general view from east, c.1900 (© RCAHMS, SC 1232830)

tecture was normally in imaginative examples of High Baronial architecture, rather than castle restoration. Sadly, Duart turned out to be the only project Harvey completed as job architect: he was killed in action during the First World War. One can only speculate whether Burnet's office may have pursued the subject of castle restoration further had Harvey survived to continue his career.

Due to the amount of historic fabric that remained at Duart, Burnet's work was concentrated largely on repair rather than rebuilding (Figure 189). Despite the knowledgeable input of Thomas Ross, the works do not, as might have been expected, reproduce forms from Scottish architecture in elaborate detail. Where architectural detail (doorways, dormers etc) is reintro-

duced, its style is 'neutral' – relatively free of decoration and recognisable as modern repairs rather than copies of contemporary elements. Perhaps the only exceptions are a seventeenth century-style door incorporating a MacLean crest and date commemorating the reoccupation of Duart, and a cast-iron beacon added to a raised part of the defensive wall. Walls were simply built up to a flat parapet and capped (with new stonework distinguished from the old) and although the roof pitches were changed, the overall appearance of the castle's exterior remained very similar to the eighteenth-century survey.

Where the Burnet scheme does make major interventions, these are in a modern idiom (Figure 190). Vaults and cross-walls were removed in the south-east range to accommodate new

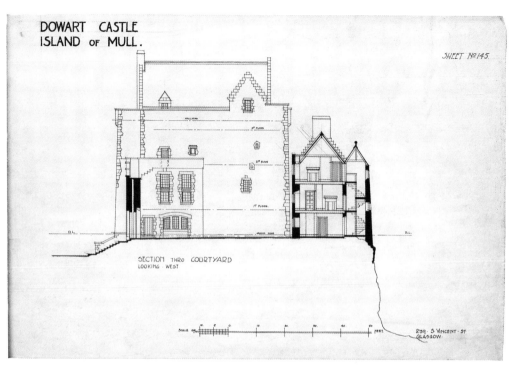

DOWART CASTLE
ISLAND of MULL.

SHEET N° 145.

SECTION THRO COURTYARD
LOOKING WEST

259· S·VINCENT·ST·
GLASGOW.

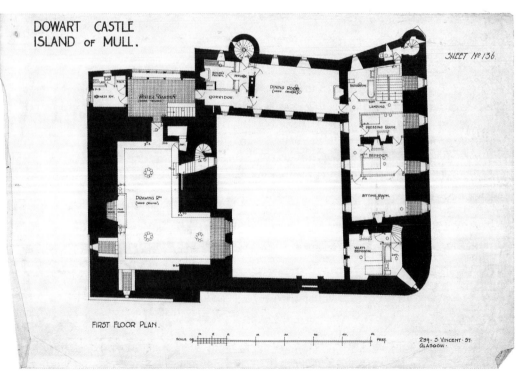

DOWART CASTLE
ISLAND of MULL.

SHEET N° 136.

FIRST FLOOR PLAN.

259· S·VINCENT·ST·
GLASGOW.

floor levels and, at the north corner of the castle, a previously external space was formed into the 'Ship Room', a largely glazed room which links the north-east range and the previously detached tower. This Ship Room, juxtaposing traditional forms with a modern scale and materials, has similarities with elements of Sir Robert Lorimer's additions at Ardkinglas or Balmanno, and Burnet had previously acknowledged the influence of Lorimer upon his work. A more uncompromising addition is the large rectangular window bay added to the tower, projecting into the courtyard and providing plentiful natural light into the principal rooms. Whilst this seems to contradict the approach of careful intervention taken elsewhere, historic photographs show the area of tower wall removed to have been in especially poor condition. Earlier buildings have butted against the tower, and poor repair work was subsequently carried out.[9] This area of the tower required significant repair and rebuilding, so perhaps this was where it was decided a major insertion could be best accommodated without unnecessarily removing historic fabric.

The castle interior skirts between the aesthetic of High Baronial architecture and known historic interiors, with large stone fireplaces, timber beam roofs and bare, white-washed walls. There is a striking similarity between the character of the main rooms at both Duart and Eilean Donan, demonstrating a similar vision for both buildings: that of the clansman sitting in his traditional seat, surrounded by ancestry, regalia and history (Figure 191).

FIGURE 190A
Opposite top. Duart Castle, Argyll: first floor plan (© RCAHMS, SC 1232810)

FIGURE 190B
Opposite bottom. Duart Castle, Argyll: section through courtyard (© RCAHMS, SC 1232811)

The Restoration of Eilean Donan

The restoration of Eilean Donan is a more complicated story. In comparison to Duart, much less of the castle's original built fabric remained as evidence to inform rebuilding (Figure 192), and the clan politics was more tangled. Since the destruction of Eilean Donan, the Clan MacRae (like the MacLeans) had established a proud military history and in many cases became notable members of British society. Amongst these was John MacRae-Gilstrap, a lieutenant-colonel in the British Army and prominent family member of the MacRaes of Conchra, one of the four MacRae septs. MacRae-Gilstrap purchased Eilean Donan Castle in 1912, with his reasoning for the acquisition stated at a ceremony celebrating the clan's return to the castle:

> The reason for rebuilding Eilean Donnain is that since it was the home in the West Highlands of Seaforth, who was undoubtedly the Chief of the Clan MacRae from time immemorial, and since the MacRaes have acted for many generations as Constables of the Seaforth's castle, the successor to the last Constable is anxious to take up residence in the old dwelling-place.[10]

Revived interest in lineage and heritage amongst the Clan MacRae sparked a debate over which sept should be leaders of a clan that, traditionally, had no chief. This peaked in 1909, when Sir Colin MacRae (of the Macraes of Inverinate) made an application to be recognised as chief to the Lord Lyon Court. This was opposed by MacRae-Gilstrap (on behalf of the Conchra sept) who argued that the MacRaes had always sworn allegiance to the MacKenzies of Seaforth. MacRae of Inverinate's bid was therefore rejected, a rift opened in the clan and rival soci-

eties were formed. Three years after these events, MacRae-Gilstrap purchased Eilean Donan Castle and, later, the nearby traditional MacRae lands of Conchra, Dornie and Ardelve. In making these purchases, MacRae-Gilstrap might be considered to have had a dual motivation: not only re-establishing the Clan MacRae as landowners in the Kintail area and their ancient role as Constables of the castle, but consequently establishing the MacRaes of Conchra as the most high-profile and therefore dominant sept within the clan itself.

Putting the reasons for rebuilding the castle to one side, how did MacRae-Gilstrap go about tackling the ruinous castle? A MacRae family account, reproduced in clan newsletters and the castle guidebook, tells that Eilean Donan was rebuilt according to a dream.[11] The mason employed to clear rubble from the castle, one Farquhar MacRae, claims to have envisaged the

FIGURE 191A
Opposite top. Eilean Donan, Ross and Cromarty: view of the Banqueting Hall, from the north-west (© RCAHMS, SC 1232812)

FIGURE 191B
Opposite bottom. Duart Castle, Argyll: interior of the Great Hall (© RCAHMS, SC581217)

FIGURE 192
Above. Eilean Donan, Ross and Cromarty: view from the south-east, c.1870 (© RCAHMS and M C Gibb, SC 1232818)

FIGURE 193
Above. Eilean Donan, Ross and Cromarty: view from
the east during reconstruction, photograph taken by
M E M Donaldson (© Highland Council,
GB1796_859_20_0766)

FIGURE 194
Opposite. Eilean Donan, Ross and Cromarty: distant
view from the north-west during reconstruction,
c.1920 (© RCAHMS, SC1063806)

castle's 'original' form, and this informed what
was built. We can only now speculate how much
of the castle was rebuilt according to this dream,
but there was also a well-known architect of the
day involved, George Mackie Watson.

Mackie Watson was chief assistant to Robert
Rowand Anderson for nineteen years and,
through the experience he gained from working
within the heart of the architectural and academic
circles of Scotland, he seems an informed choice
to rebuild a medieval castle. In Rowand Anderson's office, he worked on medieval restoration
projects such as Dunblane Cathedral and Ethie
Castle. In 1912, in independent practice, he won
the competition to restore St Magnus Cathedral
in Kirkwall, Orkney. He was also chosen by
Rowand Anderson as one of the first tutors of
architecture within the Edinburgh School of
Applied Art, a school that promoted understanding of traditional Scottish architecture amongst
its students and that established the National Art

Survey. Students were required to document
historic buildings in detail, and to use this material
as a working tool to inform the development of
new Scottish architecture.

The twentieth-century castle places each
building roughly upon the footprint of its predecessor (see Figures 188a and 188b for eighteenth-century Board of Ordnance drawings),
although these remains do not wholly dictate the
buildings today. Drawings currently on display
within Eilean Donan demonstrate that initial
design work concentrated on the tower and the
south gateway building, and historic photography
shows that the building to the south-west corner
wasn't tackled until the tower and gateway building were complete. Strangely, historic photography also shows that the tower was completely
rebuilt before the bridge between the castle and
the shore was added. The bridge only appears in
views where the gateway building is nearing
completion, and it might therefore be looked

upon as a later necessity, following an initial phase of construction (Figures 193 and 194).

There is little evidence that the castellation employed in the design was based on local precedents. For example, eight of the ten broadly contemporary castles included in Miket and Roberts' study, *Medieval Castles of Skye and Lochalsh* (1990), were in a similarly ruinous state to Eilean Donan at the start of the twentieth century, and few architectural details remained.[12] The exception may be the crenellated wallhead details running along the external S-wall, which is reminiscent of the upper walls of Dunvegan Castle on Skye. Instead, the detailing employed by Mackie Watson shows knowledge of contemporary precedents elsewhere in Scotland, many of which are illustrated in the National Art Survey. Variations of elements introduced at Eilean Donan – box machicolations, the round corner bartizan and the conical roofed cap-house – whilst typical to so many castles, are recorded in absolute detail in the survey, at places such as Lochranza and Dirleton. The gabled cap-house again has numerous historic examples, although this one is comparative to that built at Broughty Castle by Rowand Anderson in 1860.

The most unusual architectural feature is a beacon/outlook platform on the tower roof's west gable-head, which appears to double as a chimney. A beacon was found in many medieval castles (fires were lit to convey messages), but examples rarely survive today. The position and form of Eilean Donan's beacon is similar to that found on Elshieshields Tower, whilst the remains at Gilnockie Tower, both in Dumfriesshire, also deserve comparison. It seems that symbolism played a role in beacons being included in the restoration schemes for both Duart and Eilean Donan, highlighting the occupation of both castles once again.

The Mackie Watson plans on display in the castle, whilst not the final, executed version, demonstrate some interesting elements of the design (Figure 195). The drawings illustrate both the areas of the tower that were completely rebuilt and those areas where original fabric remained and was incorporated into the new building. Historic photography of the ruinous castle seems to match the retained wall sections shown on the plans. These remains, whilst fragmentary, have allowed the original wall thickness to be replicated in the new building and also

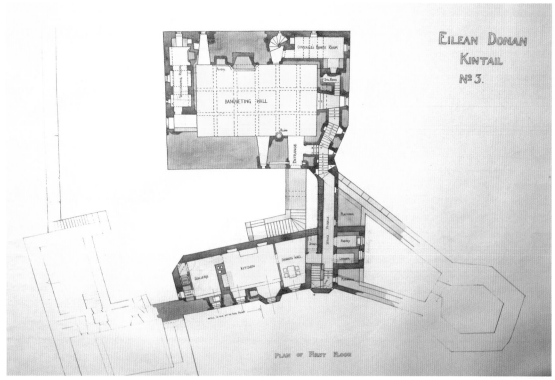

FIGURE 195
Eilean Donan, Ross and Cromarty: plan of first floor (© David Win)

dictate how and where elements could be introduced into the wall thickness. The original solid walls are incorporated into the tower up to second floor level, almost to parapet height, and rebuilt sections of wall are almost entirely inhabited between the inner and outer faces. No fewer than five staircases of various sizes lead off the principal room to spaces such as a gallery, constables' room, and a 'secret' laird's retiring room.

The character of the principal rooms within the tower is an essay in the 'Scottishness' that was illustrated earlier at Duart. The ground floor Billeting Room (shown as a billiards room in the Mackie Watson plans) is stone-vaulted, whilst the first floor banqueting hall has an exposed timber beam roof and exposed rubble walls. Within these rooms, details such as the fireplaces, lavers and niches can again be traced back as variations of details recorded in the National Art Survey at Borthwick and Liberton, amongst others.[13]

The upper two floors are entirely taken up by bedrooms: on the second floor, state bedrooms (with a series of window niches and wardrobes within the wall thicknesses) and at roof level, smaller rooms for visitors. Whilst the concession of fireplaces in each room and a bathroom on each floor is made, the overall small scale and simple whitewashed finishes of the upper floors create an aesthetic of 'medieval' simplicity, rather than comfort and grandeur. MacRae-Gilstrap retained these luxuries elsewhere, at the family's Argyllshire home of Ballimore, and nearby at Conchra, so there were no reasons for his vision to be compromised.

Functions notably absent from the rebuilt tower are kitchens and service areas. These are instead located in the southern gatehouse building. The architect's clever planning links these service areas to the tower via a narrow building range built into the thickness of the wall that divides the courtyard from the hornwork addition, therefore appearing as part of the castle defences from within the courtyard. The gatehouse building enlarges the footprint of its fifteenth-century predecessor, yet has little presence in external views of the castle, where it is expressed as a wall of enceinte. Only a few small windows and two chimneys appear above the parapet to identify the building behind. It incorporates a new, large gateway, giving a fortified point of entry to a castle whose entrance has moved repeatedly throughout its history. This is perhaps the most stylised element of the whole building: canted bays and a corbelled parapet frame a tall arched doorway with a dated, initialled MacRae coat of arms above, perhaps a twentieth-century model of defensible entrances at Rowallan, Fyvie and Dirleton. The gateway is one of a number of architectural features on the gatehouse building that appear to owe less to historic precedent. A stone, arched loggia sits to the right of this gateway at parapet level, similar in detail to new additions made by Lorimer in his restoration schemes, but a fairly odd inclusion in this place and at this height. A bellcote and rounded turret (perhaps a speaker's platform) are also incorporated on the courtyard side of the building, appearing to enliven the otherwise plain elevation (Figure 196). Perhaps tellingly, none of these features are detailed in the Mackie Watson drawings and may be later additions.

The south-west corner building of the castle is notably different in style and was the last building reconstructed. It is simple and unassuming, playing a secondary role to the tower, and today serves as modern accommodation for the Clan MacRae. There are no castellated elements here; if anything, the style of the building is mid to late seventeenth century in date, with a gridded distribution of small, segmental-arched windows. The tall, wallhead chimneys and flue design also add a distinctly modern feel, in contrast to the re-created medievalism opposite.

It might be assumed that the building encountered today has changed little since its reconstruction. However, historic photographs demonstrate that rebuilt areas of the castle, other than parts of the tower, were being finished in harl (Figure 193). This harl was not included in the historic drawings for the building and it cannot be established whether the whole building was intended to have this finish, but it does appear to have been removed for aesthetic reasons, perhaps responding to the contemporary fashion of exposing rubble to underline 'oldness'. Today harl remains on the seaward façades of the tower and the south-west corner building, and hidden areas of the west link range, but it appears to have been removed from buildings that sit within the 'key' views of the castle. This demonstrates that even since the rebuild, this castle has continued to evolve and change with fashions.

Twentieth-Century Castle Culture

It is nearly 100 years since both buildings were reacquired by their clans. Attitudes have continued to change about the treatment of ancient buildings and, in the face of modern government policy, the rebuilding of both Eilean Donan and Duart could be controversial. However, even at the time of the restorations, concerns about the principle and execution of works at ancient buildings evoked split opinions and passionate debate. For instance, in 1923, travel writer and historian M E M Donaldson, wrote of Eilean Donan:

On the first occasion we had been delighted and held by a picture perfect in every detail, for confronting us was the magnificent ruin of the castle of Eilean Donnan, then the most picturesque I have seen on the castle-strewn shores of the west coast ... but no such view is any longer obtainable. For returning several years later, I was horrified and repelled by the ruined picture which obtruded itself on the outraged surroundings, the remains of the castle being in the throes of a rebuilding which must permanently disfigure the landscape. In any modern rebuilding operations the end no less than the means to the end are alike hideous. From start to finish in the proceedings, everything is ugly; and one can only marvel at a taste which finds any satisfaction in transforming a picturesque ruin which harmonizes so completely with its surroundings into a permanent blot on the landscape. For a modern mansion house must in the nature of things be aggressive in its pretentiousness, and especially if it is to be connected with the mainland by a bridge, as is reported. How any one indentified with the country by reason of his clan can thus choose to identify himself with a proceeding usually associated with Americans or vulgarians, passes comprehension.[14]

Indeed, this was not the first criticism that was made of a restoration scheme carried out by Mackie Watson. His earlier proposed restoration of St Magnus Cathedral was pared back following

FIGURE 196
Eilean Donan, Ross and Cromarty: tower and court-yard from south-west (© RCAHMS, SC 1232813)

criticism of its impact upon the original fabric. The restoration of these castles, amongst others, contributed towards a reaction which still influences building conservation and archaeology today. But neither castle was ever protected as an Ancient Monument, and each has therefore always been treated as an evolving building. With hindsight, this evolution has come at a cost, with both archaeology and historic integrity now compromised. On the other hand, the twentieth-century works represent another important stage in the castles' ongoing process of change.

The early twentieth-century renaissance of 'Scottishness' as a fashion attracted as much criticism in certain quarters as did the restoration works. In the preface to her travel writings, M E M Donaldson again wrote:

> Infinitely more to be deplored, however, than the rubbish that Sasunnachs write about the Highlands and Saxon burlesques on the stage, is the dominion that too many strangers, distinguished only by wealth, have acquired by purchase in a country where they must for ever remain aliens. To the conservative mind of the true Celt it is grievous that in so many parts of the Highlands alien plutocrats should have supplanted clan chiefs. The dominating idea of the monied and sometimes titled nobodies from England or America, seems to be to advertise their sovereign power, and their money-archy has had the most disastrous effects upon the Gael.[15]

However, from among this group of 'alien plutocrats' came Sir Fitzroy Maclean and Lieutenant-Colonel John MacRae-Gilstrap, two prominent members of society who *were* clan descendents, however anglicised and moneyed, and who used architecture as a way of re-establishing clan identity, power and domain. The castle projects they funded are today protected as A-listed buildings of recognised national importance, partly because of the ancient fabric and their place in Scottish history but also, beyond this, as two of Scotland's most interesting early twentieth-century buildings in their own right: creations by two important figures from the forefront of Scottish architectural thinking at the time. Eilean Donan and Duart represent an important period during which wider trends in Scottish society and culture were equally manifest in the country's architecture.

On one side of Scottish culture sat the fast-evolving attitudes and knowledge within archaeology and architecture, fuelled by critical debate, the academic recording of ancient buildings, and the adoption of traditional styles to inform a new Scottish architecture. On the other side sat the romanticising of Scottish history, landscapes and traditions through literature, music and art, and, in terms of architecture, notions of rebuilding the 'castle of dreams'.

Duart and Eilean Donan castles represent the coming together of these opposing cultural trends. They played a significant part in the wider revival and reinvention of traditional Celtic and clan identities within Scottish, and British, twentieth-century culture, and demonstrate how this revival was driven not only by knowledge and history but also by trend, romanticism and patriotism.

CHAPTER FIFTEEN

Craigievar Castle
Changing Perceptions

Ann MacSween

Craigievar is one of Scotland's best known castles, one of a group of late sixteenth- and early seventeenth-century Aberdeenshire castles thought to be associated with the Bel family of stonemasons.[1] The group, which includes Castle Fraser, Midmar, Crathes and Fyvie, is characterised by a design approach which favoured vertical extension and the embellishment of the added upper storeys with corner turrets and stair towers to produce an extravagant silhouette. In Aberdeenshire, the result was a group of castles which have been portrayed as an 'architectural signifier of rank particular to northeast Scotland'.[2]

Charles McKean's view of this group of castles is that they are 'chateaux, erected at a time when, under the influence of the Gordon earls of Huntly, north-east Scotland enjoyed a period of unexampled wealth and splendour . . .'[3] Others, including Simpson,[4] while acknowledging European influences, emphasise the Scottish origins of many of Craigievar's features and the traditional leanings of the end product. However the balance of the blend is viewed, the final design undoubtedly owes much to the intellectual and geographic wanderings of its patron and his associates. This chapter examines not simply the early castle, but also the changes that have helped shape it over the past two centuries or so.

The name 'Craigievar' appears to derive from the Gaelic 'the rock of Mar'. Located about fifty kilometres west of Aberdeen, near the village of Alford in Leochel parish, the castle is situated on the east slope of Craigievar Hill. In the seventeenth century, views were important, both to and from prestigious buildings. Craigievar was sited to take in extensive views, as far as Bennachie, sixteen kilometres to the north-east, and the castle's distinctive silhouette made a statement about the prosperity and sophistication of its owner, even from a considerable distance. Close up, the building's height is accentuated by the projection of the upper storeys. Two balustraded platforms at roof level allowed the owners and their guests to take advantage of the panorama, and the experience of emerging onto the roof at such an elevation must have been an added thrill.

In its presentation as a tourist attraction, much has in the past been made of Craigievar's unaltered state, the implication being that it survives relatively intact from the time of its construction. The 1987 National Trust for Scotland guidebook, for example, states that 'Craigievar looks very much as it did in 1626, the year of its completion'.[5] While this applies in so far as the tower has changed little in profile since then, detailed survey work carried out for the National Trust for Scotland in the 1970s, and in 2009 during harling works, has shown that Craigievar has had its share of significant alterations over the 400 years since it was built.[6]

The Mortimer Tower

From at least the mid fifteenth century until the early seventeenth century, the estate of Craigievar was owned by the Mortimer family. The family began to build a castle towards the end of their ownership, but in 1610, due to a lack of funds, they sold the estate, including the unfinished building, to William Forbes. He was the younger brother of Patrick Forbes, a bishop of Aberdeen. His family owned the neighbouring estate of Corse, where Bishop Forbes' father had built a castle thirty years previously. William Forbes studied in the Arts at Edinburgh University and went on to make his fortune in the Baltic trade, earning the nickname 'Danzig Willie' ('Danzig' is modern Gdansk). In 1603 he married Margaret Woodward, daughter of the Lord Provost of Edinburgh. As with many successful merchants of the time, Forbes wanted to display his fortune through a building project.

The recent programme of works by the castle's owners, the National Trust for Scotland, provided an excellent opportunity to try to address one of the questions which had never been conclusively answered, namely how much of the castle had been built when William Forbes bought the estate. The results of the survey and analysis are summarised in *Discovery and Excavation in Scotland*.[7] That survey confirmed many of the conclusions about the building sequence from the 1973 survey carried out by the Royal Commission on the Ancient and Historic Monuments of Scotland. Although there is mention of the site from at least the fifteenth century, the 2009 survey concluded that the existing castle seems not to incorporate fabric pre-dating the

erection of a tower by the Mortimer family in the later sixteenth century. The survey also showed that the Mortimer tower survives up to the band of corbelling that encircles the castle just above the fourth floor level, and that this early phase can be recognised from the presence of chamfered surrounds and windows with ironwork grills.[8]

The early building comprised a simple rectangular tower with a wing forming an L-shape on plan, with a smaller square tower tucked into the inner angle. The ground floor of the main block contained the vaulted kitchen which, unusually, has its fireplace on a thickened exterior wall. An adjacent vaulted room in the tower and smaller rooms in the wing of the ground floor would have been used for preparation and storage. The main stair led up to the great hall, which occupies the whole of the first floor of the main block and was entered through a screens passage. A smaller, steep stair connected the preparation rooms with the hall. At first floor level the wing contains a chamber and a smaller adjacent room above the lobby, and has a similar arrangement of rooms directly above on second floor level. These rooms are on the same level as the ceiling vault of the hall, which rises through two storeys. The third floor has a large chamber and an ante-room above the hall, and a smaller chamber with an ante-room in the wing.

The Forbes Phase

William Forbes added two further storeys above third floor level which, as has been noted, comprises the heightened portion of the castle, above the first phase corbelling. False cannon-muzzle spouts and grotesque heads adorned this new build. One of the dormers is inscribed M W F, standing for 'Master William Forbes', and denoting Forbes' status as a graduate. The 2009 survey established that this early seventeenth-century phase can be identified from its entrance and window surrounds, which have rounded arrises, and from the configuration of the bars on the later windows. The survey also recovered evidence that the building was originally roofed with sandstone tiles and finished with a cream-coloured lime harl.[9]

The additional accommodation comprised a similar arrangement of rooms on the fourth floor to those directly below, while on the fifth floor were two rooms, the larger of which, a gallery, takes up the entire eastern side of the castle, stretching across the wing. Galleries like this were probably used for social purposes, for conversation and promenade, and for receptions.[10] The ceiling in this room is plain and it has been suggested that the original plasterwork may not have survived the roof repairs of the mid nineteenth century, as even the turrets have decorative plasterwork ceilings.[11] The stair continued beyond this room to the rooftop terrace, where the view could be fully appreciated.

As well as the new additions, alterations to the lower storeys were also made during Forbes' work. A chamber within the east wall overlooking the hall interior, for example, was removed. It has been suggested that it functioned as an oratory and if this was its purpose, its removal would fit with the transfer of ownership of the castle from a Catholic family to the Protestant Forbes family.[12] A large window was inserted in place of the chamber.

Inside as well as out, guests would have gained the impression that no expense had been spared. The moulded plaster ceilings were up-to-date courtier fashion, having been introduced into Scotland around the time of James VI's 1617 visit, becoming quickly popular. The number of Craigievar's ceilings and the variety of their design are impressive. The hall ceiling, for example, has the arms of William Forbes and his wife

Margaret Woodward on the crown of the vault together with profiles of Roman emperors (Figure 197). The plasterwork was the work of travelling craftsmen, and plasterwork from the same moulds used at Craigievar have been spotted at other buildings, including Glamis (in 1620) and Kellie Castle (in 1624). The hall fireplace has royal arms executed in plasterwork above it, and is regarded as one of the finest pieces of heraldry in Scotland.[13] William Forbes could display the royal coat of arms, as he was a tenant-in-chief of the crown and as such had the authority to administer justice over his lands in the name of the king. Simpson has argued that

> nothing can more tellingly underline the significance of the emergence, in that all too brief Golden Age which intervened between the wars of the Reformation and those of the Covenant, of a class of cultured lairds who based their power not on feudal privilege but on honest trade.[14]

Much of the panelled woodwork in the hall, including panels to screen the servery, also dates from this period. The adjacent chamber has Memel pine panelling, reflecting the family's business links with the Baltic, and a plaster ceiling incorporating an image of Saint Margaret, Malcolm Canmore's queen. William died in 1627, and the dates on the plaster ceilings suggest that by then Craigievar was complete.[15]

When Craigievar was built, castle architecture was understood as representing power deriving from ancestry and tradition, and the defensive references in its design are obvious. McKean has noted, however, that Craigievar was built in a period when the North-East was '. . . largely exempt from the dynastic troubles and English invasions that afflicted the districts further south'.[16] It is clear, though, that features such as

FIGURE 197
Craigievar Castle, Aberdeenshire: The hall drawn by Robert W Billings, from *The Baronial and Ecclesiastical Antiquities of Scotland*, 4 vols (1848–52), vol. 1 (© Historic Scotland)

the heavy iron yett (gate), side-hung inside the main door, and the gun-holes covering the entrance, had a more than decorative capacity. In describing Craigievar, R W Billings noted its defensive potential, even although defence was obviously not its primary purpose: 'Its uses, as a fortress against the Highland reiver rather than as a mere dwelling-house, are recalled by all its attributes of sullen strength'[17] (Figure 198).

At a time when valuables were kept inside the house, the threat of theft was very real and the ability to secure property from unauthorised entry was essential. William Forbes' son, also William (created a baronet of Nova Scotia by Charles I), who succeeded him at Craigievar, is recorded in 1644 as having moved 'his haill victuals of Fintray' to Craigievar in order that they be 'kept from plundering'.[18]

It is also recorded that in the 1630s the area was terrorised by a band of raiders who operated throughout the Highlands before a number of them, including their leader, 'Gilderoy' (Patrick MacGregor), were captured and hanged. Even this does not appear to have put an end to the raiding as the following, recounted in *History of the Troubles*, makes clear:

> He [John Dugar, a Highland freebooter] did great skaith to the name of Forbes – such as the Lairds of Corse, Leslie, Craigievar, and some others; abused their bounds, and plundered their horse, nolt, sheep, goods, and geir, because they were the instruments of Gilleroy's death; and the Forbeses concluded to watch his comeing and goeing, and to get him if they might.[19]

Eighteenth Century

Little is recorded of changes to the house during the eighteenth century, although many windows are known to have been blocked in the 1770s as a tax avoidance measure. The base of an elaborate pedimented dormer was noted at the north wall-head, and evidence for two further dormers was noted at the south end of the east wallhead – they had lit the long gallery on the upper floor.[20]

While we are used to views that show Craigievar Castle standing in isolation on its well-kept lawn, up until the late eighteenth century the castle would have been surrounded by a courtyard wall and two or more ranges of buildings. The only surviving trace of this is a stretch of the west courtyard wall which incorporates the arched entrance into the courtyard. It terminated in a round tower with a conical roof that also

FIGURE 198
Craigievar Castle, Aberdeenshire: drawing by Robert W Billings, from *The Baronial and Ecclesiastical Antiquities of Scotland*, 4 vols (1848–52), vol. 1 (© Historic Scotland)

survives, although no longer linked to the wall. Visitors would have approached along a terraced contour and through the arch. A survey of the estate, carried out in 1776 by George Brown, survives, and shows an enclosed garden in four quadrants to the north of the castle and a less formal area to the south.[21]

Excavations in 1990 by Moira Greig for the

301

National Trust for Scotland revealed evidence for the south and east walls of the courtyard. Brown's plan of 1776 also shows a north and south range of buildings. No evidence was found for stone buildings inside the courtyard wall, however, and the ranges might have been formed of timber lean-to buildings – a number of post-holes were recorded during the excavations.[22]

A slightly later estate plan by Brown, dating to 1791, shows that by this time the south range, apart from the tower, had been removed, and an additional range built at the adjacent Mains. This clearance may indicate an intention to form a garden around the castle, but by then the family's attention had turned to the rebuilding of their property at Fintray, and the *Old Statistical Account* of 1793 notes of Craigievar that 'though not at present inhabited Sir William [5th Baronet] keeps it in good repair'. Before 1800 an avenue of trees was planted on the drive to the south of the castle.[23]

Nineteenth Century

Sir William Forbes was succeeded in 1816 by Sir Arthur, his eldest son, but he died abroad in 1823 while on army service. His brother, John, returned from service as a judge with the East India Company to run the family estates, which were by then in poor financial health. He appointed Aberdeen-based John Smith, who had recently completed work on the transformation of Cluny Castle into a modern mansion house, to report on the condition of Craigievar.[24] Smith suggested that what was needed at Craigievar was only essential works, and he wrote to Sir John that Craigievar was 'one of the finest specimens of architecture in this country of the age and style in which it is built'.[25] While Smith's approach has been hailed as enlightened in that it promoted repair over rebuild, his heightening of the stair

turret as shown in James Giles' watercolour of 1840 (an alteration reversed by around 1850) hints that the relatively limited scope of the works to Craigievar were probably at least partly due to the continued diversion of the family's attention and finances to Fintray.[26]

Smith's recommendations included replacing the stone roofing tiles with Foudland slates and the enlargement of many window openings, including those in the great hall, and the installation of new sash and case windows in place of the fixed lights. The main door was replaced at this time, and the initials on the knocker are those of Sir John Forbes and his wife Charlotte Ann. It was also during this phase of works that the cream-coloured harl was replaced with its well-known pink harl, Smith recommending that the building be repointed and 'rough cast with best prepared Scotch lime to match the colour of the granite mouldings; which will greatly improve the appearance of the building as well as preserve the walls'.[27] During the recent survey, surviving traces of the original pink mortar indicated that it may have covered the stone dressings.

Craigievar became a summer and autumn holiday house only used occasionally. William Forbes, who succeeded his father while still a child, later recounted that a lasting impression of his visit to Craigievar with his father in 1842 on estate business was the box beds under the rough stone walls, and the rushes that were cut and spread on the floor every morning.[28]

During the nineteenth century, the number of visitors to the Highlands increased markedly. In addition to Scotland's landscape attractions, people were considering its rich built heritage as a reason to visit. Durie captures this mood well: 'The appeal of inherited antiquities, caves, castles and abbeys, was set in a landscape and culture endorsed by royalty. The presence of the past was preserved for profit, rather than plundered for stone, and judiciously enhanced by man-made artefacts, evocative of past personages and episodes.'[29]

In this climate, Craigievar found a new role as a local tourist destination, marked by the opening of a Visitors Book in 1848. The building retained the character of a bygone age, which was fascinating to visitors. Queen Victoria visited Craigievar twice, as did many of the European visitors to Balmoral, and the growing popularity of Royal Deeside as a tourist destination increased its visitor numbers. Craigievar was portrayed in A & C Black's *Picturesque Tourist of Scotland* (1851) as 'a grim old Flemish building', with this theme no doubt expanded during tours of the castle.[30]

In 1884 the estates passed to Sir John's eldest son, William, who succeeded as 17th Lord Sempill, and various calls on the estate's finances, including an expensive divorce, resulted in the family spending more time at Craigievar while letting out Fintray. The castle was updated with new panelling and bedsteads in place of some of the bunks, as well as with the introduction of plumbing.

Twentieth Century

Craigievar Castle's popularity was boosted in the twentieth century by two photographic campaigns in 1906 and 1938 by *Country Life*. In 1941, during the Second World War, Fintray was requisitioned and Craigievar became the home of William Francis (1893–1965), the last Lord Sempill to live at Craigievar. Many of the family's belongings moved to Craigievar with them, including the family portraits. Lady Sempill, who had trained as an artist, did much to modernise the interior decoration. Some items of furniture were cleared out, and several bedrooms had their wooden panelling whitewashed to relieve the gloom. A specially commissioned tartan carpet was added to the great hall.

Craigievar Castle was purchased from the trustees of the 18th Baron in 1963 by a consortium and presented to the National Trust for Scotland. In 1973 reharling works were carried out, and during the works some larger windows were unblocked and shotholes reopened (Figures 199 and 200). The building was reharled by dubbing out the exterior wall surfaces with cement and finishing it with a final thin coat of deep pink-pigmented cement harl.

The cement work of the 1970s, which was damaging to the fabric, was removed in 2007–9 to address the increasing humidity in the house and the associated threats to the furniture, furnishings and artwork, and, of course, to the moulded plaster ceilings.[31] The exterior walls were dubbed out with a cream lime mortar, with similarly coloured harl coats. Many coats of pale pink lime were applied, but the moulded and carved stonework was left exposed. Much of the missing carved stonework from the upper levels was reinstated, including false spouts.[32]

Changing Perceptions

The castle reopened in 2010 looking, literally, as it never had before (Figure 201). For many, the essence of Craigievar is the period of the Forbes work: the completion of the castle by a wealthy north-east businessman as his family home, to display his wealth and good taste during a time when architectural choices said much about the owner's status. The survival of so many of the castle's interior features, such as the plasterwork ceilings and the wood panelling, help greatly in the promotion of this period of Craigievar's history. But as this short history of the castle indicates, many changes were subsequently made to Craigievar, from the enlarging of some windows and blocking of others to changes in the roofing materials and the colour of the harl, and on to the

FIGURE 199
Opposite. Craigievar Castle, Aberdeenshire: general view from south, taken in 1973 (© RCAHMS, SC 445042)

FIGURE 200
Left. Craigievar Castle, Aberdeenshire: view of turret at south-west angle, taken in 1973 (© RCAHMS, SC 702559)

FIGURE 201
Below. Craigievar Castle, Aberdeenshire: photograph taken in May 2010 on completion of recent works (© Mike Scott)

twentieth-century whitewashing of some of the wood panelling. In addition there have also, of course, been major changes to the castle's original setting within a courtyard of estate buildings to its current presentation on a well-maintained lawn, the object perhaps being to help emphasise the tower's singular presence, unencumbered by more prosaic outbuildings.

The interpretation of the castle is now increasingly emphasising these changes and the castle's more recent history, and presenting these phases as also being important. The National Trust for Scotland current guidebook to Craigievar, written by Ian Gow in 2004, goes a considerable way to updating the longstanding perception of Craigievar as 'very much as it was in 1626, the year of its completion'[33] to one which reflects the castle much more as a lived-in family home over four centuries, with all the changes that inevitably brought. The recent survey work of 2009 simply adds yet another layer to our changing perceptions of Craigievar, and no doubt that process will continue.[34]

CHAPTER SIXTEEN

Castles in the Modern Age

Ian Begg

'Castles in the modern age.' We might wonder why this ancient concept of a house is still with us in the twenty-first century. There is no straight answer. The idea fascinates many and, as argued by other contributions to this book, it is a strong symbol of this unruly country of ours. It also has to be said that they can look good, and castles usually sit with great presence in the landscape.

In this chapter I want to go back a little before going forward. The late Professor Gordon Donaldson liked the old cliché: 'How do we know where we're going if we don't know where we've been?'

I very strongly believe in that sentiment, because we have so much to learn from our tradition, which has developed from our experience of life in this part of the world. This, of course, includes the light and climate of Scotland. As a working architect, I have over the years tackled many old castles or tower houses: places like Muckrach, Dairsie, Edinample, Rossend, Castle Moil, Aboyne Castle (perhaps my most enjoyable job of all), Beldorney, Tillycairn and Ashintully. During that time many people asked me if I never thought of restoring one for myself. I never did, for some inexplicable reason.

I lived most of my time in Edinburgh's New Town, but in the 1980s I moved to a flat in the Lawnmarket in Edinburgh, at 13 James Court. I had loved living in the New Town, but this was different. I knew the Old Town well but the flat, I discovered, was in a tower house; then I realised that the Old Town of Edinburgh was packed with tower houses, cheek by jowl. Fourth floor in a tower house: it felt like it, right in the heart of Scotland. I was there before the terrorist threats; God knows who is plotting against us now. Anyway, at that time we frequently had the pipes and drums of bands on the street, the almost painfully exciting music heard within the confines of the Royal Mile. I don't know if you ever hear that now. The flat was a splendid place, with very fine Georgian rooms: sitting room to the front and fine bedroom to the quiet courtyard behind. and interesting spaces between. The plan is illustrated here (Figure 202). I loved it there.

So when I wanted a new house in the country, I thought I would try to build a modern house with the feel of an old tower: the appearance of thick walls, a place that wouldn't shake in storms, and would feel good and strongly protective. I had learned, from the Lawnmarket, that the stairs would be little problem. In fact, stairs became almost a passion with me: the fascinating, clever geometric forms, and getting the landings in the right place. I found that if I followed the design of a Borromini stair I had seen in Rome, in coming to terms with the requirements of

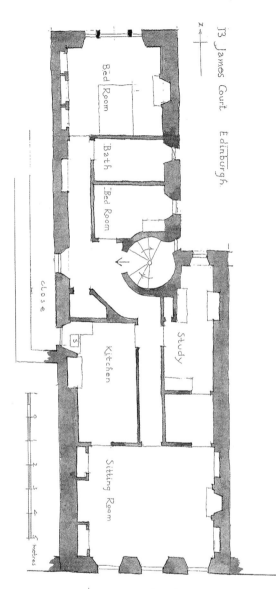

James Court

B James Court Edinburgh

close

Bed Room

Bath

Bed Room

Kitchen

Study

Sitting Room

Lawnmarket

FIGURE 202
Lawnmarket, Edinburgh, Midlothian: plan of
13 James Court (© Ian Begg)

building control, I had a perfect solution for my new place. It is a tower house called Ravens' Craig. I'm originally from Kirkcaldy, and at school there I was in Ravenscraig House. We also have ravens very close to us and our township is Craig. The name was obvious. We have been here for twenty years now, and visitors find the place very comfortable. We had a visit from a group of about fifty people on a study tour organised by the Architectural Heritage Society of Scotland. The write-up by Tom Parnell in the autumn 2010 issue of the *AHSS Magazine* (no. 28) is worth quoting:

> Our final day took us to Ian Begg's Ravens' Craig. I would admit that I was slightly apprehensive about this, but I fell in love with it. As a modern interpretation of a tower house, it works. Providing endless fascination with its many nooks and crannies, every space is used effectively and economically, in what must be an extremely complex section. It is a lot of fun, and I think that we were all very comfortable indeed.

Here is the plan of the main hall or sitting room, which sits in the core of the house (Figure 203). It has a triangular patterned ceiling and, because the equilateral triangles would dictate the precise size of the room, the dimensions of the main block of the house were established with that (Figure 204). It is not really complex.

The design process is interesting as an exercise. Starting with a relatively small footprint, every space has to be used. As you would see on a section, the ground floor has a true vault and to give stability to this, the vertical load from the roof is carried down inner walls to the springing of the arch. This gives the impression of thick walls, which is what I wanted but, being hollow, the space has to be used profitably. Rooms

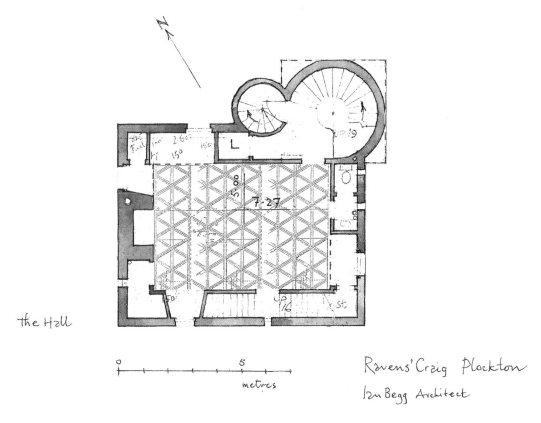

the Hall

Ravens'Craig Plockton
Ian Begg Architect

FIGURE 203
Ravens'Craig, Plockton, Ross and Cromarty: plan (© Ian Begg)

obviously have to fit over rooms, and plumbing has to be grouped so that there is only one soil pipe, and the stairs have to work, bringing landings at the right place. A sympathetic, curious building inspector is helpful and, on the other hand, building from scratch means that there is no Historic Scotland inspector breathing down your neck. The stairs keep me fit, and a second-hand lift unit bought years ago isn't installed yet. The wonder is: will it be ready when I really need it? The house was built by local tradesmen, and was a good move, as local people feel a certain attachment to the place.

About this time in the 1980s, I got a job on the High Street in Glasgow, very close to the cathedral, to build a centre for the Friends of Glasgow Cathedral, right on the site of the old Bishop's Castle or Palace. The cathedral is an Ancient Monument and under the control of Historic Scotland. The Friends of the Cathedral, primarily the congregation, needed a place to call their own. The Bishop's Castle was demolished in the eighteenth century. Here was a challenge. The requirement was a multi-purpose building and had to include the possibility of incorporating a manse for the minister of the cathedral. We were undoubtedly in old Glasgow, although the area had been savagely wrecked in the nineteenth century and the cathedral was severed from other remnants of the Old Town. It was my view that,

FIGURE 204
Ravens'Craig, Plockton, Ross and Cromarty:
view of hall (© Ian Begg)

FIGURE 205
St Mungo Museum of Religious Life and Art,
Glasgow: watercolour sketch (© Ian Begg)

without copying anything, we should give a feeling of the ancient use of the site and build a castle, making it of stone. This was my view, but there was strong backing for the idea. Just at the start of design work I was involved in a whole-of-Scotland schools project, run by the National Trust for Scotland, called 'My Place'. Magnus Magnusson and I were judges. One proposal, which ultimately won, concerned a gap site near the cathedral. It was entered by St Roch's School, Glasgow. After showing many slides of modern Glasgow to a song 'I don't belong to Glasgow!' sung to the old tune, the children changed tune and showed slides of buildings they liked. Some had arcading. I sympathised with their ideas and gained strength from that. Our proposal was traditional; I saw the new building very much as a repair of the old fabric of the city. Of course others, including many architects, saw it as a missed opportunity! It was to be a multi-purpose building, and before work was started on site the purpose changed – it was now to become the St Mungo Centre of Comparative Religion (Figure 205). It was adapted internally to suit its new use, but still retaining the space for a new manse. The exterior design remained virtually intact, and it was executed by Page & Park Architects with me looking on in an advisory capacity and attending site meetings.

It is a strong form of building at the Bell of the Brae, and is a marker for the beautiful cathedral; standing where it is, it offers good approaches to the cathedral. The small walled garden in the re-entrant angle of the St Mungo Centre, which I had planned as a knot garden, has a beautiful zen garden designed and planted by Japanese landscape gardeners, who described the space as 'perfect' (Figure 206).

The controversial but highly popular painting by Salvador Dali, 'Christ of St John on the Cross', hung in the building for many years.

Another controversial but popular building

with strong castle-like tendencies was built around the same time in the Royal Mile to my designs (Figure 207). It is an interesting case, because it was built in the Edinburgh Old Town Conservation Area – now part of Edinburgh World Heritage Site. The Scandic Hotel, now the Radisson Hotel, was the product of a Danish firm, Dancon. The boss, Jens Pilo, was an interesting man, a very strong character, and he led the whole operation. He wanted a four-star hotel in Edinburgh. It had to be Scottish, he said so forcefully, because he 'didn't want hotel guests to wonder whether they might be in Atlanta, Georgia', and he wanted it quick. He took the long-vacant gap site between Niddry Street and Blackfriars Street. It had stood empty because no developer could see how to make it pay. Jens Pilo did, and the hotel has been very successful.

The building was completed in fourteen months from the day of our founding ceremony on the long-abandoned site. The hotel and shop filled a serious gap in the Royal Mile frontage; so much so that the lower part of the High Street has become much more active and successful since. It was thought by many that the design was wrong, anti-progressive and, worst of all, 'it was pastiche'. Many folk and amenity bodies opposed the proposal, and some thought that the hotel was given a false front on a standard hotel grid plan behind. This is not so. The site was developed from the old Ordnance Survey, and the named closes are just where they were. The hotel naturally demanded level bedroom floors. There are 250 bedrooms, meeting rooms, a health club and a large car park. Part of the success of the design is that the large scale of the building is not obvious when looking at the building, which steps down kindly with the slope of the street.

Edinburgh Old Town has surprisingly few really old buildings, but it remains very much of a piece, medieval in style, because over late eighteenth, nineteenth and twentieth centuries people

have built consciously to keep the character, unashamedly using what we would now call 'pastiche', trying successfully to develop the character and scale of the place. Imagine, or – better still – take the walk, and look around you with eyes wide open, starting in the Grassmarket. Walk two thirds of the way up Victoria Street, then climb the steps to Victoria Terrace and have a short walk there. Tall buildings above and tall buildings below, with beautiful stone detail, bright paint, and fantastic views out to the south. Immediately to the north is the Royal Mile (Figure 208). Go there. There are many ways through the stone buildings. This ancient street runs from the castle at the high west end, down the continuous slope, past St Giles Cathedral to the Canongate; note the fine view out to the east and the North Sea. Just past St Giles turn north down Cockburn Street, which sweeps downhill towards the west and then north to Market Street and Waverley Station.

You get a splendid impression of the old medieval city in sympathy with the castle, yet the greater part is much later and nearer our modern age.

What I am getting at here is the dichotomy that occurs when people want an architecture of our time, and want to be modern, whatever it produces; and others, like me, who want sympathetic implants to keep the scale and character of an area like Old Edinburgh. Anyway, what has our time got to offer that is so fine as we see here?

I am going to stray abroad now but keeping to the Scottish connection.

Nearly twenty years ago a client visited me at my home, Ravens'Craig at Plockton. Much later, about five years ago, he phoned out of the blue, got me first time and asked if I remembered him, Chris Ruffle, which I certainly did. He then said: 'Well, let me remind you of a short conversation we had. I asked you if you would ever consider building another castle like Ravens' Craig? Your reply was: "Yes, – but I'd rather not

St Mungo Museum of Religious Life and Art,
Glasgow: zen garden (© Ian Begg)

Lawnmarket, Edinburgh: design sketch of Scandic
Crown hotel (© Ian Begg)

fight the climate of north-west Scotland – I would prefer to build in California.'" He went on: 'Would China do?' Deep breath! My reply was: 'Yes, I'm interested – tell me more!' The upshot was that, without doing any drawing, and within a month, my wife Ruth and I were in China (fares paid and all accommodation given) to 'look and see'.

Shanghai first, which was a great adventure in itself. When I was very young I had an uncle, Dave Ewing. He told great sea stories, although I doubt if he was ever very far from Scotland himself. Many concerned the Yangtze Kiang, as people called it then: I think that he loved the words. Well, here I was, virtually on the Yangtze, and then we flew 400 miles to the north coast of Shandong Province near Penglai. The site was very fine. A south slope on granite, looking over a wide valley growing fruit, and a lake at the bottom. The client was in the process of buying land from the government to plant a new vineyard. My job was to build a winery, or factory, to produce wine from the grapes he was going to grow. And he wanted a Scottish castle that would also be a home, with space for accommodating visitors, and a great hall to seat 100 people in Chinese banqueting style – round tables with ten people round each. (That's a big space.) Plus shop and visitors' required viewing and learning facilities; and, of course, lavatories and car and bus parking. China has no historic culture of the vine, but it is now one of the world's great wine-producing countries. China, in its race to modernise and be part of the world, is considering all aspects of its life and culture. The taste for good wine is developing fast, and this is where my client comes in. His vines would be brought from France and planted in this fine fruit-growing valley to produce quality grapes and, ultimately, fine wine, all under the supervision of Gérard Colin, a Frenchman already knowledgeable about the region and its potential.

FIGURE 208
Lawnmarket, Edinburgh: general view looking towards castle, c.1910 (© Scottish Colorfoto)

On site was the remains of a small stone quarry, creating a shallow hole in the hillside. The concept of a double-use, linked building jumped at me, and that has stuck. We were on! The site was, as I said, on the edge of a broad valley about five miles across, with hills beyond and not an industrial building in sight. Soft fruit, peaches and apricots were grown on the lowest slopes, with apples – fabulous apples – above. (Shandong province produces a third of all the concentrated apple juice consumed in the world.) At the next level, vines were going to be planted. Only about 20 hectares at present. The land here was scrub, with young trees planted for amenity reasons. It was going to be a great place for spring flowers, too. The climate, we were told, was very similar to Bordeaux in France: enough rain, hot in summer and quite cold in winter.

The winery, nearly 30 metres by 30 metres by 10 metres high, would go in the old quarry, with room hidden at the side for storage of bottles and barrels. It would have a paved roof, and the castle would stand above and behind, with the castle forecourt on the flat roof of the winery. These early design drawings have been developed and the new castle exists (Figure 209). It has been interesting work, but inevitably there have been problems and frustrations that can never be ironed out because we have a language barrier. It was expected that our working drawings would be done using computer-aided design (CAD), with all our notes on a layer that would be substituted with a different one covering all the Chinese notes. Metric is standard. In fact, the drawings were all redone on a different machine, and carelessly, and then sent to me for the tedious

FIGURE 209
Qiushan, Shandong, China: view from south west (© Ian Begg)

job of checking. In China, drawings were printed to fit the sheet so were rarely to any recognisable scale; and I have no CAD machine and work only on A3 or A4 sheets. My photocopier, fortunately, can change any scale, so a drawing that was actually to a scale of 1:38 could be changed to 1:50, but that was tiresome. Also, the basic structure had to be poured in situ concrete, because we were on the edge of an earthquake area, and changes were made with no discussion, which produced more problems. In the end, we got approvals and steamed ahead with regular communication, a steady supply of pictures to show what was happening on site, and almost constant demand for drawings and perspective sketches. My wife and I were on site on five occasions over the five years since inception.

The contractor, Mr Wang, is quite young, about fifty, very nice and very generous. Presents and banquets are part of the life. Mr Sun, who was overlooking the job, is well into his sixties, so is

from the old school, before the Cultural Revolution, and I got on particularly well with him. Quick sketching, grunts and words that the other cannot understand were an essential part of the job on site visits. And we smiled and laughed a lot (Figure 210). One visit lasted nine days and I was bloody well exhausted, drained, but the job was eventually finished with a splendid celebration.

Now is the time to ask: 'Why build a Scottish castle, anywhere?' And particularly in China? Castles are wonderfully organic in form: they grow. They are not easily read from a look at the outside, so there is an element of mystery. Even when you live in one, as I have for many years now, there is still an occasional visual or intellectual surprise, and steady enjoyment. It is calm; and others feel that too. Okay, but why a Scottish castle in China? I have thought about that. It's not something I wanted to ask my client. He is a romantic in the broad sense. He is married to a Chinese lady. I think that part of him sees his life as a seventeenth-century merchant adventurer and he *would* build a castle, wouldn't he? He was not born in Scotland. He is a Yorkshireman, but with help from me and our firm he restored a castle in Scotland; and he works as a big part of a well-known Scottish firm involved with international investment. He is a merchant adventurer!

But that is nothing like the whole answer. Why does one still build castles? Here is a very new one in China quite close to the one I have just described, also near Penglai (Figure 211). It doesn't look like it has anything to do with Scotland, and it doesn't. It was built in the name of the People's Republic of China. It was planned by men who ran the Hong Kong Stock Exchange. It says there, on the building, that it is a chateau, and it sits in a vast new vineyard. Let me give you a brief look at the very high quality of the work. But why make it look like a great European or American chateau? It must have to do with status and wanting to be worldly. It, of course, follows the enormous destruction which occurred during the Cultural Revolution. Is this a re-establishing of quality in architecture, as well as with the wine, to be seen by the West? Chateau-produced wine signifies quality in our society. The Chinese neither export their wine nor buy European, American or Australian wine – they drink their own, but they're determined to catch up, and they are doing so. This chateau is imposing, it is beautifully built, but it is largely an empty shell. It is puzzling. It is a very interesting place.

In finishing, I want to return to Edinburgh. I am thinking again of the Old Town from the castle to Holyrood, and all the closes and buildings that make up this symbol of Scotland, and the many tower houses that make a big contribution to this historical part of our country and its culture. At the same time I see the people of Mountgrange. Developers, with their modern Caltongate scheme, to the north side of the Canongate that, to me, doesn't fit; it isn't part of

FIGURE 210

Qiushan, Shandong, China: Ian Begg in winery
(© Ian Begg)

the Old Town. The economic climate has stopped the proposal for the present time, but the architect, the planning committee and the Edinburgh Council all gave approval to the project, and they will come back.

Edinburgh has a unique quality, primarily because it has two substantial and very distinct parts that are now recognised as a World Heritage Site. This is partly due to the natural topography on which the 'Medieval Old Town' and the 'Georgian New Town' were built, but it is more than that. The Old Town is informal, romantic, tight, yet has a wonderful sense of freedom, as I earlier tried to imply; while the New Town is classical, obeys rules, has space, and has beautiful formal houses. They are different, and that distinction must remain; yet it seems that some people, including architects and even some Edinburgh councillors, do not understand why so many oppose some proposals. Of course there are

FIGURE 211
Chateau Junding, Shandong, China (© Ian Begg)

others, including many architects who have their work regularly illustrated – or would like to have their work illustrated – in the architectural magazines, who approved some damaging schemes and thoroughly dislike my language of architecture. These people just cannot see what I see in this city, and I think that many, many people of Edinburgh, and our visitors, do too – people who enjoy and love this place. The more invasive projects sometimes proposed could seriously damage the character of our World Heritage site, though they can always be revised to show more sympathy for the character and scale of the existing structure and do more to reintroduce a healthy, living community. Money has a huge part to play in all this, but as we see in today's very serious financial climate, nothing is so secure as our architecture of quality.

My first wife said on a few occasions that I suffered from *folie de grandeur*. Maybe I do. I love good architecture old and modern. I wonder now if she really referred to my language of architecture, and didn't like it; as a lot of architects also feel about the way I put buildings together. Sadly, the Vienna Memorandum produced for UNESCO in 2005 seems to play into the hands of the 'Philipsteins', as I call those who haunt me, when it states that 'the urban landscape should avoid all forms of pseudo-historic design, as they constitute a denial of both the historical and the contemporary alike'. Is this is a true denial of the value of a huge body of work built in Edinburgh and many other places? I exaggerate, but this criticism, it seems to me, might even deny the architecture of the Renaissance in Rome.

Notes

Introduction

1. This quotation is from William Shakespeare's *Macbeth* (Act I, Scene VI), spoken by King Duncan before Macbeth's castle. It was inscribed on Viewhill (begun 1835), the Inverness home of the engineer Joseph Mitchell (1803–1883), FRSE, FGS and MICE.
2. Thomas Carlyle, *Oliver Cromwell's Letters and Speeches with Elucidations* (1888), p. 243.
3. A painting of the hall's interior by the brothers is reproduced in Hugh Trevor-Roper, *The Invention of Scotland* (2009), Plate 11.
4. John MacCormick, *The Island of Mull* (n.d. but 1923), pp. 117–18.
5. John Slezer, *Theatrum Scotiae* (1693), Introduction.
6. Sir Arthur Mitchell (ed.) *Geographical Collections Relating to Scotland Made by Walter MacFarlane*, 3 vols (1906–8), vol. 1, 359.
7. Sir Robert Sibbald, *Historical Inquiries Concerning the Roman Monuments and Antiquities in the north-part of Britain called Scotland . .* (1707), Preface.
8. Iain Gordon Brown, 'Critick in Antiquity: Sir John Clerk of Penicuik', in *Antiquity* (Nov. 1977), li, p. 205.
9. Jiro Nagasawa, *Dorothy Wordsworth: Journal of My Second Tour in Scotland, 1822* (1989), pp. 19, 142; J Reed, *Sir Walter Scott: Landscape and Locality* (1980), p. 19.
10. J E Bowman, *The Highlands and Islands: A Nineteenth Century Tour* (1986 edn), p. 101.
11. A. Bell, 'Reason and Dreams: Cockburn's Practical and Nostalgic Views of Civic Well-being', in A. Bell (ed.) *Lord Cockburn: a Bicentenary Commemoration* (1979), pp. 52–3.
12. J G Lockhart (ed.), *The Journal of Sir Walter Scott 1825–32* (1927 edn), pp. 490–1.
13. Bell, 'Reason and Dreams', pp. 41–2.
14. David MacGibbon and Thomas Ross, *Castellated and Domestic Architecture of Scotland*, 5 vols (1887–92), vol. 1, p. 1.
15. *Ibid.*, vol. 2, p. 3.
16. *Ibid.*, vol. 2, p. 575.
17. *Ibid.*, vol. 2, p. 67.
18. *Ibid.*, vol. 2, p. 140.
19. T W West, *A History of Architecture in Scotland* (1967), pp. 11–12.
20. S Cruden, *Scottish Medieval Churches* (1986), p. 183.
21. Giles Worsley, *Classical Architecture in Britain: The Heroic Age* (1995), p. 155.
22. Sorley MacLean, *From Wood to Ridge: Collected Poems in Gaelic and English* (1989), pp. 26–7.

Chapter 2 1603–1746: Castles No More, or '*the Honour and pride of a country*'?

1. *Register of the Privy Council*, vol. 7, pp. 26–7.
2. Robert Mylne (then working with Sir William Bruce at Holyrood) used Francini's book that same year for the design of his family monument in Greyfriars, Edinburgh.
3. 'NI DEVS AEDIFICET DOMVM' / 'except the Lord build the house'.
4. John Lowrey, 'Bruce and his Circle at Craigiehall 1693–1708' in John Frew and David Jones (eds.) *Aspects of Scottish Classicism* (1989), pp. 2–3.
5. A sixteenth-century tower had been incrementally extended, the unequal-width east and west quarters rendering the main north front slightly asymmetrical.
6. There was wide contemporary interest in and debate surrounding Mary Queen of Scots, and an extending literature – had she been a good or a bad person? Was she guilty or innocent? A betrayed Romantic heroine? In Dresden, for instance, in 1683, the poet and playwright August Adolf von Haugwitz (1647–1706) published *Schuldige unschuld oder Maria Stuarda. Königin von Schottland* [etc.].
7. Ian Gordon Brown, 'Critick in Antiquity: Sir John Clerk of Penicuik', *Antiquity*, vol. 51, no. 203 (November 1977), p. 205.
8. Harriet Harvey Wood (ed), *Watson's Choice Collection of Comic and Serious Scots Poems*, vol. i (1977), pp. 88, 107–16.
9. Cited in John MacQueen, *Progress and Poetry* (1982), p. 69.

Chapter 3 Inveraray to Abbotsford: Survival and Revival

1. National Library of Scotland: Forbes of Pitsligo Ms Acc4796/47 (7 June 1795).
2. Howard Colvin, *A Biographical Dictionary of British Architects 1600–1840* (4th edn) (2008), p. 750.

3. Charles McKean, *The District of Moray an Illustrated Architectural Guide* (1987), p. 115.
4. Cited in Miles Glendinning, Ranald MacInnes and Aonghus MacKechnie, *A History of Scottish Architecture* (1996), pp. 163, 166.
5. *Ibid.* p. 166.
6. *Ibid.*, p. 149.
7. RCAHMS, *Inventory of Argyll: 7* (1992), p. 282.
8. J Sinton (ed.) *Journal of a Tour in the Highlands and Western Islands of Scotland in 1800 by John Leyden* (1903), pp. 77–8.
9. *Ibid.*, pp. 32, 276.
10. James Reed, *Sir Walter Scott: Landscape and Locality* (1980), p. 15.
11. Sinton, *Journal of a Tour . . by John Leyden*, pp. 231–2.
12. *The Journal of Sir Walter Scott 1825–32* (1927), p. 507.
13. *Journal of Sir Walter Scott*, p. 618.

Chapter 5 Castle Reoccupation and Conservation in the Twentieth Century

1. Information from D Walker, correspondence, 20 July 2010 and November 2010.
2. For an introduction to castle scholarship in Scotland see G P Stell, 'Interpreting Scottish Castles', in *Castle Tioram: A Statement of Cultural Significance* (2006), pp. 11–14; and C McKean, 'From Castles to Calvinists: Scottish Architectural Publishing over the Last Fifty Years', *Architectural Heritage*, vol. 17 (November 2006), pp. 89–114.
3. To date, research into this era of tower house restoration has chiefly been carried out by David Walker, Alistair Rowan and Ian Gow, who have charted changing attitudes to tower houses through several articles and reports (listed below under author).
4. For a more detailed account of the history of ancient monument legislation see: I MacIvor and R Fawcett, 'One Hundred Years on! Ancient Monuments 1882–1982: A View from Scotland', *Popular Archaeology* (November 1982); I MacIvor and R Fawcett, 'Planks from the Shipwreck of Time: An Account of Ancient Monumentry, Then and Now', in M Magnusson, *Echoes in Stone* (1983); and M Glendinning, 'The Conservation Movement: A Cult of the Modern Age', *Transactions of the Royal Historical Society*, vol. 13 (2003).
5. Ancient Monuments Protection Act, 1882.
6. A S Bell (ed.), *The Scottish Antiquarian Tradition: Essays to Mark the Bicentenary of the Society of Antiquaries of Scotland and its Museum, 1780–1980* (1981), p. 198; A MacKechnie, 'Scottish Historical Landscapes', *Studies in the History of Gardens & Designed Landscapes: An International Quarterly*, vol. 22 no. 3 (July–September 2002).
7. A W N Pugin, *Contrasts* (1836).
8. J Ruskin, *The Lamp of Memory* (1849).
9. W Morris, *SPAB Manifesto* (1877).
10. For a detailed account see R Fawcett, 'Robert Reid and the Early Involvement of the State in the Care of Scottish Ecclesiastical Buildings and Sites', *The Antiquaries Journal*, vol. 82 (2002). Fawcett was chiefly responsible for researching and setting out the pre-twentieth-century history of state monument care in Scotland.
11. See Chapter 3.
12. Ancient Monuments Protection Act, 1900.

13. G W Browne, 'Notes on Newark Castle, Renfrewshire', *Proceedings of the Society of Antiquaries of Scotland*, vol. 16 (1881–2), pp. 494–504.
14. For detailed history of RCAHMS see J G Dunbar, 'The Royal Commission on the Ancient and Historical Monuments of Scotland, The First Eighty Years', *Transactions of the Ancient Monuments Society*, vol. 36 (1992), pp. 13–77.
15. Baldwin Brown served as a RCAHMS commissioner from 1908 to 1932. See G Baldwin Brown, *The Care of Ancient Monuments* (1905), and D J Breeze, 'Gerard Baldwin Brown (1849–1932): The Recording and Preservation of Monuments', *Proceedings of the Society of Antiquaries of Scotland*, vol. 131 (2002), pp. 41–55.
16. For a detailed account see F Mudie, D Walker and I MacIvor, *Broughty Castle and the Defence of the Tay* (2010).
17. J Gifford, *Buildings of Scotland: Perth & Kinross* (2007).
18. HMSO, *Ancient Monuments and Historic Buildings, Report of the Inspector of Ancient Monuments for the Year Ending 31st March 1913.*
19. For a more detailed historical overview see D Walker, 'The Adaptation and Restoration of Tower Houses: An Historical Review from the Reign of Charles II to the Present', in R Clow (ed.), *Restoring Scotland's Castles* (2000), pp. 1–29.
20. For a broader overview of this period see Miles Glendinning, Ranald MacInnes and Aonghus MacKechnie, *A History of Scottish Architecture* (1996).
21. L Weaver, 'Midmar Castle and Barra Castle, Aberdeenshire', *Country Life* (23 November 1912), pp. 710–15.
22. See H Richardson, 'Lorimer's Castle Restorations', *AHSS Journal* (1992), pp. 64–73. Additional information from G Stell, March 2008.
23. L G Thomson, 'The Late Sir Robert Lorimer and his Work', *Quarterly Journal of the Royal Incorporation of Architects in Scotland*, no. 31 (1929), 63–76. Leslie Grahame Thomson adopted the name MacDougall from 1953.
24. Glendinning et al., *History of Scottish Architecture*, p. 342.
25. J Mackechnie, *The Clan Maclean, A Gaelic Sea Power* (1954), p. 21.
26. *Dean Castle Guide*, Kilmarnock & Louden District Council, n.d.
27. Glendinning et al., *History of Scottish Architecture*, p. 386.
28. G Scott Moncrieff (ed.), *The Stones of Scotland* (1983), p. 4.
29. D Walker, 'The Adaptation and Restoration of Tower Houses: A Historical Review', typescript, October 1994.
30. For a more detailed account of this movement see D Watters and M Glendinning, *Little Houses: The National Trust for Scotland's Improvement Scheme for Small Historic Homes* (2006).
31. The Marquess of Bute, *A Plea for Scotland's Architectural Heritage: Speech Delivered in Edinburgh* (1936).
32. See *NMRS 1941–1991, National Monuments Record of Scotland Jubilee: A Guide to Collections* (1991).
33. J Stirling Maxwell, *Shrines & Homes of Scotland* (1937), p. 4. Stirling Maxwell was recorded in 1938 as the former AMB chair: see *Scottish Biographies* (1938).
34. I MacIvor, *Blackness Castle* (1982); J Gifford and F A Walker, *Buildings of Scotland: Stirling and Central Scotland* (2002); *RCAHMS Tenth Report with Inventory of Monuments and Constructions in the Counties of Midlothian and West Lothian* (1929), pp. 192–5.

35. D Watters, 'The Scottish National War Memorial', *The Architectural Heritage Society of Scotland Magazine*, issue 12 (2001), pp. 34–5; P Savage, 'An Examination of the Work of Sir Robert Lorimer', unpublished PhD thesis (1973).

36. G P Stell, 'Interpreting Scottish Castles', in *Castle Tioram: A Statement of Cultural Significance* (2006), pp. 11–14; additional information from G P Stell, March 2008, and D Walker, November 2010.

37. V Gordon Childe and W Douglas Simpson, *Illustrated Guide to Ancient Monuments in the Ownership of The Ministry of Works, Volume VI: Scotland* (1952).

38. J G Dunbar, 'The Royal Commission on the Ancient and Historical Monuments of Scotland'. David Walker notes that, in the 1920s and 1930s, the guardianship programme had a lot to do with the friendship of Sir Herbert Maxwell at RCAHMS, Sir John Stirling Maxwell at the Ancient Monuments Board, and Sir Lionel Earle at the Office of Works (correspondence with D Walker, November 2010).

39. *Ancient Monuments Board for England, Scotland and Wales, First Annual Reports* (1954).

40. *Report of the Committee on Houses of Outstanding Historic or Architectural Interest* (1950).

41. The 1950 report suggested that the HBC 'might take over the duties of the Royal Commission on the Ancient and Historical Monuments of Scotland or be closely associated with that Commission; and advisory panels might be set up as necessary from the present membership of these bodies and the Ancient Monuments Board for Scotland'. *Report of the Committee on Houses of Outstanding Historic or Architectural Interest* (1950), p. 80.

42. Walker recalls a collective approach at HBC, with representation not always being 'clean cut'. He attended alternately 'every third meeting of the HBC from 1966' with Michael Gibb and Gavin Goodfellow. Stewart Cruden was assessor from 1953, and he and Iain MacIvor wrote the reports. When conservation grant was introduced in 1972, Gibb, Walker and Goodfellow were brought in to augment the team, and although not yet Chief Investigator, Walker usually attended until he became assessor in 1978. Stewart Cruden remained an assessor until his retirement in 1980. HBC secretary Harry Graham had an important role in determining policy from 1972, as had Robert Matthew as the Secretary of State advisor, the Earl of Crawford as chairman, and Ronald Cant and Sir James Dunbar Nasmith as the key members of council. As assessor, Walker did not 'set the standards for the work, only the design'. The technical standards were set by William Boal as principal architect, George Hay, Douglas Hogg, Ingval Maxwell and Neil Hynd. Where a castle was scheduled, Iain MacIvor and Richard Fawcett advised on design elements. (Correspondence with D Walker, November 2010.)

43. The bulk of the data relating to HBC tower house grant-aiding activities comes from: HBC *Annual Reports*, 1953–2001; 'Scottish Development Department, Historic Buildings Branch, Notes for BBC Current Account Programme', typescript, 17 February 1978; D Walker, 'The Adaptation and Restoration of Tower Houses: A Historical Review', typescript, 29 August 1994; Historic Buildings Branch, 'The Restoration of Ruined or Disused Castles and Country Houses of Fifteenth, Sixteenth and Seventeenth

Centuries: Information Paper Revised to July 1985', typescript; correspondence with D Walker, 28 January 2008 and 1 March 2011.

44. Correspondence with D Walker, 20 July 2010.

45. *Ibid.* According to Walker, consolidation at a cost of £10,000 was ruled out as unaffordable a few years earlier 'The loss of it concentrated Stewart Cruden and Iain MacIvor's minds as much as the conservation lobby.'

46. See I Gow, *Scotland's Lost Houses* (2006); and I Gow, 'Lost Houses Introduction', draft typescript, n.d.

47. A Rowan and D Walker, 'New Castles for Old: The Restoration of Tower Houses in Scotland I', *Country Life* (14 February 1974), pp. 298–301, and 'Restoring Tower Houses II, Abergeldie, Balfluig, and Udny', *Country Life* (21 February 1974), pp. 362–5.

48. The monies for HBC grants came from the minister of Public Buildings and Works up until July 1966, and thereafter the Secretary of State for Scotland: the HBC only made recommendations for grant giving. (Correspondence with D Walker, 1 March 2011.)

49. Walker later recalled that the key problem in the 1970s was 'that we could not persuade estates to spend large sums of money on structures of no beneficial uses. This was in part how re-roofing came to be accepted.' (Correspondence with D Walker, November 2010.)

50. Correspondence with D Walker, November 2010. Walker later recalled: 'We always insisted on grant-aided schemes being evidence-based.'

51. *Ibid.*

52. *Ibid.*

53. *Ibid.*; M Lindsay, *The Castles of Scotland* (1986).

54. R Clow (ed), *Restoring Scotland's Castles* (2000).

55. D Pringle, 'The Restoration of Tower Houses', typescript, 1998.

56. J Inglis, 'Scotland's Castles, Times of Change, 1945–2009', *The Architectural Heritage Society of Scotland Magazine* (Autumn 2009).

57. 'Restoration Earns Fine for Businessman', *Scotsman*, 12 January 1996. Dairsie Castle was de-scheduled in 1997.

58. R Fawcett, *The Conservation of Architectural Ancient Monuments in Scotland, Guidance on Principles* (2001).

59. I MacIvor, 'The Decision to Restore the Hall', in R Fawcett (ed.), *Stirling Castle: The Restoration of the Great Hall* (2001).

60. G Scott-Moncrieff, 'Introduction', in S Forman, *Scottish Country Houses and Castles* (1967).

61. See *The Architecture of the Scottish Renaissance*, RIAS Edinburgh International Festival Exhibition Catalogue (1990); A Mackechnie, 'Scots Court Architecture of the Early Seventeenth Century', unpublished PhD thesis, University of Edinburgh (1993); I Campbell, 'Linlithgow's "Princely Palace" and its Influence in Europe', *Architectural Heritage*, vol. 5 (January 1994), pp. 1–21; D Howard, *The Architectural History of Scotland: Scottish Architecture from the Reformation to the Restoration, 1560–1660* (1995).

62. C Mckean, 'From Castles to Calvinists', p. 89.

63. Data from G P Stell, *Castle Tioram: A Statement of Cultural Significance* (2006).

Chapter 6 Radical Restorations of the Late Twentieth Century

1. Alastair Campbell, *A History of Clan Campbell, Vol. 2: From Flodden to the Restoration* (2002), pp. 203–4.
2. Strictly, refusal of consent would lie with the Secretary of State – now, Scottish Ministers – but acting on the inspector's advice.

Chapter 8 The Refashioning of Glamis, 1668–1684

1. J Macky, *Journey through Scotland* (1723), pp. 140–2.
2. Based on Earl Patrick's own notes, it is generally thought that work began at Glamis in 1670. There are, however, building accounts for substantial works dating back to 1668. NRAS 885/148/1/37.
3. D MacGibbon and T Ross, *The Castellated and Domestic Architecture of Scotland, Volume 11* (1887), p. 113ff.
4. Echoes of the stair exist in the slight curved shapes in the wall between the two wings. For further information about such 'great towers' see C McKean, 'The Scottish Mediaeval Country Seat', in P. Barnwell (ed.), *The Mediaeval Great House in Britain* (Donington, 2011).
5. H G Slade, *Glamis Castle* (2000), p. 28.
6. M Glendinning, A MacKechnie and R MacInnes, *A History of Scottish Architecture* (1996), p. 71.
7. *Ibid.*, p. 73.
8. H Colvin, 'The Beginnings of the Architectural Profession in Scotland', *Architectural History* vol. 29 (1986), pp. 168–82.
9. Slade, *Glamis*, p. 41.
10. A H Miller (ed.), *The Book of Record* (1890), p. 29.
11. K Newland, 'The Acquisition and Use of Norwegian Timber in Seventeenth Century Scotland, with Reference to the Principal Building Works of James Baine, His Majesty's Master Wright', unpublished PhD thesis, Dundee University (2010), provides a detailed examination of the construction or reformatting of Glamis and Brechin Castles and Panmure House.
12. C Wemyss, 'The Scottish Treasury Commission and its impact upon the development of Scottish Country House Architecture 1667–1682', unpublished PhD thesis, Dundee University (2010), examines the aristocratic context, the significance of government posts, and the architectural and cultural agendas of both the Scots nobility and that of the 'new men'.
13. *Book of Record*, p. 19.
14. Alloa Tower, Town Façade: RHP13258.
15. *Book of Record*, p. 33.
16. Matthew Davis, 'Scottish North-East Renaissance Bel-houses – Was There a School of Architecture Operating in the North-East of Scotland during the Turn of the Seventeenth Century?' unpublished PhD thesis, University of Dundee (2010).
17. J Cornforth, 'Was there a Scottish Baroque ?', *Country Life* (June 1989).
18. Margaret Stewart, 'The Earl of Mar and Scottish Baroque', *Architectural Heritage*, vol. 9 (November 1998), pp. 16–30.
19. A MacKechnie, 'Scottish Historical Landscapes', *Studies in the History of Gardens and Designed Landscapes*, vol. 22 no. 3 (July–September 2002), pp. 214–39.
20. Margaret Stewart, 'The Metaphysics of Place in the Scottish Historical Landscape: Patriotic and Virgilian themes, c.1700

to the Early Nineteenth Ventury', in *Studies in the History of Gardens*, vol. 22 no. 3 (July–September 2002), p. 247.
21. For more on this and these terms, see C McKean, *The Scottish Chateau* (2004), chapter 4.
22. The best available analysis of the building work at Glamis, Brechin and Panmure is in Newland, 'Acquisition and Use of Norwegian Timber'.
23. *Book of Record*, p. 19.
24. See M. Young, 'Rural Society in Scotland from the Restoration to the Union c.1660–1707', unpublished PhD thesis, University of Dundee (2004).
25. *Book of Record*, p. 18.
26. See Davis, 'Scottish North-East Renaissance Bel-houses'.
27. *Book of Record*, p. 39. Also M. Brown, 'The Gardens of Glamis – An Aerial View', *Proceedings of the Society of Antiquaries of Scotland*, vol. 135 (2005), pp. 19–39, picture 10.
28. *Book of Record*, p. 24.
29. *Book of Record*, p. 40.
30. C Dingwall, *Glamis Castle – A History of the Designed Landscape* (2000), p. 11.
31. Newland, 'Acquisition and Use of Norwegian Timber', p. 211, information deriving from Paul Brockbank.
32. Strathmore was entirely ambiguous about this; and the term 'mounthoolie' is used quite frequently in Scotland. He appears also to have used this term for the family burial vault in the kirk, so this interpretation differs from those of both Slade and Newland. However, what is incontestable is that the block containing the charter room and library held a highly symbolic importance for Strathmore.
33. I am much indebted to Andrew Nicoll for this notion.
34. *Book of Record*, p. 40.
35. *Book of Record*, p. 43.
36. *Book of Record*, p. 38.
37. *Book of Record*, p. 41.
38. NRAS 885/148/1/82.
39. Slade considers that Earl Patrick added the top two storeys, but neither the building accounts nor the *Book of Record* sustain this. If he went to the trouble to detail the 7-foot additional height he made to the east wing, he surely would have mentioned a two-storey addition to the ancestral tower.
40. *Book of Record*, p. 42.
41. M Apted, 'Arnold Quellin's Statues at Glamis Castle', *Antiquaries Journal*, vol. 64 (1984), pp. 53–61.
42. See Newland, 'Norwegian Timber Trade'.

Chapter 9 Caisteal Inbhir-Aora / Inveraray Castle

1. *Oxford Dictionary of National Biography* (2004), vol. 9, p. 733.
2. Batty Langley, *Ancient Architecture / Restored, and Improved, by A Great Variety of Grand and Usefull Designs, Entirely New in the Gothick Mode for the Ornamenting of Buildings and Gardens* (1742), pp. 277–8.
3. *Ibid.*, p. 321.
4. Batty Langley, *Ancient Masonry, Both in the Theory and Practice, Demonstrating the Useful Rules of Arithmetic, Geometry, and Architecture, in the Proportions and Orders of the Most Eminent Masters of All Nations* (1736).
5. Lochleven Castle had been restored or consolidated in the previous century, but this was because it found new value as

a Picturesque Romantic ruin for viewing, and not for simply its intrinsic architectural value as an 'antique'.

6. 'A lot of noise about very little and a lot of men killed uselessly' was Frederick the Great's verdict on the battle (Michael Orr, *Dettingen 1743* (1972), p. 71).

7. Also said to belong to this campaign is the soldier's song 'Will ye go to Flanders, my Mally-O?'; which derived in turn from a Gaelic pressgang song, 'Mo Mhàili bheag òg' ('My Little Young Maili/Mally') (information from Allan MacDonald, Glenuig).

8. It is unclear whether Stair himself made a 'Dettingen' plantation at Newliston House, though a partly surviving union flag layout there may date from his time. A union flag arrangement had been the model of the prize-winning but unimplementable design for Edinburgh's New Town in 1766. The modern 'Dettingen Roundabout' road intersection at Cumnock reflects the old name living on at the Dumfries House estate.

9. 'CAL. OCT. ANNO DOM. MDCCXLVI POSUIT A. A. DUX / GULIELMUS CUMBRIAE DUX NOBIS HAEC OTIA FECIT.'

Chapter 11 From Blair Castle to Atholl House to Blair Castle

1. John, 7th Duke of Atholl (ed.), *Chronicles of the Atholl and Tullibardine Families*, vol. 3 (Edinburgh, 1908), p. 420.

2. Bruce P. Lenman, 'From the Union of 1707 to the Franchise Reform of 1832', in R A Houston, and W W J Knox (ed.) *The New Penguin History of Scotland* (2001), p. 305.

3. *Chronicles*, vol. 3, p. 368n.

4. His elder brother, William, marquess of Tullibardine and, in the Jacobite peerage, duke of Rannoch, had been attainted in 1716 for his part in the Jacobite Rising of the year before.

5. *Chronicles*, vol. 1, pp. 190–8, 206, 282, 286–98, 307; *Ibid.*, vol. 3, pp. 193, 195–7.

6. [Daniel Defoe], *A Tour Thro' the Whole Island of GREAT BRITAIN*, vol. 3, pt. 2 (1727), p. 219.

7. The account of the building history of Blair Castle before the eighteenth century is based on that in *Chronicles*, vol. 5, Appendix, pp. xli–xlvii.

8. Howard Colvin, *A Biographical Dictionary of British Architects*, 4th edn (2008), pp. 329–30. Douglas' plans and elevation of the east front are in the Atholl Muniments, Blair Castle, Perthshire, D2.14(1–4).

9. Quoted in Ian G Lindsay, and Mary Cosh, *Inveraray and the Dukes of Argyll* (1973), p. 354.

10. Atholl Muniments, Blair Castle, D2.13(36), 'Estimates of Blair Castle 1736'.

11. Colvin, *Biographical Dictionary*, p. 1070. Winter's plans and elevations of the east front are in the Atholl Muniments, Blair Castle, D2.14(9–12).

12. *Chronicles*, vol. 2, p. 474; Atholl Muniments, Blair Castle, D2.13(39), 'The Divisions and Dimensions of the Offices and Rooms built in 1743 & 1744'.

13. *Chronicles*, vol. 3, pp. 378–9; Atholl Muniments, Blair Castle, 40.IV.39, memorandum, 17 July 1748.

14. *Chronicles*, vol. 3, pp. 236–44.

15. *Ibid.*, vol. 3, pp. 336–7.

16. *Ibid.*, vol. 3, pp. 368 and n., 378–81.

17. *Ibid.*, vol. 3, pp. 379–81; Atholl Muniments, Blair Castle, 40.IV.69, memorandum, 25 September 1751; Atholl Muniments, Blair Castle, D2.13(38), 30 January 1753; plans and elevations in Atholl Muniments, Blair Castle, D2.13(47), D2.13(61), D2.13(63), D2.14(7).

18. Atholl Muniments, Blair Castle, 40.III.22, letter from Thomas Clayton, 31 March 1750; Atholl Muniments, Blair Castle, 40.II.D(4).35, account of Thomas Clayton, 21 September, 1751.

19. Atholl Muniments, Blair Castle, 40.II.D(4).39, account of Thomas Clayton, 20 June, 1753; Atholl Muniments, Blair Castle, 40.IV.96, Thomas Clayton to James, 2nd Duke of Atholl, 11 August 1755; Arthur Oswald, 'Blair Castle', *Country Life* (11 November 1949), p. 1438.

20. Atholl Muniments, Blair Castle, 40.IV.64, 'Memorandum . . 29 Novr. 1750'; Colvin, *Biographical Dictionary*, p. 799.

21. Oswald, 'Blair Castle', 1437.

22. Atholl Muniments, Blair Castle, 40.IV.96, Thomas Clayton to James, 2nd Duke of Atholl, 11 August 1755, 40.III.33, Thomas Clayton to Major [Humphrey] Harrison, 29 January 1756, 40.IV.11, memorandum, 5 March 1756; Geoffrey Beard, *Decorative Plasterwork in Great Britain* (1975), p. 87.

23. Beard, *Decorative Plasterwork*, p. 87.

24. Oswald, 'Blair Castle', p. 1437.

25. Atholl Muniments, Blair Castle, 40.II.D(4)39, account of Thomas Clayton, 20 June 1753–10 July 1756; Beard, *Decorative Plasterwork*, 88.

26. Oswald, 'Blair Castle', p. 1436.

27. Atholl Muniments, Blair Castle, 40.IV.90, 6 February 1755.

28. Elevations in Atholl Muniments, Blair Castle, D2.11(1) and D2.11(2).

29. *Chronicles*, vol. 4, pp. 483–7; Valerie Fiddes and Alistair Rowan, *David Bryce* (1976), pp. 115–16.

Chapter 12 Balmoral

1. David Duff, *Victoria in the Highlands* (1968), p. 78.

2. R W Clark, *Balmoral* (1981), p. 21.

3. Illustrated in Duff, *Victoria*, facing page 80.

4. Francis Groome, *Ordnance Gazeteer of Scotland*, 5 vols, n.d, vol. 1, p. 69.

5. Ivor Brown, *Balmoral* (1955), p. 36.

6. Duff, *Victoria*, p. 74.

7. *Ibid.*

8. Earl of Wemyss, *Gosford House* (2010), p. 43.

9. Delia Miller, *Queen Victoria's Life in the Scottish Highlands* (2003).

10. Miller, *Queen Victoria's Life*, p. 61.

11. These proposals survive in the Royal Archives, Windsor.

12. Miller, *Queen Victoria's Life*, p. 57.

13. RCAHMS collections ref UND/116/1.

14. Original ground floor plan published in Clark, *Balmoral*, and in Robert Kerr, *The Gentleman's House: Or How to Plan English Residences, from the Parsonage to the Palace, with Tables of Accommodation and Cost, and a Series of Selected Plans* (1864), Plate 18.

15. Kerr, *The Gentleman's House*, p. 65.

16. Royal Collection Windsor.

Chapter 13 Edinburgh Castle and the Remaking of Medieval Edinburgh

1. 'Argyle' is nowadays generally standardised as 'Argyll'.
2. *Report of Her Majesty's Commission of Inquiry into the Condition of the Crofters and Cottars in the Highlands and Islands of Scotland*, Parliamentary Papers, 1884, c.3980.
3. Recent research has shown that the roof is oak. A Crone and D Gallagher, 'The late Medieval Roof over the Great Hall in Edinburgh Castle', *Medieval Archaeology*, vol. 52 (2008) pp. 231–60. Gore-Booth and Napier may have been misled by knowledge that chestnut was present in the recently restored Tower of London.
4. *Scotsman*, 11 December 1883, p. 5.
5. G Morton, *Unionist Nationalism. Governing Urban Scotland, 1830–1860* (1999).
6. The main branch of the family was later to become noted for contributing Constance Markievicz to the Dublin Easter Rising of 1916 and the Irish Dail of 1919. James Gore-Booth had served with the Royal Artillery in India in the1860s, and this may have given him some affinity with Napier. *The Times*, 18 January 1861.
7. R J Morris, 'The Capitalist, the Professor and the Soldier: The Re-making of Edinburgh Castle, 1850–1900', *Planning Perspectives*, vol. 22, issue 1 (January 2007) pp. 55–78.
8. He refers here to the recent 'restoration' of St Giles Cathedral which had been financed by the publisher–printer and one-time Lord Provost William Chambers.
9. 'Edinburgh Architectural Association: Visit to Edinburgh Castle', *Scotsman*, 18 February 1884, p. 6.
10. *Report of Her Majesty's Commission of Inquiry . . Highlands and Islands of Scotland*. He took evidence in Edinburgh, 22–24 October, and only a brief trip to Tarbert on 26 December remained to be made.
11. E A Cameron, 'Communication or Separation? Reactions to Irish Land Agitation and Legislation in the Highlands of Scotland, c.1870–1910', *English Historical Review*, vol. 70, no. 487 (June 2005) pp. 633–66.
12. T W Mason, 'Nineteenth Century Cromwell', *Past and Present*, no. 40 (July 1968), pp. 187–91.
13. *Scotsman*, 28 December 1883, p. 4.
14. *Scotsman*, 31 January and 14 March 1884. Shaw Lefevre was First Commissioner of Works in Gladstone's government. He had promoted the first Act for the Preservation of Ancient Monuments in 1883 (*Oxford Dictionary of National Biography*, 2004–2010). Dick Peddie was MP for the Kilmarnock Burghs, 1880–5, and member of a leading firm of Edinburgh architects. He was closely linked with the Society for the Preservation of Ancient Buildings (*Dictionary of Scottish Architects*: see www.scottisharchitects.org.uk).
15. *Scotsman*, 28 December 1883, p. 4.
16. *Scotsman*, 9 April 1884, p. 9.
17. *Scotsman*, 10 April 1884, p. 7.
18. Morris, 'The Capitalist'; J Gifford, C McWilliam and D Walker, *The Buildings of Scotland. Edinburgh* (1984); E Hulse (ed.), *Thinking with Both Hands: Sir Daniel Wilson in the Old World and the New.* (1999). Most of Wilson's papers were destroyed in a fire at the University of Toronto. The surviving Daniel Wilson scrapbooks in the Toronto Public Library (S65) show his continued interest in Edinburgh affairs.
19. *Scotsman*, 28 December 1883, p. 4.
20. See John Grant's Letter to the Editor, *Scotsman*, 17 December 1883, p. 6.
21. G Morton, 'Civil Society, Municipal Government and the State: Enshrinement, Empowerment and Legitimacy. Scotland 1800–1929', *Urban History*, vol. 25 no.3 (December 1998), pp. 348–67.
22. The records are in Edinburgh University Library. See Morris, 'The Capitalist'.
23. War Office to William Nelson, 19 August 1885, MS 1734 f.9. This collection is in the National Library of Scotland.
24. W W Robertson to Hippolyte Blanc, 14 September 1885, NLS MS 1734 f.17.
25. Report of the Committee for the Restoration of St Margaret's, April 1886, NLS MS 1735, f.85.
26. Copies of Drawings of Buildings of Edinburgh Castle lent by Major Gore-Booth, NLS Map Library, MS 1739/1–6 and Proposed Restoration, NLS MS 1739/7.
27. R S Gowland to William Nelson, 2 September 1885, NLS MS 1734 f.64.
28. Andrew Clark, War Office to William Nelson, 19 February 1886, NLS MS 1735 f.1.
29. Daniel Wilson to Hippolyte Blanc, 21 May 1886, NLS MS 1735, f.114.
30. NLS MS 1735, f.152.
31. Ingress Bell to Hippolyte Blanc, 1 October and 7 October 1885, NLS MS1735, f.29.
32. Ingress Bell to Hippolyte Blanc, 20 October 1885, NLS MS 1734 f.65.
33. Hippolyte Blanc British Museum Reading Room Ticket and order slips, NLS MS 1734 f.49.
34. David Wilson to William Nelson, NLS MS 1734 f.107.
35. William Nelson to Hippolyte Blanc, 14 September 1885, NLS MS 1734 f.15.
36. William Nelson to Hippolyte Blanc, October 1886, NLS MS 1734 f.38. The Georg Braun and Franz Hogenberg map c.1582 showed a rather stylised pitched roof. A sketch derived from it may have been what Malcolm was looking at.
37. Hippolyte Blanc to Daniel Wilson, 4 November 1885, NLS MS 1734 f.74.
38. Paper on the Argyle Tower, NLS MS 1735 f.152.
39. The room as it was rebuilt by Nelson and Blanc now contains a picture of 'Argyle's Last Night' by W R Ward (1816–1879), a historical narrative painter who also contributed to the Palace of Westminster. This was apparently bought in the 1980s, although it would have been appropriate to Nelson's purposes. My thanks to Peter Yeoman of Historic Scotland for this information.
40. Report of the Committee for the Restoration of St Margaret's, NLS MS 1735 f.85.
41. Napier to Hippolyte Blanc, MS 1735 f.57.
42. Hippolyte Blanc to Daniel Wilson, 4 November 1884, NLS MS 1734 f.74.
43. Daniel Wilson to Hippolyte Blanc, 5 December 1884, NLS MS 1734 f.99.
44. Morris, 'The Capitalist'.
45. Daniel Wilson to Hippolyte Blanc, NLS MS 1734 f.129.
46. A Keay with R B Harris, 'The White Tower, 1642–1855 and 1855–2000', in Edward Impey (ed.), *The White Tower* (2008), pp. 179–344; P Hammond, 'Epitome of England's History.

The Transformation of the Tower of London as a Visitor Attraction in the Nineteenth Century', *Royal Armouries Yearbook*, vol. 4 (1999) pp. 144–74.

Chapter 14 Duart and Eilean Donan Castles

1. The Royal Commission on the Ancient and Historical Monuments of Scotland (RCAHMS), *Argyll: An Inventory of the Monuments*, vol. 3: Mull, Tiree, Coll and Northern Argyll (excluding the early medieval and later monuments of Iona) (1980), no. 339.
2. See the 'Brief History' page, Duart Castle official website: http://www.duartcastle.com/castle/castle_briefhistory.html.
3. RCAHMS, *Argyll*.
4. R Miket and D L Roberts, *The Medieval Castles of Skye and Lochalsh* (1990), pp. 74–92.
5. Ibid.
6. National Library of Scotland, Board of Ordnance drawings, MSS 1648 no. Z.3/28, Lewis Petit, 1748.
7. National Library of Scotland, Board of Ordnance drawings, MSS 1648 no. Z.3/26, Lewis Petit 1741 & 1748.
8. 'At Duart Castle', *Time*, 8 January 1934.
9. RCAHMS, archive no. AG/4727: Duart Castle, south-east wall of tower-house, before 1911.
10. J MacRae-Gilstrap, 'Eilean Donnain Castle', *Sgurr Uaran* [Clan MacRae Society of North America Newsletter] (1932).
11. Conchra Charitable Trust, *Eilean Donan Castle: Official Guide* (1999), p. 4.
12. Miket and Roberts, *Medieval Castles*, pp. 74–92.
13. R R Anderson, *Examples of Scottish Architecture from the Twelfth to the Seventeenth Century: A Series of Reproductions from the National Art Survey Drawings* four vols (1921–33), vol. 2, Plates 31–7; RCAHMS, National Art Survey of Scotland Collection, archive no. EDD 145/6: Liberton Tower, South and East Elevations and Section, c.1900.
14. M E M Donaldson, *Wanderings in the Western Highlands and Islands* (1923), pp. 193–5.
15. Ibid., p. 195.

Chapter 15 Craigievar Castle: Changing Perceptions

1. D Howard, *The Architectural History of Scotland: Scottish Architecture from the Reformation to the Restoration, 1560–1660* (1995), p. 214.
2. S Fraser, 'Galleries, Gardens and Gates: Transforming the House of Muchall into a Setting for Lordship', in notes accompanying 'A Lad O'Pairts: A Day Conference in Memory of Ian Shepherd', Aberdeen University, 11 December 2010, p. 48.
3. C McKean, 'The Scottishness of Scottish Architecture: Building for People and Places', in J M Fladmark (ed.), *Heritage: Conservation, Interpretation and Enterprise* (1993), p. 81.
4. W D Simpson, *Craigievar Castle: The Rock of Mar: An Illustrated Account* [National Trust for Scotland guidebook] (1978), pp. 10–11.

5. M Ellington, *Craigievar Castle* [National Trust for Scotland guidebook] (1987), p. 3.
6. Geoffrey Hay and Geoffrey Stell, *Craigievar Castle: A Preliminary Report* (RCAHMS, 1973); T Addyman, K Macfadyen, S Phillips and A Gow, 'Craigievar Castle', in *Discovery and Excavation in Scotland* (New Series), vol. 10 (2009), pp. 25–6.
7. Ellington, *Craigievar Castle*, p. 3.
8. Addyman et al., 'Craigievar Castle', p. 25.
9. Addyman et al., 'Craigievar Castle', pp. 25–6.
10. I Gow, *Craigievar Castle* [National Trust for Scotland guidebook] (2004), p. 22.
11. Ellington, *Craigievar Castle*, p. 22.
12. Addyman et al., 'Craigievar Castle', p. 28.
13. Ellington, *Craigievar Castle*, p. 12.
14. Simpson, *Craigievar Castle*, p. 18.
15. Gow, *Craigievar Castle*, p. 4.
16. McKean, 'The Scottishness of Scottish Architecture', p. 81.
17. R W Billings, *The Baronial and Ecclesiastical Antiquities of Scotland*, 4 vols (1848–52), vol. 1, p. i.
18. Ellington, *Craigievar Castle*, p. 7.
19. Ellington, *Craigievar Castle*, p. 5; quotation cited in Billings, *Baronial and Ecclesiastical Antiquities*, vol. 1, p. 1.
20. Addyman et al., 'Craigievar Castle', p. 25.
21. National Archives of Scotland (NAS), RHP13779.
22. M K Greg, 'Excavations at Craigievar Castle, Aberdeenshire', *Proceedings of the Society of Antiquaries of Scotland*, vol. 123 (1993), pp. 381–93.
23. NAS RHP13780; Gow, *Craigievar Castle*, p. 24; personal communication, Shannon Fraser.
24. William A Brogden, 'John Smith and Craigievar Castle', in I Gow and A Rowan (eds), *Scottish Country Houses 1600–1914* (1995), p. 235.
25. John Smith to Sir John Forbes, Baronet of Craigievar, 16 November 1824: NAS 90250/41/32.
26. Brogden, 'John Smith and Craigievar Castle', p. 235; Ian Gow, *Scottish Houses and Gardens from the Archives of Country Life* (1997), p. 36. For the changes to the stair tower compare J Giles, *Drawings of Aberdeenshire Castles* [Aberdeen, The Third Spalding Club] (1936), Plate LXIV, with the illustration by R Billings, this volume, Figure 198.
27. Brogden, 'John Smith and Craigievar Castle', p. 235.
28. Visitor's Book, 1903: personal communication, Ian Gow.
29. A J Durie, *Scotland for the Holidays* (2003), p. 45.
30. A and C Black [publishers], *Picturesque Tourist of Scotland* (1851), p. 39.
31. M Maclellan, 'Facing the Future', *NTS Magazine* (Spring 2009), p. 37.
32. Addyman et al., 'Craigievar Castle', p. 26.
33. National Trust for Scotland and Historic Houses Association for Scotland, *Scottish Renaissance Interiors* (1987), p. 64.
34. Addyman Archaeology, 'Craigievar Castle, Aberdeenshire: Historic Building Survey and Analysis 2007–9', Report for the National Trust for Scotland (forthcoming).

Reading List

The widest collection of individual castle studies are those published in the *Proceedings of the Society of Antiquaries of Scotland*, notably essays by W Douglas Simpson and Harry Gordon Slade. Historic Scotland's guidebook series, and that of the National Trust for Scotland, also comprise individual detailed studies. Local guidebooks, such as those for Drumlanrig or Lennoxlove, are also useful sources of studies, while some castles – such as Glamis and Culzean – have dedicated history books. The wider historical and cultural context that brought about these buildings is provided both by national histories, such as Michael Lynch's *Scotland: A New History* (1992) and by volumes of collected essays, such as Jenny Wormald's *Scotland: A History* (2005), plus the wider series of essays contained in the *Scottish Historical Review* and Scottish Text Society publications (1882–), the *Innes Review* (1950–), and references within each of these. The best modern architectural area studies are those in the Buildings of Scotland series, spearheaded by John Gifford, and the Royal Incorporation of Architects in Scotland ('RIAS') guides, whose series was inaugurated by Charles McKean. *Architectural Heritage*, the journal of the Architectural Heritage Society of Scotland, contains a series of relevant papers (their volume 18 is included below).

Airs, Malcolm (ed.). *The Victorian Great House* (2000).

Airs, Malcolm (ed.), *The Edwardian Great House* (2001).

Anderson, R R. *Examples of Scottish Architecture from the 12th to the 17th Century: A Series of Reproductions from the National Art Survey Drawings*, 4 vols (Edinburgh, 1921–33).

Architectural Heritage, volume 18: 'Scotia-Europa Interactions in the Late Renaissance' (2007).

The Architecture of the Scottish Renaissance (RIAS Edinburgh International Festival Exhibition Catalogue, 1990).

Bailey, Rebecca M. *Scottish Architects' Papers: A Source Book* (1996).

Bath, Michael. *Renaissance Decorative Painting in Scotland* (2003).

Bell, A S (ed.). *The Scottish Antiquarian Tradition: Essays to Mark the Bicentenary of the Society of Antiquaries of Scotland and its Museum, 1780–1980* (1981).

Billings, Robert William. *The Baronial and Ecclesiastical Antiquities of Scotland*, 4 vols (1848–52).

Blanning, Tim. *The Romantic Revolution* (2010).

Brown, Jennifer M (ed.). *Scottish Society in the Fifteenth Century* (1977).

Bolton, A T. *The Architecture of Robert and James Adam*, 2 vols (1922).

The Buildings of Scotland series:

Borders by Catherine Cruft et al. (2006).

Central Scotland and Stirling by John Gifford and Frank Walker (2002).

Dumfries and Galloway by John Gifford (1996).

Edinburgh by John Gifford et al. (1984).

Fife by John Gifford (1988).

Glasgow by Elizabeth Williamson, Anne Riches and Malcolm Higgs (1990).

Highland and Islands by John Gifford (1992).

Lothian (except Edinburgh) by Colin MacWilliam (1978).

Perth and Kinross by John Gifford (2007).

Brown, G Baldwin. *The Care of Ancient Monuments* (1905).

Brown, Ian G. 'Critick in Antiquity: Sir John Clerk of Penicuik', *Antiquity*, 51 (Nov. 1977).

Brown, Ian G. *The Hobby-horsical Antiquary* (1980).

Brown, Ian G. (ed.) *Abbotsford and Sir Walter Scott: The Image and the Influence* (2003).

Brown, Keith M. *Bloodfeud in Scotland 1573–1625: Violence, Justice and Politics in an Early Modern Society* (1986).

Brown, P Hume. *Early Travellers in Scotland* (1891).

Burton, J Hill and Masson, D, et al. (eds). *The Register of the Privy Council of Scotland*, 37 vols (1877–).

Caldwell, David H (ed.). *Scottish Weapons and Fortifications* (1981).

Campbell, Ian. 'A Romanesque Revival and the Early Renaissance in Scotland c.1380–1513', *Architectural History* [journal of the Society of Architectural Historians of Great Britain], 54:3 (1995).

Campbell, Ian. 'Linlithgow's "Princely Palace" and its Influence in Europe', *Architectural Heritage*, 5 (1995), pp. 1–21.

Cavers, Keith. *A Vision of Scotland: The Nation Observed by John Slezer* (1993).

Correspondence of Sir Robert Kerr, First Earl of Ancrum and his son William, Third Earl of Lothian (ed. David Laing), 2 vols (1616–49 and 1649–67) (1875).

Colvin, Howard. *A Biographical Dictionary of British Architects, 1600–1840* (4th edn, 2008).

Clark, James Toshach (ed.). *Genealogical Collections Concerning Families in Scotland, Made by Walter Macfarlane, 1750–1751*, 2 vols (1900).

Clow, Robert (ed.). *Restoring Scotland's Castles* (2000).

Coventry, Martin. *The Castles of Scotland* (2006).

Craig, Cairns (general editor). *A History of Scottish Literature*, 4 vols (1987).

Cruden, Stewart. *The Scottish Castle* (1960 and later editions).

Cocksey, J C B. *Alexander Nasmyth HRSA: A Man of the Scottish Renaissance* (1991).

Daiches, David. *Sir Walter Scott and His World* (1971).

Davis, Matthew. 'The Bel family and their Renaissance Tall-houses', *Architectural Heritage*, 16 (2005) pp.1–13.

Davis, Michael C. *The Castles and Mansions of Ayrshire* (1991).

Davis, Michael C. *Scots Baronial Mansions and Castle Restorations in the West of Scotland* (1996).

Devine, T M. *The Scottish Nation 1700–2007* (2006).

Davis, Michael C. *Clearance and Improvement: Land, Power and People in Scotland 1700–1900* (2006).

Dictionary of Scottish Architects 1840–1980, available online at: www.scottisharchitects.org.uk

Dingwall, Christopher. *Glamis Castle: A History of the Designed Landscape* (2000).

Dixon, Philip. 'Towerhouses, Pelehouses and Border Society', *Archaeological Journal*, 136 (1979), pp.240–52.

Dunbar, John G. *The Architecture of Scotland* (1966 and rev. edn, 1978).

Dunbar, John G. *William Bruce* [exhibition catalogue] (1970).

Dunbar, John G. 'The Building Activities of the Duke and Duchess of Lauderdale, 1670–82', *Archaeological Journal*, 132 (1975), pp.202–30.

Dunbar, John G. *Scottish Royal Palaces: The Architecture of the Royal Residences during the Late Medieval and Early Renaissance Periods* (1999).

Fawcett, R. *The Conservation of Architectural Ancient Monuments in Scotland, Guidance on Principles* (2001).

Fawcett, R. (ed.). *Stirling Castle: The Restoration of the Great Hall* (2001).

Fawcett, R and Rutherford, Allan. *Renewed Life for Scottish Castles* (2011).

Fiddes, Valerie and Rowan, Alistair (eds). *Mr David Bryce* (1976).

Foster, S, Macinnes, A and MacInnes R (eds). *Scottish Power Centres* (1998).

Frew, John and Jones, David (eds). *Aspects of Classicism* (1989).

Higgot, John (ed.). *Medieval Art and Architecture in the Diocese of St Andrews* (1994).

Hill, Oliver. *Scottish Castles of the Sixteenth and Seventeenth Centuries* (1953).

Gifford, John. *William Adam 1689–1748* (1989).

Giles, James. *Drawings of Aberdeenshire Castles* (1936).

Glendinning, M, MacInnes, R and MacKechnie, A. *A History of Scottish Architecture* (1996).

Gow, Ian and Rowan, Alistair (eds). *Scottish Country Houses 1600–1914* (1995).

Gow, Ian. *Scotland's Lost Houses* (2006).

Hannan, Thomas. *Famous Scottish Houses: The Lowlands* (1928).

Historic Scotland guidebook series, various authors.

Historic Scotland / Batsford series:

    Edinburgh Castle by Iain MacIvor (1995).

    Fortress Scotland and the Jacobites by Chris Tabraham and Doreen Grove (1995).

    Medieval Scotland by Peter Yeoman (1995).

    Scotland's Castles by Chris Tabraham (1997, 2005).

    Stirling Castle by Richard Fawcett (1995).

Hussey, Christopher. *The Work of Sir Robert Lorimer* (1931).

Innes, Cosmo (ed.). *The Black Book of Taymouth* (1855).

Innes, Cosmo (ed.). *The Book of the Thanes of Cawdor* (1859).

Innes Review (1950–).

Kenyon, John R. *Castles, Town Defences and Artillery Fortifications in the United Kingdom and Ireland, a Bibliography 1945–2006* (2008).

King, David. *The Complete Works of Robert and James Adam and Unbuilt Adam* (2001).

King, David James Cathcart. *Castellarium Anglicanum*, 2 vols (1983).

Langley, Batty. *Ancient Masonry, both in the Theory and Practice, Demonstrating the Useful Rules of Arithmetic, Geometry, and Architecture, in the Proportions and Orders of the Most Eminent Masters of All Nations* (1736).

Langley, Batty. *Ancient Architecture Restored, and Improved, by A Great Variety of Grand and Usefull Designs, Entirely New In the Gothick Mode For the Ornamenting of Buildings and Gardens* (1742).

Lewis, J. 'Excavations at Bothwell Castle, Lanarkshire, 1981', *Glasgow Archaeological Journal*, 11 (1984), pp.119–28.

Lewis, J. 'Excavations at Bothwell Castle, North Lanarkshire', *Proceedimgs of the Society of Antiquaries of Scotland*, 127:2 (1997), pp.687–95.

Lewis, Michael J. *The Gothic Revival* (2002).

Liddiard, R. *Castles in Context: A Social History of Fortification in England and Wales, 1066–1500* (2005).

Lightowler, Edward. *The Michael Kirk Gordonstoun and its Historical Background* (1980).

Lindesay, R, of Pitscottie. *The Historie and Cronicles of Scotland* (Scottish Text Society, 1899–1911).

Lindsay, Ian, and Cosh, Mary. *Inveraray and the Dukes of Argyll* (1973).

Lindsay, M. *The Castles of Scotland* (1986).

Lloyd, Sampson and Brown, Cameron. *Scottish Castles* (2008).

Lockhart, J G. *The Life of Sir Walter Scott, Bart.* (1893 and other editions).

Lynch, Michael. *Scotland: A New History* (1992).

Lynch, Michael (ed.). *The Oxford Companion to Scottish History* (2004).

MacAuley, James. *The Gothic Revival 1745–1845* (1975).

MacAuley, James. *The Classical Country House in Scotland 1660–1800* (1987).

Macdonald, Murdo. *Scottish Art* (2000).

MacGibbon, D. and Ross, T. *The Castellated and Domestic Architecture of Scotland from the Twelfth to the Eighteenth Century*, 5 vols (1887–92).

MacKechnie, Aonghus. 'Sir David Cunningham of Robertland: Murderer and 'Magna Britannia's' First Architect', *Architectural History*, 52 (2009), pp.79–115.

MacKechnie, Aonghus. 'Renaissance Scotland's Martial Houses', *History Scotland*, 10:5 (September–October 2010), pp.48–54; and 10:6 (November–December 2010), pp.36–43.

MacKechnie, Aonghus. 'Scottish Historical Landscapes', *Studies in the History of Gardens & Designed Landscapes: An International Quarterly*, 22:3 (July–September 2002), pp.214–39.

Macinnes, Allan I. *Clanship, Commerce and the House of Stuart, 1603–1788* (1996)

Mackenzie, W Mackay. *The Medieval Castle in Scotland* (1927).

Maclean-Bristol, Nicholas. *From Clan to Regiment: 600 Years in the Hebrides, 1400–2000* (2007).

MacMillan, Duncan. *Scottish Art* (1990).

MacQueen, John. *Progress and Poetry: The Enlightenment and Scottish Literature* (1982).

MacQueen, John. *The Rise of the Historical Novel: The Enlightenment and Scottish Literature* (1989).

MacRae-Gilstrap, I M. *The Clan MacRae: With its Rolls of Honour and of Service in the Great War* (1923).

McNeill, Tom. *Castles in Ireland: Feudal Power in a Gaelic World* (1997).

McNeill, P G B and MacQueen H L. *Atlas of Scottish History* (1996).

Maxwell-Irving, Alastair M T. *The Border Towers of Scotland: Their History and Architecture* (2000).

McKean, Charles. *The Scottish Chateau: The Country House of Renaissance Scotland* (2001).

McKean, Charles. 'A Scottish Problem with Castles', *Historical Research*, 79:204 (May 2006).

McKinstry, Sam. *Rowand Anderson, The Premier Architect of Scotland* (1991).

The Middle Ages in the Highlands (1981).

Mills, John, et al. *Rosehaugh: A House of its Time* (1996).

Mesqui, Jean. *Châteaux forts et fortifications en France* (1997).

Miket, R and Roberts, D L. *The Medieval Castles of Skye and Lochalsh* (1990).

Millar, A H (ed.). *The Book of Record: A Diary Written by Patrick First Earl of Strathmore and Other Documents Relating to Glamis Castle, 1684–1689* (1890).

Mitchell, Arthur and Clark, James T (eds). *Geographical Collections Relating to Scotland Made by Walter Macfarlane*, 3 vols (1906–8).

Moss, Michael. *The Magnificent Castle of Culzean and the Kennedy family* (2002).

Mudie, Francis, Walker, David M and MacIvor, Iain. *Broughty Castle and the Defence of the Tay* (2010).

Mylne, R S. *The Master Masons to the Crown of Scotland* (1893).

Nicoll, James. *Domestic Architecture in Scotland* (1908).

Oram, Richard, and Stell, Geoffrey (eds) *Lordship and Architecture in Medieval and Renaissance Scotland* (2005).

Oram, Richard. 'Castles, Concepts and Contexts: Castle Studies in Scotland in Retrospect and Prospect', *Château Gaillard*, 23 (2008), pp.349–60.

The Oxford Dictionary of National Biography, 60 vols (2004); also available online at www.oxforddnb.com

Paul, J Balfour. *The Scots Peerage*, 9 vols (1904–14).

Purser, John. *Scotland's Music* (rev. edn, 2007).

Reed, James. *Sir Walter Scott: Landscape and Locality* (1980).

Ross, Stewart. *Scottish Castles* (1990).

The Royal Commission on the Ancient and Historic Monuments of Scotland (RCAHMS) *Inventory* series:
    Argyll, 7 vols (1971–92)
    Berwick (revised 1915)
    Caithness (1911)
    Dumfries (1920)
    East Lothian (1924)
    City of Edinburgh (1951)
    Fife, Kinross and Clackmannan (1933)
    Kirkcudbright (1914)
    Midlothian and West Lothian (1929)
    Orkney (1946)
    Outer Isles (1928)
    Peebles (2 vols, 1967)
    Roxburgh (1956)
    Selkirk (1957)
    Shetland (1946)
    Stirlingshire (2 vols, 1963)
    Sutherland (1911)
    Wigtown (1911)

RCAHMS. *Argyll Castles in the Care of Historic Scotland* (1997).

Royal Incorporation of Architects in Scotland (RIAS) *Illustrated Architectural Guides* series:
    Aberdeen by W A Brogden (1998 edn.)
    Aberdeenshire Donside and Strathbogie by Ian Shepherd (2006)
    Argyll and Bute by F A Walker (2003)
    Ayrshire & Arran by R Close (1992)
    Banff & Buchan by C McKean (1990)
    Borders & Berwick by Charles Strang (1994)
    Central Glasgow by C McKean et al. (1989)
    Clackmannan & the Ochils by Adam Swan (1987)
    Deeside & The Mearns by Jane Geddes (2001)
    Dumfries and Galloway by John Hume (2000)
    Dundee by C. McKean and D M Walker (1993 edn)
    Edinburgh by C. McKean (1992 edn)
    Falkirk and District by Richard Jaques (2001)
    The Kingdom of Fife by G L Pride (1990)
    Central Glasgow by Charles McKean, David Walker and Frank Walker (1989)
    Greater Glasgow by Sam Small (2008)
    Gordon by Ian Shepherd (1994)
    Midlothian by Jane Thomas (1995)
    The Monklands by J Peden (1992)
    The District of Moray by Charles McKean (1987)
    North Clyde Estuary by Frank A Walker and Fiona Sinclair (1992)
    Orkney by L Burgher (1991)
    Perth & Kinross by Nick Haynes (2000)
    Ross & Cromarty by E Beaton (1992)
    Shetland by M Finnie (1990)
    South Clyde Estuary by F A Walker (1986)
    Stirling & the Trossachs by C McKean (1985)
    Sutherland by E Beaton (1995)
    West Lothian by R Jacques and C McKean (1994)
    The Western Seaboard by Mary Miers (2008)
    Savage, Peter. *The Edinburgh Collection of Drawings from the Office of Rowand Anderson, Edinburgh* (1977).

Savage, Peter. *Lorimer and the Edinburgh Craft Designers* (1980).

Scottish Historical Review (1890–).

Scottish Text Society (1882–).

Seton, G. *The History of the Family of Seton* (1896).

Simpson, W D. 'The Architectural History of Bothwell Castle', *Proceedings of the Society of Antiquaries of Scotland*, 59 (1925), pp.165–93.

Simpson, W D. 'Bothwell Castle Reconsidered', *Transactions of the Glasgow Archaeological Society*, 11 (1947), pp.97–116.

Simpson, W D. *The Province of Mar* (1943).

Simpson, W D. *The Earldom of Mar* (1949).

Simpson, W D. 'The Donjons of Conisborough and Bothwell', *Archaeologia Aeliana* (4th series), 32 (1954), pp.100–15.

Sinclair, Fiona J. (ed.). *Charles Wilson, Architect, 1810–63* (1993).

Slade, Harry Gordon. *Glamis Castle* (2000).

Slezer, John. *Theatrum Scotiae* (1693).

Stark, David. *Charles Rennie Mackintosh & Co.* (2004).

Stell, Geoffrey. 'The Scottish Medieval Castle: Form, Function and "Evolution"', in Keith J Stringer (ed.), *Essays on the Nobility of Medieval Scotland* (1985), pp.195–209.

Stell, Geoffrey , Shaw, John and Storrier, Susan (eds). *Scottish Life and Society: A Compendium of Scottish Ethnology*, vol. 3: *Scotland's Buildings* (2003).

Stell, Geoffrey. 'Castle Tioram: A Statement of Cultural Significance' (2006), available online from the Historic Scotland website: http://www.historic-scotland.gov.uk/index/news/ indepth/castletioram/castletioram-documents.htm

Stell, Geoffrey. 'The Scottishness of Scottish Towers', *Europa Nostra Scientific Bulletin*, 63 (2010), pp.57–68.

Stirling-Maxwell, John. *Shrines and Homes of Scotland* (1938).

Stevenson, John James. *House Architecture* (1880).

Stewart, M C H. 'The Metaphysics of Place in the Scottish Historical Landscape: Patriotic and Virgilian Themes, c.1700 to the Early Nineteenth Century', *Studies in the History of Gardens and Designed Landscapes* (2002), pp.240–64.

Stewart, M C H. 'The Earl of Mar and Scottish Baroque', *Architectural Heritage*, 9 (1998), pp.16–30.

Stringer, K J (ed.). *Essays on the Nobility of Medieval Scotland* (1985).

Tabraham, C. 'The Scottish Medieval Towerhouse as Lordly Residence in the Light of Recent Excavations', *Proceedings of the Society of Antiquaries of Scotland*, 118 (1988), pp.267–76.

Tait, A A. *The Landscape Garden in Scotland* (1980).

Thomson, Katrina. *Turner and Sir Walter Scott: The Provincial Antiquities and Picturesque Scenery of Scotland* (1999).

Thomson, T and Innes, C. *Acts of the Parliaments of Scotland* (1814–75).

Transactions of the Glasgow Archaeological Society (1857–).

Tranter, Nigel. *The Fortified House in Scotland*, 5 vols (1962–70).

Trevor-Roper, Hugh. *The Invention of Scotland: Myth and History* (2008).

Turner, Olivia Horsfall (ed.). *The Theatre of the Empire: The Architecture of Britain and Her Colonies in the Seventeenth Century* (forthcoming, 2012).

Watt, Donald, et al. (eds). *Walter Bower: Scotichronicon*, 9 vols (1987–97).

Wemyss, Charles. 'Merchant and Citizen of Rotterdam: The Early Career of Sir William Bruce', *Architectural Heritage*, 16 (2005), pp.14–30.

Wormald, Jenny. *Lords and Men in Scotland: Bonds of Manrent, 1442–1603* (1985).

Wormald, Jenny (ed.). *Scotland: A History* (2005).

Zeune, Joachim. *The Last Scottish Castles* (1992).

Chapter 1 Foundations of a Castle Culture: Pre-1603

Billings, Robert William. *The Baronial and Ecclesiastical Antiquities of Scotland*, 4 vols (1848–52).

Cruden, Stewart. *The Scottish Castle* (1960 and later editions).

Dixon, Philip. 'Towerhouses, Pelehouses and Border Society', *Archaeological Journal*, 136 (1979), pp.240–52.

Kenyon, John R. *Castles, Town Defences and Artillery Fortifications in the United Kingdom and Ireland, a Bibliography 1945–2006* (2008).

King, David James Cathcart. *Castellarium Anglicanum*, 2 vols (1983)

MacGibbon, D. and Ross, T. *The Castellated and Domestic Architecture of Scotland from the Twelfth to the Eighteenth Century*, 5 vols (1887–92).

Mackenzie, William Mackay. *The Mediaeval Castle in Scotland* (1927).

McKean, Charles. 'A Scottish Problem with Castles', *Historical Research*, 79:204 (May 2006).

McNeill, Tom. *Castles in Ireland: Feudal Power in a Gaelic World* (1997)

Maxwell-Irving, Alastair M T. *The Border Towers of Scotland: Their History and Architecture* (2000).

Maxwell-Irving, Alastair M T. 'How Many Tower-Houses Were There in the Scottish Borders? A Few Observations', *Proceedings of the Society of Antiquaries of Scotland* (forthcoming).

Mesqui, Jean *Châteaux forts et fortifications en France* (1997).

Oram, Richard and Stell, Geoffrey (eds). *Lordship and Architecture in Medieval and Renaissance Scotland* (2005).

RCAHMS. *Argyll Castles in the Care of Historic Scotland* (1997).

Stell, Geoffrey. 'Late Medieval Defences in Scotland', in David H Caldwell (ed.), *Scottish Weapons and Fortifications* (1981), pp.21–54.

Stell, Geoffrey. 'The Scottish Medieval Castle: Form, Function and "Evolution"', in Keith J Stringer (ed.), *Essays on the Nobility of Medieval Scotland* (1985), pp.195–209.

Stell, Geoffrey. 'Castle Tioram: A Statement of Cultural Significance' (2006), available online from the Historic Scotland website: http://www.historic-scotland.gov.uk/index/news/indepth/castletioram/castletioram-documents.htm

Stell, Geoffrey. 'The Scottishness of Scottish Towers', *Europa Nostra Scientific Bulletin*, 63 (2010), pp.57–68.

Stell, Geoffrey. 'Scottish Castellology and Castellologists: A Brief Historical Introduction', *Castellologica Bohemica*, forthcoming

Tabraham, Chris. *Scotland's Castles* (1997, 2005).

Zeune, Joachim. *The Last Scottish Castles* (1992).

Chapter 2 1603–1746: Castles No More, or 'the Honour and pride of a country'?

Bath, Michael. *Renaissance Decorative Painting in Scotland* (2003).

Buildings of Scotland series (by John Gifford et al.).

Burton, J Hill and Masson, D, et al. (eds) *The Register of the Privy Council of Scotland*, 37 vols (1877–).

Colvin, Howard. *A Biographical Dictionary of British Architects 1600–1840* (4th edn, 2008).

Cruden, Stewart. *The Scottish Castle* (1960 and other editions).

Dunbar, John G. *William Bruce* (exhibition catalogue, 1970).

Dunbar, John G. 'The Building Activities of the Duke and Duchess of Lauderdale, 1670–82', *Archaeological Journal*, 132 (1975), pp.202–30.

Frew, John and Jones, David (eds). *Aspects of Classicism* (1989).

Glendinning, M, MacInnes, R and MacKechnie, A. *A History of Scottish Architecture*. (1996).

Gifford, John. *William Adam 1689–1748* (1989).

Gow, Ian and Rowan, Alistair (eds). *Scottish Country Houses 1600–1914* (1995).

Historic Scotland guidebook series

MacGibbon, D. and Ross, T. *The Castellated and Domestic Architecture of Scotland from the Twelfth to the Eighteenth Century*, 5 vols (1887–92).

MacKechnie, Aonghus. 'Sir David Cunningham of Robertland: Murderer and 'Magna Britannia's' First Architect', *Architectural History*, 52 (2009), pp.79–115.

MacKechnie, Aonghus. 'Renaissance Scotland's Martial Houses', *History Scotland*, 10:5 (September–October 2010), pp.48–54; and 10:6 (November–December 2010), pp.36–43.

McKean, Charles. *The Scottish Chateau: The Country House of Renaissance Scotland* (2001).

McKean, Charles. 'A Scottish Problem with Castles', *Historical Research*, 79:204 (May 2006).

Mackenzie, W Mackay. *The Medieval Castle in Scotland* (1927).

RCAHMS county *Inventory* series.

Slezer, John. *Theatrum Scotiae* (1693).

Turner, Olivia Horsfall (ed.). *The Theatre of the Empire: The Architecture of Britain and Her Colonies in the Seventeenth Century* (forthcoming, 2012).

Zeune, Joachim. *The Last Scottish Castles* (1992).

Chapter 3 Inveraray to Abbotsford: Survival and Revival

Bolton, A T. *The Architecture of Robert and James Adam*, 2 vols (1922).

Daiches, David. *Sir Walter Scott and his World* (1971).

King, David. *The Complete Works of Robert and James Adam and Unbuilt Adam* (2001).

Lockhart, J G. *The Life of Sir Walter Scott, Bart.* (1893 and other editions).

MacAuley, James. *The Gothic Revival 1745–1845* (1975).

MacAuley, James. *The Classical Country House in Scotland 1660–1800* (1987).

MacKechnie, Aonghus. 'Scottish Historical Landscapes', *Studies in the History of Gardens & Designed Landscapes: An International Quarterly*, 22:3 (July–September 2002), pp.214–39.

Reed, James. *Sir Walter Scott: Landscape and Locality* (1980).

Thomson, Katrina. *Turner and Sir Walter Scott: The Provincial Antiquities and Picturesque Scenery of Scotland* (1999).

Chapter 4 'Old Scotch': Victorian and Edwardian High Baronial

The Royal Commission on the Ancient and Historical Monuments of Scotland holds the surviving drawings of William Burn (Scottish works); Charles Wilson; Peddie & Kinnear; J M Dick Peddie; Sydney Mitchell & Wilson; and Robert Lorimer. It also holds copies of the drawings for many of the buildings discussed in this chapter. The Royal Institute of British Architects holds some of the drawings for Burn's English works and the preliminary sketch plans for many of his Scottish houses.

Edinburgh University Library holds the surviving drawings of William Henry Playfair and the R Rowand Anderson collection, which also embraces the Thomas Brown, Maitland Wardrop and Charles Reid practices. The University of Glasgow holds the drawings of John Archibald Campbell and the job-books of John Honeyman and his partners John Keppie and Charles Rennie Mackintosh; and the Mitchell Library, Glasgow (Strathclyde Archives) holds the surviving drawings of Campbell Douglas & Sellars and Alexander Nisbet Paterson.

Illustrations of many, but not all, of the buildings discussed in this chapter will be found in the Royal Incorporation of Architects in Scotland/Rutland Press series of architectural guides. More detailed accounts of the surviving buildings will be found in the Buildings of Scotland series, and a very few have been the subject of articles in *Country Life* and *Scottish Field*.

Biographical details and lists of works for the architects discussed in this chapter will be found in the online *Dictionary of Scottish Architects*, at www.scottisharchitects.org.uk. Anthony Slaven and Sydney Checkland's *Dictionary of Scottish Business Biography* (1990) provides background for some of the industrial and mercantile clients, while Burke's *Peerage* and *Landed Gentry* will provide summary details for the landed ones: in many cases reference to the earlier editions will be required. A very few clients, most notably the Tennants, have been the subject of biographies.

Academy Architecture (ed. A Koch) (1890–1914).

Airs, Malcolm (ed.). *The Victorian Great House* (2000).

Airs, Malcolm (ed.). *The Edwardian Great House* (2001).

Bailey, Rebecca M. *Scottish Architects' Papers: A Source Book* (1996).

Bradley, Paul. *The Country Houses of William Burn*, unpublished PhD thesis, University of Nottingham (2004).

Calder, Alan. *James MacLaren, Arts and Crafts Pioneer* (2003).

Carruthers, Annette (ed.). *The Scottish Home* (1996).

Davis, Michael C. *The Castles and Mansions of Ayrshire* (1991).

Davis, Michael C. *Scots Baronial Mansions and Castle Restorations in the West of Scotland* (1996).

Dean, Marcus, and Miers, Mary. *Scotland's Endangered Houses* (1990).

Fiddes, Valerie and Rowan, Alistair (eds). *Mr David Bryce* (1976).

Green, Simon, 'William Leiper's Houses in Helensburgh', *Architectural Heritage*, vol. 3 (1992), pp.32–42.

Gow, Ian. *The Scottish Interior* (1992).

Gow, Ian. *Scotland's Lost Houses* (2008).

Gow, Ian and Rowan, Alistair (eds), *Scottish Country Houses 1600–1914* (1995).

Hussey, Christopher. *The Work of Sir Robert Lorimer* (1931).

Kerr, Robert. *The English Gentleman's House* (1864–71), Scottish section, Part 4, Chapter 11.

MacKechnie, Aonghus (ed.). *David Hamilton, Architect, 1768–1843* (1993).

McKinstry, Sam. *Rowand Anderson, The Premier Architect of Scotland* (1991).

Mills, John, et al. *Rosehaugh: A House of its Time* (1996).

Nicoll, James. *Domestic Architecture in Scotland* (1908).

Savage, Peter. *The Edinburgh Collection of Drawings from the Office of Rowand Anderson* (1977).

Savage, Peter. *Lorimer and the Edinburgh Craft Designers* (1980).

Sinclair, Fiona J. (ed.). *Charles Wilson, Architect, 1810–63* (1993).

Stark, David. *Charles Rennie Mackintosh & Co.* (2004).

Stevenson, John James. *House Architecture* (1880).

Walker, David W. *Peddie & Kinnear*, unpublished PhD thesis, University of St Andrews (2002).

Chapter 5 Castle Reoccupation and Conservation in the Twentieth Century

Ancient Monuments and Historic Buildings, Report of the Inspector of Ancient Monuments for the Year Ending 31st March 1913 (published by HMSO) (1914).

Baldwin Brown, G. *The Care of Ancient Monuments* (1905).
Bell, A S (ed.). *The Scottish Antiquarian Tradition: Essays to Mark the Bicentenary of the Society of Antiquaries of Scotland and its Museum, 1780–1980* (1981).
Breeze, D J. 'Gerard Baldwin Brown (1849–1932): The Recording and Preservation of Monuments', *Proceedings of the Society of Antiquaries of Scotland*, 131 (2002), pp.41–55.
Childe, V Gordon and Simpson, W Douglas. *Illustrated Guide to Ancient Monuments in the Ownership of the Ministry of Works, Volume VI, Scotland* (1952).
Clow, R (ed.). *Restoring Scotland's Castles* (2000).
Dunbar, J G. 'The Royal Commission on the Ancient and Historical Monuments of Scotland, The First Eighty Years', *Transactions of the Ancient Monuments Society*, 36 (1992).
Fawcett, R. *The Conservation of Architectural Ancient Monuments in Scotland, Guidance on Principles* (Historic Scotland, 2001).
Glendinning, M. 'The Conservation Movement: A Cult of the Modern Age', *Transactions of the Royal Historical Society*, 13 (2003).
Glendinning, M, MacInnes, R and MacKechnie, A. *A History of Scottish Architecture* (1996).
MacIvor, I, and Fawcett, R. 'One Hundred Years On! Ancient Monuments 1882–1982: A View from Scotland', *Popular Archaeology* (November 1982).
Magnusson, M (ed.). *Echoes in Stone* (1983).
McKean, C. 'From Castles to Calvinists: Scottish Architectural Publishing over the Last Fifty Years', *Architectural Heritage*, 17 (2006).
Mudie, F, Walker, D, and MacIvor, I. *Broughty Castle and the Defence of the Tay* (2010).
Richardson, H. 'Lorimer's Castle Restorations', *AHSS Journal* (1992).
Stell, Geoffrey. 'Castle Tioram: A Statement of Cultural Significance' (2006), available online from the Historic Scotland website: http://www.historic-scotland.gov.uk/index/news/indepth/castletioram/castletioram-documents.htm
Stirling Maxwell, J. *Shrines and Homes of Scotland* (1937).
Watters, D and Glendinning, M. *Little Houses, The National Trust for Scotland's Improvement Scheme for Small Historic Homes* (2006).

Chapter 7 Bothwell Castle in the Thirteenth and Early Fourteenth Centuries

Cruden, S. 'Scottish Medieval Pottery: The Bothwell Castle Collection', *Proceedings of the Society of Antiquaries of Scotland*, 86 (1951–2), pp.140–70.
Dixon, P. 'The Donjon of Knaresborough: Tthe Castle as Theatre', *Château Gaillard*, 14 (1990), pp.121–39.
Lewis, J. 'Excavations at Bothwell Castle, Lanarkshire, 1981', *Glasgow Archaeological Journal*, 11 (1984), pp.119–28.
Lewis, J. Excavations at Bothwell Castle, North Lanarkshire', *Proceedings of the Society of Antiquaries of Scotland*, 127 (2) (1997), pp.687–95.
Liddiard, R. *Castles in Context: A Social History of Fortification in England and Wales, 1066–1500* (2005).
MacGibbon, D. and Ross, T. *The Castellated and Domestic Architecture of Scotland from the Twelfth to the Eighteenth Century*, vols 1 and 5 (1887 and 1892).
Oram, R D and Stell, G P (eds). *Lordship and Architecture in Medieval and Renaissance Scotland* (2005).
Oram, R D. 'Castles, Concepts and Contexts: Castle Studies in Scotland in Retrospect and Prospect', *Château Gaillard*, 23 (2008), pp.349–60.
Simpson, W D. 'The Architectural History of Bothwell Castle', *Proceedings of the Society of Antiquaries of Scotland*, 59 (1925), pp.165–93.
Simpson, W D. 'Bothwell Castle Reconsidered', *Transactions of the Glasgow Archaeological Society*, 11 (1947), pp.97–16.
Simpson, W D. 'The Donjons of Conisborough and Bothwell', *Archaeologia Aeliana* (4th series), 32 (1954), pp.100–15.
Tabraham, C. *Scotland's Castles* (1997, 2005).
Viollet-le-Duc, E E. *An Essay on the Military Architecture of the Middle Ages. Translated from the French by M MacDermott* (1860).

Chapter 8 The Refashioning of Glamis, 1668–1684

Apted, M. 'Arnold Quellin's Statues at Glamis Castle', *Antiquaries Journal*, 64 (1984), pp.53–61.
Brown, M. 'The Gardens of Glamis – An Aerial View', *Proceedings of the Society of Antiquaries of Scotland*, 135 (2005), pp. 19–39.
Colvin, H. 'The Beginnings of the Architectural Profession in Scotland', *Architectural History*, 29 (1986), pp. 168–82.
Cornforth, J. 'Was There a Scottish Baroque ?', *Country Life* (June 1989).
Davis, M. 'Scottish North-East Renaissance Bel-houses – Was There a School of Architecture Operating in the North-East of Scotland during the Turn of the Seventeenth Century?' unpublished PhD thesis, University of Dundee, 2010.
Dingwall, C. *Glamis Castle: A History of the Designed Landscape* (2000).
Glendinning, M, MacInnes, R and MacKechnie, A. *A History of Scottish Architecture* (1996).
MacGibbon, D. and Ross, T. *The Castellated and Domestic Architecture of Scotland from the Twelfth to the Eighteenth Century*, vol. 2 (1887).
MacKechnie, Aonghus. 'Scottish Historical Landscapes', *Studies in the History of Gardens & Designed Landscapes: An International Quarterly*, 22:3 (July–September 2002), pp.214–39.
McKean, C A. *The Scottish Chateau* (2004).
Miller, A H. (ed.) *The Book of Record* (1890).
Newland, K. 'The Acquisition and Use of Norwegian Timber in Seventeenth Century Scotland, with Reference to the Principal Building Works of James Baine, His Majesty's Master Wright,' unpblished PhD thesis, Dundee University (2010).
Slade, H G. *Glamis Castle* (2000).
Stewart, M C H. 'The Metaphysics of Place in the Scottish Historical Landscape: Patriotic and Virgilian Themes, c.1700 to the Early Nineteenth Century', *Studies in the History of Gardens and Designed Landscapes* (2002), pp.240–64.
Stewart, M C H. 'The Earl of Mar and Scottish Baroque', *Architectural Heritage*, 9 (1998), pp.16–30.
Wemyss, C. 'The Scottish Treasury Commission and its Impact upon the Development of Scottish Country House Architecture 1667–1682', unpublished PhD thesis, Dundee University (2010).

Chapter 9 Caisteal Inbhir-Aora / Inveraray Castle

Lewis, Michael J. *The Gothic Revival* (2002).
Lindsay, Ian, and Cosh, Mary. *Inveraray and the Dukes of Argyll* (1973).
MacAuley, James. *The Classical Country House in Scotland 1660–1800* (1987).
Macinnes, Allan I. *Clanship, Commerce and the House of Stuart, 1603–1788* (1996)
MacKechnie, Aonghus. 'Scottish Historical Landscapes', *Studies in the History of Gardens & Designed Landscapes: An International Quarterly*, 22:3 (July–September 2002), pp.214–39.
Oxford Dictionary of National Biography (2004), vol 9, pp.726–33.
Royal Commission on the Ancient and Historical Monuments of Scotland. *Argyll: An Inventory of the Monuments*, vol. 7: Mid Argyll and Cowal: Medieval and Later Monuments (1992).
Walker, Frank Arneil. *The Buildings of Scotland: Argyll and Bute* (2000).

Chapter 10 Culzean Castle

Moss, Michael. *The Magnificent Castle of Culzean and the Kennedy Family* (2003)

Chapter 11 From Blair Castle to Atholl House to Blair Castle

Atholl Muniments at Blair Castle, Perthshire
Atholl, John, 7th Duke of (ed.). *Chronicles of the Atholl and Tullibardine Families* (1908).
Fiddes, Valerie and Rowan, Alistair (eds). *Mr David Bryce* (1976).

Chapter 12 Balmoral

Brown, Ivor. *Balmoral: The History of a Home* (1955).
Clark, Ronald W. *Balmoral: Queen Victoria's Highland Home* (1981).
Duff, David. *Victoria in the Highlands: The Personal Journal of Her Majesty Queen Victoria* (1968).
Miller, Delia. *Queen Victoria's Life in the Scottish Highlands: Depicted by her Watercolour Artists* (2003).

Chapter 13 Edinburgh Castle and the Remaking of Medieval Edinburgh

Gifford, J. McWilliam, C. and Walker, D. *The Buildings of Scotland: Edinburgh* (1984).
Morris, R J. 'The Capitalist, the Professor and the Soldier: The Re-making of Edinburgh Castle, 1850–1900', *Planning Perspectives*, 22 (January 2007) pp.55–78.
Morris, R J. *Scotland 1907. The Many Scotlands of Valentine and Sons, Photographers* (2007).

Chapter 14 Duart and Eilean Donan Castles

Anderson, R R. *Examples of Scottish Architecture from the 12th to the 17th Century: A Series of Reproductions from the National Art Survey Drawings*, 4 vols (Edinburgh, 1921–33).
Clow, R (ed.). *Restoring Scotland's Castles* (2000).
Davis, M C. *Scots Baronial: Mansions and Castle Restorations in the West of Scotland* (1996).

Donaldson, M E M. *Wanderings in the Western Highlands and Islands* (1923)
Gifford, J. *The Buildings of Scotland: Highland and Islands* (1992)
MacGibbon, D. and Ross, T. *The Castellated and Domestic Architecture of Scotland from the Twelfth to the Eighteenth Century*, 5 vols (1887–92).
MacLean, J P. *A History of the Clan MacLean from its First Settlement at Duard Castle, in the Isle of Mull, to the Present Period Including a Genealogical Account of some of the Principal Families together with their Heraldry, Legends, Superstitions etc* (1986).
MacNeil, R L. *Castle in the Sea / The MacNeil of Barra* (revised edn, 1975).
MacRae, Rev. *A History of the Clan Macrae* (1899)
MacRae-Gilstrap, I M. *The Clan MacRae: With its Rolls of Honour and of Service in the Great War* (1923).
Miket, R and Roberts, D L. *The Medieval Castles of Skye and Lochalsh* (1990).
RCAHMS. *Argyll: An Inventory of the Monuments*, Volume 3: Mull, Tiree, Coll and Northern Argyll (excluding the early medieval and later monuments of Iona) (1980), no. 339.
RCAHMS, National Art Survey of Scotland Collection, archive no. EDD 145/6.
Savage, P. *Lorimer and the Edinburgh Craft Designers* (1980).
Walker, F A. *The Buildings of Scotland: Argyll and Bute* (2000).

Chapter 15 Craigievar Castle: Changing Perceptions

Addyman, T, Macfadyen, K, Phillips, S and Gow, A. 'Craigevar Castle', *Discovery and Excavation in Scotland* (New Series), 10 (2009), pp.25–6.
Billings, R W. *The Baronial and Ecclesiastical Antiquities of Scotland*, vol. 1 (1852).
Brogden, William, A 'John Smith and Craigievar Castle', in Gow, I and Rowan, A (eds), *Scottish Country Houses 1600–1914* (1995).
Ellington, M. *Craigievar Castle: National Trust for Scotland Guide* (1987).
Fraser, S. 'Galleries, Gardens and Gates: Transforming the House of Muchall into a Setting for Lordship', in notes accompanying 'A Lad O'Pairts, a Day Conference in Memory of Ian Shepherd', Aberdeen University, 11 December 2010 (2010).
Gow, I. *Craigievar Castle* [National Trust for Scotland guidebook] (2004).
Gow, I. *Scottish Houses and Gardens from the Archives of Country Life* (1997).
Greg, M K. 'Excavations at Craigievar Castle, Aberdeenshire', *Proceedings of the Society of Antiquaries of Scotland*, 123 (1993), pp.381–93.
Howard, D. *The Architectural History of Scotland: Scottish Architecture from the Reformation to the Restoration, 1560–1660* (1995).
McKean, C. 'The Scottishness of Scottish Architecture: Building for People and Places', in Fladmark, J M (ed.), *Heritage: Conservation, Interpretation and Enterprise* (1993).
Simpson W D. *Craigievar Castle: An Illustrated Account* [National Trust for Scotland guidebook] (1978).

Chapter 16 Castles of the Modern Age

Glendinning, M, MacInnes, R and MacKechnie, A. *A History of Scottish Architecture* (1996).

Royal
Commission on the
Ancient and
Historical
Monuments of
Scotland

Royal Commission on the Ancient and Historical Monuments of Scotland

For over 100 years, RCAHMS has been collecting, recording and interpreting information on Scotland's architectural, industrial, archaeological and maritime heritage – creating an archive that offers a unique insight into the special nature of Scotland's places. Many millions of items, including photographs, maps, drawings and documents are made widely available to the public via the Web, through exhibitions and publications, and at the RCAHMS search room in Edinburgh.

Records relating to Scotland's castles form a significant part of RCAHMS collections, and since its formation in 1908, castles have had a privileged position in terms of architectural survey and recording. RCAHMS commitment to recording Scotland's rich and diverse castle culture continues today. Its scope remains geographically and chronologically extensive, ranging from the survey of the archaeological remains of Scotland's earliest castles to the recording of today's conservation programmes.

How and why castles have been recorded by RCAHMS has, of course, shifted over time, but the commitment to make records available to the general public has remained a constant. The seventy-year inventory project proved a golden era of castle recording. RCAHMS was established to conduct area-by-area inventories of pre-eighteenth century monuments, as a preliminary to state protection. It was essentially the first attempt at systematic nationwide listing, stemming from the Ancient Monuments Act of 1882. Through detailed period-hatched measured surveys, photography and documentary research, a new understanding of castle development was achieved. In 1913, RCAHMS lost its preservation remit, but the published inventories developed into an important research-based recording project, which ended in 1992.

In 1966, RCAHMS merged with the Scottish National Buildings Record, and as a result archive gathering and threat-based survey were greatly expanded. The collecting of important architectural drawings and photography of nineteenth- and early twentieth-century castles was pursued vigorously, and the recording of castles under threat of alteration or demolition was strengthened in 1968 with the formation of the Threatened Building Survey. The introduction of oblique aerial photographic surveys brought a new aspect to castle recording. The fruits of these RCAHMS programmes of work can be found in the numerous illustrations within this volume.

Contact Details

Royal Commission on the Ancient and
Historical Monuments of Scotland
John Sinclair House
16 Bernard Terrace
Edinburgh
EH8 9NX
tel 0131 662 1456
fax 0131 662 1477
info@rcahms.gov.uk
www.rcahms.gov.uk

Top. Kellie Castle, Fife: Sketch by Robert Lorimer of 1888
(© RCAHMS, SC 1055475)

Above. Earlshall Castle, Fife: photographic view from *The Kingdom of Fife* (1860), a published collection of calotypes by Thomas Rodger (© RCAHMS, DP 058252)

Top. Drum Castle, Aberdeenshire: watercolour view, showing extensions by David Bryce of 1875 (© RCAHMS, SC 800700)

Above. Aboyne Castle, Aberdeenshire: view from south, showing restoration work by architect George Truefit. From a scrap book album compiled c.1875–85 (© RCAHMS, DP 075632)

Top. Tantallon Castle, East Lothian: aerial view taken in 1994 (© RCAHMS, SC 800165)

Left. Kelburn Castle, Ayrshire: view from south-west taken in 2009 (© RCAHMS, DP 062256)

Index of Castles
and Associated Buildings

General Index

Dunnottar Castle: drawing by David M Walker (© David M Walker)